Curriculum Planning and Development

- **James A. Beane**

  St. Bonaventure University, New York

- **Conrad F. Toepfer, Jr.**

  State University of New York at Buffalo

- **Samuel J. Alessi, Jr.**

  *Director of Curriculum Evaluation and Development,
  Buffalo (New York) City School District*

 Allyn and Bacon, Inc.
Boston   London   Sydney   Toronto

Series editor   Susanne F. Canavan
Developmental coordinator   Lauren Whittaker
Production administrator   Kazia Navas
Production coordinator   Nancy Benjamin

Library of Congress Cataloging-in-Publication Data

Beane, James A., 1944-
   Curriculum planning and development.

   Includes bibliographies and index.
   1. Curriculum planning—United States.   I. Toepfer,
Conrad F., 1933-   .   II. Alessi, Samuel J., 1944-
III. Title.
LB1570.B379   1986   375′.001′0973   85-28713
ISBN 0-205-08745-0

Printed in the United States of America.
10 9 8 7 6 5 4 3 2   91 90 89 88 87

Credits

Various citations from the following works are used with permission as indicated.

Page 171: Aiken, W. *The Story of the Eight Year Study.* Copyright McGraw-Hill Book Company, 1941. Reprinted by permission of McGraw-Hill Book Company.

Page 183: Alberty, H. and Alberty, E. *Reorganizing the High School Curriculum.* Reprinted with permission of Macmillan Publishing Company. © The Macmillan Publishing Company, 1962.

Page 424: Attica, New York. "School Goals" by permission of the Attica Central School.

Page 85: Bestor, A. "The Distinctive Function of Schools," *Daedalus* (1959): 75–90. Reprinted by permission of *Daedalus,* Journal of the American Academy of Arts and Sciences, Boston, MA.

Page 233: Bloom, B. et al. *Taxonomy of Educational Objectives: Handbook I: Cognitive Domain.* Copyright © 1956 by Longman Inc. Reprinted by permission of Longman Inc., New York.

Credits continue on page 444, which constitutes a continuation of the copyright page.

We dedicate this work

Professionally, to our teacher, colleague, and friend,
Robert Spencer Harnack

Personally, to our parents,
John and Catherine Beane
Conrad and Ethel Toepfer
Samuel and Jeanette Alessi

And to our present and futures with
Jim, Jason, and John Beane
Barbara Brodhagen
Jeannie, Kathy, Mike, Julie, and Julian Michael Toepfer
Kathy, Lisa, Claire, Geoff, and Sarah Alessi

Contents

List of Frames

Preface

The systematic study of curriculum is a twentieth-century phenomenon. In the past, concerns about what happened in schools were mostly limited to descriptions of what courses or subjects ought to be studied. Today we find curriculum planning and development much improved but still in the process of change and refinement.

This book adds to the growing body of literature that began over eighty years ago. It stands on the shoulders of ideas developed and reworked by thousands of students of the curriculum field. Clearly, it does not claim to invent any "new wheels." Rather, it considers what ought to be done as well as what is done in the name of curriculum improvement. Our work here deals with consideration of fundamental, persisting ideas in the curriculum field viewed from emerging and evolving challenges facing education and society today. Our profession has often been inclined to change to new ideas largely because of their newness. For this and other reasons, many fundamental curriculum approaches have never been systematically and fully implemented. Despite their successes in beginning practice, numbers of these approaches were replaced with more recent organizational concepts.

For many years, curriculum specialists have debated Herbert Spencer's question "What knowledge is of most worth?" Indeed, for many that query has almost come to define what the curriculum field is about. In this book we suggest focusing conceptualization of the curriculum field through the question "How much of what kind of learning is required to get where?" In other words, this book not only addresses the issue of compelling knowledge and skills, but also considers why, to what degree, and to what ends they should be learned. However, the book is also set within the context of schools that attempt to educate young people. Thus, in order to consider our question adequately, we have also described ideas about the form schools might take and how learning experiences may be planned, implemented, and evaluated.

The book follows what we believe to be a useful format for thinking through the many issues related to curriculum planning and development. The introduction raises some future concerns, and the first two chapters blend two aspects of our study. One is a look at how curriculum ideas appear in the present context of schools. The second is an attempt to define the meaning of curriculum, curriculum planning, and other related ideas.

Chapters 3–7 explore how concepts in curriculum planning and development might be applied in schools. To clarify this issue, we suggest a broad framework that delineates the content and process of curriculum planning. Included in these chapters are discussions of the foundations of curriculum, the purposes of education, professional knowledge needed for curriculum development, organization of the school program, and design of specific curriculum plans to support teaching–learning situations.

Chapter 8 describes some of the important ideas and issues in curriculum evaluation. Chapter 9 looks at ways in which curriculum planning may be made more effective through cooperative efforts, professional growth, and organizational structures developed to respond to curriculum issues. Chapter 10 focuses on emerging issues such as school criticisms, youth issues, and modern technology as the basis for imagining what we must do in curriculum planning to make our school programs more responsive in the future.

One book can hardly explain all that is known or could be said about curriculum, and ours is no exception. Our purpose has been to describe and discuss what seem to be the most persistent issues and needs in curriculum planning and development. To do this we have explored some issues in considerable detail while treating others in a more cursory fashion. For more information about these latter topics, we encourage readers to consult the sources listed in the bibliography at the end of each chapter.

The book may prove most useful in two types of settings. One is the many courses taught each year in graduate education programs, courses that have such titles as curriculum planning, curriculum development, curriculum issues, curriculum trends, and the like. The second setting is schools themselves, where teachers and other professionals seek guidance as they work on curriculum. If present trends toward shifting responsibility for advanced teacher education from universities to schools continue, the book may also serve as a useful resource for inservice and staff development programs. Beyond these primary settings, the book might be used with upper-level undergraduate students who as prospective teachers will shortly have major responsibilities in the area of curriculum planning and development. We believe that such use of this book would help broaden their understanding of curriculum planning beyond the frequently observed narrow conceptions of a single subject or a daily lesson plan. Since curriculum planning and development are important to any educational program, the book may also prove useful to those concerned with education in the helping professions, business, public agencies, and so on. While our focus is schools, the principles we discuss apply in other settings as well.

Finally, we have tried to write this book in an invitational tone that encourages readers to relate their own professional experiences to what we have described. In most cases, where an issue or an idea is discussed, we present various alternatives that the reader may consider in formulating a personal vision of curriculum planning and development. The activities following each chapter are designed specifically for that purpose. In the end, we believe that this approach is necessary to convey the richness and diversity of the curriculum field and to promote further inquiry into its many aspects.

Acknowledgments

We are indebted to all who helped us in undertaking and completing this venture. Special thanks are gratefully extended to the following.

We wish to acknowledge the contributions of Margaret Quinlin, Jeff Johnston, and Hiram Howard for their confidence, help, and encouragement in getting this project off the ground. Particular appreciation is due to Sue Canavan, Lauren Whittaker, Kazia Navas, and Nancy Benjamin, who saw things through, showing great patience and understanding along the way.

We are equally appreciative to James Johnson, Mary Jo Henning, Ronald Doll, Glen Hass, Harold Shane, Anabelle Robbins, William Morrison, and J. T. Dillon for reviewing our manuscript. Their comments, directions, and encouragement are reflected throughout, although we take responsibility for the final content and interpretations.

Any doubts about the nutritional value of pizza with double cheese should be dispelled because of its high efficiency in fueling our collaborative working sessions on the manuscript! We also wish to thank our friend Brad Frederick for his willingness to drive in any weather conditions to get this necessary sustenance for our deliberations.

Our dearest thanks go to Barb Brodhagen, Jeannie Toepfer, and Kathy Alessi for their roles as "proofreaders," "reviewers," and "camp counsellors" as work on this project progressed.

Last, and certainly not least, our warm thanks to Marilyn Stepp for her keyboarding skills and for living with the mechanics of this project.

J.A.B.
C.F.T.
S.J.A.

INTRODUCTION

The purpose of planning, it has been said, is to bring the context of the future into the present and make decisions about that future now. As an ancient Chinese proverb states, "Even a journey of a thousand miles must begin with a single step." The destination of a journey becomes its objective, and a journey without a destination becomes a wandering or an unplanned search. Consider the needs of education. *To what degree are school programs planned to meet objectives? Are they truly developed as means to reach a destination or set of goals, or are they merely an unplanned search for some better ways to deal with present needs?*

This book will deal with the concepts and skills of curriculum planning that educators need to enhance the experiences of learners. School–communities that develop this capacity can better define goals that address the needs of learners and the problems of society. Through the planning process, educators can improve their skills to make curriculum plans and develop school programs that respond to those goals.

Consider the criticisms of education that characterized the first half of the 1980s. The critics identified problems, but did so largely outside of a planning context that could address their concerns. Over the years, most contemporary school programs were arrived at through reactions to critics or crises rather than through systematic curriculum planning. It is important that we recognize that the future is neither unalterable nor unavoidable. In a very real sense, the future is determined by present actions and steps taken in addressing concerns about that future.

A number of educational futures are possible. The worst possibility would be for schools and their communities simply to react to conditions without planning those reactions in terms of goals suggested by present and anticipated needs. The nature and state of education two decades from now can be planned more effectively. Typically we have tended to predict rather than plan the future of education. Educators have seldom planned actions to increase or decrease the likelihood of those predictions. It is this element of control that curriculum planning can address and support.

THREE SCENARIOS

■ ■   As a prelude to dealing with the concepts and skills needed to improve curriculum planning of our educational futures, let us consider three possible scenarios of what education could be in the year 2005. Any of these scenarios, as well as a number of others, could largely come to pass by that time. We present the scenarios without bias or determination as to whether one would be better or worse than the others. However, the choices that schools and communities make in the coming years, and the degree to which educators develop curriculum planning skills, will largely determine what education in the year 2005 will actually be.

■   **2005: The Homogenized School**

As education became a serious political issue in the 1980s, popular opinion centered around several ideas about the form and function of schools. One idea involved the belief that the schools had become too diversified in an attempt to meet the needs of youth, particularly in the affective domain and through programs dealing with the needs of handicapped learners. Many citizens questioned whether students were being sufficiently exposed to the traditional academic subjects and skills they remembered from their own years in school.

Besides feeling pressure from public criticisms, educators agreed that they were being asked to do too much for youth, including services that had previously been performed by other youth agencies. Also, additional questions were being asked about educational arrangements such as promotion policies, grouping and grading practices, elective programs, exploratory courses, and discipline procedures. These criticisms had been heard before over the years, but coupled with economic, political, and social conditions, the response by federal and state authorities was swift and dramatic.

Now in the year 2005, the suggestions of earlier educational reform movements have coalesced in a reorganized national school system. The nationally standardized curriculum mandated for all schools reflects the belief that the academic courses that all students take contain the fundamental and essential knowledge and values that they all need. The omission now of exploratory and social development courses highlights this fact. Required reading of the "great books" and memorization of historical events underscore the belief that the past is the key to the future. The prominence of mathematics and science coincides with the national priority of technological and economic advantage in the world marketplace. The school is now officially recognized as being responsible for intellectual development; it is not expected to consider personal needs, social growth, or major social problems in curriculum planning.

The National Testing Program (NTP) consists of basic competency tests at the elementary level and standardized subject-area examinations in the secondary academic courses, the passing of which is required for high school graduation. The tests themselves are constructed and administered by the American Testing Company, which was formed by combining the Educational Testing Service (ETS) and the National Center for the Assessment of Education (NCAE). This national assessment program derives from four goals. First, it ensures that the program in every school covers the required skills and subject matter in the national curriculum. Second, it provides colleges and employers with standardized information about prospective students and workers. Third, it provides the public with statistical data for ranking school districts across the country. Fourth, and perhaps most important, results of various tests at the elementary and middle-level schools identify the type of high school that students will attend.

This process of assigning students to different high schools represents a major difference between the present secondary school system and that used for most of the twentieth century. The first tier is for students who score in the upper 20 percent on the national exams. The program consists of advanced and highly technical courses comparable to at least the old advanced academic programs. The second tier consists of regular academic programs geared for those scoring in the middle range on the national tests. The third tier is intended for those who score in the lowest range on the national tests. Most of these students will enter low-skill-level jobs after completing their years in school. The program in this tier consists of basic academic subjects and remedial skill instruction. Movement of students between tiers occurs rarely since the national tests are generally regarded as final decision points. For this reason, many students who might be close to a higher tier take advantage of the nationally accredited, private tutoring centers located in most communities. Originally, these agencies were developed by computer companies to supplement school instruction where parents felt that the latter was insufficient. Today, however, they combine home computer instruction with personal tutoring designed specifically to raise scores on the National Testing Program exams.

Curriculum planning and development also are markedly different from what they were in the twentieth century. Once local and state education agencies agreed to follow the national curriculum format, they began to seek more specific direction in implementing the program. To meet this need, the federal government currently

contracts with several major universities for scholars and other subject-area specialists from one or more departments of the particular
university to develop curriculum plans. Once approved by the federal Department of Education, the curriculum plans are presented at
regional conferences to various state department representatives and
master teachers from local districts. These teachers then disseminate them to local teachers in their districts.

In addition to its responsibilities in establishing national curriculum standards and plans, the Department of Education is responsible for licensing teachers. This process, like curriculum
development, involves contractual arrangements with several major
universities that have been accredited by the federal agency. Li-
censed teachers are required to complete both a bachelor's and a
master's degree in a particular subject area. They are required to
pass a national teacher examination and serve an internship under
a master teacher. In contrast to licensing procedures common in the
twentieth century, prospective teachers are currently not required to
take coursework in pedagogy. Teaching techniques and related skills
are learned during the teaching internship, and since curriculum development is centralized at the federal level, broader concepts
in educational pedagogy are not required in federal licensing
standards.

In sum, the present system of education reflects major changes
from that common in the earlier parts of the twentieth century. At
the core of the present system is the concept of centralization
through the national curriculum and the related testing and teacher
licensing program. Since the national curriculum is concerned with
academic preparation, teachers are no longer considered responsible
for affective or psychomotor development. Furthermore, the schools
have finally been freed from the need to respond to social issues and
thus are not subject to the varieties of community or state interests.
The enduring values of the perennialist tradition are preserved, at
least in the schools, and educational accountability across the land
is ensured. *John Dewey's dream has been realized: the community
has available for all of its children that which the best and wisest
parent would want.*

■ 2005: The Community School Emerges

A century ago John Dewey recommended that schools and their
communities develop programs to help children meet their needs
and those of their society. Never popularly accepted, this approach
was virtually lost in the 1980s movement to establish a national
system of schools based primarily upon intellectual and academic
norms. However, the youth upheaval at the end of the 1980s and the

findings of the National Commissions on the Quality of Life for Youth and Society mobilized the nation's resources for youth needs to a degree never imagined.

No one ever imagined that the Student School Strike initiated by minority high school students in several major cities in February 1989 would succeed. However, within three months the support of 88 percent of students in the nation's urban, suburban, and rural communities closed America's high schools. Hopes that students would return to school for the 1989/90 school year proved unfounded. The strike continued into the 1989/90 school year, and over half of the nation's middle grades programs also were closed. This reflected young adolescent concerns about the largely academic emphasis in middle grades schools. The majority of school-age youth did not have adults at home during the school day. This meant that parents could neither enforce nor monitor their children's activities. After all, that was what schools were supposed to do.

The Carnegie and other foundations quickly established commissions to study this problem. On September 15, 1989, the President established the National Commission on the Quality of Life for Youth (NCQLY) and called upon students to return to school pending preliminary findings of the Commission. Students refused because there was no youth representation on the Commission. The President agreed to involve youth in deliberations of the Commission but would not agree to actual student membership on it. At 3:00 P.M. on October 1, 1989, 85 percent of the National High School and Junior High School Honor Society members burned their membership cards to protest the failure of the adult sponsors of the Honor Societies to endorse student representation on the Commission and their demands for involvement in determining educational goals and school programs. Clearly, efforts of governmental and adult insistence to combat the strike had failed. It was obvious that students would not relent on their demands that they be given parity involvement in planning school goals and programs.

The effectiveness with which students networked to communicate, generate, and disseminate information via modems to computers in their homes and other available settings impressed the adult world. Students whom school testing programs had identified as "insufficiently able" and excluded from school computer education programs now demonstrated their abilities to learn these skills. Coverage by the national news media showcased the responsible and effective conduct of striking youth. The Grey Panthers and other organizations for the elderly became strong supporters of the strike's goals. Other adults, however, were dividing into groups that either favored the student concerns or recommended a stern end to this disruption.

During the first week of December 1989, the National Student Coalition (NSC) released a list of central, essential issues. It was hoped that agreement on the items and a formula to involve students in deliberating how these areas would become regular school concerns could be reached to end the strike. The list was disseminated through a week-long series of national news releases. The areas of concern included resolving the growing alienation of youth and lack of support and interaction with adults; dealing with youth unemployment problems with attention to differing needs of minority and nonminority settings; the need for a guaranteed annual wage for youth who increasingly can obtain only part-time jobs with no retirement, medical or other benefits following completion of school; the need for guaranteed public financing of retraining for people whose jobs and careers are displaced by technocracy; the development of volunteer programs to utilize "people" talents and abilities of employably displaced persons, with a guaranteed annual wage and social benefits to enable such people to retain a viable self-esteem and feeling of worth; the need to address the growing numbers of youth suicide cases; and the need for school programs and the government to deal with these accelerating problems. It was suggested that schools become centers to confront these problems during after school and evening hours. Schools were recommended as primary resources to offer education and retraining programs for adolescents and adults in resolving these problems in every U.S. community.

That same week, one state decided to crack down on students whom its supreme court declared in violation of the compulsory education laws. School-aged students on the streets would be directed to and kept in schools by security personnel, and the parents of dissenting students would be cited as violating their legal responsibility to enforce their children's school attendance. National guard troops had to quell a tragic riot that erupted in one large city in that state. Hundreds of arrests, injuries and three deaths shocked the nation. The President ordered a halt to any efforts that might possibly incite further violence.

The findings of the Carnegie Commission were published on December 17 and included most of the concerns disseminated by the NSC two weeks previously. In the wake of the riot, the National Congress of Parents and Teachers and the National Conference of Christians and Jews had jointly endorsed the student concerns as priorities for survival of the national society. The NCQLY agreed to accept these concerns and endorsed the establishment of representative student participation in school–community planning activities. State legislatures also moved to adopt the students' proposals in state educational laws in a growing effort to resolve the student strike. A national reopening of schools was celebrated in January 1990 with plans to pursue the related needs of youth and adults and plan the "Countdown to the Third Millennium."

Assessment of the relationship of school programs to societal needs led to a reenvisioning of many dimensions of the school–community relationship. The decade of the 1990s was characterized by growing involvement of youth and youth advocates in expanding the role of education in the school–community setting. In 2005 we have n the benefit of planning educational programs upon bases such as the emerging needs curriculum approach, human developmental needs, developmental neuropsychological learning data, life-long learning opportunities, and the effective use of schools as centers for youth and adult activities in the community. For eight years now, the dollar support of education has increased thanks to the replacement of local property tax financing of education by a national, graduated income tax formula. Senior citizens and people on limited incomes are exempt from this taxation, but schools have greater resources than ever before. This has largely eliminated the former adversarial relationships that arose among citizens when school budgets impacted on local property taxation limits. Students in every American community now have equalized per-pupil financial support of their education. Regional and local cost-of-living differences are handled by formulas that adjust and equalize the funding of educational support money in real dollar amounts.

Parent education programs now assist parents in understanding and dealing with the normal changes in children's needs, abilities, and behaviors across their schooling years. Pupil–teacher ratios have decreased, and schools now have access to community psychiatric, psychological, mental health, medical, and social work expertise as needed. The coordination of all community agencies with schools has provided responsive, effective youth services to a degree never before possible.

In sum, the present educational system reflects a commitment to excellence in improving the quality of life for youth. Attention to meeting the personal and social needs of youth as they grow and develop has provided a basis for better intellectual achievement among them, and the vast majority are working up to their potential. Remedial help is provided as needs appear, and continuous progress allows students to grow at their own ability rates. This has interestingly resulted in the kind and degree of improvement in academic achievement envisioned twenty-two years ago in the government report *A Nation at Risk*. However, the means that now have achieved these results are virtually 180 degrees away from the procedures recommended in that report. The efforts of that era focused on intellectual and academic achievement separately and above all else. History will report that it took student refusal to submit to such demeaning programs to bring the nation to realize that the education and development of youth must be a holistic enterprise. *John Dewey's dream has been realized: the community has available for all of its children that which the best and wisest parent would want.*

■ 2005: The Corporate School

Futurist planners sitting in boardrooms around the country still liked to reminisce about how unbelievably easy it had been to replace the public school system. Of course, all the factors had gone in their favor—economic, technological, and societal. There had been a few anxious moments, sporadic incidents of social unrest, and a handful of setbacks, but overall, everything had proceeded almost exactly as planned.

In the 1980s, a dozen of the most powerful corporations had uncharacteristically put aside their competitive instincts and budgeted $1 million each to begin a cooperative research and development project whose major goal was the replacement of public education. Each year, as plans advanced and success seemed even more assured, the corporation increased its contributions to what became known simply as "The Project." Certainly the profit motive was an initial impetus for involvement, but as research continued, even the most jaded of bureaucrats became genuinely excited by the potential of the Project's results. Technologically, everything fell into place.

While the schools were still debating whether to use computers in classes, the Project had developed a supermicrochip that stored the equivalent of a million volumes of information on a silicon wafer the size of a watch crystal. While teacher textbook committees were trying to decide which publishing company's books to adopt for use in their particular schools, Project students had access to *every* book in print, as well as films, videotapes, newsreel footage, lectures, and demonstrations, all digitally stored in Project computers. While schools planned the best way to teach students keyboarding for computer orientation, the Project perfected speech input/output, with computers and people interacting in normal conversational question-and-answer format. Anything that needed hard copy confirmation was printed out, perfectly spelled and punctuated, at a rate of four *pages* per second on high-quality laser printers. By the mid-1990s, however, even the spoken input had become obsolete, being replaced by the Project's direct brain-to-database interface. First available as a small headset, this was soon available as a surgical implant that could be performed in a quick, painless, and inexpensive procedure on an outpatient basis. Explained to nonprofessional users as an adaptation of technology linking infrared, laser, and satellite communications, the practical implant was to give an individual direct and immediate access to a network of computer services that would have been unimaginable in 1989. The effect on education was dramatic.

In 2005, the network access was linked to an extensive library of holographic resource units, covering every subject area and interest center with skill levels from early childhood to what had earlier been considered as postgraduate-level work. Students wanting or required to do work in a particular field interacted one-to-one or in small groups with three-dimensional holograms of the leading experts in that field. Programming and stored database scenarios were so extensive that only in the rarest cases did students ask a question or introduce an answer for which the network had no immediate response. When such a situation did occur, Project records immediately flagged the control computer and the student was put into live contact (holographically) with an expert—usually within a turnaround time of thirty minutes. Entries also marked that student as a likely prospect for special development in the future.

Education was, for the first time in our history, truly individualized and personalized. Students could use the system at any time of the day or night. Computers carefully timed responses and chose activities (usually simulated) to match the student's previous achievement, learning style, level of cognitive skills, and interests, and predicted her or his intellectual ability level. All of these data were constantly updated and revised as students continued to use the system. Students had access, through holographic simulation, to the most advanced and current apparatus, equipment, and techniques—and all of this was done at far less cost than what was required to run the more inefficient schools of the 1980s and early '90s.

There had been concerns along the way. Very early on, financing was through a subscription service, similar to early cable television plans. For extra premiums, subscribers had access to better-known experts and more extensive libraries of data. In the early 1990s, this practice resulted in a dual society—those who could afford the Project and those who could not. The ones who couldn't were legally required to remain in public schools. But the gap in achievement caused social upheaval. A court case tested the Project's discrimination against low-income families. By 1995, after careful consideration of the merits and incredible achievements of those students who had been with the Project, the federal government passed enabling legislation that provided stipends to all families with children. They could choose to give their stipends to a "traditional" school or to the Project, an unforeseen application of the

"voucher" tax tuition credit system debated in the 1980s. Few chose
the traditional schools, and fundamentalist groups were the last to
try and maintain a separate and distinct system of schools.

Eventually economics won out. The savings in utilities, teacher
salaries, administrative costs, busing, equipment, supplies and materials, and unique programs for special education were staggering. A
movement began to shut down all publicly financed schools. For a
while, there was concern about students who would be home by
themselves and wouldn't bother to participate in any educational
program. For a very brief period, such students, identified by examining records kept by the Project, were assigned to the remaining
school buildings. During this period, such schools were called "lock-
ers," referring to their resemblance to juvenile detention centers.
Two factors, however, caused this period to last no more than eighteen months.

First, as is always the case, the cost of premium technology
continued to decline. Since more and more parents gave their stipends to the Project, profit enabled the corporate sponsors to offer
everyone, at the same lower price, their ultimate network. There
were no more distinctions based upon ability to pay. And this network was so exciting, and so well matched to the developmental
needs, characteristics, and interests of each student, that all students did participate—usually to an extent beyond that mandated in
the minimum competency tests set up as part of the ongoing Project
evaluation.

The second factor, more subtle but ultimately more important,
started to have an impact about 2001. To maintain services and to
produce and manufacture goods and products for our society required only 10 percent of the existing potential workforce. The rest
could be done with robots and sixth generation (thinking, reasoning,
analytic) computers. The three-day workweek finally gave way in
2001 to the USASS—the United States Annual Support Stipend. Almost 90 percent of families in the country had no working members.
Everyone began to participate in the Project and its virtually unlimited activities. Lifelong learning became more of a recreation than a
necessity. In many senses, basic or general education was more of a
social mark than a requisite for success.

Reading—given a choice of visual or auditory presentation of
information—was unnecessary. Writing (spelling, rules of punctua-
tion)—given the option of dictating or merely *thinking* through a
text, and being given a choice of appropriate synonyms if desired—
was also unnecessary. Memorizing facts was totally senseless since
anyone could have immediate access to all factual information—
current and accurate—merely by querying the Project networks.
Artistic forms of representation—drawing, painting, musical

composition—required no more than imagination. Anything that could be visualized mentally could be reproduced by computer graphics. Any musical composition that could be imagined could be played through a combination of computer-enhanced synthesizers.

In sum, education as a necessity, in 2005, has been replaced by education as a lifestyle. The only remaining critical decision is whether to participate in the Project by headset with limited access vocal amplifier (LAVA) or to choose the newest-model surgical implant, which has the range to give users general access to all international networks (GAIN), no matter where the user happens to be, much as portable radios were able to receive transmissions in any location.

The Project identifies the "best and brightest," and they are specially trained in order to continue developing and improving Project networks. The TPWs (ten-percent workforce) are selected from the next highest group of Project participants in order to maintain and improve technological service and production. For the bulk of society, schools are memories of grandparents, school taxes have been eliminated, and education—now able to address each individual's most fundamental needs and interests—is central to life. *John Dewey's dream has been realized: the community has available for all of its children that which the best and wisest parent would want.*

Against the background of these scenarios, let us now examine the concepts, skills, and processes of curriculum planning. We hope that the reading and study of this text will facilitate your abilities as an effective curriculum planner during your personal journey through our profession.

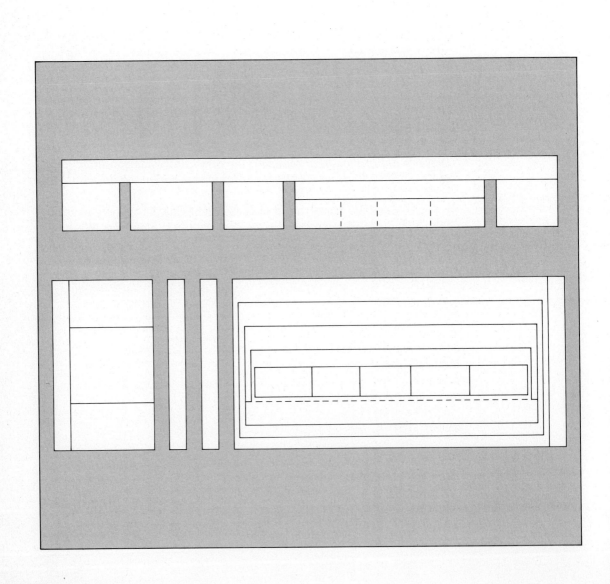

1

Organizing and Defining the Curriculum

Virtually all citizens in our society share one common experience. At one time or another in their lives, they have attended school. For some the experience ended after elementary school, while others have continued through middle school, high school, and higher education. Still others have joined the increasing number of people who have returned to school as adults through continuing education programs. However, although attending school is a common characteristic, the actual nature of the experience varies widely. One needs only to listen to adults recall their schools, or to visit a few schools in different locations, to notice a seemingly endless diversity in the kinds of programs that make up schools.

Obviously, opinion differs widely about what constitutes a "good" school. Some schools seem to focus entirely on separate subjects such as English, mathematics, science, and history. Others seem more concerned with the personal and social development of learners. Many blend these two approaches in a balanced program. Furthermore, within any school one might find all three approaches operating from one grade or classroom to another. The continuing debate over what makes a "good" school program is just one of the many issues of concern in the curriculum field. Because school programs represent the context in which learning takes place, this issue is one of the most prominent.

The diversity among approaches to curriculum organization, the form of the school program, is the major topic of Chapter 1. In an attempt to describe some different forms of curriculum organization, we devote the first part of this chapter to three sets of situations. Each one portrays a different type of curriculum organization, and each should give you a flavor of the diversity one may find in schools. After presenting the situations, we analyze their content, particularly the differences between those situations organized around subjects and those organized around the experiences and in-

terests of learners. To add to the sense of diversity, the second part
of the chapter includes a discussion of some of the different ways in
which the term "curriculum" is defined. Awareness of the different
types of curriculum organization and of different interpretations of
"curriculum" itself thus begins our study of curriculum.

As a result of reading Chapter 1, you should be able to:

1. Describe different types of curriculum organizations
2. Cite patterns of curriculum organization to which you have
   been exposed as student or teacher
3. Distinguish between approaches that focus on separate
   subjects and approaches that emphasize the interests and
   experiences of learners
4. Identify four categories of definitions of curriculum
5. Describe the advantages and disadvantages of each type of
   definition

ORGANIZING THE CURRICULUM: NINE SITUATIONS

■ ■ This section describes three situations at each of the three levels of
the school system. The situations deal with curriculum organization
issues at elementary, middle, and high school levels. As teachers work
on curriculum, they need to deal with learning issues ranging from
subject-centered to student-centered concerns. In some of the situations
that follow the focus is on subject-matter concerns, while in others,
more attention is given to the personal needs of learners.

As you will see, curriculum planning involves the organization
of instruction and learning arrangements in a variety of settings at
each of the levels of schooling considered here. The elements in some
of these situations may be familiar to you. Drawing on your personal
experiences in educational settings will help you to understand those
patterns of curriculum organization. However, you should also reflect
carefully on those situations not familiar to you as they describe other
kinds of curriculum organization. All of these examples are important
to understanding what it means to work on curriculum.

As educators gain a broader experience in planning and teaching,
it becomes apparent that they need to be able to work in differing
curriculum organizations. Subject- and experience-centered curriculum organization each have appropriate places in the school program.
As educators develop the skills to plan varied situations at their level
of teaching, they will gain a deeper insight into what it means to work
on curriculum. As you consider each case, keep the following questions
in mind.

Do particular situations represent patterns of curriculum orga-
nization familiar to you?
What factors in the situations are familiar to you?
Which settings focus on subjects?
What settings focus on the more personal needs of learners?
What issues or questions are being addressed?

■ **Curriculum Settings at the Elementary School Level**

☐ *Scene One*   This scene deals with three teachers. They are fourth-
grade teachers in an elementary school working to organize the program for the year in a two-day planning workshop before the opening
of the school year. Their goal is to make sure they cover the material
at certain times in the year so that each completes the program by
June. Since texts and other instructional materials must be shared,
they have planned a schedule so that they can have the materials they
need at different times throughout the school year. After the first day,
they have identified common curriculum goals and programs in each
subject area and agreed upon their personal needs for instructional
materials. The district adopted a new basal reading series, and they
have been working to develop an outline for the program. They also
have divided papers and other disposable instructional materials
equally, and have synchronized how they will use the new reading
program.

The second day, the three teachers work individually on an outline of their teaching activities for the year. Once the sequence has
been established, their attention turns to organizing the first unit of
study in each subject they teach. Careful attention is given to making
certain each subject gets equal time. Each teacher prepares a daily
schedule so that every subject will be offered in the same time frame
each day. Consistency of time schedule each day throughout the year
allows the teacher to have firm control of the situation and allows
students to know what to expect each day. This way, pupils and the
teacher can concentrate on the subject matter at a particular time of
the day and then move on to the next planned activity.

In reviewing this scene, we observe a situation that emphasizes
the subject-centered approach in developing learning activities. Careful attention is given to preciseness of organization and to the time
allotted to each content-area study. Schedule consistency is sought
after, and in this case it is carefully ensured. Curriculum organization
of this nature regards systematic organization as essential to the effective study and interpretation of the content in each subject area.
The organization of such subject-centered learning experiences is simple, easily understood, and based on the content area alone. It does not

relate to other content areas taught to students at other times in the daily schedule. The teachers in this setting can easily evaluate learning and performance by their students in terms of the careful and exact program they have planned. Only minimal effort is required to build each year's program from the previous one. Subject-centered curriculum is quite easily revised and kept current from year to year. Adopting new textbooks can be handled in the way the new reading program was instituted here.

In this kind of curriculum organization, the mastery of the content, in and of itself, is the central purpose. This goal predominates over all others in organizing, teaching, and measuring learners in their mastery of content and subject matter taught. The planning done by each teacher was done only after the subject concerns at the fourth-grade level were agreed upon. Subsequently, the three teachers individually worked out their content outlines for the year in terms of the time schedule and procedures of their own choice. Procedures for the year are established before meeting each class, and the program for the year is set forth by each teacher for his or her own class. Although subject matter is a key element in any kind of curriculum organization, in this example it is the primary and dominant focus for the planning of instruction. These elements are central to the subject-centered point of view.

☐ *Scene Two*   This scene deals with the third-grade teachers in an elementary school. They are working together after school on an afternoon following the first quarter of the school year. They are evaluating the success of their students during that period and are considering whether any adjustments in the third-grade program need to be made for the next quarter. Their program features a modified self-contained program. In the self-contained program, students stay with their teacher for instruction in social studies, science, and English language arts. Students leave their self-contained classrooms and are mixed with students from the other third-grade classes in reading and mathematics. This allows instruction in reading and math to be organized by levels of mastery. In building the levels program in each grade, small groups of students can work through the levels at their own rate of progress throughout their elementary school years.

Leveling in reading and math is used because of the skill base necessary in both of those subject areas. Each teacher focuses on a specific level and thus can provide more responsive and specific teaching to meet the differing abilities of youngsters within that level. This allows students to learn at their own paces, but still cover essential skills in their development in reading and math. Part of the work teachers must do now is to examine the individuals in the various levels groups to see whether changes in placements must be made for the second quarter. In various cases, referrals will be made to the school remedial reading specialists, if the teachers feel that individuals need such help.

In the self-contained part of the program, teachers will begin a new unit of study. English language arts, social studies, and science are taught in relation to unifying themes. The unifying theme for the second quarter will be "People and Transportation." Students return from the mix of leveling in reading and math to their self-contained classroom for this part of the third-grade program. They will study the development of transportation in social studies, basic scientific concepts needed for transportation discoveries, and literature, spelling, and vocabulary dealing with transportation in English language arts. Planning of the use of reading materials, films, visuals, and other instructional materials must be considered by the teachers as they plan their individual self-contained classroom units from the total resource unit available for studying "People and Transportation."

In reviewing this scene, we observe a departure from the exact subject-centered program depicted in the first situation. Subject matter is an important part of the curriculum organization presented in this second situation. The reading and math levels programs are subject-centered, but not totally preplanned for the year as was the case in the first example. Here a more flexible arrangement for dealing with the changing needs of learners in a subject-centered setting is a concern of teachers. This replaces a need to have an entirely presequenced program. Thus, the use of subject matter is modified by teacher concerns for learning needs based on the experiences of individual students. The self-contained program in English language arts, social studies, and science introduces a modified aspect of the experience-centered curriculum. The curriculum organization in this environment is therefore a combination of subject- and experience-centered approaches. Many classrooms combine, in varying degrees, aspects of both these approaches. In this situation, the teachers have used both of these approaches to meet specific curricular needs. The skill development needs in reading and math caused them to utilize a modified, subject-centered approach in those areas. Likewise, they felt that the experience-centered approach that correlated learnings in three content areas around a unifying theme provided a broader learning experience in those areas. Curriculum organization can be varied and may utilize more than one approach to planning instruction. In this example, such an eclectic basis for the curriculum organization was described.

☐ *Scene Three* This scene deals with a second-grade teacher working with her class. In this school, teachers develop a set of general objectives for the elementary school both on a grade-level basis and on a vertical basis across the grades included in the school. These general objectives are then translated into specific subject-matter objectives in the same fashion. Within these agreed-upon purposes, teachers may then begin to develop curriculum organization for their own classes. This allows for differentiated means to achieve the general and specific objectives.

Teachers in this school organize curriculum in a means–ends relationship. The achievement of learning objectives in general and specific subject matter areas is a focal concern. However, the specific learning experience and subject matter materials utilized are not in any way prescribed, as long as the learning objectives are achieved. The second-grade teacher in this situation begins teaching a unit of study with detailed discussion and interaction with students. She seeks to identify the current concerns and interests of individual students, and unifying interest centers among groups of students in the class. These interests may deal with concerns about world, national, and local society, as well as the personal interest centers of students. The teacher then relates these interest centers to subject-matter materials through a unifying topic or theme, as was described in the previous situation. In this case, the unifying theme is "Community Helpers." Students will study community helpers, including police, fire, sanitation, mail, and transportation workers. The range of such helpers will be expanded in terms of the personal experiences of students with community health, social work, family counselors, and the like. Thus, the experience of students may become a screen or organizer for selecting content for study.

As the unit is planned by the teacher with student input, and is initiated, skill and development must be included. However, skill development in areas such as reading and math is taught in relation to the experiences studied. There is no predetermined skill or level of skill program separate from the subject matter covered within the unifying theme. Skill-level concerns are developed from the content used for study and learning in the unit itself. Thus, the teacher has been able to develop skill-level learnings for the students. Both subject- and experience-centered objectives for the second grade are simultaneously achieved. However, the fashion and manner in which this second-grade teacher achieved those objectives will differ throughout the year, from unit to unit. Her means to those ends will also differ from every other second-grade teacher's since the curriculum organization guidelines in this school allow for such differentiated response. The primary concern is to achieve the agreed-upon learning objectives.

In reviewing this scene, we see a departure from the modified experience-centered approach in the previous situation. In this instance, the teacher is heavily emphasizing the experience-centered curriculum approach in developing the program for students. Although subject matter is as essential as it was in both the previous situations, here it is used strictly as a means to achieve the learning objectives. Its selection is specific to the interests and concerns of students in this particular class. Their experiences become increasingly important as screens, selectors, and organizing centers for learning. They also are significant determinants of the subject matter most appropriate and relevant for study by those students. Thus the subject matter takes on increasing personal significance as a means to learn and to achieve. In such a setting, we can see that personal, experience-centered learning is closely related to the perceived problems, needs, and interests of students. Individual and group needs can become means to utilize the resources of the physical and social environment in which students live. Such learning experiences can facilitate the unification of school and community concerns and common interests.

The experience and professional preparation that educators need to be able to plan effective programs in both subject- and experience-centered approaches are important issues. In the examples of these first three situations, we can see that working on curriculum involves organizing learning within a wide range of settings. Although individual preferences will emerge within individual teaching styles, it is essential that teachers be able to develop both subject- and experience-centered curricular organizations. Such versatility is an important dimension in developing effective school programs.

■ Curriculum Settings at the Middle Grades Level

□ *Scene One* This scene deals with a meeting of a junior high school English department. The school year has ended and the department is planning some revisions in the English language arts program for the coming school year. There is a concern that teachers in this seventh-through ninth-grade school have not been adhering to the course outlines in English. In some cases, teachers of above-average groups have been including some of the ninth-grade literature in eighth-grade classes. This has led to problems of duplication or repetition, or the need for ninth-grade teachers to find alternate selections. After considerable study, the department votes to keep a strict adherence to the sequence of literature in the program and not to teach any piece out of its grade-level designation. Several optional literary works are agreed upon as supplementary pieces for each grade level, but they are not works to be studied in the other grades in the school.

Discussion then turns to the sequence of unit elements in the three grades. It is decided that the short-story unit should be moved from eighth to seventh grade because of its success in motivating students. The biography unit from seventh grade is moved to eighth grade because it depends upon literary skills more easily developed in the short-story unit that has just been moved to seventh grade. Because of its difficulty and concerns with understanding imagery, the poetry unit is moved from eighth to ninth grade. It is hoped that the literary skills necessary for greater success in poetry can be better learned in moving from short stories, through biography, to poetry over the three-year literary sequence in the junior high school. Such piecemeal interchange of subject units is known as "cut and paste" curriculum reorganization. Teachers then organize into grade-level committees to agree upon the sequence of all English language arts units in grammar, composition, and literature. This is done to make certain that individual teacher schedules allow for the passing of text and other instructional materials on a rotating schedule, with no conflict from teacher to teacher in each grade.

In reviewing this scene, we can once again see the manipulative advantages to be found in a subject-centered curriculum organization. As changes in the units or program elements are agreed upon, the replacement of items or reorganization of these elements is quickly and effectively done. Once such a scope and sequence are decided, teachers have virtually no advance planning to do for introducing units of study during the school year. Furthermore, subject units can be easily rearranged using the "cut and paste" method. Note that in the decision to reorganize the sequence of biography, poetry, and short-story units across the three junior high grades, the goal was to arrange the units in increasing difficulty based upon skills that could be readily developed from year to year. No attention was paid to the experience base of students or the degree to which their maturation indicates any increased abilities to think at higher levels. The emphasis in this situation is upon subject matter—with no priority for experience. The logical organization created by planning in this example will undoubtedly improve the program and result in learning gains. We see that concern for the appropriate arrangement of subject matter is an important factor in subject-centered curriculum organization.

☐ *Scene Two* This scene deals with two teachers in a middle school. One teaches English language arts and the other teaches social studies. Both teachers have seventh- and eighth-grade classes as part of their assignment. The school is organized in a departmentalized structure, but this year both teachers have some common groups. They each have two seventh- and two eighth-grade classes in which the same students have each teacher at different times during the day. The two teachers are both graduates of secondary education programs, and they have worked in the middle school together for several years. Some teachers have begun to move into team planning and teaching arrangements as an option available within the school schedule. The two teachers here are curious about this idea of teaming. Since they have a planning period at the same time, they decide to use it to develop a possible pilot experience in teaming.

They decide to plan a unit of study for the two seventh-grade classes that they share. Since American literature and American history are the seventh-grade curriculum areas, they decide to plan a unit in which an aspect of history can be the frame for literary study. The classes do not meet back-to-back with both teachers, so the emphasis of correlation must carry from teacher to teacher when the classes do meet. The unit organizes the study of *Johnny Tremain* and *Common Sense* in the seventh-grade English class to occur at the time students are studying the American Revolutionary War with the social studies teacher. The unit is a simple correlation of literature studied against the historical time frame with which both literary works deal. Vocabulary and word use from the social studies material are also included in aspects of the English class. Compositions and written assignments in both classes are given language grades as well as substantive evaluation. The use of subject matter is related to the experiential base of both classes.

The success of this initial effort leads the two teachers to plan a unit for the next year. This time they decide to try a similar effort in eighth grade using the study of the novel *A Tale of Two Cities* in correlation with the study of the French Revolution in the social studies class. The teachers consider the second attempt even more successful since they can use the skills they learned in the seventh-grade setting as a basis to improve and refine their planning of the second effort. They decide to ask that they be given common seventh- and eighth-grade classes again the following year so that they can plan several more units.

In this scene, we see another alternative for organizing learning experiences. Both teachers are concerned with subject-matter mastery in their respective content areas. However, because of beginning efforts to team in their school, they decide to try correlating two subject areas, English language arts and social studies. They select one unit for initial planning and development. The unit does not sacrifice any subject learning, but helps students see relationships between two subject matter areas. Thus the experiences gained by students in the one class and content area become important to the other. As a result, their learning of subject matter takes on a greater context of meaning. As the two teachers feel they had an initial success in this first venture, they plan a second. From their successes, they feel there is value in combining concepts and materials from their areas, and they plan to extend that approach in their teaching in the following year.

□ *Scene Three*   This scene deals with a seventh-grade teacher in a middle school. Students in this grade take mathematics and physical education daily from specialist teachers in those areas. This teacher works in a block-time program that allows him to organize spelling, English language arts, reading, social studies, and health for half of his students' school day.

The teacher has decided to plan with students a unit of study around critical problems in the local community. This will allow the teaching of spelling, reading, English language arts, social studies, and health around the expressed interests and concerns of students. A week is taken to discuss student concerns. During this time, individuals and groups engage in the study of materials, local newspapers, and the media to identify major areas that the class can then prioritize. The second week is spent in studying these data, developing a set of goals for the unit, and planning activities. These include large-group, small-group, and individual activities.

A six-week unit is developed around such consensus problems as unemployment, toxic waste dumping, providing for senior citizens, educating the community, and organizing for community action. Field trips and interviews with governmental leaders, employers, labor union leaders, and workers in the media are organized through small- and large-group projects. Several individuals develop a community service project with a local organization for the elderly and then begin a volunteer program with an area home for the elderly. Speakers from various community groups and organizations come and speak to the class. Local public service telecasting develops several programs utilizing students and their study. Students propose a program for community education on these issues, including several possible adult community education courses for the local continuing education program. The unit culminates in the school with an open house for parents and the community to visit and see what student learnings in the unit have achieved and produced.

In reviewing this case, we see that students use their base of experience to plan with their teacher a range of learning activities around personal interests and concerns under a unifying theme. Subject matter becomes important and specific to provide students with information necessary to expand their experience base in such activities. The subject matter comes from traditional sources as well as the resources of their community. Learning is action-oriented to provide students with skills that will enhance their base of experience for further learning in school and community. Teacher skills in such an experience-centered program include expertise not only in subject matter, but also in process development and guidance. Although teacher roles in such active-learning curriculum organization shift from initiation to cooperative planning, the teacher's pedagogic skills are absolutely necessary. This is not "kids doing whatever they want to do."

It is based on generating interest centers for the learning of content and skills in the subject-matter areas involved. This concept is the crucial element in experience-centered curriculum organization.

■ Curriculum Settings at the High School Level

□ *Scene One* This scene deals with a teacher of elementary algebra in high school. This is the first day of class in the new school year, and she is orienting a group of ninth-grade students to their year with her. She makes an initial presentation about the scope and sequence of the algebra course, the requirements for grades, credit for homework and assignments, and penalties for missed work, and then she distributes the textbook. In turning to the students for questions and discussion of her outline of the course, a range of concerns are raised. The class contains students who have come to the high school from a number of different public middle schools in the district, some from parochial schools, and some transfer students. Some students indicate they used the book as a resource in their eighth-grade math class and have done several parts of the book as extra assignments.

Others are concerned that they have not covered several areas that the teacher said she assumed they understood. The teacher offers this latter group the option of dropping algebra and taking a general math course instead so that they might take algebra as tenth-graders. Some students accept this, but others feel they should be able to have a review and perhaps some teaching of those areas and still stay in the algebra course. Some ask why the class cannot be organized on a unit approach for a while, like the one they had in eighth grade, and then allow students to move into the algebra sequence. The diverse background of the majority of students leads to more concern and dissatisfaction with the course as proposed. The environment begins to deteriorate as students express some general grumbling, cynical remarks, and negative feelings. The teacher becomes angry and silences the group. She comments that this is high school and that in adult life you have to accept the choices you face. She expresses regrets for their poor and varied preparation for high school. Then she states that if elementary and middle level schools developed higher standards and made students work, they would not find high school so difficult. She indicates that the course will be offered as she initially outlined it. She will be willing to give extra help after school to students who feel they are lacking in some of the prerequisites she sees for the course. Also, she states that those who may have studied some algebra before, or even parts of the book, may have a slight advantage. However, she will teach the information the way it really should be taught.

At this point, some students ask for passes to their counselor to see about dropping the course. Those remaining go through a brief introduction and are given a homework assignment for the next day.

In reviewing this situation, we see an attitude that may be inherent in an individual teacher's exclusive use of the subject-centered approach. Even in a subject-centered orientation, the previous experiences and learnings of students need to be considered. In the junior high school example dealing with the English department, concern was given to reordering the sequence of units from year to year based upon student experience and success. Such consideration must be given to readiness, especially when students are entering the next unit of a school system. A subject-centered curriculum organization must have vertical articulation among the elementary, middle grades, and high school units. If the variance that students bring to the setting described in this case cannot be regulated, perhaps such differentiation in student subject matter must be accommodated. This could be facilitated by several beginning algebra courses for students with differing backgrounds. The students with some algebra experience, those with none, and those still needing some prerequisite learning could be scheduled into the appropriate courses or sections. With such accommodation, both students and teachers could then proceed in a continued, realistic subject-centered mathematics program. The situation described here is a subject-centered approach, but even so, it is obvious that consideration should be given to the previous experiences of learners.

□ *Scene Two*   This scene deals with a teacher of American history. He is beginning the year's program with his eleventh-grade class. The course deals with "Problems of Democracy." The teacher believes that students can organize their study best around their interests and in terms of their previous study of American history. This requires extensive planning with students to organize the course around the collective concerns and experiences of the class.

Following the first day of orientation, the class begins to plan and identify eight topics and interest areas that they feel have the greatest impact upon the nation today and that they believe will be serious issues in the coming decade. Following two days of activity as a committee of the whole, they have identified sixteen possible topic centers. They divide the topics into eight pairs, and they break into an equal number of working groups. The teacher takes a day to outline, discuss, and teach group process skills before the eight working committees begin their study. The library and other extra-class resources are used for two days, with groups checking with the teacher to give progress reports. The class then comes together on the seventh day to share their progress. A number of the topics are dropped, and several are combined into single topics. The next day groups meet to rank topics, and the following day the class comes together to agree upon the final eight. The teacher works with the topics that evening to see how much of the required American history content to be covered can be woven into the pattern of the eight topics selected. The next day he presents his plan to take a day or two to pursue those aspects of the required American history content that could not be woven into the eight issues. This would complement the work studied in the eight organizing centers. The class then organizes to begin studying the first topic. A time line is developed, and committee assignments are made for specific group work that will be part of the unit. The class is now organized to begin its "Problems of Democracy" course.

In reviewing this scene, we see an interesting combination of aspects from both subject- and experience-centered approaches. Student planning is utilized to screen and prioritize the history to be learned and to develop major organizing centers for that purpose. Personal experiences of the students and previous study and learnings in American history are utilized to draw the subject-matter concerns into realistic focus. This removes the need for either a completely topical or chronological approach to the course. In working together in the two weeks of planning, students gain experiences in decision making, both in small groups and in the class as a whole. They identify the ways in which they can work with each other, and they develop an understanding of group process that will be one technique used in the course. Subject matter will be the means to achieve the learning objectives they have defined in the eight topics finalized in this project. The teacher has organized supportive historical study into intervening study, which shall be offered in addition to the eight topics selected. We can see the importance both of subject matter and of developing common experiences among class members as points of departure in beginning this course. The balance and blending between student interests and subject content constitute an essential ingredient in this kind of curriculum organization.

☐ *Scene Three* This scene deals with a group of ninth-graders who have expressed a doubt about whether to choose the district's vocational or academic program, which begins in tenth grade. A vocational exploration experience is designed for this purpose and offered during the final two periods of the day. This allows students to be able to leave school for field trips and work exploration experience. The first two weeks involve orientation and daily visits to the vocational school, where they are given a survey of the program offered there. The third week is given to meetings with vocational and career counselors at the school to determine work and educational requirements for careers in those fields. Career demands and expectations, as well as job supply in the areas, are also clarified.

In the fourth week in school, students begin to plan the career and work experiences they would like to study in the course. Each student can gain four nine-week experiences. Actual work settings are visited, and students can schedule their time in each placement. As students develop some initial background in the elements they choose to study, they may assist in work at actual job sites. This is all subject to strict safety standards and to confirmation by appropriate vocational teachers that the students have the background to participate in even such beginning activities. If students begin to develop a serious interest in a given experience, they may take a second nine-week experience at an intermediate level in that area. However, at least two separate placements in different vocational areas are required to provide an exploratory experience. General academic learnings in the remainder of their day in the school can be correlated around the interest centers and experiences of students in this vocational exploration program. Fully 60 percent of the students eventually choose the district's vocational program, while 40 percent choose to attend the academic high school program.

In reviewing this final scene, we see an experience-centered program developed as the result of careful planning to help students clarify their future educational direction. Experiences such as these must be realistic in terms of the expectations students will find in real vocational and career settings. Likewise, the nature and demands of study and preparation to enter these career areas must be clearly seen in terms of the work that is required. *Exploratory education at any level must allow a student to investigate potential interests.* It is critical that student decisions to apply to vocational programs be made in full understanding of the preparation as well as the work experience related to that vocational area.

The planning of such an experience-centered program requires constant revision to be certain that the experiences offered students reflect the dynamics of changing student interests and needs. Curriculum organization in such settings must also be responsive to change in both occupational and vocational preparation areas. Together, these represent a critical dimension in an experience-centered approach.

■ Analysis of the Situations

The situations we have presented deal with patterns of curriculum organization one might find at elementary, middle grades, and high school levels. Subject-centered situations, experience-centered situations, and situations that modified and combined both approaches were sketched. The degree of correctness in the examples is not an issue. Each was appropriate for the learning objectives involved. However, some clarification on the nature of subject matter and experience seems in order at this point. Edward Krug gives a good general statement of the nature and purpose of subject matter:

> Subjects are categories of knowledge or skill arranged for teaching purposes. The term does not have precise limitations since it is sometimes used to indicate an instructional field and at other times used to indicate a particular division of that field like chemistry or physics. Obviously, this kind of organization of classroom studies implies subject matter, but other kinds do not exclude it. (1957, p. 103)

The situations described gave varying examples of subject-centered curriculum organization in which the learning of the subject matter, or content, was the central objective.

In the case of experience, John Dewey's statement is central to considering its role in curriculum organization:

> The nature of experience can be understood only by noting that it includes an active and passive element peculiarly combined. On the active hand, experience is a trying, a meaning which is explicit in the connected term experiment. On the passive, it is undergoing. When we experience something we act on it; we do something with it; then we suffer or undergo the consequences. We do something to the thing and then it does something to us in return; such is the peculiar combination. The connection between these two phases of experience measures the fruitfulness or value of the experience. Mere activity does not constitute experience. It is dispersive, centrifugal, dissipating. Experience as trying involves change but change is meaningless transition unless it is consciously connected with the return wave of consequences which flow from it. When an activity is continued into the undergoing of consequences, when the change made by action is reflected back into a change made in us, the mere flux is loaded with significance. We learn something. It is not an experience when a child merely sticks his finger into a flame; it is experience when the movement is connected with the pain he undergoes in consequence. Henceforth the sticking of the finger into the flame means a burn. Being burned is a mere physical change, like the burning of a stick of wood, if it is not perceived as the consequence of some other action. (1916, p. 163)

Thus, experience-centered curriculum organization is concerned with the consequences or growth in learning provided by a particular learning experience. In that regard, content and subject matter are essential components if the learning experience is to be achieved. Earl Kelley bridges the interaction of subject matter and experience which is the concern of curriculum organization in any kind of setting:

Since we know now that the student learns in accordance with his own purposes and experiences which he cannot in fact truly perceive in any other way, we must necessarily look to a modification of the role and usefulness of subject matter. We now know that the subject matter will be perceived as the student can perceive it, no matter what we do, and that no two students will perceive a given fact the same way.

This does not mean that subject matter will not be used, or that it becomes unimportant. We cannot teach without teaching something, or students learn without learning something. No piece of subject matter, no fact of human knowledge, is bad in itself. It is good or bad only in relation to the person learning it, and to the possibility of his learning it. The question becomes one of asking who the subject matter is for, whether or not he has the purpose and experience to acquire it, what its acquisition will do to and for the learner and why it should be learned. (1947, p. 99)

The role of subject matter and experience is a central consideration in organizing curriculum plans. The examples presented here have attempted to portray different emphases in the possible relations between those two concerns. Teacher skill in using the various approaches is gained from experience in situations such as those elementary, middle grades, and high school settings that have been described here. But just because of their pivotal roles in organizing the curriculum, one should not assume that subject matter and experience are the only elements in that complex process. Many others will be presented in later chapters. For now, we turn to an examination of how this field defines curriculum.

DEFINITIONS OF CURRICULUM

■ ■   The question of what ought to be the curriculum of the school has been at issue for several centuries. Almost everyone seems to have an opinion about what students ought to learn or what they ought to study. Strangely enough, however, we have arrived at the present without a widely accepted definition of the term "curriculum" itself. In education we talk about "curriculum planning," "curriculum development," "curriculum evaluation," and many other types of curriculum-related activities. Given the lack of a consistent definition of curriculum, one might well ask what are we planning, developing, or evaluating? This does not mean that there is no such definition at all. In fact, as Frame 1.1 indicates, many definitions have been proposed.

The *Oxford English Language Dictionary* tells us that the term "curriculum" is borrowed from the Latin, originally referring to a race course used by chariots. We can imagine a group of patricians wending their way to the Circus Maximus talking about the length and form of the "curriculum" and debating about which chariot driver has the best skill for traversing such a course. Thus, our use of the term "curriculum" today is a metaphor, describing not a race course, but some notion of the course of events in school. When we finish school and begin applying for jobs, we usually send along with an application our *curriculum vitae,* or résumé, which describes the course of events in our lives. In the school, there is no single course of events. There are plans for learning, scheduled classes, athletic programs, ideas that students learn, and so on. Furthermore, each of these may be different for various groups of individuals. To define curriculum simply as "the course of events" in school does not resolve the confusion over its meaning. Although that concept probably lies at the root of various definitions, there is still the question of "which course of events?"

The definitions of curriculum found in Frame 1.1 illustrate some that have been proposed. A listing of all the attempts at definition would take many pages, perhaps filling a book by itself. Fortunately, many definitions have enough in common that we can place them into categories and study them in that way. With few exceptions, definitions of curriculum fall into one of four categories: (1) curriculum as a product, (2) curriculum as a program, (3) curriculum as intended learnings, and (4) curriculum as the experiences of the learner.

■ **Curriculum as Product**

It is not unusual when visiting a school to be invited to look at the "curriculum of the school." As the invitation is issued, the tour guide hands over a thick document, referring to it as the "language arts curriculum," the "science curriculum," or some other "curriculum." Such documents may include a listing of courses, syllabi for various courses, lists of skills and objectives, titles of textbooks, and so on. Whatever the contents, however, the document presumably describes the curriculum or course of events in the school. If there are several such documents, each one describing a different program or course of study, they may collectively be referred to in the plural as the "school curricula."

The definition of curriculum as a product thus derives from the idea that such documents are the results of curriculum planning, curriculum development, or curriculum engineering. In other words, if these documents are the results of *curriculum* planning, development or engineering, then they must be the curriculum.

The advantage of this definition of curriculum is that it allows us to think of that term in a concrete and definite way. Also, it provides direction for curriculum planning and development by specifying their purpose as the production of a document. When compared with other

Curriculum Is Defined in Many Ways

[Curriculum is] that series of things which children and youth must do and experience by way of developing abilities to do the things well that make up the affairs of adult life; and to be in all respects what adults should be.
                                                Bobbit, *The Curriculum*, 1918

Curriculum is all of the experiences children have under the guidance of teachers.
                        Caswell and Campbell, *Curriculum Development*, 1935

Curriculum consists of all the means of instruction used by the school to provide opportunities for student learning experiences leading to desired learning outcomes.
                                        Krug, *Curriculum Planning* (rev. ed.), 1957

A curriculum is a plan for learning. . . .
                        Taba, *Curriculum Development: Theory and Practice*, 1962

Curriculum encompasses all learning opportunities provided by the school.
                Saylor and Alexander, *Curriculum Planning for Modern Schools*, 1966

Curriculum is a structural series of intended learning outcomes. Curriculum prescribes (or at least anticipates) the results of instruction. It does not prescribe the means . . . to be used in achieving the results.
                        Johnson, "Definitions and Models in Curriculum Theory," 1967

---

definitions, however, it has two disadvantages. First, it limits the idea of "curriculum" to specific programs or courses of study as described in these documents. Second, it presumes that the documents can describe all the possible "courses of events in the school."

■ Curriculum as Program

A second category of curriculum definitions includes those which use the term in reference to the program of the school. Here, the course of events in school is viewed as the means used by the school to carry out its purposes. At its narrowest extreme, the curriculum as program refers to the *courses of study* offered by the school, including both required and elective courses. Those who define curriculum this way might also refer to an individual student's curriculum, meaning the courses being taken by that student. Narrow as it may be, this definition of curriculum is probably the most widely held in schools. However, the curriculum as program might also be conceived in a broader

Curriculum [is] "the educational program of the school" with attention to the elements of (1) program studies, (2) program of experiences, (3) program of services, and (4) hidden curriculum.

Oliver, *Curriculum Improvement* (2nd ed.), 1977

[Curriculum embodies] all of the teaching–learning experiences guided and directed by the school.

Harnack, *The Teacher: Decision Maker and Curriculum Planner*, 1968

Curriculum is the formal and informal content and process by which learners gain knowledge and understanding, develop skills, and alter attitudes, appreciations and values under the auspices of that school.

Doll, *Curriculum Improvement: Decision Making and Process* (4th ed.), 1978

[Curriculum is] that reconstruction of knowledge and experience systematically developed under the auspices of the school (or university), to enable the learner to increase his or her control of knowledge and experience.

Tanner and Tanner, *Curriculum Development: Theory into Practice* (2nd ed.), 1980

The curriculum is all of the experiences that individual learners have in a program of education whose purpose is to achieve broad goals and related specific objectives, which is planned in terms of a framework of theory and research or past and present professional practice.

Hass, *Curriculum Planning: A New Approach* (3rd ed.), 1980

Curriculum [is] a plan or program for all experiences which the learner encounters under the direction of the school.

Oliva, *Developing the Curriculum*, 1982

way. If the purpose of the school is learning, and if curriculum is the means of carrying out that purpose, then one must consider the fact that students learn from aspects of the school other than just the courses of study or classroom activities. For example, learning presumably takes place in clubs and activities, in athletic programs, in the guidance program, and so on. The point could probably be pressed to include the cafeteria, the hallways, the buses, and the principal's office since students undoubtedly "learn" in these settings also. The broader interpretation of curriculum as programs refers to all aspects of the school in which learning takes place.

The advantages of defining curriculum as program include (1) the fact that the curriculum can be easily described in concrete terms and (2) the recognition that learning takes place in many different settings in the school. The latter idea may also lead to a careful analysis of what students learn in settings other than courses of study. While this definition is obviously broader than curriculum as product, it has the similar disadvantage of implying that what is contained in our plans for the various school programs describes what students actually learn. As we shall see, this assumption has been challenged by other "curriculum" definers.

■ Curriculum as Intended Learnings

A third category of curriculum definitions includes those which use the term in reference to the learnings that are intended for students. In other words, curriculum may be defined as "what is to be learned." Proponents of this definition claim that what is to be learned should be considered separately from how it is to be learned. In addition, when educational planning occurs, the what (curriculum) always precedes the how. These proponents also suggest that curriculum does not include consideration of why something is to be learned. As defined here, then, curriculum refers to knowledge or content, skills, attitudes, and behaviors that students are supposed to learn in school. Although this definition is obviously more conceptual than the curriculum as product, the "intended learnings" are often described in documents. Included may be student objectives for learning or lists of facts, principles, concepts, and understandings from various subject fields. When reference is made to the means for learning, such as activities, proponents of this definition would say that one has left the area of curriculum and entered the realm of instruction. We will be considering the relationship between curriculum and instruction later. For now we simply note that some "curriculum definers" see a distinct difference between the what and how of learning and limit the idea of curriculum to the former.

The advantages of defining curriculum as intended learning outcomes are that (1) curriculum becomes a concept or idea rather than a product, and (2) it puts curriculum into a more manageable focus by limiting its scope. The disadvantage of this definition is its insistence that the what and how of learning can and ought to be treated separately. This view may contribute to fragmented planning and may detract from a comprehensive view of learning.

■ Curriculum as Experiences of the Learner

The fourth category of definitions represents a major departure from the other three. While largely different from one another, those already described all have in common the idea that curriculum is something developed or planned prior to teaching–learning situations. Here, however, curriculum refers to the experiences of the learner that are outcomes of the planned situations. This definition has its roots in the idea that what is planned is not always what actually happens. Thus, the course of actual events or the "curriculum" can only be found in the learnings that students take away from various experiences. Proponents of this category would suggest that the three definitions previously discussed are actually *curriculum plans*. Presumably, any description of *the* curriculum would require an after-the-fact analysis of the student's learning experiences.

To illustrate this category, imagine that a football team is coached by an individual who espouses the goal of building character and teamwork through the sport. However, week after week the coach plays only the best players and consistently "runs up the score" against less talented teams. Although the plan called for character and teamwork, the players actually learn that the purpose of sport is to win at all costs, including humiliation of the opponent. In other words, the actual course of events is something far different from what was intended. The curriculum is obviously what the participants learned rather than the plan. Proponents of this category would claim that the same kind of analysis could be applied to the classroom in terms of the differences between what the teacher plans and what students actually learn.

The advantages of this definition are that (1) it focuses on learning and the learner, rather than teaching, and (2) it includes all of the experiences of learners both planned and unplanned. The disadvantages are that (1) it is more abstract and complex than the other definitions, and (2) it makes the curriculum of a school so comprehensive that it cannot be described in simple terms or short phrases.

It is unlikely that the differences of opinion about the meaning of "curriculum" will soon be completely resolved. For both the beginning student of curriculum and the experienced curriculum theorist, the task is the same—to explore the consequences of each definition for curriculum planning and development, perhaps finding in one or another enough to warrant personal commitment. Without trying to resolve the conflict, we might suggest that it may be useful when referring to curriculum to use more specific terms such as the "planned curriculum" or the "learner's curriculum." This practice might at least alleviate the differences between the first three categories and the last.

Furthermore, in analyzing the four categories, consideration might be given to two observations. As shown in Figure 1.1, the definitions can be placed on a continuum ranging from the concrete to the abstract. Thus, while "curriculum as experiences of the learner" may be more desirable to some than "curriculum as product," the former can be more difficult to understand and/or explain. Figure 1.1 also shows that the four definitions may be placed on another continuum ranging from a school-centered focus to a focus on the learner. In this case, analysis may depend upon one's view of which ought to receive higher priority— a clearly definable plan or program, or an endless variety of experiences that are centered on learning but that are tremendously difficult to describe.

FIGURE 1.1   Definitions of Curriculum Range from Abstract to Concrete and from School-Centered to Learner-Centered

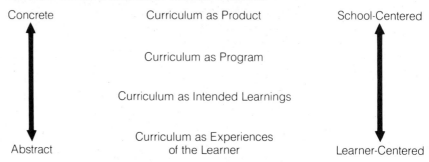

The differences of opinion regarding the definition of curriculum may seem frustrating, particularly in light of the fact that a consensus about accepting one or another will probably not be reached. At first glance, one might well ask how the field can ever get on with its work if agreement cannot even be reached regarding what it is about. Indeed, the lack of agreement on this and other views has caused some observers to wonder about the state of the curriculum field. Philip Jackson vividly portrayed the problem of ambiguity in the curriculum field in the following tongue-in-cheek sketch:

> They had traveled a long way. Their horses bore marks of the journey; flanks caked with mud, manes matted with dust. At last, the end was near. Dismounting, the pair walked the final few yards on foot. At the edge of the cliff, they paused and gazed upon the scene below. The younger of the two, tugging at his partner's arm, broke the silence.
>
> "Behold," he said, gesturing at the view that lay before them, "Yon lies the field of curriculum. So vast and inviting. Such a worthy object of contemplation. So ready for the harvest, ripe for the hands of willing workers. But wait! What's this? Can it be? Why is there not more movement? Why does it lie so still? Tell me, good father, is it . . . is it alive? Or is it . . . could it be . . . (gulp!) . . . dead?"
>
> Meanwhile, back on the cliff at the end of the trail, the older traveler turned and looked incredulously at his younger companion. "What's got into you, son?" he asked. "That ain't no field of curriculum. Them is plain old summer squash as far as the eye can see. Field of curriculum! Well, I never! All that university book-learning must have gone to your head. Well, you're home now, son, so you can talk normal again. Just mind your words and speak up loud and clear. You should have plenty to talk about."
>
> After a long pause the older man again broke the silence. "Let's go now," he said.
>
> The pair turned, walked back to their horses, remounted, and began the long descent into the valley. Neither spoke on the way down. (1980)

On the other hand, the differences of opinion about the definition of curriculum and other issues may be viewed as an advantage. Elliot Eisner and Elizabeth Vallance (1974) admit that such differences may present a "conceptual jungle" to students of curriculum, but also point out that "the richness of issues and values in the field provides an arena that can be . . . a dynamic and stimulating resource." Indeed, a field in which consensus is easily reached risks stagnation since new ideas that do not conform to set standards may be rejected without careful consideration of their value. The continuing dialogue about meanings is just the kind of forum that encourages the possibility of fresh ideas and new insights.

Perhaps the most fruitful message to be gleaned from the recognition of differing definitions of curriculum is the following. Even if one selects one definition to have "most favored status," one should still recognize that several definitions do exist and are just as favored by others. Thus, they cannot be rejected lightly since all have both advantages and disadvantages.

CHAPTER SUMMARY

The study of curriculum involves learning not only about central ideas, but also about the diversity of opinion within each one. Chapter 1 has included a consideration of two major topics. The first was curriculum organization, or the form that school programs take. A series of situations illustrated three different curriculum organization patterns at the elementary, middle, and high school levels. The major difference among patterns was the varying emphasis placed on separate subjects or on the interests and experiences of learners. As discussed in the commentary following the descriptions, subject matter is found in all approaches but is used differently from one approach to another.

The second topic considered in Chapter 1 was the definition of the term "curriculum." As we have seen, the term has been defined in many ways, although most definitions fall into one of four categories: (1) curriculum as product, (2) curriculum as program, (3) curriculum as intended learning, and (4) curriculum as experiences of the learner. The debate over how curriculum ought to be defined will probably continue to be unresolved. However, the diversity of opinion need not be frustrating. Rather, it should be seen as representing the richness of the field, and as a source of fresh ideas and new insights.

Having read Chapter 1, you should be able to:

1. Describe different types of curriculum organization

2. Cite patterns of curriculum organization to which you have been exposed as student or teacher
3. Distinguish between approaches that focus on separate subjects and approaches that emphasize the interests and experiences of learners
4. Identify four categories of definitions of curriculum
5. Describe the advantages and disadvantages of each type of definition

SUGGESTED ACTIVITIES

1. Have the group review the classroom situations presented in this chapter and discuss any pertinent situations they recall from their own school experiences. Ask them to discuss and report the following to the class.
   a. Did they recall having experiences that involved the subject-centered, experience-centered, and combined approaches similar to those described in the situations?
   b. Did they recall more experiences similar to one of the situations than the others?
   c. Did they have any opinions about whether as children they individually preferred being in or learned better in any one of the specific kinds of settings?

Discuss what this means for teachers in planning to meet individual student learning needs and preferences of children and youth.

2. Divide the large group into educators concerned with elementary, middle level, or high schools. Have each small group discuss and report the following to the class.
   a. What do they see as the advantages and disadvantages of either heavily subject-centered or experience-centered learning activities for learners at their level?
   b. Do any of them feel the combined modification of both subject- and experience-centered approaches is better for all learners?
   c. Why do they feel this to be the case?
   d. Do they feel teachers should develop some learning experiences that use each of the three approaches described in the situations for their level?
   e. Why do they feel this to be the case?

3. Summarize and discuss what members of the groups in Activities 1 and 2 felt were the strengths and weaknesses of the subject-centered approach, experience-centered approach, and combined modification of both approaches at elementary, middle level, and high

schools. In what ways did the choices and preferences differ in each group? Consider how the answers may or may not reflect changing emphases in learning needs of students as they grow through their years in school. Does this suggest differing concerns for developing learning activities at each level?

4. Frame 1.1 lists twelve definitions of curriculum. Have interested members of the class work in groups and find examples of school practices for each definition. Discuss ways in which these definitions can be helpful to teachers in planning learning activities for students.

5. Have interested members of the class break into groups and identify examples of school practices that represent curriculum as product, curriculum as program, curriculum as intended learning, and curriculum as the experiences of the learner. Convene the groups, and share and compare the examples they identified.

Discuss how the twelve definitions of curriculum presented in Frame 1.1 can be listed under the categories of curriculum (as product, as program, as intended learning, and as the experience of the learner) in terms of their presentation in Figure 1.1.

6. Have each member of the group ask two or three teachers and two or three laypersons to define the term "curriculum." Classify these definitions according to the four major categories discussed in Chapter 1. Which category accounted for the majority of definitions? Were any definitions outside the four categories? Might any be classified in more than one category?

7. Have members of the large group select a personally preferable definition of curriculum. Form small groups on the basis of each category. Have these groups formulate a rationale supporting their choices. Develop an informal debate with each group presenting its position. Then invite individuals to change groups based upon the arguments presented. The clustering of groups will not represent a visual demonstration of opinion within the large group. (The group should be reminded of the continuing diversity of opinion about definitions outlined in this chapter.)

REFERENCES

Bobbitt, F. *The Curriculum*. Boston: Houghton Mifflin, 1918.

Beauchamp, G. *Curriculum Theory*. 3rd ed. Wilmette, Ill.: Kagg Press, 1975.

Caswell, H., and Campbell, D. *Curriculum Development*. New York: American Book Company, 1935.

Dewey, J. *Democracy and Education*. New York: Macmillan, 1916.

Doll, R. C. *Curriculum Improvement: Decision Making and Process*. 4th ed. Boston: Allyn and Bacon, 1978.

Eisner, E., and Vallance, E. *Conflicting Conceptions of Curriculum*. Berkeley, Calif.: McCutchan, 1974.

Hass, G. *Curriculum Planning: A New Approach*. 3rd ed. Boston: Allyn and Bacon, 1980.

Harnack, R. *The Teacher: Decision Maker and Curriculum Planner*. Scranton, Pa.: International Textbook, 1968.

Jackson, P. "Curriculum and Its Discontents." *Curriculum Inquiry* 10 (1980): 159–172.

Johnson, M. "Definitions and Models in Curriculum Theory." *Educational Theory* 17 (1967).

Kelley, E. *Education for What Is Real*. New York: Harper & Brothers, 1947.

Krug, E. *Curriculum Planning*. Rev. ed. New York: Harper & Brothers, 1957.

Oliva, P. *Developing the Curriculum*. Boston: Little, Brown, 1982.

Oliver, A. *Curriculum Improvement*. 2nd ed. New York: Harper & Row, 1977.

Saylor, J. G., and Alexander, W. *Curriculum Planning for Modern Schools*. New York: Holt, Rinehart and Winston, 1966.

Taba, H. *Curriculum Development: Theory and Practice*. New York: Harcourt Brace Jovanovich, 1962.

Tanner, D., and Tanner, L. *Curriculum Development*. 2nd ed. New York: Macmillan, 1980.

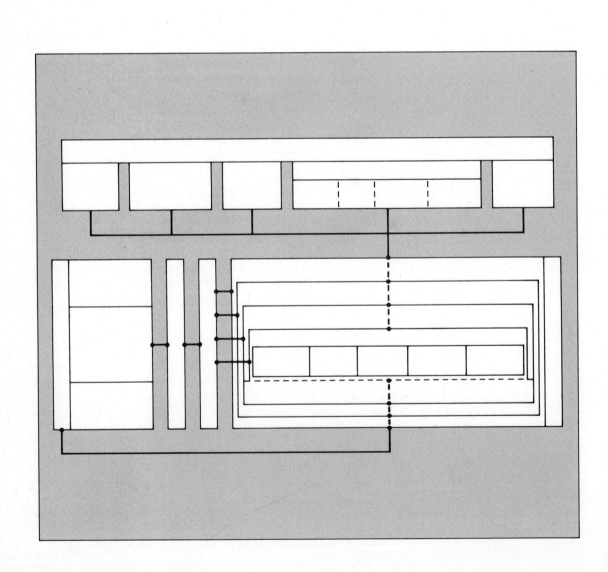

2

Working on Curriculum

In Chapter 1, we saw that the curriculum field is one of diversity. Its study involves not only learning about central themes and topics, but learning the differences of opinion within them. In Chapter 2, the sense of diversity will continue in a different context—the action phase of the curriculum field.

The first section describes situations depicting curriculum work. Each one represents a different level at which such work is done, and each illustrates several different forms of curriculum planning. Those who have had teaching experience will probably have participated in settings like one or more of these.

The second section extends the list of definitions begun in Chapter 1. Whereas the discussion there focused on the term "curriculum" itself, here we will consider several curriculum-related terms and phrases, including "curriculum planning," "curriculum development," "instruction," "curriculum evaluation," "hidden curriculum," and "out-of-school curriculum." The definition of these terms is not simply an exercise in semantics. A working knowledge of them is not only part of studying curriculum, but essential for effective participation in curriculum work.

The third section of this chapter describes some of the persistent issues in the curriculum field. Here we will see what happens when curriculum terminology, curriculum work, and possibilities for curriculum organization are subjected to different value systems held by various groups. For our purposes, three fundamental issues have been selected: subject matter versus the learner, participation in curriculum decision-making, and the definition of "basics" in learning. These and other issues will then serve as recurring themes in subsequent chapters. Thus, the action phase of curriculum work represents the second stage in our study of curriculum.

As a result of reading Chapter 2, you should be able to:

1. Describe several different levels and forms of curriculum work
2. Identify some of the principles of curriculum planning
3. Define some of the phrases related to curriculum, such as "curriculum development," "instruction," "curriculum evaluation," "hidden curriculum," and "out-of-school curriculum"
4. Discuss some of the persistent issues in the curriculum field and different opinions within each

CURRICULUM PLANNING: SEVEN SCENES

■ ■   The planning of learning experiences, or curriculum planning, is one of the most important professional activities in education. In fact, outside of the actual teaching–learning situation, it is probably the most important activity since it largely determines the day-to-day life of learners in school.

The majority of this section is devoted to seven situations involving curriculum planning. They present curriculum planning activities at the national level, the state level, the school-system-wide level, the building level, the teacher team level, the individual teacher level, and the classroom level with cooperative planning between students and teachers.

Each situation describes a particular level or form of such planning, and together they represent a comprehensive, although not exhaustive, look at what it means to work on curriculum. As you will see, curriculum planning involves both long- and short-range decision-making. It includes participation by diverse groups and takes place at many different levels. The purpose of the seven situations is to give the reader a familar context in which to consider the meaning of curriculum planning. After presenting the situations, we discuss the common threads or patterns that run through them and that thus define curriculum planning.

Whether one is a classroom teacher, curriculum coordinator, subject-matter supervisor, or school administrator, it is necessary to understand the implications of curriculum planning at each of these levels. There is an interaction among all of these levels that has an eventual impact on the teaching–learning environment at the classroom level. Teachers, at different times, may participate in curriculum planning at many of the levels described here. The situations are illustrations of "what it means to work on curriculum." As you consider each one, keep the following questions in mind.

At what level is the curriculum planning activity taking place?
What group (groups) is (are) represented in that situation?

What issues or questions are being addressed?

For what purpose(s) is the curriculum planning being done?

Does the situation sound familiar in terms of your experiences?

■ Curriculum Planning at the National Level

□ *Scene One* This scene deals with a group of scholars from universities around the country, all from some particular subject area, such as biology or history. They have come together because they are dissatisfied with the nature of elementary or secondary education in their subject areas and want to do something about it. Eventually, they decide to develop and disseminate a recommended set of plans for teaching their particular subjects. Initially, they identify what they consider to be the important subject matter, facts, principles, concepts, and understandings they believe ought to be taught. Next, they decide on a sequence in which the subject matter ought to be taught, from specific to general or from easy to difficult. Following this, they make recommendations for activities through which students might best learn the subject matter, including experiments, discussions, and lectures. Finally, they list what they believe to be the best materials for studying their area and some possible tests that learners might take to check their progress. All of this is then put together in sets of teaching–learning materials, which are tested by a group of teachers and then disseminated to schools throughout the country.

In this situation, the projected group of scholars have considered what should be taught in a particular subject area and have identified related activities, materials, and measuring devices. This kind of activity represents one form of curriculum planning, done in this case at the national level. Such curriculum planning was particularly popular following the launching of the satellite *Sputnik* by the Russians in 1957, and the approach continued through the 1960s. At the time, it was concluded that this technological event demonstrated the superiority of Russian over American schools. It was projected, therefore, that American schools needed to enhance the teaching of subject areas, particularly mathematics and science. Who could better do the required curriculum planning than eminent scholars in the subject fields? Such projects were subsequently undertaken in fields like biology (BSCS biology), chemistry (Chem Bond), physics (PSSC Physics), and mathematics (SMSG Math). The underlying assumption was that once developed, such curriculum projects or packages could be put in the hands of teachers and quality education would be assured. Further, the materials were touted as "teacher-proof" since it was believed that teachers with less than desired skills or knowledge would be working from the plans of true scholars. The same kind of thinking emerged in the early 1980s as politicians, the media, and other sources questioned the economic strength of the United States in the world marketplace. Concern over the rising industrial power of Japan and other nations prompted the development of national reports such as *A Nation at Risk* from the Commission on Excellence in 1983. In turn, many states acted quickly to mandate new courses and higher standards. Teacher competence was also questioned, and some critics suggested that curriculum plans and guides should be developed at the state level to counteract the lack of teaching skill.

In reviewing this situation, it is important to be aware that such curriculum planning prompted a variety of reactions. Following are some questions you should address in formulating your own analysis.

Do you feel that national-level curriculum projects can account for the characteristics of learners in local schools where the projects are supposed to be used?

Are you confident that subject-area scholars are sufficiently knowledgeable about learner characteristics to prepare curriculum plans for use in schools?

Do you feel that subject-area scholars are better equipped than teachers to develop curriculum plans in their area of specialization?

How do national-level curriculum plans influence the professional role of teachers?

Do you think it is possible to develop curriculum plans that would be successful even when used by relatively unskilled teachers?

Although curriculum planning at the national level is the most remote from the classroom, it is one level and form of curriculum planning. Therefore, any description of "what it means to work on curriculum" would be incomplete without it.

■ Curriculum Planning at the State Level

□ *Scene Two* In this scene, a group of educators (teachers, principals, curriculum coordinators, and others) come together as a committee formed by a state education department. Their task is to recommend what ought to constitute the overall program of elementary schools across the state. A series of meetings of the group over the course of several months culminates in the production of a booklet. The publication is sent to all school districts as the recommended model for the elementary school curriculum.

The booklet reflects the deliberations and decisions of the group. First, they have decided that the elementary school includes three subgroups of learners: early childhood, middle childhood, and late childhood. In turn, each group is described in terms of specific developmental, physical, social, and cognitive characteristics. Then, for each group, a review is provided of how each of the statewide goals for education might be approached. The review might include what children should have already learned in relation to each goal, as well as a variety of activities that could be used to further development toward the goal at each level. In addition, general ideas at all levels are presented regarding topics such as classroom atmosphere, scheduling, cooperative planning, school organization, teaching techniques, and curriculum evaluation. In other words, the committee has taken two approaches to the elementary school curriculum. One deals with contributions that may be made at each level to the attainment of broad goals. The other deals with curriculum considerations that cut across each of the subgroup levels.

In reviewing this situation, we see that the committee has considered the characteristics of learners and the broad goals of education. In combining the two, focus is drawn upon how the curriculum of the elementary school ought to be planned and structured. This kind of activity can offer valuable guidance to both improvement and assessment. Since it involves recommending program ideas and suggestions, it represents one level and form of curriculum planning often done at the state level. Other state-level activities that influence curriculum or involve actual curriculum planning include dissemination of curriculum guides on various topics, holding statewide curriculum conferences, mandating new areas that are to be taught in schools, and deciding on graduation requirements or minimum skill levels.

The role of the states in developing or regulating local school programs has been a matter of some controversy. In formulating your own reaction to this situation, consider the following questions.

Do you feel that local school districts should have the prerogative of setting up their own programs based upon local needs and preferences?

Are statewide programs and standards necessary to ensure the quality of education for learners across a state?

How would you rate the quality of curriculum guides or plans developed at the state level in your own state?

Do you feel that state-level personnel are more qualified to develop curriculum plans than local teachers?

How do state-level curriculum guides and mandates affect the role of the teacher at the local level?

Most educators agree that cooperation between the state and local levels can do much to enhance curriculum planning. In any event, virtually all state departments of education or instruction are involved in curriculum planning to some degree. Thus, curriculum planning at this level is a necessary ingredient in considering "what it means to work on curriculum."

■ Curriculum Planning at the System-Wide Level

☐ *Scene Three*   This scene deals with a group from a local school district who have come together to discuss the district's program in citizenship education. Included are elementary, middle level, and high school teachers, the district curriculum coordinator, and several citizens. Under sponsorship of the system-wide curriculum planning council, the group has been charged to evaluate the overall citizenship education program and decide how it might be improved.

The discussion begins with an overview of the goals involved in citizenship education. The overview includes general agreement about the definitions and concepts involved and the relationships among local, national, and global citizenship. Following this, representatives from the various levels present reports describing what each level includes in its citizenship program and how its program contributes to the overall goals.

At a second meeting, the participants review the materials developed in the first meeting, identifying what they believe to be the strengths of the program as well as the gaps that need to be filled. Before the next meeting, each level representative meets with colleagues to discuss the committee's work and to gather recommendations for improving the program. In the meantime, members of the committee visit nearby schools that have exemplary citizenship education programs, and the curriculum coordinator gathers materials from various professional resources that focus on citizenship education. At a third meeting, the level representatives report on their discussions with colleagues. Reports are given on visits to other schools, and the materials are distributed. Over the next few months, the committee meets several times and, as a result of its various activities, develops a set of recommendations for the system-wide council concerning the status and improvement of the district's citizenship education program. Among the recommendations are the need to clarify the goals of the citizenship program, the need to sponsor committees at various levels to develop curriculum plans, the need to articulate these plans across levels, the need to sponsor visitations by teachers to other schools, and the need to identify ways in which learners might participate more actively in community activities under the sponsorship of the schools. At this point, the committee disbands, although several of its members will assume active roles in carrying out the recommendations.

In reviewing this situation, we see that the committee members carried out several activities. For example, they studied and refined goals associated with a particular program, considered the nature of what students might already be learning about citizenship, identified areas in need of improvement, and recommended steps for improving the program. Although not developing plans for specific learners, the group nonetheless considered the purposes of a program and the related means for achieving those purposes. In other words, the committee engaged in curriculum planning, albeit at the system-wide level. Such activity clearly represents one level and form of curriculum that is used by many school districts. In this case, a standing system-wide curriculum planning council, with representation from school and community and from all levels, meets regularly to consider curriculum issues that affect the whole district. In turn, the council sponsors curriculum development projects, professional growth activities, and special study groups dealing with issues like school climate and community relations.

The sum of these projects promotes an atmosphere in which cooperative and comprehensive curriculum planning is encouraged, and this facilitates planning at more specific levels as part of a coherent and articulated structure. In analyzing this situation, consider the following questions.

> What are some present problems or ideas in your local district that might be referred to a system-wide curriculum planning council?
>
> In what ways might such a council support your work as a professional educator?
>
> If you were responsible for setting up a curriculum council, what methods would you use to solicit representation from various groups such as citizens, teachers, and administrators?
>
> What educational issues, if any, would you identify as not appropriate for consideration by a curriculum council?

It is unfortunate that all local districts do not have such a council. However, those that do serve as excellent examples of how curriculum activities can be enhanced locally. For this reason, system-wide curriculum planning represents a critical operational component in understanding "what it means to work on curriculum."

■ Curriculum Planning at the Building Level

□ *Scene Four* This scene deals with a group of parents, teachers, administrators, counselors, and students from a particular school. They have come together to develop a new discipline policy for the school. Initially, some participants express a concern about the need to regulate the behavior of students whom they believe are disruptive. They feel that there is a need to develop a comprehensive set of rules and regulations to deal with students. However, other participants point out that such a set of rules would mean that virtually all student life in school would be heavily regulated. Thus, students would have few opportunities to make responsible decisions for themselves. In the end, the group understands that the personal and social learnings that grow out of the school's governance structure are at least as important as those gleaned from the academic program. Furthermore, since these personal and social experiences are learning experiences, they are part of the curriculum. As a result, the group begins its deliberations, not by listing possible rules and regulations for student behavior, but by deciding what they believe students should learn about responsible participation in group settings.

This situation represents a form of curriculum planning that results from the fairly recent recognition that students learn a great deal from what is termed the "hidden curriculum." The hidden curriculum includes such institutional features as governance structure, grouping patterns, grading procedures, and teacher expectations. Since features like these do result in learning, whether they are planned or unplanned, they need to be considered in conscious efforts to plan the curriculum. That is to say, they must be planned in terms of purposes, activities, evaluation devices, and so on. The same holds true for athletic programs, cafeteria procedures, busing arrangements, and all other aspects of school life in which students participate and thus have learning experiences.

In reviewing this situation, we see that all aspects of the school program need to be subjected to the same careful planning and review as are given to content and subject-matter areas. In examining these areas of the hidden curriculum, we can identify the impact of learning experiences in such areas. Where the importance of such learnings has been ignored, schools have failed to identify the range of positive and negative learnings that students acquire from such experiences. Recognizing the influence of these hidden-curriculum learnings has been an important step in understanding the impact of the school upon learners. In reviewing this situation, consider the following questions.

What persons do you feel should serve on a curriculum council within your own school?

Should students be included on a building-level curriculum council? If so, in what capacity, and how would you select representatives?

What present problems or ideas in your local building might be addressed by a curriculum council?

What do you believe are some of the more powerful features of your school that influence the hidden curriculum?

To what extent are aspects of the hidden curriculum in your school considered to be sources of learning for students?

As those who plan activities come to the realization of the importance of such learning, the relationship of the hidden curriculum to the planned learnings of the stated curriculum can be better understood. We have seen here a subtle but important dimension of "what it means to work on curriculum."

■ **Curriculum Planning at the Teacher Team Level**

☐ *Scene Five* This scene deals with a group of teachers who have come together to discuss the possibility of carrying out a unit on Colonial Living that will involve all eighth-grade students. Each teacher represents a different subject area, and all have agreed to participate in development and implementation of the unit. Prior to the meeting, they have been asked to think about how their area might contribute, and each is now asked to share that thinking with the group. As a result of the discussion, a listing of areas and contributions is developed:

> *Social Studies:* origins of colonies and their relation to England, similarities and differences in colonial government, colonial trade
>
> *Language Arts:* types of communication, language patterns, stories about colonial figures, newspaper and book samples from colonial times
>
> *Science:* medical treatments and medicines, superstitions, family genealogy
>
> *Mathematics:* weights and measures, trade and currency, shipping routes and invoices
>
> *Home Economics:* family living styles, clothing construction, common foods and their production and preparation
>
> *Physical Education:* recreation, sports, games played by colonial children
>
> *Industrial Arts:* home construction, farming tools, blacksmithing and other trades
>
> *Art:* representative works of art from the period, use of art materials such as dyes
>
> *Music:* common types of music, favorite songs, typical songs sung by children, musical instruments
>
> *Other:* activities such as spinning and weaving, candlemaking, and soapmaking

Further discussion is held regarding the timing of various activities, including such things as field trips and films, as well as who will be responsible for each of the ancillary activities. Also, the library-media specialist is asked to develop a list of available in-school resources that learners may use and to put them in a centralized place for the duration of the unit. Finally, it is decided that the unit will begin with a meeting between the teachers and all eighth-grade students to give an overview of the plans. The unit will culminate with an open house for parents, including a display of projects and a colonial-style dinner.

This type of activity is known as interdisciplinary curriculum planning since it involves contributions from various subjects or disciplines of knowledge. In reviewing this situation, consider the following questions.

What would you see as the benefits of cooperative interdisciplinary planning in your school?

How would you feel about serving as a member of such a team? What might hinder your volunteering to participate?

What factors do you believe might detract from the effectiveness of an interdisciplinary team?

What aspects of your present curriculum plans might be correlated with other teachers or areas?

Although currently growing in popularity at the middle school and junior high level, the interdisciplinary idea has a long history in the curriculum field and has enjoyed popularity at various times in the past sixty years. Obviously, then, the activity described in this situation represents one level and form of curriculum planning. It is another component in studying "what it means to work on curriculum."

■ **Curriculum Planning by the Individual Teacher**

☐ *Scene Six* This scene is one that repeats in hundreds of thousands of rooms every night as a teacher sits alone thinking about possible learning activities that might be used during the next few days or weeks. In this case, a teacher is trying to make a decision about learning objectives—what the teacher would like a group of students to learn. In the area of subject matter or content, the teacher will have to make decisions about important facts, principles, concepts, and understandings that should be emphasized. The teacher must also plan different kinds of activities and resources and ways to measure how well learners have accomplished various objectives. At some time, the teacher may search through various journals looking for ideas about activities, gathering background information, or consulting with other teachers. In the end, the teacher decides on long- and short-term objectives as well as the timing of various activities. The teacher must then develop a set of plans for use on a daily, weekly, and longer basis. In designing this kind of plan, a number of items must be considered, such as the characteristics of the learners, the sequencing of activities, the appropriateness of various learning materials, and the availability of resources.

In reviewing this situation, we must recognize that the planning orientation of prospective teachers is often limited to daily lesson planning. All too often, little attention is paid to how these relate to long-term unit plans. This orientation is frequently reinforced by school officials who emphasize and often inspect daily plans without regard to long-term implications. As a result, many teachers may have difficulty understanding the relationship between short- and long-range plans and, in addition, may not realize the need for the latter. The planning done by the individual teacher is probably the most critical in the range of curriculum planning forms. This is because it largely determines the actual experiences learners have in relation to the school. Daily lesson planning is certainly one form of curriculum planning, but it is only one aspect of that which should be done by the individual teacher.

Of all the types of curriculum planning we have described so far, this one is probably the most common inasmuch as virtually all teachers develop plans for the particular learners with whom they work. In analyzing this level of planning, consider the following questions.

> In developing curriculum plans for your teaching, do you consider both long- and short-term learning objectives?
> What is the greatest problem you encounter in your curriculum planning?
> About how much time do you spend on curriculum planning? Is that time sufficient? If not, what would be?
> What format do you use for formulating curriculum plans? How does your format compare with that of other teachers?
> How often do you teach without having prepared curriculum plans?
> Do you feel that preparation of careful curriculum plans enhances your teaching?
> How often do you depart from your plans in teaching situations?

We must be aware that planning done by the teacher needs a more comprehensive view than is often held. This understanding of long- and short-range planning of instruction is an essential element in defining "what it means to work on curriculum."

- **Cooperative Curriculum Planning at the Classroom Level**

□ *Scene Seven*   This scene deals with a teacher and a group of learners. They are meeting for the first time, or at the beginning of a new unit they are about to undertake. The teacher initiates the discussion by informing the group that they will be studying commercial media, particularly television, during the next five weeks and asks for ideas about what specific topics or issues might be addressed. After a short period of silence, individuals begin suggesting possibilities: how programs are selected, how commercial ads are made, how a person becomes a television performer, and so on. As the discussion continues, the topics become more sophisticated: how commercial media affect our daily lives, how much truth there is in advertising, whether it is possible to keep certain programs from being shown, how much influence the government has over commercial media. After developing a long list of possibilities, the group divides them into three categories: those that will be addressed by the whole group, those that might be dealt with in small groups, and those that are of interest only to certain individuals and thus will be taken on independently. Next, the group discusses ideas for activities that will help them address the issues already decided upon. A range of possibilities is suggested: visiting local television and radio stations, developing simulated commercials, holding a debate about the government's role in media, writing of a screenplay for a videotaped program on life in school, testing various products to see if they are accurately portrayed in commercials, keeping personal logs of television and radio listening habits, and surveying other students about their views of media. Following this discussion, the group identifies ways to gather learning resources. They include searching school and town libraries for materials regarding commercial media; contacting federal, state, and local officials about laws governing media; examining catalogs for films, tapes, and other materials related to media; and talking with their parents about any pertinent resources they might know. Finally, the group draws up a formal set of plans, summarizing all of its discussions about what might be done. Included is a list of the specific topics, problems, or issues that will be addressed, an indication of who will be addressing each, the activities that will be done in relation to specific topics (including approximate times when they will be done), ideas for resources that might help with each topic, and ideas for any special projects that might be done during the unit. Having taken one or two days to develop these plans, the group is now ready to implement them in carrying out the unit.

In reviewing this situation, we observe a technique known as pupil–teacher planning or teacher–student planning. Here the teacher is guiding a group in formulating plans as to how they might study a particular topic. The teacher and learners work together to decide any combination of the "what, how, who, where, and when" questions regarding the unit they are undertaking.

The involvement of learners in curriculum planning has been the subject of much debate. In formulating your analysis of this situation, consider the following questions.

> In what ways, if any, have you involved learners in curriculum planning?
>
> What factors might inhibit learner participation in curriculum planning?
>
> What benefits do you believe might result from learner participation in curriculum planning?
>
> Do you believe learners should play a role in curriculum planning? If no, why not? If yes, what kind of role?

Whether one believes in its use or not, pupil- or student-teacher planning does represent a level and form of curriculum planning. Its proximity to the actual group of learners and the possibilities for including learner interests in plans lead some of its proponents to conclude that it is the ultimate level of curriculum planning.

Be that as it may, working with a group of learners to develop or refine plans represents a classroom methodological component of the definition of curriculum planning. It is this instructional planning interaction between teacher and students that is so vital to understanding "what it means to work on curriculum."

PRINCIPLES OF CURRICULUM PLANNING

■ ■ The scenes just described do not represent all the possible variations on levels and forms in which curriculum planning may take place. However, they do illustrate "what it means to work on curriculum," and they clarify the meaning of curriculum planning.

In order to determine what curriculum planning involves, we may thus examine what the situations have in common with regard to such factors as participation, issues considered, process elements, and purposes. Where consistent patterns emerge, we may then identify the characteristics or principles of curriculum planning and finally arrive at a definition of the term *curriculum planning*.

PRINCIPLE 1 The situations described several different levels and a number of different groups. In its broadest sense, curriculum planning is a complex activity involving the interplay of ideas from the curriculum field and other disciplines. However, as was the case in each situation, the ultimate purpose of curriculum planning is to describe or refine the learning opportunities available to students.

Therefore: curriculum planning is ultimately concerned with the experiences of learners.

PRINCIPLE 2   In each of the situations, the participants were concerned not only with what students ought to learn, but also with how they would learn it. Curriculum plans that define concepts or ideas without considering action are incomplete since learning must eventually involve doing. In like manner, plans that merely describe action without considering purpose are also incomplete since otherwise learning activity runs the risk of aimlessness. This interrelationship of content and process accentuates the need to consider curriculum and instruction not as distinct entities, but rather as interdependent concepts in the planning process.

Therefore: curriculum planning involves decisions about both content and process.

PRINCIPLE 3   Within the areas of curriculum and instruction, there are many specific issues and topics that may be subject to curriculum planning. As indicated in the situations presented, such areas might include identifying broad purposes for a program, identifying curricular approaches that might be used, carrying out a program evaluation, or deciding about the need for new programs. In addition, curriculum planning focuses on the various components of teaching–learning situations, including the selection of organizing centers or themes, and the identification of objectives, content, activities, resources, and measuring devices for teaching–learning situations. It should be noted that curriculum planning typically involves decisions about some combinations of areas and issues since it is difficult to consider any one in isolation; for example, the identification of activities is done in relation to objectives, and the selection of organizing centers should be done in light of broad goals. In addition, curriculum planning involves decisions about both regular programs of the school and the hidden curriculum—the institutional features of the school from which students learn a great deal about themselves and their relations with others.

Therefore: curriculum planning involves decisions about a variety of issues and topics.

PRINCIPLE 4   Prior to the 1920s, popular thinking held that curriculum planning was to be done by scholars or administrators, and the implementation by teachers. Today, however, most educators have come to realize that curriculum planning is not the sole responsibility or privilege of any one group. Rather, we recognize that worthwhile contributions can be made by a number of groups, and plans are often enriched as a result of varied participation. As evident in the situations we have presented, participants in curriculum planning may include teachers, students, administrators, curriculum coordinators, citizens, scholars, state education personnel, and others. It is true that not all groups need to be involved in every aspect of curriculum planning, but it is important to remember that appropriate groups should be represented whenever possible so that the variety of ideas and suggestions might be improved. Furthermore, we must also recognize that the key participant in curriculum planning is the teacher who will ultimately be responsible for putting the plans into action.

Therefore: curriculum planning involves many groups.

PRINCIPLE 5   As noted, each of the situations represented an example of curriculum planning. Thus, we can conclude that legitimate curriculum planning takes place at many levels, from the national to the classroom. However, the further such planning is from the specific teaching–learning situation, the less specific it can be in terms of the individual needs or characteristics of particular learners. This does not necessarily mean that national level activity is less valuable than local. Rather, it means that the scope of planning is more or less focused. For example, the identification of national goals for education represents an important contribution to the idea of culturally shared values. On the other hand, plans to enable all learners to achieve those goals must be developed if the goals are to have any real meaning. Finally, the variety of levels at which curriculum planning takes place provides the means by which many more groups have an opportunity to participate in the process than would be possible if such planning took place at only one or two levels.

Therefore: curriculum planning takes place at many levels.

PRINCIPLE 6   As a collection, the situations described several different phases in the planning process. These include the identification of broad purposes, the definition of organizing centers, the selection of specific activities, and the evaluation of programs, including recommendations for their improvement, which in turn require additional decision making. While participants may enter the process at any phase, their efforts naturally lead to other phases, and thus the process becomes continuous. When decisions are not evaluated or when evaluation does not lead to program improvement, the process ceases and curriculum plans may be stagnant or obsolete. Thus, the view of curriculum planning as a continuing process is critical if educational programs are to be dynamic and current.

Therefore: curriculum planning is a continuous process.

The term *curriculum planning* has been defined in many ways. (See Frame 2.1.) Each definition is based upon its author's perception of the nature and purpose of the process, and thus each has a place in the curriculum field. The definition we find most useful is based upon actual curriculum planning activities such as those described in the situations presented. In light of those, we suggest the following definition:

Curriculum planning is a process in which participants at many levels make decisions about what the purposes of learning ought to be, how those purposes might be carried out through teaching–learning situations, and whether the purposes and means are both appropriate and effective.

DEFINITIONS OF CURRICULUM-RELATED TERMS

■ ■   The term *curriculum* is used in a variety of contexts. The education community frequently uses such phrases as "curriculum planning," "curriculum development," "instruction," "curriculum evaluation," "out-of-school curriculum," and "hidden curriculum." This section discusses these terms in order to clarify further the language of the curriculum field and to expedite reading of chapters which follow.

Two terms have already been defined in previous sections. One is *curriculum organization,* or the way in which the program of the school, the intended learnings, or the planned experiences of the learner are structured. The second is *curriculum planning,* a process in which participants at many levels make decisions about what the purposes of learning ought to be, how those purposes might be carried out through teaching–learning situations, and whether the purposes and means are both appropriate and effective.

The terms *curriculum planning* and *curriculum development* are often used interchangeably. Since this is so, some curriculum "definers" obviously believe that they represent the same activity. However, others believe that they are different. The distinction is further compounded by the use of the term *instruction.* We view the relationships among curriculum planning, curriculum development, and instruction as shown in Figure 2.1. Each is concerned with the others, but each has a major focus. We view *curriculum planning* as a generic concept

Curriculum Planning: No Single Definition

Curriculum planning is the orderly study and improvement of schooling in light of stated objectives.

—Krug, *Curriculum Planning* (rev. ed.), 1957

Curriculum planning is the process whereby . . . arrangements of learning opportunities or curriculum plans are created.

—Saylor and Alexander, *Curriculum for Modern Schools*, 1966

Curriculum planning consists of all the processes necessary to plan for and write a curriculum.

—Beauchamp, *Curriculum Theory* (rev. ed.), 1975

Curriculum planning is the process of gathering, sorting, selecting, balancing, and synthesizing relevant information from many sources in order to design those experiences that will assist learners in attaining the goals of the curriculum.

—Hass, *Curriculum Planning: A New Approach* (3rd ed.), 1980

Curriculum planning is the preliminary phase of curriculum development when the curriculum workers make decisions and take actions to establish the plan that teachers and students will carry out.

—Oliva, *Developing the Curriculum*, 1982

that may describe activity ranging from the identification of broad goals to the description of possibilities for specific teaching–learning situations. In this sense, all of the situations at the beginning of this chapter were referred to as forms of curriculum planning. *Curriculum development,* on the other hand, is mainly concerned with the design of plans for actual teaching–learning situations. It is based upon the broad goals and identifies ways to translate those goals into a coordinated and coherent program of learning experiences. *Instruction* is developed from broad goals and curriculum plans and focuses on methodological questions such as teaching techniques and the implementation of activities, resources, and measuring devices used in specific teaching–learning situations. Thus, curriculum planning is a generic concept that includes both curriculum development and instructional design. Curriculum development encompasses instructional design, and instructional design denotes a highly specific activity focused on methods of teaching and learning.

Other definitions also require attention here. One involves the term *curriculum evaluation.* Its frequent use is largely due to a recognition that the continuous improvement of programs and learning depends upon their continuous evaluation. *Curriculum evaluation* re-

FIGURE 2.1   The Relationships among Curriculum Planning, Curriculum Development, and Instruction

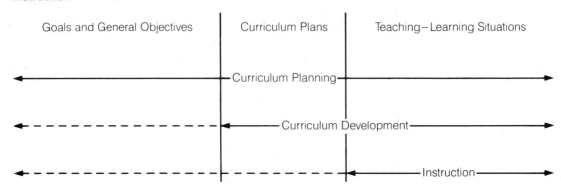

fers to the process by which the planned curriculum and the learner's curriculum are judged in terms of their adequacy and effectiveness. There are several methods used to carry out curriculum evaluations, and more will be said about them in Chapter 8.

As noted in Scene Four, another term, of more recent vintage, is "hidden curriculum." Curriculum observers have come to recognize that virtually every school situation offers students opportunities to learn about themselves and their relationships to others. Furthermore, these learnings are not always planned or intended in curriculum plans. Instead, they grow out of the day-to-day life of the school and its organization. Such features as school climate, grouping, rules and regulations, and grading are not simply procedures for organizing life in school. They also suggest values and attitudes that students may acquire. For example, if rules and regulations are rigid, comprehensive, and fixed from year to year, students may eventually learn that they are incapable of making decisions for themselves. On the other hand, if students are involved in a continuing process of deciding how they can best live together while in school, they may learn that they are capable of governing their own lives. Because such learnings are embedded in features of the school rather than in curriculum plans, they are often referred to as the *hidden curriculum*. More will be said about this aspect of curriculum in Chapter 6.

A third and even more recent term is "out-of-school curriculum." Most educators realize that in today's world, young people learn a great deal from their experiences with television and other media, varying lifestyles, and changes in family structure. Learnings may also result from home experiences (for example, computers), community groups (for example, scouting), and other settings. Furthermore, these learnings often are more dramatic than those found in the school, and frequently they carry over into the school in the form of attitudes, behaviors, and supplementary knowledge. Such learnings require the attention of educators since they often represent a major portion of the learning experiences of young people. The power of *out-of-school curriculum* in the lives of learners is certainly increasing. It will undoubtedly receive more and more attention in the curriculum field in years to come.

The terms defined in this section do not exhaust all the contexts in which curriculum is the root idea. However, they do provide a flavor of the many ways in which the term is used in conjunction with various topics or processes. In succeeding chapters, other usages will be discussed and those described here will recur frequently. One of the characteristics of a field of study is the emergence of a commonly used language to describe its elements and procedures, and obviously the curriculum field is no exception to this rule.

PERSISTENT ISSUES IN THE CURRICULUM FIELD

■ ■ By now it should be clear that many unresolved issues have persisted in the curriculum field for years. Not the least of these is the question of definition of terms, including "curriculum" itself. In this section, we will add to the sense of diversity already established by illustrating some additional basic issues on which opinion varies. These issues, however, are not limited to definitions. Rather, they focus on examples of the practical questions that arise in curriculum planning and development. In one form or another, they arise in committee meetings, faculty lounges, and public forums. Hardly an issue of any professional journal appears without at least one article that refers to one of these areas of concern.

■ Subject-Centered versus Learner-Centered Curriculum

In designing curriculum plans, participants are often confronted with the question of whether those plans should be derived from one or another subject area or from the learner's more personal and immediate world of experiences. In our Chapter 1 examples, we described differing types of curriculum organizations at each school level that were based upon this issue.

The idea of focusing curriculum plans on separate subjects has a long tradition in education, particularly at the secondary level. Virtually all of us attended schools in which we passed from one classroom to another, each offering a particular subject—English, social studies, mathematics, science, and so on. Furthermore, subjects were usually broken down into more specific topics. In mathematics, we studied arithmetic, algebra, geometry, trigonometry, calculus, and the like. The subject-area approach to curriculum development is based upon the idea that the various subjects contain essential knowledge, the mastery of which makes a person "educated." Thus, the most appropriate method of education is to explore various subject areas and "learn" what is contained in them.

The progressive education movement of the 1930s, however, introduced the concept of a learner-centered curriculum. Here, the curriculum would be based not on separate subjects, but rather on the emerging world of the learner. The important issues for proponents of this organization are the interests, needs, problems, and concerns of the learner. For example, curriculum plans for elementary school children might center on such issues as the family, the neighborhood, the school, habits for good health, and other child-centered topics. Plans for middle grades learners might focus on getting along with peers or on physical change during this stage of development, and so on. Plans for high school students might center on self-identity questions, global awareness, plans beyond high school, and so forth.

The debate between advocates of the subject- and the learner-centered curriculum should not be interpreted as questioning whether subject matter should be mastered or dismissed. The fact is that subject matter (e.g., facts, principles, concepts) is always a part of teaching and learning, whether it involves the facts of world history or the concepts of physical development. John Dewey attempted to resolve this issue by arguing that the issue of subject versus learner is not an either/or question. The task, according to Dewey, was to work with subject matter that was of use to the learner both in the immediate sense and in gradually expanding horizons of new realizations. Despite the efforts of Dewey and others, the issue continues to be a source of debate in the curriculum field. Perhaps the reason it has not been settled is that it actually has to do not with mere methods, but with philosophies of education. The different philosophies that undergird each position will be described further in the section on philosophic foundations of the curriculum in Chapter 3.

■ Who Should Plan the Curriculum?

A second persistent issue involves the question of who ought to have the right and responsibility for developing curriculum plans. In the Chapter 2 situations, we clearly implied that many groups are involved in curriculum planning: scholars, teachers, administrators, learners, citizens, state education department personnel, and so on. While all these groups do participate, in reality there is debate over the question of balance and even whether some groups ought to participate at all.

It would seem decidedly logical that teachers ought to be involved.

Yet some people believe that teachers ought to be implementors of plans while scholars and/or administrators ought to do the actual planning. Others believe that curriculum planning ought to involve professionals and thus exclude citizens. Still others believe that citizens, particularly parents, should have a say in what and how young people learn. Some would exclude scholars and state and federal officials, arguing that curriculum planning should or can be done only on the local level. Still others debate over whether the learners, as consumers of the plans, should have a say in what happens. In short, positions on this question range from including only one group to including all of the groups to some degree.

In recent years, this issue has been compounded by the emergence of politics in curriculum planning. Various groups have sought power in that process, ranging from those representing national religious movements to local groups interested in specific materials used in teaching and learning. Within the profession, a new job title has even emerged—"curriculum developer." Although selected issues or topics may serve as the focus for these recent events, the fundamental issue is still: Who should plan the curriculum? Thus, while the political debate persists, the reality is that all groups are involved to some degree. The coordination of involvement of these groups to improve curriculum planning will be discussed further in Chapter 9.

■ **What Are the Basics in Learning?**

Perhaps the most compelling educational issue we have faced since the 1970s revolves around the question of "basics" in learning. Displeased over the alleged decline in reading, writing, and mathematics test scores, many critics decried the emphasis on "relevant" learner-centered curriculum plans in the late 1960s, extending the cry for reform beyond basic skills to a renewed emphasis on traditional subject areas. Of particular interest was the rapidity with which these ideas caught hold in the schools. Despite the claim that they were the result of public pressure, concern over basic skills and traditional subjects was obviously shared by many professional educators as well.

Some members of the public and of the profession responded to this movement by describing a broad definition of the basics. It included not only those skills previously mentioned, but also such areas as values, citizenship, problem-solving, and global awareness. This view was not an attempt to defuse the more limited perspective; it was intended to provide an expanded idea of comprehensive curriculum.

Proponents of the first position centered their attention on improvement of standardized achievement and subject test scores. But even here there was debate over the nature of the "basics." Were "basics" to include only reading, writing, and mathematics? Should they be derived from skills needed in the adult world or those necessary to enter that level? Or should they be derived from the school context, including skills and subjects normally taught in schools?

The debate over the definition of skills, their source, and the level of their achievement has been going on for many years. The study of curriculum history seems to show that these issues arise almost every decade, and one or another view has had most-favored status at various times. These constantly shifting priorities are the source of one of the common clichés in education: "The pendulum is always swinging from one position to another." One of the recurrent themes within the curriculum field is the pursuit of balance in the curriculum. For many educators, this is not an either/or question, but rather one of maintaining a sense of balance between specific skills and broad concepts, and between traditional subjects, emerging social issues, and personal needs of learners. In subsequent chapters, this issue and the means for achieving balance in the curriculum will be more fully discussed.

The issues described here do not exhaust those which have persisted across the years in the curriculum field. Rather, they represent the kinds of questions that remain unresolved and are likely to continue as such. Like the question of definitions, they may give rise either to frustration or to a sense of diversity and richness in the field.

CHAPTER SUMMARY

Chapter 2 considered four major topics. The first involved a description of several levels and forms at which curriculum work is done. As shown in the situations presented, these include (1) the national level, (2) the state level, (3) the district level, (4) the school level, (5) the team or grade level, (6) the individual teacher level, and (7) the classroom level. Furthermore, the situations depicted different degrees of participation by various groups and different kinds of decisions.

The second section of Chapter 2 focused on curriculum planning as a concept. In the discussion following the situations, the levels and forms were analyzed to reveal six principles of curriculum planning:

1. Curriculum planning is ultimately concerned with the experiences of learners.
2. Curriculum planning involves decisions about both process and content.
3. Curriculum planning involves decisions about a variety of issues and topics.
4. Curriculum planning involves many groups.
5. Curriculum planning takes place at many levels.
6. Curriculum planning is a continuous process.

In light of these principles, *curriculum planning was defined as a process in which participants at many levels make decisions about what the purposes of learning ought to be, how those purposes might be carried out through teaching–learning situations, and whether the purposes and means are both appropriate and effective.*

The third major topic considered in Chapter 2 was the definition of several curriculum-related terms. These included "curriculum planning," "curriculum development," "instruction," "curriculum evaluation," "hidden curriculum," and "out-of-school curriculum." As was the case with "curriculum" itself, the definition of the related terms revealed differences of opinion about their meanings. Awareness of the terms and their different uses is not only a part of the study of curriculum, but an important skill for participating in curriculum work.

The fourth topic covered in this chapter was some persistent issues in the curriculum field. To illustrate areas of continuing debate, three issues were briefly discussed: (1) subject matter versus the learner, (2) who should participate in curriculum decision making, and (3) what are the basics in learning. In each case, different positions on the issues were reflected, as well as efforts to resolve those positions. These and other issues will appear as recurring themes in subsequent chapters.

Having read Chapter 2, you should be able to:

1. Describe several different levels and forms of curriculum work
2. Identify some of the principles of curriculum planning
3. Define some of the phrases related to curriculum, such as "curriculum development," "instruction," "curriculum evaluation," "hidden curriculum," and "out-of-school curriculum"
4. Discuss some of the persistent issues in the curriculum field and different opinions within each

SUGGESTED ACTIVITIES

1. At the end of each of the curriculum planning situations in this chapter is a set of questions for analysis. These questions should be used for discussion in the large or small groups. Before doing so, participants should develop (in brief form) their own responses to the questions.

2. Conduct a survey within the large group, using the principles of curriculum planning. The survey should question the degree to which each principle is actually represented in local planning. Use the survey for a discussion of local curriculum planning efforts.

3. Using the principles of curriculum planning, have small groups identify (1) specific examples of the positive use of each principle and (2) examples of cases where each principle was ignored. The examples should be drawn from participants' local school experience. Combine the small-group lists into a master list for large group consideration.

4. Ask participants to find out how much money is allocated in their district budget for curriculum planning. Compare this amount on a percentage basis to other categories, such as interscholastic sports or music equipment. What does this reveal about the local district commitment to curriculum planning?

REFERENCES

Beauchamp, G. *Curriculum Theory.* 3rd ed. Wilmette, Ill.: Kagg Press, 1975.

Dewey, J. *The Child and the Curriculum.* Chicago: University of Chicago Press, 1902.

Hass, G. *Curriculum Planning: A New Approach.* 3rd ed. Boston: Allyn and Bacon, 1980.

Kelley, E. *Education for What Is Real.* New York: Harper & Brothers, 1947.

Krug, E. *Curriculum Planning.* Rev. ed. New York: Harper & Brothers, 1957.

Oliva, P. *Developing the Curriculum.* Boston: Little, Brown, 1982.

Overly, N. *The Unstudied Curriculum: Its Impact on Children.* Washington, D.C.: Association for Supervision and Curriculum Development, NEA, 1970.

Saylor, J.G., and Alexander, W. *Curriculum Planning for Modern Schools.* New York: Holt, Rinehart and Winston, 1966.

Schubert, W.H. "Knowledge about Out-of-School Curriculum." *The Educational Forum* 45 (1981).

Snyder, B. *The Hidden Curriculum.* Cambridge, Mass.: MIT Press, 1970.

PROLOGUE TO CHAPTERS 3–17

A Framework for Curriculum Planning

Thus far, we have considered some of the themes and issues that are fundamental to the study of curriculum. In Chapter 1, various types of curriculum organization were portrayed through a series of situations in elementary, middle, and high school settings. In Chapter 2, a second set of situations depicted curriculum planning at several levels from the national to the classroom. In both chapters, we also discussed definitions of terms used in the curriculum field. Throughout, we emphasized that the curriculum field is one of diversity. The many ideas and viewpoints in the field are often perplexing. However, they also make the study of curriculum rich and exciting.

THEORIES ABOUT CURRICULUM PLANNING

■ ■ Over the years, many attempts have been made to outline the key elements in curriculum planning as well as how those elements interrelate. These theories or models are typically sketched from one of two viewpoints. The first is a *description* of what seem to be the ideas or actions commonly used in the process of curriculum planning in schools or other educational settings. The second is a *prescription* of what ought to be done in curriculum planning. In both cases, the purpose of theory or model development is to improve, by sharing ideas, the quality of curriculum work.

The curriculum field generally acknowledges the work of Ralph Tyler as foundational in the area of theory development. As a result of his work on the Eight Year Study in the 1930s, Tyler formulated a rationale for curriculum evaluation consisting of four questions that he believed should be addressed in curriculum planning.

1. What educational purposes should the school seek to attain?
2. What educational purposes can be provided that are likely to attain these purposes?
3. How can the educational experiences be effectively organized?

4. How can we determine whether these purposes are being attained? (1950, pp. 1–2)

Since it has guided the majority of curriculum plans and projects over the past three decades, Tyler's rationale has probably been the most influential of the collection of curriculum planning theories. Other theorists, such as Virgil Herrick (1950) and Hilda Taba (1962), added to Tyler's model by delineating some of the specific ideas that they felt should be considered within each of the four questions. These included specification of such things as sources of educational purpose, types of curriculum organization, and means for conducting evaluation. Others, such as Elliot Eisner (1967) and Herbert Kliebard (1968), acknowledged Tyler's contribution but criticized the rationale, mainly on grounds that it was either too simplistic or too limiting. Joseph Schwab (1970) pointed out a problem that may arise from any rationale or model for curriculum planning. That is, in describing the process of curriculum work, a model usually appears to involve a series of steps to be followed in a linear or sequential way. For example, one might conclude that Tyler's four questions have to be answered in the order in which they are written. In reality, however, curriculum planning involves a complex set of ideas and elements that are so interrelated that decisions about one influence and derive from the others. Furthermore, it is generally conceded that when teachers engage in curriculum development, they often begin by designing either the content to be mastered or activities related to the particular course or unit under consideration. Thus, to propose a linear model proceeding from purposes to activities denies much of curriculum work in the real world. This line of reasoning has led other theorists, such as J. Galen Saylor and William Alexander (1974), to propose curriculum planning through a "systems" model in which all components are considered in each step of the process.

A GENERAL FRAMEWORK

■ ■ In Chapters 3 through 7, we will discuss components in curriculum planning based upon a general "framework." We have chosen the term *framework* rather than *theory* or *model* partly to avoid the implication of a linear process and partly because we realize that space prohibits discussing all of the possible interrelationships and nuances in curriculum planning. Furthermore, a framework blends the realities of practical curriculum work with ideas for how components ought to be considered. Our framework follows the thinking of such theorists as Tyler (1950), Herrick (1950), Edward Krug (1950, 1957),

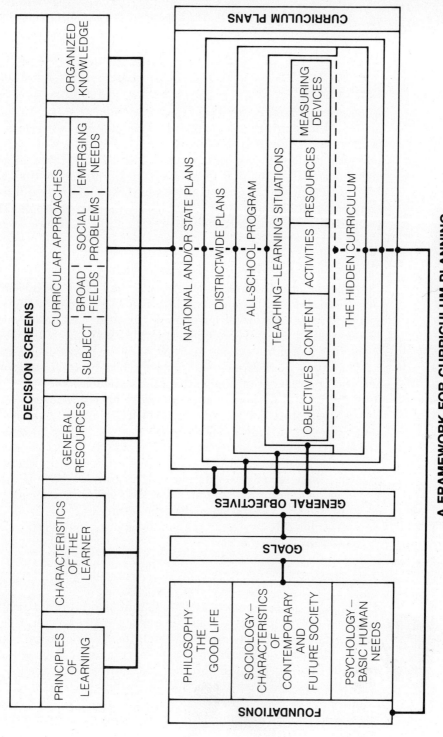

A FRAMEWORK FOR CURRICULUM PLANNING

and Robert Harnack (1968). We hope that our constant reminder to avoid a linear interpretation overcomes some of the problems that others have perceived to grow out of earlier work.

■ Foundations

Education is based upon three broad foundational areas. These areas—philosophy, sociology, and psychology—deal with concerns common to the needs both of individuals and society. Curriculum planning deals with a specific focus of each of these three foundational areas. Philosophy is focused as "the philosophy of the good life," sociology as "the characteristics of contemporary and future society," and psychology as "the basic human needs" of people. These foundations of the curriculum are discussed in Chapter 3.

■ Goals

Perhaps the broadest area of curriculum work is the definition of overall goals for education. Based upon the three foundation areas, goals represent the larger purposes of education and are developed at national, state, and district-wide levels. Goal statements at each level, it is hoped, reflect one another, with the national and state goals guiding local development, and the latter contributing to the former. The number of illustrative goal statements is certainly not lacking. Several national statements have been developed over the years, every state has a list of purposes for its educational system, and since accrediting agencies require them, virtually all school districts have local goal statements. Two problems persist, however. One is that specific curriculum planning is often done without considering these broad goal statements. The other problem is that broad goals are often viewed as too ambiguous to implement through specific curriculum plans. The nature and content of goals, as well as ideas to overcome the problems just mentioned, will be discussed in Chapter 4.

■ General Objectives

Educational goals represent the broad purposes toward which all teaching–learning activities are directed. For the learner, this means that as he or she moves through the developmental stages from child to adult, a wide variety of learning situations will contribute to realization of the broad goals. In this sense, the question that arises is, What will happen at each step along the way? Since educational programs are divided into levels that match developmental stages, curriculum planning partly involves identifying what each level will contribute to the larger goals. For example, elementary educators must consider what children might do at their stage of development which will lead toward broader goals. Middle level educators must be concerned with contributions at the transescent, or emerging adolescent, stage. Statements about the contributions at each level to the broad goals are known as general objectives. This term denotes their placement between general goals and the specific objectives that are used in teacher–learning situations. General objectives serve two purposes. First, by clarifying what broad goals mean at a particular level, general objectives help to bridge the gap between those broad goals for education and the specific activities of teachers and learners. Second, general objectives serve as guiding purposes for curriculum planning activity at a given level. Given the problem of the gap between goals and action, the contribution that general objectives make to bridging that gap means that they are a critical feature in the curriculum framework. More about general objectives, including sample statements, will be said in Chapter 4.

■ Decision Screens

As teachers and others develop curriculum plans for specific teaching–learning situations, they need to consider five areas that should influence their decisions. The first area involves clarifying the characteristics of the particular learners for whom the plans are intended. Here thought is given to the chronological and developmental age of the learners, their interests, previous achievement, learning styles, cognitive level, social maturity, physical development, and any other pertinent characteristics. This clarification is important since the effectiveness of curriculum plans largely depends upon whether they are appropriate for the intended learners.

The second issue involves reflection on principles of learning. Here consideration may be given to how people learn, under what conditions learning might best occur, and other important aspects of the learning process. While these principles are not written out each time curriculum plans are developed, they must be kept in mind constantly so that learners have the best chance possible to carry out the plans.

The third area involves consideration of the general resources available to support teaching–learning activities included in the curriculum plans. Some resources may be found inside the school, while others may be located in the outside community. The former could include money, specific facilities or equipment, and media and other materials. Outside the school, one might find places to visit, people with special knowledge or talent, useful materials, and other resources.

The fourth consideration involves the type of curricular approach that might be used. Depending upon the purposes of the plans, one or more approaches may be chosen: one based on separate subjects, a second on correlation of two or more subjects, a third on social problems, and a fourth on emerging personal or social needs of the learner. Each approach is appropriate in certain circumstances, and the choice of which to use is an important decision.

Finally, the fifth area involves consideration of ways in which organized knowledge from specific disciplines might be used in planning teaching–learning situations. Regardless of the curricular approach being used, subject knowledge or subject matter is a key component. Even when objectives focus on the personal or social needs of learners, facts, principles, concepts, and understandings related to those needs must be addressed. All of these screens, their characteristics, and their appropriate use will be discussed in Chapter 5.

■ Components of Curriculum Plans

In light of goals and decisions about preplanning issues, curriculum plans may begin to take shape. Decisions must be made about the organization of the all-school program, including specification of requirements, staffing, grouping, scheduling, and other concerns. These will be considered in Chapter 6.

Finally, the topics, themes, problems, or issues that will serve as specific organizing centers upon which those plans will focus must be selected. As curriculum plans for effective teaching–learning situations are developed around a particular *organizing center,* they focus on five components. The first component is a statement of learning *objectives* or proposed outcomes of the plans. The second component is *content:* the important facts, principles, concepts, and understandings related to the organizing center and objectives. The third component involves the many *activities* that might be used to accomplish the objectives. The fourth component involves possible *resources* that may be used to address the objectives. The fifth component is *measuring devices,* or the means to determine whether and to what degree objectives have been accomplished. These components, and various ideas and viewpoints regarding each one, will be discussed in Chapter 7.

It is important to note that although our framework is a systematic one, it does not necessarily imply that curriculum planning must move through the elements step by step. The fact is that curriculum plans already exist in schools. Further planning usually evolves from problems or ideas involving one or another element anywhere in the framework. However, the framework should and can be used for two major purposes. First, it may serve as a checklist to determine whether all important elements are being considered in curriculum planning. Second, it may be used as an evaluation tool to determine whether the various levels of curriculum planning are connected to one another. With this in mind, we now turn to our consideration of a comprehensive curriculum planning framework.

REFERENCES

Eisner, E. "Educational Objectives: Help or Hindrance?" *School Review* 75 (1967): 250–66.

Harnack, R. *The Teacher: Decision Maker and Curriculum Planner.* Scranton, Pa.: International Textbook, 1968.

Herrick, V. "Concept of Curriculum Design." In *Toward Curriculum Theory,* edited by V. Herrick and R. Tyler. Chicago: University of Chicago Press, 1950.

Kliebard, H. "Curricular Objectives and Evaluation: A Reassessment." *The High School Journal* 51 (1968): 241–247.

Krug, E. *Curriculum Planning.* New York: Harper & Row, 1950.

———. *Curriculum Planning.* Rev. ed. New York: Harper & Row, 1957.

Saylor, J. G., and Alexander, W. *Planning Curriculum for Schools.* New York: Holt, Rinehart and Winston, 1974.

Schwab, J. *The Practical: A Language for Curriculum.* Washington, D.C.: National Education Association, Center for the Study of Instruction, 1970.

Taba, H. *Curriculum Development: Theory and Practice.* New York: Harcourt Brace Jovanovich, 1962.

Tyler, R. *Basic Principles of Curriculum and Instruction.* Chicago: University of Chicago, 1950.

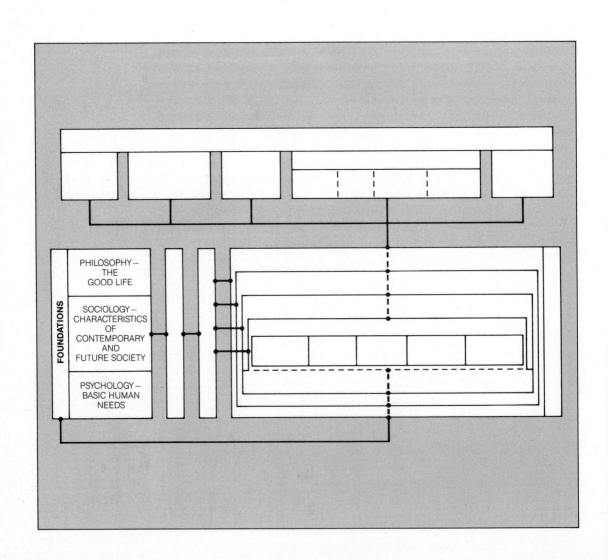

FOUNDATIONS

PHILOSOPHY—
THE
GOOD LIFE

SOCIOLOGY—
CHARACTERISTICS
OF
CONTEMPORARY
AND
FUTURE SOCIETY

PSYCHOLOGY—
BASIC HUMAN
NEEDS

3

Foundations of Curriculum

The development of curriculum plans depends partly on ideas that grow out of three fields: philosophy, sociology, and psychology. Together, these three have traditionally been considered as foundations of curriculum planning. Their understanding is crucial to the study of curriculum. For this reason, Chapter 3 looks at each area and at its relation to the curriculum field.

Philosophy involves inquiry into the nature and meaning of life. Such thinking includes ideas about the nature of human beings, the source of values, and the role and purpose of education in determining "the good life." One's philosophy largely determines one's view of learners, the purpose of education, and the importance of various learning activities. *Sociology* is the study of society and social issues in the past, present, and future. It provides valuable clues about the characteristics of contemporary life and the future in which learners will lead the rest of their lives. Sociology aids in understanding relationships among people and between people and society. It also helps curriculum planners make appropriate decisions about how the school will relate to society. *Psychology* involves the study of basic human needs, attitudes, and behaviors. It provides insight into the characteristics of the young people with whom we work. This understanding of humanness is a valuable aid in determining the nature of learners. Also, it is an important base for identifying the types of curriculum arrangements that will most benefit growth and development.

The three foundation areas contribute to curriculum plans that help individuals grow and develop so that they may lead satisfying lives within the context of society. This does not exclude the development of ideas and skills to improve society, since the pursuit of a satisfying life may involve reshaping one's environment. Whatever the case, those involved in curriculum planning should have a clear idea of each of the foundation areas so that their decisions are as sound as possible.

Our consideration of the three foundations will continue the theme of diversity begun in Chapters 1 and 2. This is necessary since in each area there are many different ideas and viewpoints. We will note here as before, however, that diversity is one of the factors that helps to make the curriculum field both dynamic and exciting.

As a result of reading Chapter 3, you should be able to:

1. Describe various philosophies and their implications for the curriculum field
2. Describe reasons why an understanding of philosophy is important for curriculum work
3. Identify philosophical issues that need to be considered in curriculum planning today
4. Identify the importance of sociology for the curriculum field
5. Describe various social trends and issues that should be considered in curriculum planning
6. Describe the importance of basic human needs in curriculum planning and development
7. Identify particular issues in the contemporary needs of youth that should be considered in curriculum planning

FOUNDATION 1: PHILOSOPHY—THE GOOD LIFE

■ ■ Curriculum decisions involve the consideration of several topics and issues. As we have seen in Chapters 1 and 2, these topics include the purposes for learning, the sources of subject matter, characteristics of the learner, the nature of the teaching–learning process, and others. Such decisions are not made in a vacuum; rather, they are based upon fundamental beliefs that arise from one's philosophy of education. For this reason, philosophy is recognized as one of the major foundation areas in curriculum.

Some educators seem to believe that the study of philosophy is not a useful activity. They feel that philosophy is an abstract field that has little, if anything, to do with the practical problems faced in school. Certainly this is a shortsighted view since what we do in education is, and ought to be, guided by what we believe is important and appropriate for learning and learners. As a matter of fact, even those who question the usefulness of philosophy typically are willing to give reasons why they do what they do. In other words, even these critics actually have a philosophy of education.

In this section, we will explore several different philosophies of education that influence curriculum decisions. As you will see, all of them have several components in common even though they represent widely different ways of thinking. Among these components are the following:

1. Beliefs about the nature of people, particularly the young, regarding their natural or inborn characteristics
2. Beliefs about the sources of truth and values that ought to guide living
3. Beliefs about what constitutes a good and satisfying life
4. Beliefs about what is important for people to learn
5. Beliefs about the role of the school in society
6. Beliefs about the role of the teacher in the learning process

The fact that there are several different philosophies of education means that there is wide disagreement about specific beliefs in each of the six points just listed. What is ultimately important is that those responsible for curriculum decisions attempt to clarify what they believe about each of the issues. If they are unclear or confused about their own beliefs, then their curriculum plans may also be unclear and confusing. One important step in developing a personal philosophy of education is to understand the various alternatives that others have developed over the years. We will next illustrate the major philosophic positions that have influenced curriculum planning. Since we are considering these positions in the context of curriculum planning, we have treated them in broad, general terms. The study of philosophy itself examines the finer distinctions within, and the overlap among, the philosophies considered here.

■ Alternative One

Suppose you believed that people are inherently good, that they are born with a natural tendency to do what is good and right. While people are born with this tendency toward goodness, ideas about what is good or right arise from some source outside them. The source of goodness might be some concept of God, nature, or the universe. Whatever the source, it must be naturally related to human beings since they are born with it.

If we apply these ideas to education, we can begin to clarify some beliefs involved in one possible philosophy of education. We could say that children are inherently good and that they have within them a tendency to do what is good and right. However, that sense is contained within and needs to be brought out. In other words, children need help in discovering what that spiritual goodness is so that they can actually apply it to their lives. Thus, the purpose of education would be to bring the learner to a point where the natural spirit is recognized in relation to God, nature, the universe, or some other external source. In this way, the learner is on the path to a good and satisfying life in which he or she lives according to those enduring values.

In order to accomplish this purpose, the school would be set up so that it is consistent with enduring values. Life in the school would represent a continuous opportunity for learners to see what those values mean in action. For example, young people would be led not only to see the goodness within themselves, but also to understand that they must respect the goodness that others naturally possess. Teachers would act as role models of the enduring values and would respect the inherent goodness of learners. If schools were set up this way, they would be an important part of society since they would be one of the agencies or institutions that lead people toward a good and satisfying life.

When considering the organization of the school and curriculum plans, it is important to remind ourselves of the idea that even though young people are born with inherent goodness, they must be given guidance in bringing it to the surface. The school must be highly structured and include only those ideas that demonstrate enduring values. For example, materials used for reading instruction should not only develop that skill, but should portray worthwhile values as well. Learning would be centered around broad ideas, particularly those contained in great works of literature, so that learners come to see the relationships among various aspects of the universe. Learners who are "discipline problems" would be led to see the effect of their behavior on others and the way in which it disrupts the enduring values of the community. After all, while the emphasis is on self-realization of enduring values, those values already exist and must be respected. Since the community consists of individuals who are either moving toward those values or have already discovered them, disruption of the community is also disruptive of the values.

This set of beliefs about education is based on the traditional philosophy of *idealism*. The roots of idealism can be found in the work of Plato, who believed that truth and values are eternal and that human beings are engaged in a continuous process of discovering them. He further believed that ideas were already contained within people, and that people needed to be helped to bring to the surface what they already knew. The philosophy of idealism was furthered by René Descartes, George Berkeley, Immanuel Kant, Georg Hegel, and others. This philosophy has had less impact on education than others, though it can be found to some degree in the ideas of A. S. Neill. (See Frame 3.1.)

Since it is based on broad ideas and concepts, idealism runs counter to the beliefs of those who feel that important learnings are specific facts from various subject areas. The latter "philosophers" find it hard to believe that such knowledge already resides within the learner.

A. S. Neill on the Summerhill School (1977)

Well, we set out to make a school in which we should allow children freedom to be themselves. In order to do this, we had to renounce all discipline, all direction, all suggestion, all moral training, all religious instruction. We have been called brave, but it did not require courage. All it required was what we had—a complete belief in the child as a good, not an evil, being. For almost forty years, this belief in the goodness of the child has never wavered; it rather has become a final faith.

My view is that a child is innately wise and realistic. If left to himself without adult suggestion of any kind, he will develop as far as he is capable of developing. Logically, Summerhill is a place in which people who have the innate ability and wish to be scholars will be scholars; while those who are only fit to sweep the streets will sweep the streets. But we have not produced a street cleaner so far. Nor do I write this snobbishly, for I would rather see a school produce a happy street cleaner than a neurotic scholar.

What is Summerhill like? Well, for one thing, lessons are optional. Children can go to them or stay away from them—for years if they want to. There is a timetable—but only for the teachers.

The children have classes usually according to their age, but sometimes according to their interests. We have no new methods of teaching, because we do not consider that teaching in itself matters very much. Whether a school has or has not a special method for teaching long division is of no significance, for long division is of no importance except to those who want to learn it. And the child who wants to learn long division will learn it no matter how it is taught.

■ Alternative Two

Suppose you believed that people are inherently ignorant. In order to lead a good life, they must be led to learn about the reality of the world since that reality represents the source of truth and values. Suppose that you further believed that people are inherently rational and that given the proper guidance they are capable of learning what they should. Rationality is what allows otherwise ignorant people to become capable of participating in society and its culture. However, if not led to know what they should, people will remain ignorant and thus tend toward unfulfilled or even evil lives.

Applied to education, these ideas begin to reveal a second possible philosophy of education. To begin with, the child is viewed as an ignorant person who must be directed toward worthwhile knowledge. Left to their own interests, children would probably remain ignorant since they would likely pursue only frivolous topics. Since what is "important" is contained in the reality of the world, children must be taught what is already known about that world. In this way, education becomes a matter of reality rather than speculation. What is already "known" is revealed in what scholars in various subject areas have discovered. Thus, all children would be taught the content of various subject areas so that they too know what is worth knowing.

Since one must be educated away from ignorance into enlightenment, those who have already undergone education are in a much better position to know what should be learned than those who are still in the process. Thus, the teacher is the central person in education. It is the responsibility of the teacher to identify worthwhile knowledge and impart it to students. This must be done through direct methods since the "ignorant" child cannot be expected to understand subtle or indirect learning procedures. If the teacher can simultaneously teach subjects and deal with the interests of learners, he or she may do so. However, the latter must not interfere with the important knowledge, nor should the personality of the learner interfere. The paramount responsibility of the teacher is to teach knowledge about the world to learners.

As an institution, the school should reflect the permanent and enduring values that have been handed down through history. Such virtues as diligence and honesty must be learned since they are valued in the real world and have been for many centuries. Furthermore, thinking and intellect are of prime importance as they are necessary to overcome ignorance. When children stray from these values, they must be brought into line. Once learned, bad habits are not easily overcome and only serve to prolong the possibility of continued ignorance. On the other hand, worthwhile knowledge and habits learned through education become the foundation for what is to follow in life. In other words, education is preparation for a "good life."

This set of beliefs about education is based upon the philosophy of *realism*. Originally developed by Aristotle, it begins with the idea that truth can be discovered by studying the world of matter or reality. Thus, science and philosophy are both important since the former is a method for objective study of reality. That idea, combined with the view of humans as rational animals and the notion of enduring values that exist in the world, serves as the basis for realism. This philosophy has been furthered by a number of thinkers, and thus it takes several different forms. For example, Thomas Aquinas, a religious philosopher, leaned heavily on Aristotle's ideas in proposing that one could prove the existence of God by observing or studying the real world.

Historically, the ideas associated with realism have had a powerful impact on schools. They have given rise to a specific educational philosophy known as *perennialism*. At the heart of this way of thinking are ideas such as required subjects, use of the "great books" as materials, and direct, formal teaching. In fact, one can safely say that perennialism has been an extremely influential source of ideas for school practices and procedures. (See Frame 3.2.)

Robert Hutchins on the Basis of Education (1953)

We cannot talk about the intellectual powers of men, though we can talk about training them, or amusing them, or adapting them, and meeting their immediate needs, unless our philosophy in general tells us that there is knowledge and that there is a difference between true and false. We must believe, too, that there are other means of obtaining knowledge than scientific experimentation. If knowledge can be sought only in the laboratory, many fields in which we thought we had knowledge will offer us nothing but opinion or superstition, and we shall be forced to conclude that we cannot know anything about the most important aspects of man and society. If we are to set about developing the intellectual powers of men through having them acquire knowledge of the most important subjects, we have to begin with the proposition that experimentation and empirical data will be of only limited use to us, contrary to the convictions of many American social scientists, and that philosophy, history, literature, and art give us knowledge, and significant knowledge, on the most significant issues.

If the object of education is the improvement of men, then any system of education that is without values is a contradiction in terms. A system that seeks bad values is bad. A system that denies the existence of values denies the possibility of education. Relativism, scientism, skepticism, and anti-intellectualism, the four horsemen of the philosophical apocalypse, have produced that chaos in education which will end in the disintegration of the West.

The prime object of education is to know what is good for man. It is to know the goods in their order. There is a hierarchy of values. The task of education is to help us understand it, establish it, and live by it.

■ **Alternative Three**

Suppose you believed that human beings are not born with either inherent goodness or ignorance. Instead, they have the beginning physical and mental equipment that allows them to participate in the world around them. Suppose that in a broader sense you believed that society and culture emerged in the same pattern, not from any fixed values, as it became increasingly "civilized." In this sense, whatever values and ideas are currently believed would be considered tentative since further social development might refine or change them. In arguing this case, you might point out that one time it was generally believed that the earth was flat, but subsequent scientific research proved that it is not. Even beliefs that are central to human values may prove untrue later on. Thus, truth and values are not fixed or eternal, but rather the result of evolving human experience.

Applying this philosophy to children, then, you might believe that they come to know what they know and behave as they do as a result

79

of interacting with the world around them. Like society, their beliefs and understandings would not be fixed, but open to further experience by which they might be refined or changed. Education would not simply consist of having children learn eternal truths, enduring values, or fixed bodies of subject matter. Instead, it would involve experiences that would promote increasing interaction with the world around the children. And from interaction with that environment, their values, beliefs, and knowledge would become progressively more mature. By learning the skills and attitudes involved in intelligent interaction with the environment, the child would not only be able to live a satisfying life now, but would be able to enjoy a good life later.

Suppose you further assumed that the false knowledge that was believed true in the past ("the earth is flat") should not lead us to belittle previous societies, but should be seen as based on the best information available given the current state of scientific research. By the same token, you might assume that children know and understand as much as they can, given the limits of their experience and their physical and mental development. They cannot know or understand what adults can until they grow and develop physically, mentally, and through the experience of interaction with the environment. As in society, this process cannot be forced in giant leaps of knowledge and understanding. It must come with gradual, evolving growth and insight.

Given these beliefs, you might devise a system of education based upon helping children to understand themselves and their world more fully as they pass through each stage of development. What the young child sees is the immediate, concrete world, consisting of people he or she knows and of objects used in daily life. The education of these children might thus emphasize learning about other people and learning how objects fit into or work in the environment. As they develop further, children and young people might learn about the interdependence of people, reasons why the environment functions as it does, and how it can be modified. At these later stages, young people might also explore beliefs and values, not only from the standpoint of their own society and time, but from others as well. This kind of education would consist of learning based upon the expanding interests, knowledge, and experiences of young people.

What is to be learned under this set of beliefs is not, then, any fixed body of subject matter or set of enduring values. What is to be learned is that which helps the child to understand more fully his or her interactions with the environment at that point in his or her development. Thus, the role of the teacher is not simply to disseminate information, but to construct situations that involve both direct experience with the child's world and opportunities to understand those experiences. The teacher promotes a continuing cycle of interaction with the environment. This is followed by reflective thought about what might be learned from the interaction. Of critical importance would be the idea that the experience (both interaction and reflective thought about it) would be based upon the world of the child rather than the world of adults. After all, the world of the child only seems simplistic when viewed through the eyes of an adult. To the child, even the simple world of known people and objects is full of wonders that must be understood before more complex issues can be pursued.

This set of beliefs about education is based upon the philosophy of *pragmatism*. The best-known proponent of this philosophy was John Dewey (see Frame 3.3), although his work followed that of Jean-Jacques Rousseau, Charles Pierce, and William James, and has, in turn, been promoted by educators such as William Kilpatrick and Louis Raths. The philosophy of pragmatism has been carried out through so-called progressive education, which promoted such ideas as the child-centered school and interest-centered education. Although pragmatism has roots in the European philosophy, the application of pragmatic philosophy to schools has been largely an American phenomenon. This is because the idea of tentative values emerging from intelligent and evolving human experience is a basic principle of democracy. This philosophy of education has had a major impact on education here and abroad. Many educators readily admit their allegiance to Dewey's ideas. As we shall see in later chapters, pragmatic philosophy has found a central place in several concepts and practices in the curriculum field.

■ Alternative Four

Suppose you believed that life has no particular logic or enduring meaning. People exist, and in the course of their lives they develop ideas and values that are highly personal and not necessarily connected with any organized social pattern. Life is simply a continuing series of situations that individuals may respond to in any number of ways rather than on the basis of enduring values or morals. In other words, life is an absurd paradox in which there is no particular order. Suppose you further believed that ideas, values, and institutions are merely attempts by people to create some kind of organized life. They are not permanent or independent, but rather developed as individual responses to various situations. Thus, values and institutions cannot be depended upon since not only can they be developed differently by different people, but they may also change from one situation to another. Taking this view one step further, suppose you concluded that human beings may be rational, but they use their rationality mostly to justify their individual values and behavior. Finally, suppose you believed that given no permanent values, people are free to choose their own and are thus responsible for their own actions. One cannot

John Dewey on Education and School
(1897)

I believe that all education proceeds by the participation of the individual in the social consciousness of the race. This process begins unconsciously almost at birth, and is continually shaping the individual's powers, saturating his consciousness, forming his habits, training his ideas, and arousing his feelings and emotions. Through this unconscious education the individual gradually comes to share in the intellectual and moral resources which humanity has succeeded in getting together. He becomes an inheritor of the funded capital of civilization. The most formal and technical education in the world cannot safely depart from this general process. It can only organize it or differentiate it in some particular direction. . . .

I believe that this educational process has two sides—one psychological and one sociological; and that neither can be subordinated to the other or neglected without evil results following. Of these two sides, the psychological is the basis. The child's own instincts and powers furnish the material and give the starting point for all education. Save as the efforts of the educator connect with some activity which the child is carrying on of his own initiative independent of the educator, education becomes reduced to a pressure from without. It may, indeed, give certain external results, but cannot truly be called educative. Without insight into the psychological structure and activities of the individual, the educative process will, therefore, be haphazard and arbitrary. If it chances to coincide with the child's activity it will get a leverage; if it does not, it will result in friction, or disintegration, or arrest of the child nature. . . .

I believe that the only true education comes through the stimulation of the child's powers by the demands of the social situations in which he finds himself from the standpoint of the welfare of the group to which he belongs. Through the responses which others make to his own activities he comes to know what these mean in social terms. The value which they have is reflected back into them. For instance, through the response which is made to the child's instinctive babblings the child comes to know what those babblings mean; they are transformed into articulate language and thus the child is introduced into the consolidated wealth of ideas and emotions which are now summed up in language. . . .

I believe that the school is primarily a social institution. Education being a social process, the school is simply that form of community life in which all those agencies are concentrated that will be the most effective in bringing the child to share in the inherited resources of the race, and to use his own powers for social ends.

I believe that education, therefore, is a process of living and not a preparation for future living. . . .

blame one's actions on others since we have freedom of choice in a world that is disorganized anyway.

Applied to education, these beliefs reveal a fourth possible philosophy of education. To begin with, the child is an individual who must seek some kind of meaning in an otherwise meaningless world. Since there are no enduring values and ideas to depend upon, the child must be helped to create his or her own ideas rather than discover those of others. Thus, education must center on the perceptions and feelings of the individual in order to facilitate understanding of personal reactions or responses to life situations. In this way, the individual may begin to address such questions as "Who am I, why am I here, and where am I going?" As ideas or beliefs are formed, the learner is encouraged to take action so that ideas can be applied to life. Thus, the idea of commitment is promoted.

Of primary concern in this process is the importance of the individual. Since life is based upon personal meanings, the nature of education should be largely determined by the learner. Individuals should not be forced into required programs or made to conform to the interests of others. Whatever the learner feels he or she must learn should be respected and facilitated by the school. Also, learners must be helped to see that knowledge is not certain; rather it is uncertain and open to question.

Within this set of beliefs, the teacher takes on a nondirective role. The teacher is a partner in learning and, in fact, can learn much from students. As a professional, the teacher serves as a resource, facilitating the individual's search for personal meaning rather than imposing some set of values or interests. Of paramount importance are the personal feelings, perceptions, and emotions of the learner. After all, in a confusing world there is much tension and anxiety. Rather than ignore how this affects children, the teacher must help them to understand their own reactions and responses to life situations.

This set of beliefs about education is based upon the philosophy of *existentialism*. Although this philosophy had its beginnings in the nineteenth-century work of Søren Kierkegaard, it is largely recognized as a twentieth-century phenomenon developed by such thinkers as Jean-Paul Sartre and Martin Buber. Existentialism has gained greater popularity in recent years as people have experienced the ambiguity of our increasingly complex world. Today, many educators talk about focusing on the individual, promoting diversity in the curriculum, and emphasizing the personal needs and interests of learners. However, existentialism has found only a limited place in the real life of the school. We must remember that the school is a social institution maintained to provide common education for young people. Hence, it is based upon the idea of group living and social values. In fact, the existentialist believes that the school is a product of people's ideas. The school has been put where it is to promote order in society. Thus, by its very nature, the school as an institution is generally antithetical to existentialism. As Van Cleve Morris (1954) pointed out, "we might even conclude that Existentialism would have no traffic with education in any shape or form. Indeed, the case might even be developed that Existentialism is the very denial of education as we understand it today." Nevertheless, many procedures used in the so-called affective curriculum continue to show the influence of this philosophy on educational practice.

■ **Two Additional Alternatives**

The four major philosophies of education just described all have roots in classical philosophic positions. Each begins with a particular view of human nature and the sources of values and truths, and then proceeds to ideas about what those mean for education. Before concluding our look at the philosophic foundations of curriculum, we should make note of two more alternatives, *essentialism* and *reconstructionism*. These two might be better termed educational theories than philosophies since each begins immediately with ideas about education rather than human nature and truth. However, their influence on curriculum in the twentieth century has been just as powerful as the four major philosophies. Thus, they have a legitimate place in this section.

▢ *Essentialism*　The viewpoint known as essentialism evolved mainly as a criticism of progressive education. Although its proponents might be viewed as realists or idealists, they do not totally reject progressive methods. The main theme of essentialism is that education should prepare the learner to adjust to present conditions in society. Since young people are "in training" for adulthood, the school must assume a benevolent role in directing their education. Thus, school learning should consist of mastering subject matter that reflects currently available knowledge in various subject-area disciplines. Since teachers know that subject matter while learners do not, the teacher plays a highly directive role. This consists mainly of disseminating information to students. Furthermore, standards must be set for students so that they master enough knowledge and skill to prepare them for adulthood. To reflect the real world, essentialists maintain that nothing succeeds like hard work. While learners might have various personal problems, these must be overcome or set aside in favor of the necessary knowledge and skill requirements. Finally, the curriculum might include vocational and special subjects since these too are part of adulthood. Although these should also be organized on the basis of rigorous standards, they do not have the high standing of academic subjects. (See Frame 3.4.)

Arthur Bestor on the Function of
Schools (1959)

The school, the college, and the university were created to perform a specific and recognized function. Their facilities and techniques—classrooms, libraries, laboratories, recitations, lectures, seminars, and examinations—were designed and developed for the particular purpose of intellectual training. To enable the school to carry out any other function, it must be altered and adapted, and its performance in the new role is usually haphazard, fumbling, and defective. Moreover, if intellectual training is pushed aside or neglected by schools and colleges, society is thereby impoverished of intellectual training, because it possesses no other resources, no other agencies, no other techniques for making up the loss. That the primary function of the educational system is to furnish intellectual training is as completely self-evident as any statement that can possibly be made about the function of a social institution, whether one approaches the matter from the point of view of logic or history or sociology. . . .

The questions I am asking have reference to the curriculum of the school— the organized course of study conducted in the classroom and directed by the teacher. Young people are under the supervision of the school for certain hours in addition to those for which classroom work is scheduled. During these hours, many kinds of activities can be carried on and, if necessary, can be required: athletics, debate, shopwork, cooking, driver training, and so on. These are extracurricular activities. They are highly desirable, and in planning them the distinctions I have made between job training, social conditioning, and intellectual training have no particular relevance. In its extracurricular activities, the school may properly cater to any of the "felt needs" of young people. It may consciously undertake to foster and advance social purposes broader than those of intellectual training. Through its extracurricular activities, indeed, the school can often be extremely effective in redirecting the energies of young people, which otherwise may take an erratic course.

In recent years, the essentialist position has been stated vociferously by critics who claim that educational standards softened during the 1960s and early 1970s. The most notable achievements of the essentialists have been the widespread implementation of competency-based programs, the establishment of grade-level achievement standards, and the movement to reemphasize academic subjects in high schools and colleges. In many ways, the ideas of essentialism lie behind attacks on the quality of education by the media and by local pressure groups. The phrase "back to the basics" reflects the desire for a return to traditional methods of education, which are largely associated with essentialism. The recent popularity of that phrase illustrates just how powerful the influence of essentialism is on education.

☐   *Reconstructionism*   The position known as reconstructionism evolved
mainly as a response to what its proponents viewed as major problems
in society. The reconstructionists believe that because the school is
attended by virtually all youth, it can be used as a means to shape the
attitudes and values of each generation. As a result, when youth become adults they will share certain common values, and thus society
will be reshaped. In other words, the school is to be used as the means
to reshaping or "reconstructing" society. Furthermore, the reconstructionists are explicit about the types of values that are to be developed—
namely, those which are democratic. Among these are emphasis on
participatory problem-solving, concern for social welfare, and the application of systematic planning techniques. The school should become
a microcosm of a truly democratic society, and hence a premium is put
on group work and cooperative pupil–teacher planning. Subject matter,
rather than something to be mastered, is used as a vehicle for studying
social problems that serve as the central focus of the curriculum. The
separate subject curriculum is balanced, if not replaced, by the study
of social problems, and subject matter from various fields is used as it
is pertinent to those problems. In some cases, students may take direct
action toward solving problems in their local communities. In cases
where this is not possible, the students will at least carry ideas and
attitudes for solving social problems with them when they leave the
school.

The reconstructionist point of view has its roots in Dewey's book
Reconstruction in Philosophy (1920). However, it was most emphati-
cally stated by George Counts (1932) in a booklet entitled *Dare the
Schools Build a New Social Order?* (See Frame 3.5.) The title of that
work implied the belief that the schools could change society if they
chose to do so. The contents consisted of a challenge to carry out the
mission. Aside from the curriculum implications of reconstructionism,
its advocates also suggested that teachers view themselves as a major
political force in the struggle to solve social problems. Many schools
adopted programs based on this theory, and some teachers heeded the
political call by carrying their social reform ideas into the community.
As a result, such teachers were often labeled radicals, and the school
programs that they developed were attacked as unpatriotic.

Nevertheless, the theory of reconstructionism has survived and
can be seen today in courses such as "Problems of Democracy," in
school-sponsored community service projects, and in classes where students actively participate in planning. More recently, the interest in
developing "futures study" programs reflects this theory since such
programs usually promote concern for social problems and the need to
solve them. Disillusionment with society among young people in the
1960s contributed to a major rebirth of reconstructionist thinking during that period, and should that spirit emerge again, reconstructionism
will undoubtedly be in favor once more.

George Counts on Schools and the Social Order (1932)

. . . The age is pregnant with possibilities. There lies within our grasp the most humane, the most beautiful, the most majestic civilization ever fashioned by any people. This much at least we know today. We shall probably know more to-morrow. At last men have achieved such a mastery over the forces of nature that wage slavery can follow chattel slavery and take its place among the relics of the past. No longer are there grounds for the contention that the finer fruits of human culture must be nurtured upon the toil and watered by the tears of the masses. The limits to achievement set by nature have been so extended that we are today bound merely by our ideals, by our power of self-discipline, by our ability to devise social arrangements suited to an industrial age. If we are to place any credence whatsoever in the word of our engineers, the full utilization of modern technology at its present level of development should enable us to produce several times as much goods as were ever produced at the very peak of prosperity, and with the working day, the working year, and the working life reduced by half. We hold within our hands the power to usher in an age of plenty, to make secure the lives of all, and to banish poverty forever from the land. The only cause for doubt or pessimism lies in the question of our ability to rise to the stature of the times in which we live.

Our generation has the good or the ill fortune to live in an age when great decisions must be made. The American people, like most of the other peoples of the earth, have come to the parting of the ways; they can no longer trust entirely the inspiration which came to them when the republic was young; they must decide afresh what they are to do with their talents. Favored above all other nations with the resources of nature and the material instruments of civilization, they stand confused and irresolute before the future. They seem to lack the moral quality necessary to quicken, discipline, and give direction to their matchless energies. In a recent paper Professor Dewey has, in my judgment, correctly diagnosed our troubles: "The schools, like the nation," he says, "are in need of a central purpose which will create new enthusiasm and devotion, and which will unify and guide all intellectual plans."

This suggests, as we have already observed, that the educational problem is not wholly intellectual in nature. Our progressive schools therefore cannot rest content with giving children an opportunity to study contemporary society in all of its aspects. This of course must be done, but I am convinced that they should go much farther. If the schools are to be really effective, they must become centers for the building, and not merely for the contemplation, of our civilization. This does not mean that we should endeavor to promote particular reforms through the educational system. We should, however, give to our children a vision of the possibilities which lie ahead and endeavor to enlist their loyalties and enthusiasms in the realization of the vision. Also our social institutions and practices, all of them, should be critically examined in the light of such a vision.

- ### Educational Philosophy in the Real World of Schools

Most teachers have at one time or another been in faculty room discussions or formal meetings where colleagues have expressed strong personal views about education. Phrases such as the following are thus familiar:

> "Students have to be told what to do or they won't learn anything."
> "Kids should have more choices so that learning will be more interesting for them."
> "Mr. Jones has so many activities going on in his classroom that it is utter confusion."
> "Students should be taught how to think, not what to think."
> "Standards in this school are going down. Students don't have basic skills anymore."

As we have seen in the descriptions of various educational philosophies, these statements are actually expressions of one philosophy or another.

Many educators have also, at times, found themselves in conflict with prevailing views in their schools about what and how students should learn. Often they will say, "I don't agree with the philosophy of this school." Such a statement is an accurate observation of one of the most difficult problems for educators. In any given school, one can usually find different teachers and administrators who represent several or all of the different educational philosophies. While such diversity may be healthy, those educators in the philosophical minority often feel uncomfortable. In this situation, they may cling bravely to their personal beliefs, adopt those of the majority, or develop an eclectic philosophy that combines ideas from two or more viewpoints.

Frequently, when the topic of philosophy comes up, someone says, "Philosophy is for universities and schools of education—it doesn't have anything to do with the real world." In the two cases just cited, we have seen that this statement is far from the truth. In fact, educational philosophy is an important concept that has a critical and continuing place in the real world of schools.

Ideas about curriculum and teaching do not arise in a vacuum. Such ideas are actually based upon views of human nature, sources of values, worthwhile knowledge, and the roles of the teacher and the school. Put together, these topics constitute the ingredients of a philosophy of education.

If one is unclear about one's philosophy of education, curriculum plans and teaching procedures may be inconsistent or confused. For this reason, development and awareness of a personal philosophy of education are a crucial professional responsibility. Furthermore, educators need to be constantly open to new ideas and insights that may lead to revision or refinement of their philosophies.

Knowledge of different educational philosophies is also important as a tool for curriculum evaluation. As programs or methods are reviewed, questions ought to address what those programs assume about learners and learning as well as about values and knowledge. Behind these questions should be critical appraisal:

- Is this what we really believe about learners?
- Is the knowledge we are asking learners to achieve really worthwhile?
- Do our curriculum plans reflect the values we mean them to?

As we interact with other educators about important ideas, we ought to ask ourselves what philosophic ideas they seem to be expressing. In this way, our discussions might focus on basic issues rather than simply arguments about the pros and cons of some particular program or teaching technique.

Becoming aware of our own and other philosophies of education also allows us to go beyond the day-to-day activities of schooling and become participants in the larger view of our profession. This is not to say that those day-to-day activities are not important. Indeed, they are the arena for interaction with learners, which is, after all, our most important task. However, as professionals we should also have a sense of our overall purpose and place in society. We have an obligation to understand the reasons behind what we do and how our actions affect learners and society.

Finally, the issues and themes involved in philosophy include consideration of what constitutes a good and satisfying life. In each of the philosophies described, some such view was reflected. Presumably, schools contribute to the ability of the young to achieve a good life. Thus, philosophy serves as a foundation area to be considered in formulating educational goals. In the next chapter, we will consider possible goals, and the place of educational philosophy in curriculum planning will become even more obvious.

FOUNDATION 2: SOCIOLOGY—CHARACTERISTICS OF CONTEMPORARY AND FUTURE SOCIETY

■ ■   If children and youth had no lives away from the school, educators could simply ignore the social world as an influence on curriculum plans and outcomes. However, the fact is that young people do live in a world larger than the school, and that world influences both their interests and their attitudes. Furthermore, the school is an institution that is maintained by society partly for the purpose of helping the young adapt to and prepare for life in the larger society. For these reasons, those responsible for developing curriculum plans must consider the characteristics of contemporary society as well as characteristics that are forecast for the future. The latter point is especially crucial since today's young people will live most of their lives in the twenty-first century.

In this section, we will identify several social issues in terms of both their contemporary context and future forecasts about them. Before we do so, however, two factors related to social issues are worth mentioning. First, young people not only live in the larger world outside the school, but learn a great deal from experiences in that part of their lives. Sources of out-of-school learning include television, parents, the community, friends, and institutions such as government and church. Too often, when we think of learning, we think only of what is gained from the in-school curriculum. Experiences outside of school are viewed as peripheral and, when "negative," as interfering with school learning. For the learner, however, both are part of a total collection of learnings in which the two may be complementary or, in some cases, conflicting. In other words, in-school and out-of-school learnings may be viewed as consistent, but they may also be seen as opposed to one another. The latter case, of course, gives rise to the complaint that what is learned in school has little to do with the real world. In any event, educators must begin to give more attention to the reality of what William Schubert (1981) terms the "out-of-school curriculum."

The second factor involves recognition of the role of the school in helping to meet society's needs. The resolution of social problems depends upon citizens who have the skill, knowledge, and inclination to tackle them. Young people represent an important resource for resolving social issues through the contributions that they can make now and as adults of tomorrow. Thus, by virtue of the kind of education it provides, the school may be a major factor in the improvement of society by helping young people to develop the capacity to respond intelligently to social problems. In this way, the curriculum serves not only the needs of the learner, but also the needs of society. This function of the school, incidentally, need not reflect only the reconstructionist point of view described earlier in this chapter; a particular solution to social problems is not described here. The idea expressed simply reflects the fact that the school can and does serve a purpose in the society of which it is a part. Those responsible for curriculum planning must decide what kinds of skills, knowledge, and attitudes are called for by society's needs. Should curriculum plans promote conformity to existing social values? Should they encourage questioning of those values? Should specific social problems be studied in the school? If so, should one or another view of them be emphasized? Questions like this represent an important part of the overall consideration of the characteristics of contemporary and future society in curriculum planning.

With these two factors in mind, we will now turn to an examination of several social issues that curriculum planners need to consider. Those selected do not represent a total list of possibilities. Rather, they illustrate some important issues about which sensitive educators are concerned.

■ Technology

Over the past several decades, technology has taken on increasing importance in our lives. Often, when we think of technology, we think only of the emergence of "hi-tech" computers. However, the vast array of technology includes much more, from mechanical conveniences in the home to sophisticated devices used in health care to the support systems for space travel. The devices of technology are everywhere, and we have come to depend on them for work, leisure, communications, transportation, and virtually all other aspects of living.

The purpose of technology is to enhance the quality of living for human beings. What this means is that technology is supposed to work for us. To a large extent, this purpose has been served. Instant communications around the globe allow direct and immediate interaction among people. Computers provide a means for storing vast amounts of information and instantly retrieving it. Robots and other devices have taken on many of the menial tasks that humans have formerly had to perform. Mechanical organs have prolonged the lives of terminally ill patients. Television has brought both entertainment and education into our homes. Such a litany of technological wonders could alone fill an entire book. Indeed, technology has enhanced the quality of our lives.

At the same time, however, technology has created problems. Workers have found themselves unemployed, replaced by machines. Televisions and other entertainment devices have contributed to the sedentary use of leisure time. Further, both commercials and regular programs often consist of meaningless or questionable content. Fast-food restaurants frequently serve meals that lack nutritional value. Like the list of advantages, one of disadvantages could fill an entire book.

The one thing that we can expect of technology is that its development will continue. As a result, technology will probably become even more deeply rooted in our lives. No doubt we will have more television channels, more artificial organs, more sophisticated computers, and so on. This means that young people are growing up in a world that is very different from that of a generation or two ago—a world that will continue to stretch the imagination of even the most forward-looking people.

The increasing presence of technology in our world poses several important questions for those involved in curriculum planning:

- To what extent is the school responsible for introducing learners to technology?
- To what extent should the school involve learners in a critical analysis of the advantages and disadvantages of technology?
- Should the school attempt to develop skills involved in using technology?
- How can technology be used in promoting more effective learning?
- How should the school deal with technology-related learning that young people acquire outside the school (e.g., from television)?
- To what extent should learners use technology (e.g., word processors, computerized spelling checkers) to carry out school activities?

■ Family Structure

Traditionally, the family has been viewed as the core of our society's complex fabric. The picture of the family consisting of both natural parents and their children has been a dominant theme in social values and social institutions. However, this picture is rapidly fading, replaced by a much more complicated diversity of family structures. Separation, divorce, and childbirth without marriage have led to a tremendous increase in the number of single-parent homes. Adoption and foster parenthood have provided homes for children who might otherwise grow up in institutions apart from their natural parents. Multifamily homes and communes have become settings for those who feel limited by the possibilities of nuclear family life. Geographical mobility has negated the centrally located, extended family of grandparents, aunts and uncles, and other relatives. In short, the traditional nuclear and stable family has largely been replaced by one less structured and more transient.

These changes have been compounded by others involving family roles. Where once the father worked while the mother managed the home, we now find increasing numbers of families in which both father and mother work. This phenomenon has been brought on by the need for additional income and by the desire of many women to pursue careers outside the home. With the increase in the number of working mothers has come a corresponding increase in the number of day-care centers, preschool programs, and other agencies that care for children while their parents work.

The school as we know it today evolved in the context of the traditional family structure. Presumably, parents could be depended upon to provide a stable and predictable environment for young people. Mothers could be expected to become involved in school activities as an aspect of their child-rearing responsibility. When children had problems in school, parents could be called upon to devote time and energy to support the school's values and efforts. In sum, the family and the school were to work hand in hand in the growth and development of the young. Today, these expectations are no longer certain. As the family has changed, so has its role and function in relation to the school.

The change in family structure poses several questions for those concerned with curriculum planning:

- What responsibilities previously expected of the family should the school now assume?
- When family living is addressed in curriculum plans, what kind of family structure should be portrayed?
- To what extent should parents be expected to supplement curriculum plans through learning in the home?
- To what extent should the schools assume responsibility for the development of morals and values previously expected of parents?

■ Working in the Information Society

Alvin Toffler, in his book *The Third Wave* (1981), has noted that our society is entering a new phase. The first phase or "wave" in our history was agricultural. The second wave was represented by the industrial phase, from which we are now emerging. The third wave, which we are now entering, can be characterized by a number of trends. Among these is the fact that ours is a society based increasingly on information or knowledge.

In the first two phases, our economic, social, and political lives were largely tied to a workplace in which goods were produced. What was important, then, was the amount and value of material products that could be marketed. As technology has gradually replaced human production, increasing premium has been placed upon the quantity and value of new ideas and the means for using them.

The development of new ideas and knowledge was, of course, important in the first two phases. However, the future will bring new demands upon society with regard to information. First, work will be needed to identify how new technology can be used to benefit people. For example, we now have the means to communicate simultaneously with people in various parts of the globe. However, we also need to know how this ability can be used to promote world peace and unity. Second, in previous phases emphasis was placed on information specialists who developed knowledge in highly specific fields. Today we understand that knowledge in one field may also have implications for another. As a result, new information generalists are needed who can identify relationships among various fields. For example, a small group of researchers is now developing the field of biopolitics, which will explore the possibility of human biology influencing political elections and preferences. Third, as technology becomes more capable of performing human services, workers will be needed who can facilitate that process. For example, as computer technology delves more deeply into medical diagnosis, there will be increasing demand for medical technicians who can use machines to generate information about personal health profiles.

In addition to the creation of new kinds of jobs, the information society will influence other aspects of the workplace. At one level, such influence will be directed at using computers and other information-processing devices to replace clerical workers with more highly efficient machines. At another level, the locale of the workplace will also be affected. In both the agricultural and industrial phases, workers had to be brought to a central location where goods were produced. Given the availability of communications technology, this kind of centralization will no longer be necessary. Instead, people will be able to work cooperatively on information-based projects while located in various places. For example, some information workers may simply work at home using microcomputers. In some cases they may be in a single community, and in others they may be spread around the globe. Increasingly, the title "multinational corporation" will apply not only to marketing locations, but also to geographical spread of the work force.

Finally, increasing value will be placed upon persons who can "network" their credentials to fill emerging needs in the information society. In the past, for example, persons who were prepared to work in education went into teaching, administration, and other purely educational jobs. However, we might expect that in coming years, many individuals will combine their educational backgrounds with such areas as computer skills or media journalism to create software for technology-aided education.

Underlying all this is a serious challenge to the work ethic that has pervaded both our society and our schools. Among the values the schools have promoted are those related to the productive industrial worker. Such behaviors as punctuality, loyalty, acceptable appearance, and the like have been taught as preparation for life. In the decentralized information society, workers will find themselves largely working alone, setting flexible work hours, and servicing more than one employer. Thus, the old work-ethic behaviors may become as obsolete as the old jobs. Furthermore, in the near future many people will find themselves out of work, replaced by technology. Many of these people will have difficulty finding new jobs because they lack certain skills or because there simply are no jobs. No doubt this will threaten the self-esteem of those who have learned that self-dignity depends heavily upon having a job. Thus, the combination of technology and the information society may lead to the need to rethink the traditional work ethic and its place in our society.

Issues related to working in the information society raise several questions for curriculum planning:

- What should be the balance between specialization and generalization in the curriculum?
- What occupational fields might emerge for which some preparation may be done in school?
- What work-related values should the school promote, if any at all?
- What skills may be necessary to live a satisfying life in the information society?

■ Changing Sex Roles

Probably no social phenomenon has been more controversial in recent years than the women's movement. This movement has been based upon two desires of women: to achieve equal rights with men in many areas where sex discrimination exists and to have access to roles that have historically been reserved for men. Although the Equal Rights Amendment was not added to the Constitution, the effort to dispel sex-role stereotypes has had a profound effect on society, both in the United States and other countries.

Symptoms of the breakdown in sex-role stereotypes can be found in many areas of life. Women have begun to appear in executive positions in both business and the professions. Increasing numbers of married women are choosing to pursue careers outside the home. Women are competing and demonstrating excellence in sports for which they had previously been thought physically unfit. Furthermore, women are being portrayed in less stereotyped roles in the commercial media. These are but a few examples, but alone they are enough to imply that sex roles are changing in our society.

As women assume new roles and demonstrate excellence in them, we can expect to see stereotyping reduced even more. This trend will undoubtedly create some dissonance in society for those who continue to cling to old stereotypes. On the other hand, women will have opportunities to pursue much more diverse and dynamic lives. Many will continue to want to work in the home, but others will have enlarged opportunities in business, politics, the professions, sports, and other avenues of life. Although the "old-boy network" may disappear, it will be replaced no doubt by the "old-person network."

This trend is in a transitional stage since sex equity has not yet been fully achieved. Among those groups that still cling to sex-role stereotyping are, apparently, young people. For example, adolescents as a group continue to portray the "ideal" male as dominant, assertive, and competent, while depicting the "ideal" female as warm, expressive, and nonassertive. Furthermore, they continue to aspire to careers that are largely sex-role-stereotyped. Confronted with the ambiguous identity issues of adolescence, young people apparently find some certainty in this aspect of their self-concept (Wylie, 1979).

The changing perception and reality of sex roles raises several issues for those involved in curriculum planning:

- Should curriculum plans be used as a means to dispel sex-role stereotypes?
- What represents equitable sex-role portrayal in curriculum materials and activities?
- To what extent should young people be expected to participate in activities that conflict with sex-role stereotypes?
- Which aspects of curriculum plans are based on unfair sex-role bias, and how should these be revised?

■ **Cultural Diversity and Pluralism**

Our society has traditionally been characterized as a "melting pot," bringing together peoples of diverse cultural and ethnic backgrounds. Presumably, the "melting" process meant not only that such groups would coexist, but that they would rally around certain values. Among these values were democracy and national patriotism. In assuming the values and customs, ethnic and cultural groups were asked to abandon their unique characteristics in the interest of a unified society.

Today, the melting-pot idea has been replaced by what some sociologists call the "salad bowl." This metaphor reflects the increasing trend away from the idea of a homogeneous culture toward one of diversity and plurality. The trend can be recognized in several symptoms. One is the proliferation of hyphenated or specified identities, such as Polish-Americans, black Americans, Italian-Americans, Asian-Americans, and so on. One need only read bumper stickers to realize the increasing emphasis on dual identity. Another symptom is the emergence of ethnic festivals, which have become regular events in large cities. A third is the rebirth of regional interests represented, for example, by the revival of arts and crafts that were unique to various geographical areas. The trend toward cultural diversity has its roots in three phenomena. First, our society, in general, is moving toward diversity in values and lifestyles; being different is now a socially sanctioned idea. Second, people have developed a new interest in their own histories, and they seek to know their own personal heritage. Third, telecommunications has reminded people of their links with cultures in other parts of the world.

The trend toward cultural diversity and ethnic pluralism raises several questions that are pertinent to the future of our society. Is it possible to depend on unity of critical values in a society that otherwise prizes diversity? Which values are so critical that our society cannot exist without them? What if one subculture does not prize one or more of these critical values? These questions, of course, pertain not just to cultural diversity but to lifestyle diversity as well.

Traditionally, the school has been viewed as the major social agent in the melting-pot process. Earlier in this century, the schools were given the responsibility for teaching new language and customs to immigrant groups. This and related functions meant that immigrants were assimilated into our culture through the schools. More recently, government and the courts have directed the schools to develop bilingual and multicultural programs. Thus, the school is caught in an ambiguous position between its traditional role and the emerging trend toward diversity. This raises several questions for curriculum planning:

- How should the school portray cultural values?
- Should some cultural values be given greater emphasis than others?
- To what extent should curriculum plans be revised to reflect cultural diversity?

■ Changing Lifestyle Values

Until recent years, people in our society have generally engaged in fairly predictable life patterns. They grew up at home, went to school, got married, settled into lifetime careers, developed roots in a community, and ended their life cycle in quiet retirement. Today, people have begun to seek more diversity in lifestyles, seeking new pathways and alternative routes. Virtually every phase of the traditional pattern has been opened to question and action. The changing family structure has widely affected the nature of the child's home. Increasing numbers of parents are sending their children to alternative schools or teaching them at home. Nonmarriage and divorce have become at least as popular as marriage. Most people experience at least a half-dozen job changes in their work careers, and this number is expected to grow. Transience has replaced permanence in communities, and condominiums compete with homes. Elder citizens have taken on new and exciting roles that are changing perceptions of old age. Even death has not been untouched as medical technology stretches the expected lifespan.

Recently, one of the authors had the opportunity to visit with a group of adolescents. One question they were asked was, "What values are most commonly held or prized among your peers?" The answer was, "None, really. . . . Everybody has their own values, and as long as they don't interfere with other people's, that's okay." This statement reflects what appears to be a major trend toward diversity rather than conformity in lifestyle values. These values range from those which might be considered liberal or progressive to those which might be viewed as ultraconservative. If the 1960s could be characterized by concern for social welfare, the 1970s and early 1980s reflected self-fulfillment and self-realization. Magazine racks were filled with a flood of new titles that demonstrated diversity of lifestyle and self-improvement. In a world that is increasingly complex and ambiguous, individuals seem to seek some personal meaning and relevance for their lives. As technology frees people from work, increased leisure time is used for this purpose. Thus, we see people giving serious attention to physical fitness, health foods, and a myriad of other lifestyle characteristics.

This trend toward diversity in life patterns and values implies some interesting questions for our society. Traditionally, our lives have been focused on commonality and even conformity. One could depend upon others to act in largely predictable ways, and group pressure acted in behalf of that certainty. Today, such concepts as loyalty and patriotism are a matter of opinion rather than security. Among the many institutions that are affected by the new individualism is the school. The reason for this is that schools have served as a major source for promoting common values among youth. In light of this, the current trend toward diversity in life patterns and values raises several questions for those involved in curriculum planning:

- Which values should curriculum plans emphasize?
- Should life in the school reflect the range of diversity that is evident in society?
- How should curriculum plans address the various lifestyles and values?
- Is it possible for an institution that consists of large groups to maintain a program that also serves individual purposes?
- What response, if any, should the school make to values and lifestyles that differ widely from those which it generally reflects?
- What guidance should be given for identifying ways to use leisure time to achieve more satisfying lives?

■ A Coming Transformation?

Futures forecasters generally agree that our society is in transition from an industrial to a postindustrial phase. Identifying the general direction that the new phase will take is particularly challenging since there is no historical precedent for postindustrialism. There is widespread agreement about continuing advances in technology and greater diversity in lifestyles. However, there is also a good deal of disagreement about the general shape that our society might take in the new phase. Doomsday forecasters suggest that we are rapidly disintegrating in the area of morality and values. They predict that we will fall like the Roman Empire under the weight of hedonism. Less pessimistic observers sense that we are at a crossroads in our history and need to plan systematically the kind of future we would like. If we do not take action, they say, we might be vulnerable to some form of dictatorship that will shape society for us. Optimistic forecasters suggest that technology will develop to the point where it will solve our technical problems and allow us to pursue happier and more satisfying lives.

One of the most interesting treatments of this dilemma is that provided by futurists like Willis Harmin (1972) and Robert Bundy (1976). Their observations are based upon a two-step analysis of the present transition. First, they note that the industrial age has brought us enormous benefits in such areas as communications, medicine, and transportation. However, it has also led to inequitable distribution of wealth, economic insecurity, environmental problems, a short-range mentality, and a priority on technology rather than people. The postindustrial society, they suggest, may involve not only a new phase, but a large-scale transformation. Where power and decision making were largely centralized, they would become decentralized and participatory. Where technology previously engaged in unbridled growth, its development would be limited to what serves people's needs. Where people were dependent on institutions, they would become more self-reliant. Where all roads had led to the city, increasing numbers of people would choose rural life. Where material affluence was a major goal, the needs of people would take a higher priority. These and other trends reflect what Harmin has described as an emerging "person-centered society." The key issue here is that such a society would mean a major shift in values away from those associated with the industrial society.

For those involved in curriculum planning, such a shift raises several questions:

- What visions of the future ought to be reflected in curriculum plans?
- What role should the school play in our transitional society?

■ Which values, if any, should the curriculum emphasize?

■ How should the school respond to pressures to emphasize one set of values or another?

FOUNDATION 3: PSYCHOLOGY—BASIC HUMAN NEEDS

■ ■ Throughout this book we emphasize the need to recognize diversity among learners. However, it is also the case that people, including those who are young, share certain common characteristics. Among these are basic psychological needs which are necessary for individuals to lead a full and happy life. The third foundation of curriculum, then, is found in the basic human needs associated with sound mental health. Physical health needs are generally recognized and frequently dealt with through programs on fitness, nutrition, and health problems. Mental health needs, such as those for acceptance, belonging, security, and status, have been widely studied but less emphasized in the schools. If the curriculum is to help learners pursue a full and happy life, educators must consider how it will contribute to meeting basic human needs and how, in turn, those needs affect what happens in school. In this section we will describe some of the ideas that have been developed in relation to this foundation area.

■ Self-Actualization

Almost fifty years ago, Abraham Maslow (1937) began his monumental study of how basic human needs result in the development of personal drives and motivation. His theory of human motivation deals with psychological needs, safety needs, social needs, need for esteem, and the need for self-actualization. These five categories are hierarchical, and one can begin to deal with the self-actualization process, for example, only after progressing through the other four categories. Maslow used the notion of self-actualization to characterize people's need for self-fulfillment in life by actualizing or achieving their own potentiality. He concluded that one's desire to know and understand is a basic human need the fulfillment of which is a precondition of self-actualization.

In *Motivation and Personality* (1954), Maslow detailed the processes involved in maximizing self-actualization. He states: "What man can be, he must be" (p. 91). This requires that individuals be assisted to realize their potential by pursuing those activities which will positively fulfill their basic human needs. Curriculum plans should provide learning activities that allow youngsters to identify those things they can do well and should also assist them to succeed in other activities that are difficult for them—but nonetheless relate to fulfilling their individual needs. In this regard, self-actualization should not be construed as being limited to the fulfillment of one's particular talents and abilities. It deals with the fundamental task of each person to develop her or his identity and total self. Put another way, self-actualization assists youngsters to find out who they are and who and what they want to become.

In making curriculum plans and developing school programs, attention should be given to assist all students in maximizing their achievement of these needs to the greatest degree possible. By attending to these needs, schools can more effectively facilitate the achievement of content and subject-matter goals.

The fact that the school organizes its own community of adults and youngsters from the community at large allows it to organize appropriate patterns of human interaction even where those may not be present in the larger society. Thus the school can plan activities that bring together community personnel and resources from both school and community for particular learners to pursue their needs and interests while learning basic curriculum content. Normally these patterns do not exist for youngsters in the community, and no one would attempt to orchestrate efforts to meet such needs of individuals or groups of youngsters.

Thus, the school can provide youngsters with opportunities to explore and fulfill needs for acceptance, belonging, expression, participation, satisfaction, and status in pursuing its educational objectives. Learners are thus helped to find personal meaning in the learning experiences offered by the school. As educators find success in this area, their professional perspective on how to develop more effective and meaningful learning experiences for students will also be enhanced.

In *Perceiving, Behaving, Becoming* (1962), Maslow further commented:

> A society or culture can either be growth-fostering or growth-inhibiting. The sources of growth and of humanness are essentially within the human person and are not created or invented by society, which can only help or hinder the development of humanness, just as a gardener can help or hinder the growth of a rosebush, but cannot determine that it shall be an oak tree. (p. 46)

Those responsible for curriculum planning must pay attention to the concept of self-actualization. We all recognize the importance of school and community goals for learners. However, self-actualization also includes satisfying the desire to know and understand in relation to personal needs and interests. Moreover, when personal purposes are ignored, learners seem to be less successful in meeting those goals that the school and community desire. As curriculum plans reflect a balance between institutional and personal needs, the impact on both may be substantially enhanced.

■ **Developmental Tasks**

Another concept, that of developmental tasks, is one of the most specific approaches to considering human needs in organizing curricula. Robert Havighurst (1950) defined this concept as follows: "A developmental task is a task which arises at or about a certain period in the life of the individual, successful achievement of which leads to his happiness and to success with later tasks, while failure leads to unhappiness in the individual, disapproval by society, and difficulty with later tasks" (p. 6). Havighurst suggests that the needs of individuals are governed by their stage of development and age, and also grow out of needs to respond to societal expectation. He cites the origination of these tasks as follows: ". . . developmental tasks may arise from physical maturation, from the pressure of cultural processes upon the individual, from the desires, aspirations, and values of the emerging personality, and they arise in most cases from combinations of these factors acting together" (p. 8). Havighurst identified tasks for the stages of infancy, early childhood, middle childhood, adolescence, and adulthood. This approach affords teachers a means to identify persisting basic human needs that learners face in their progress through their school years. Frame 3.6 lists those tasks of children and youth.

Havighurst suggests that a developmental task occurs at the point or time of intersection of a basic need with society's expectations of the time at which this task should be achieved. The list in Frame 3.6 of the developmental tasks appropriate for each stage of growth and development should serve as a guideline in estimating when particular basic human needs of youngsters may be expected to appear. Educators should become more understanding of behaviors manifested by a learner indicating her or his readiness and need to deal with a particular developmental task. As we are able to facilitate the learner's achievement of these needs/tasks, her or his total success in school programs can be increased.

■ **The Fully Functioning Self**

In his chapter in *Perceiving, Behaving, Becoming* (1962), Earl Kelley considers the school's role in assisting each youngster to achieve the potential of his or her "fully functioning self." He maintains that

> The self is built almost entirely, if not entirely, in relationship to others. While the newborn babe has the equipment for the development of the self, there is ample evidence to show that nothing

Developmental Tasks for the School-Age Years
Havighurst, 1950

- **Infancy and Early Childhood**

    1. Learning to walk
    2. Learning to take solid foods
    3. Learning to talk
    4. Learning to control the elimination of body wastes
    5. Learning sex differences and sexual modesty
    6. Achieving physiological stability
    7. Forming simple concepts of social and physical reality
    8. Learning to relate oneself emotionally to parents, siblings, and other people
    9. Learning to distinguish right and wrong and developing a conscience

- **Middle Childhood**

    1. Learning physical skills necessary for ordinary games
    2. Building wholesome attitudes toward oneself as a growing organism
    3. Learning to get along with age-mates
    4. Learning an appropriate masculine or feminine social role
    5. Developing fundamental skills in reading, writing, and calculating
    6. Developing concepts necessary for everyday living
    7. Developing conscience, morality, and a scale of values
    8. Achieving personal independence
    9. Developing attitudes toward social groups and institutions

- **Adolescence**

    1. Achieving new and more mature relations with age-mates of both sexes
    2. Achieving a masculine or feminine social role
    3. Accepting one's physique and using the body effectively
    4. Achieving emotional independence of parents and other adults
    5. Achieving assurance of economic independence
    6. Selecting and preparing for an occupation
    7. Preparing for marriage and family life
    8. Developing intellectual skills and concepts necessary for civic competence
    9. Desiring and achieving socially responsible behavior
    10. Acquiring a set of values and an ethical system as a guide to behavior

resembling a self can be built in the absence of others. Having a cortex is not enough; there must be continuous interchange between the individual and others. Language, for example, would not be possible without social relationships. Thus, it is seen that man is necessarily a social being. (p. 9)

In considering the need to accept and like one's self, Kelley discusses how adults in the youngster's life should deal with the conscious self. As a youngster's "self" reaches out toward facilitating factors and withdraws from endangering ones, the need for positive interaction with adults to help the youngster with this process should be obvious. When the school and its programs function in this manner, learners will more readily perceive educational opportunities as possible, supportive factors. This will occur, however, only as we plan and develop learning and other school activities around the basic needs of the level of youngsters our particular school serves (e.g., young children, emerging adolescents, or maturing adolescents). In this way, students will be assisted in their needs to progress toward becoming fully functioning selves. This possibility is well expressed in a statement by Karen Horney (1945), which ought to be considered in fashioning one's personal philosophy as an educator:

My own belief is that man has the capability as well as the desire to develop his potentialities and become a decent human being, and that these deteriorate if his relationship to others and hence to himself is, and continues to be, disturbed. I believe that man can change and keep on changing as long as he lives. (p. 19)

Kelley defines the characteristics of the fully functioning self as follows:

The fully functioning personality thinks well of himself.
The fully functioning personality thinks well of others.
The fully functioning personality therefore sees his stake in others.
The fully functioning personality therefore sees himself as part of a world in movement—in process of becoming.
The fully functioning personality, having accepted the ongoing nature of life and the dynamic of change, sees the value of mistakes.
The fully functioning personality, seeing the importance of people, develops and holds human values.
The fully functioning personality knows no other way to live except in keeping with his values.
Since life is ever-moving and ever-becoming, the fully functioning personality is cast in a creative role. (1962, pp. 18–20)

Educators might consider using these characteristics as guidelines or expectations for ways in which the goals of the curriculum could be effectively achieved. Implementing activities that assist the learner in developing these characteristics will also enhance the achievement of other goals.

■ The Needs Theory

The work of Louis Raths on needs theory spanned a quarter of a century and synthesized both the identification of needs in learners and approaches that teachers could use in dealing with those needs. While acknowledging that the emotional needs of children can be extensive, in his final work on the needs theory (1972) Raths identified the eight persisting emotional needs of children as follows:

1. The need for love and affection.
2. The need for achievement.
3. The need for belonging.
4. The need for self-respect.
5. The need to be free from deep feelings of guilt.
6. The need to be free from deep feelings of fear.
7. The need for economic security.
8. The need for understanding of self. (p. 25)

Research conducted widely with Raths's eight emotional needs resulted in approaches and techniques that teachers can use to meet and facilitate these needs in the school setting. Problems of frustration may result when learning activities have not been organized to provide information and procedures with which teachers and students may work. Raths's observation about the teacher's role and responsibilities in dealing with these needs in the school setting should be clearly understood.

Is it your job to meet the emotional needs of children in your room? The answer is no. You really have no more responsibility in this matter than the personnel of other social institutions, and much less responsibility than parents. In fact, your priority job is to promote learning. Now, if something gets in the way of learning, including how to get along with others, quite obviously you have a responsibility to do something about it. If the vision of a particular child is suspected as a cause, you try to do something about it. If his hearing is bad, you do something about it. In the same way, if frustrated needs seem to be blocking the learning process, you will want to do something about it. . . . Are you expected to be a clinical psychologist or analyst or psychiatrist? By all means NO! You will do the things that can normally be expected of teachers in group situations and in the typical teacher–child or teacher–parent interview. If you have any reason to suspect that a child has some very deep psychological problems, you do have a responsibility to take the matter up with school officials. (1972, pp. 64–65)

Raths felt that teachers ought not to overlook or hide symptoms, but should try to identify cases of "unsocial behavior." As unmet needs can be identified and avenues for their acceptable pursuit provided, each youngster's own thought, growth, and development will progress better. Very often, if attention is paid to these needs rather than to surrounding conditions that may make for minor disagreements, student difficulties can be more readily overcome. As such problems are resolved and the student needs properly satisfied, progress toward learning objectives in the teaching–learning situation can be more effectively pursued.

Raths's needs theory has as its end objective the development of an environment in which learners feel genuinely secure. In developing school programs that take into account and help resolve the emotional needs of children, the school becomes an emotionally secure environment. When schools develop such an environment, teachers and students develop an increased attraction to learners because their needs and those of the school–community become more closely aligned and complementary. Raths's work is an important source that can help educators consider the emotional needs aspect with which children must deal. As the learner copes effectively with and fulfills these emotional needs, the satisfaction of other basic human needs in her or his pursuance of learning can be more successfully accomplished.

■ Readiness Concerns

The issue of readiness to deal with experiences related to one's basic human needs is frequently overlooked. Ira Gordon addressed the relationship between readiness and a youngster's ability to meet basic human needs successfully. He saw the school as an open-energy system with continuous exchange and feedback among youth and adults. Such a school could respond more effectively to learner needs. This responsiveness must be based upon the readiness of learners to deal with specific needs and to handle challenges of specific observed:

> Needs, drives, and urges represent potentialities, pushes, and overall directions. They do not operate in a social vacuum. Meeting these needs requires the interaction process, first with the family and later with the society as a whole. The self is developed through these transactions with the environment. (1969, p. 35)

Gordon envisioned the school as an open-energy system and society's formal channel to help youngsters deal with and meet these needs. The achievement of basic human needs should result in the youngster's developing an increasing capacity for intelligent self-direction. Both school and society should be prepared to reward such growth by delegating appropriate increases in authority for which youngsters can become responsible. Teachers must become proficient in judging both the sensory and cognitive readiness of the learner for increasingly challenging situations. As this ongoing task of matching readiness to opportunity becomes accurate, the learner's need to develop an increased sense of achievement, confidence, and satisfaction is positively fulfilled.

Cognitive levels matching is a recent approach that matches learning challenges to the student's cognitive level at a given time in her or his school years. The approach allows teachers to develop and present learning activities that more appropriately match a student's readiness to think and learn. Learning activities developed in this manner minimize instances of overchallenge and underchallenge of student abilities and develop learning experiences more compatible with the student's human needs.

The psychological foundation of curriculum is concerned with basic human needs. School programs should respond to these basic human needs of youngsters at every stage during their development. Those responsible for curriculum planning must always take the nature and level of the learner into account, as well as the materials that are to be planned and organized in any learning activity. The planning of a sequence that results in learning should be a highly interactive process involving the curriculum planner, the teaching activity, and the active participation of the learner. Teaching and learning are virtually impossible to separate in the school setting. While various theories may make their own separation of these notions, the arguments are little more than semantic considerations and, in themselves, not important to curriculum planning. Curriculum planning may involve a range of situations from the teacher interacting with learners to learners interacting with a microcomputer on a learning activity planned and programmed by the teacher. It is the nature of the teaching–learning interaction that is critical to learning.

The effectiveness of the learning experience is determined by many variables, including the activity's level of difficulty, the learner's prior experience and skills, and the teacher's understanding and capacity to adapt the lesson to these variables. This results in the desired situation described by Edward Krug (1950): "The curriculum comes to life in the classroom, school, or community teaching situation, in the pupil-teacher relationships, and in the activities carried on. Good teaching and good learning are the reasons for which all other aspects of curriculum development exist" (p. 8).

CHAPTER SUMMARY

In Chapter 3, we have explored three areas that are foundations of the curriculum field: philosophy, sociology, and psychology. Each field is important since it contributes to ideas that are critical in curriculum planning.

The discussion of philosophy included a look at several different viewpoints. Each one represented a different perspective about the nature of human beings, the source of knowledge, and the role of education in human growth and development. We also suggested that philosophy has a valuable place in the practical realities of school since one's educational philosophy largely determines the views one has about teaching and learning.

Since young people learn a great deal outside of the school, and since the school functions in relation to society, our discussion recognized sociology as the second major foundation of curriculum. Like philosophy, sociology is not some abstract subject far removed from the real life of the school. Our society is in a state of transition, filled with uncertainty and ambiguity. Educators see this every day in their interactions with youth in the school. Like the society at large, young people reflect a wide diversity of values, lifestyles, and interests. At the same time, they often seem confused and uncertain about what they should believe or do. What they learn from parents, friends, government, television, and other sources sometimes complements but often conflicts with what they learn in school.

In developing goals and curriculum plans, educators must consider both contemporary society and the future in which young people will live their lives. Attention must be paid to such issues as technology, family structure, work, lifestyles, and other aspects of society. At the same time, thought must be given to how the school, an institution that developed in the industrial age, will respond to the growing diversity of the emerging postindustrial society. Whatever the outcome of these deliberations, sociology presents a challenging and exciting field for curriculum planners.

Our discussion of the psychological foundation has indicated that curriculum and school programs can become more effective as they consider the nature of basic human needs and assist youngsters in meeting those needs. Finally, we showed how the various viewpoints about basic human needs are manifested in ideas about learning.

Having read Chapter 3, you should be able to:

1. Describe various philosophies and their implications for the curriculum field
2. Describe reasons why an understanding of philosophy is important for curriculum work
3. Identify philosophical issues that need to be considered in curriculum planning today
4. Identify the importance of sociology for the curriculum field
5. Describe various social trends and issues that should be considered in curriculum planning today
6. Describe the importance of basic human needs in curriculum planning and development
7. Identify particular issues in the contemporary needs of youth that should be considered in curriculum planning

SUGGESTED ACTIVITIES

1. Have members of the group identify which, if any, of the "schools of philosophy" discussed in this chapter reflect their own personal educational philosophy. In cases where particular members of the group do not readily see relationships of their own positions to these areas, ask if they would be willing to describe their own personal educational philosophy to the group. Have the rest of the group discuss ways in which they see that these individual philosophies do and do not relate to the philosophical areas presented in this chapter.

2. Have interested members of the class discuss philosophical ideas that are related to current educational programs such as gifted and talented education, special education, vocational education, efforts to correct racial imbalance in schools through busing, and so on. Identify the ways in which the objectives of these programs are related to the philosophic positions presented in this chapter.

3. Organize two groups of interested class members to discuss the following in terms of the information presented in this chapter on educational philosophy issues. One group is to consist of class members who work in nonpublic educational settings. They are to organize a discussion of the differences they see in the philosophical bases of their schools from those of the public schools. The second group is to include members of the class who work in public schools. They are to discuss what they see as the primary philosophical bases of public schools in our society. After the groups make their reports, discuss any philo-

sophically based differences that the two presentations suggest for planning and developing school programs.

4. Have members of the group list current social trends that they feel are having the greatest impact on children and youth. Randomly organize the class in groups to identify the five most important trends, which they should then arrange in priority by combining their individual lists. Convene the total group and identify the social trends most commonly listed in each group. What does the class rank as the ten most important trends for schools and their communities to consider in their curriculum planning activities?

5. Discuss what current social trends the class feels are most likely to continue in the immediate future. What new social trends do members of the groups believe will emerge in the near future? In what way do they feel these will affect children and youth, and how will schools have to respond in dealing with these trends?

6. Discuss the ways in which the group sees the developmental tasks concept (Frame 3.6) helpful in planning learning activities that relate to personal and social tasks and issues important to youngsters at particular times in their growth and development. After this discussion, organize the class into groups that are primarily concerned with early childhood, middle childhood (transescence), or adolescence. Ask each group to identify the contemporary issues and tasks that they view as most important to the social development of the age group with which they work. Have them identify any contemporary changes or additions they would make to the developmental tasks list that Havighurst identified for their students' age group. Reconvene the groups and discuss what, if any, changes the groups identified.

7. Discuss ways in which basic human needs (e.g., acceptance, belonging, expression, participation, satisfaction, and status) are important in curriculum planning in schools today. Identify ways in which teachers and schools need to deal with these needs in today's environment for children and youth.

8. Have interested members of the group identify what they consider to be changes in the kinds of human needs students demonstrate in schools today from those recalled from their own experiences as students. In what ways do they see these needs today are similar or different from those of their own youth? In what ways do they feel that society is better or less able and/or prepared to deal with these basic human needs today? In what ways do they see there is a need for schools to change or expand their roles in helping students meet these needs today?

9. Discuss with the group what they feel to be the most critical basic human needs of youth that schools can properly address today. Following this discussion, organize the class into groups that are primarily concerned with early childhood, transescence, or adolescence. Ask the groups to consider and rank those needs identified by the group at large in terms of needs issues of students for their students' age group. Reconvene the group and discuss how and why these needs are seen to vary for children at different ages.

REFERENCES

Bestor, A. "The Distinctive Function of Schools." *Daedalus* 88 (1959): 75–90.

Brubacher, J. (ed.). *Philosophies of Education.* Forty-first Yearbook of the National Society for the Study of Education, Part I. Chicago: University of Chicago Press, 1942.

Bundy, R. (ed.). *Images of the Future.* Buffalo, N.Y.: Prometheus Books, 1976.

Clayton, T. *Teaching and Learning: A Psychological Perspective.* Englewood Cliffs, N.J.: Prentice-Hall, 1965.

Counts, G. *Dare the Schools Build a New Social Order?* New York: John Day, 1932.

Dewey, J. "My Pedagogic Creed." *The School Journal* 54 (1897): 77–80.

———. *Reconstruction in Philosophy.* New York: Henry Holt, 1920.

Gordon, I. *Human Development from Birth through Adolescence.* New York: Harper & Row, 1969.

Harmin, W. "The Nature of Our Changing Society: Implications for Schools." In *Curriculum and Cultural Revolution,* edited by D. E. Purpel and M. Bellinger. Berkeley, Calif.: McCutchan, 1972.

Havighurst, R. *Developmental Tasks and Education.* New York: Longmans, Green, 1950.

Horney, K. *Our Inner Conflicts.* New York: W. W. Norton, 1945.

Hutchins, R. *The Conflict in Education.* New York: Harper & Row, 1953.

Kneller, G. *Introduction to the Philosophy of Education.* New York: John Wiley & Sons, 1964.

Kelley, E. "The Fully Functioning Self." In *Perceiving, Behaving, Becoming: A New Focus for Education.* The 1962 Yearbook of the Association for Supervision and Curriculum Development, A. Combs, Chairman. Washington, D.C.: Association for Supervision and Curriculum Development, 1962.

Krug, E. *Curriculum Planning.* New York: Harper & Row, 1950.

Maslow, A. "Dominance-Feeling, Behavior and Status." *Psychological Review* 44 (1937): 404–429.

———. *Motivation and Personality.* New York: Harper & Row, 1954.

———. "Some Basic Propositions of a Growth and Self-Actualization Psychology." In *Perceiving, Behaving, Becoming: A New Focus for Education.* The 1962 Yearbook of the Association for Supervision and Curriculum

Development, A. Combs, Chairman, Washington, D.C.: Association for Supervision and Curriculum Development, 1962.

Morris, V. C. "Existentialism and Education." *Educational Theory* 4 (1954).

Naisbitt, J. *Megatrends: Ten New Directions Transforming Our Lives.* New York: Warner Books, 1982.

Neill, A. S. *Summerhill: A Radical Approach to Child Rearing.* New York: Pocket Books, 1977.

Park, J. *Selected Readings in the Philosophy of Education.* 4th ed. New York: Macmillan, 1974.

Raths, L. *Meeting the Needs of Children: Creating Trust and Security.* Columbus, Ohio: Charles E. Merrill, 1972.

Rich, J. *Readings in the Philosophy of Education.* Belmont, Calif.: Wadsworth, 1966.

Schubert, W. "Knowledge about Out-of-School Curriculum." *The Educational Forum* 45 (1981): 185–198.

Toffler, A. *The Third Wave.* New York: William Morrow, 1981.

Venable, T. *Philosophic Foundations of the Curriculum.* Chicago: Rand McNally, 1967.

Wylie, R. *The Self Concept.* Vol. 2. Lincoln: University of Nebraska Press, 1979.

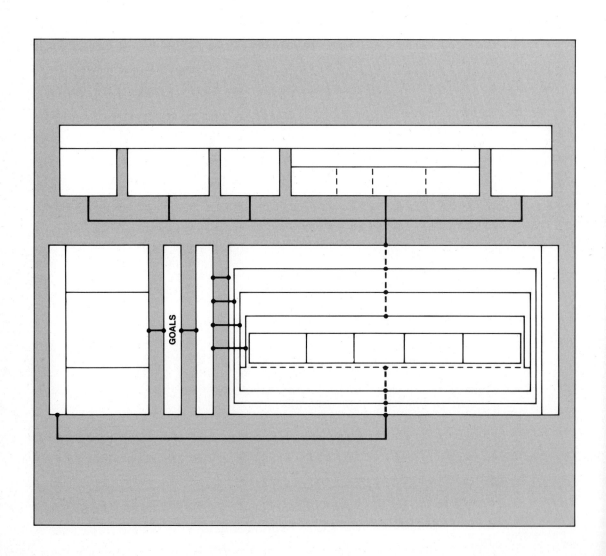

4

Developing Educational Goals

The plans and activities involved in everyday school life do not arise in a vacuum. They are formulated and carried out as a means to achieve some larger purposes. *Goals* represent the broadest or most general level at which educational purposes are developed. In this chapter, we will consider issues relating to the development of educational goals. Included in the analysis are types of goals, procedures for their development, examples of goal statements, and criteria for analyzing existing goal statements.

As a result of reading Chapter 4, you should be able to:

1. Differentiate types of educational purposes
2. Describe the purpose of broad goals
3. Describe the role of goals in curriculum planning
4. Identify examples of goal statements
5. Describe procedures for developing broad educational purposes
6. Describe procedures for analyzing broad educational purposes
7. Describe the purposes of general objectives
8. Identify examples of general objectives

TYPES OF GOALS

■ ■ Over the years, there has been some confusion about the difference between goals and other statements of educational purposes. Many different ideas have been suggested for resolving this confusion. In keeping with the curriculum framework described earlier, we will use the following definitions in relation to statements of educational purposes.

> *Goal:* a broad or general statement reflecting the ultimate ends toward which the total educational program is directed
>
> *General objective:* a statement reflecting the purposes of a particular unit or level of the school program, such as elementary, middle level, or high school
>
> *Specific objective:* a statement reflecting a short-range or more immediate purpose involved in a specific teaching–learning activity, such as a unit or daily plan

Although developed in relation to various levels of the educational process, these three types of purposes should be highly interactive. General objectives should contribute to the attainment of the goals; likewise, specific objectives should lead toward achievement of general objectives. Similarly, the process of defining specific objectives may indicate a need to revise, refine, or clarify general objectives or goals. Attention to the interactive nature of various educational purposes ensures coordination and consistency in curriculum plans. The lack of such attention may lead to confusion about what form curriculum plans ought to take.

Typically, goals are developed in two forms: learner goals and institutional goals. *Learner goals* describe the kinds of behaviors, knowledges, skills, and attitudes we hope learners will acquire as a result of their experiences in the total educational program. Furthermore, goals are intended for all learners, although, in reality, some may attain them more fully than others. The important factor is that all learners have opportunities to pursue the goals to whatever level is possible for them. Samples of full goal statements will be discussed later in this chapter. At this point, we may note that most typically include, among others, statements such as the following:

- Development of mental and physical health
- Development of citizenship skills
- Understanding of and respect for others
- Mastery of basic communication skills

Institutional goals define the role of the school in helping young people attain learner goals as well as clarify the school's role in society.

Institutional goals outline in broad terms what the school will do. Typically, institutional goals include statements such as the following:

- To ensure equal educational opportunity for all learners
- To provide a healthy and supportive environment for learners
- To offer educational opportunities for all citizens
- To contribute to the improvement of community life

In Chapter 3, we noted the place and power of the out-of-school curriculum in learning. In light of this, those responsible for developing goals should recognize that the out-of-school curriculum may influence goal attainment. In some cases, the home, the community, the church, and other agencies may help learners attain goals. In other cases, they may inhibit goal attainment. For example, a supportive home environment may enhance mental health, whereas a nonsupportive home may actually contribute to poor mental health.

It must also be recognized that institutional goals are often influenced by forces outside the school. For example, the provision of equal educational opportunity for all learners is a goal that follows not only from the concept of public education, but also from Supreme Court rulings about the function of schools. External influences, particularly court rulings, sometimes conflict with local opinion about the function of schools. In most cases the courts have acted in the best interests of young people and in keeping with democratic principles. Although some schools have thus been forced to act against their will, the two factors just named transcend local opinion. In fact, they are vital to identifying worthwhile institutional goals.

While learner goals and institutional goals represent two different types of purposes, they obviously should function in an interactive way. Learner goals represent the behaviors, knowledge, skills, and attitudes we hope young people will attain. Institutional goals define what the schools will do so that the learner goals may be realized as fully as possible. Together, they provide guidance for specific curriculum plans that constitute the heart of the educational process.

DEVELOPING GOALS

■ ■   Given the critical place of goals in curriculum planning, it is important that they be developed carefully and systematically. In order to ensure that this is the case, three principles should be kept in mind. First, goals should be based upon the foundation areas of philosophy, sociology, and psychology. Second, goals should be developed through the participation of a variety of groups. Third, goal statements should be as succinct as possible and, where necessary, provide clarification of their meaning.

■ Applying the Foundations

The use of the various foundations areas in developing goals is reflected in three questions.

1. What constitutes a good and satisfying life to which schools may contribute?
2. What are the characteristics of contemporary and future life with which learners must deal?
3. What basic human needs must be met in order for learners to experience health, growth, and development?

Ideas about the nature of a good and satisfying life are derived largely from one's philosophy. Depending upon the particular philosophic viewpoint, "good" and "satisfying" may take on different meanings. For the realist or idealist, such a life is based upon some set of enduring values and the extent to which life is consistent with them. For the pragmatist, a good and satisfying life might revolve around continuing participation in experiences that add to the meaning of life and the clarification of personal and social values. For the existentialist, such a life might involve self-fulfillment in a complex and confusing world. Beyond this, ideas about a good and satisfying life may involve other variables. For example, people might prize economic security, intellectual activities, social welfare, individuality, and other concepts. Whatever the case, educational goals must be developed in light of philosophic views in order that the goals reflect the kind of life to which schools will contribute.

Sociological considerations suggest the nature of the contemporary and future society in which learner's lives do or will take place. Thus they help to clarify the behaviors, knowledges, skills, and attitudes necessary for effective functioning in society. In developing goals, attention must be given to such concepts as lifestyles, technology, global interdependence, work, and the nature of institutions. We have seen in Chapter 3 that our society is in transition from the industrial phase to some form of postindustrial life. As a result, the concepts listed above are in a state of flux, and our world has become increasingly complex. If trends of the past few decades continue, we can expect that today's young people will live in a world vastly different from the one we have known. Although the future is relatively uncertain, current trends do suggest that it will involve increasing diversity, technological advancement, and information richness. It may also center more on human needs than did the industrial society. In any event, those responsible for developing goals must make certain that they have an eye on the future if the goals are to represent a realistic view of the social purposes of education.

Psychology illuminates the human needs that must be met to ensure healthy growth and development. In order to experience self-actualization, people need to have a sense of belonging, participation, and personal dignity in their environment. In addition, they need to be free from feelings of guilt and fear, and they need to have a clear self-concept and positive self-esteem. Each of these concepts suggests specific human purposes toward which the schools should strive. They also imply the kind of environment that ought to characterize the school—namely, one in which self-actualization is nurtured. Along with this, however, we must consider recent findings in the neurosciences that indicate that physiological development also contributes to psychosocial growth. Careful analysis of the nature–nurture balance will ensure that educational goals reflect the aspects of "humanness" that they ought to foster and support.

■ Participation in Goal Development

Parents send their children to school to receive a quality education. They and other citizens provide financial and political support to maintain schools as an important part of our society. Young people depend on schools to help them meet their interests and needs now and for the future. The education profession is based upon a commitment to providing good schools for quality education. Other groups with special interests are concerned that schools help young people acquire various skills, knowledges, attitudes, and behaviors. Seemingly all people have an interest and stake in what the schools do. Thus, they are concerned about the nature of educational goals.

By virtue of that concern and the fact that schools are maintained by the society, virtually everyone has a right to participate in the formulation of educational goals. The problem with this point of view is that different groups have different opinions about what those goals ought to be. Furthermore, some groups speak louder than others, and their opinions may serve special interests rather than those of young people and the general society. Effective and worthwhile goals, however, depend upon a consensus of ideas so that people may be mutually commited to them. Thus, *the key to the process of goal development is participation based upon educated opinion.* To consider how this might be achieved, consider some steps a local community might take to develop a set of goals.

1. A steering committee is formed including representation from groups such as citizens, teachers, students, administrators, and the school board.
2. The steering committee studies existing goal statements and important concepts from the foundations areas. This infor-

mation is then organized into a format by which it may be presented to other groups.

3. A series of open meetings is held for citizens, educators, students, and others. At each meeting, the steering committee reviews pertinent information from the foundations areas. Individuals and groups are then invited to submit suggestions for educational goals.

4. The steering committee then analyzes goals suggested within its own groups as well as goals from others. From these a working draft of a set of goals is developed.

5. The working draft is presented to various groups in open meetings similar to those of step 3. Reactions are invited for input into a finalized set of goals.

6. The steering committee develops a finalized set of goals based on step 5. These are then submitted for approval by the school board.

7. The set of goals is then publicized in the local media and presented in a series of open public meetings. At this point, additional work may also be undertaken to set priorities or further clarify the goals.

This process or one like it guarantees that all interested parties have an opportunity to suggest educational goals. Representation on the steering committee provides direct input for groups in all phases of the project. At the same time, two traditional problems in goal development are addressed. First, the goal development process is based upon information gleaned from the foundations areas rather than mere opinion. Second, the broad-based participation reduces the chance that one or another special-interest group will have an undue say in the content of the goals. In the end, such a process does much to ensure that goals are developed through a participatory process and on the basis of educated opinion. By these means, concerned groups will be committed to the goals, and their value to further curriculum planning will be greatly enhanced.

■ **Clarifying Goal Statements**

By definition, goals are broad and general statements about educational purposes. For this reason the language used in goal statements often includes ambiguous terminology. For example, one goal might indicate that learners will "develop skills necessary for effective citizenship in a democracy." Not only does the concept of democracy have many meanings, but there is a multitude of opinions about what constitutes effective citizenship skills. For some this may mean knowing the Bill of Rights and the branches of government. For others such

skills might involve participation in elections or other aspects of the
political process. Still others may think of skills such as the planning
and participation that are involved in improving communities. Where
such differences of opinion about goals exist, it is little wonder that
they are looked upon simply as platitudes that have nothing much to
do with specific curriculum plans. To add to the usefulness and meaning
of goal statements, it is frequently helpful to clarify them with additional information. This is done by providing examples of skills, knowledges, attitudes, or behaviors related to particular goals. The following
additions clarify the previously stated goal.

Goal: To develop skills necessary for effective citizenship in a
democracy. This goal will be accomplished by:

1. gaining knowledge about how our political system operates
2. understanding the functions of the branches of government
3. understanding basic principles set forth in the Constitution
4. developing planning, participation, and decision-making skills

Another goal statement might be developed as follows:

Goal: To develop a sense of self-worth. This goal will be accomplished through:

1. clarifying aspects of the self-concept
2. developing personal values
3. developing positive self-esteem
4. acquiring skills involved in self-evaluation
5. understanding aspects of the environment which influence self-
   perceptions

Additional examples of clarifying items related to goal statements
will be illustrated in sample lists of goals in the next section. At this
point, it is important to understand the role such items play in specifying the meaning of particular goals. In this way the goals may be
more useful in developing specific curriculum plans for learners.

SAMPLE GOAL STATEMENTS

The sample goal statements in this section include national, state, and
local levels. Since they span several decades, particular items may
seem out of date. However, our purpose here is only to illustrate the
kinds of goal statements that groups at each level have developed.

■ **National Level**

Perhaps the most quoted national goal statement was developed by the Educational Policies Commission of the National Education Association in 1938. The statement included four broad goals and clarifying statements for each. Two of these goals appear in Frame 4.1 while the entire statement can be found in Appendix B.

In 1944, the Educational Policies Commission issued a second statement, which expanded upon the four main categories in the earlier version. This statement was entitled "Imperative Educational Needs of Youth," and it included the items given in Frame 4.2.

Both of the previous statements listed learner goals. An excellent example of one that includes institutional goals was issued by the American Association of School Administrators in 1966. The statements, listed in Frame 4.3, were intended to identify points at which the educational program of American schools was in need of special attention.

The content of goal statements is influenced by trends at the time they are developed, as well as by certain values that are viewed as timeless. For this reason, statements in the 1980s might include some items from lists such as those already shown, plus others of more contemporary concern, such as computer literacy and technological competence. In Chapter 10 and in the Epilogue, we will consider issues for contemporary and future curriculum planning. Among these will be a suggested goal statement for the 1980s and beyond.

■ **State Level**

Since individual states are largely responsible for education within their boundaries, each maintains a set of goals to guide educational decision making at the state level. State-level goals for learners tend to be largely similar, although regional differences may influence institutional goals. Virtually all states support the acquisition of citizenship skills by learners. On the other hand, some may attach greater importance than others to bilingual education, depending upon the proportion of residents for whom English is a second language. For our purposes, we will present two state goal statements representative of learner goals.

The first example, shown in Frame 4.4, is Pennsylvania's "Twelve Goals of Quality Education." One of the interesting aspects of this statement is that Pennsylvania conducts a statewide assessment program to identify the degree to which students in local schools are attaining the goals. Of particular note is the fact that the assessment includes both academic and nonacademic areas.

Goal Statement of 1938 Educational Policies Commission

■ **The Objectives of Self-Realization**

The Inquiring Mind	The educated person has an appetite for learning.
Speech	The educated person can speak the mother tongue clearly.
Reading	The educated person reads the mother tongue effectively.
Writing	The educated person writes the mother tongue efficiently.
Number	The educated person solves his problems of counting and calculating.
Sight and Hearing	The educated person is skilled in listening and observing.
Health Knowledge	The educated person understands the basic facts concerning health and disease.
Health Habits	The educated person protects his own health and that of his dependents.
Public Health	The educated person works to improve the health of the community.
Recreation	The educated person is participant and spectator to many sports and other pastimes.
Intellectual Interests	The educated person has mental resources for the use of leisure.
Esthetic Interests	The educated person appreciates beauty.
Character	The educated person gives responsible direction to his own life.

■ **The Objectives of Human Relationship**

Respect for Humanity	The educated person puts human relationships first.
Friendships	The educated person enjoys a rich, sincere, and varied social life.
Cooperation	The educated person can work and play with others.
Courtesy	The educated person observes the amenities of social behavior.
Appreciation of the Home	The educated person appreciates the family as a social institution.
Conservation of the Home	The educated person conserves family ideals.
Homemaking	The educated person is skilled in homemaking.
Democracy in the Home	The educated person maintains democratic family relationships.

Imperative Educational Needs of Youth (1944)

1. All youth need to develop salable skills and those understandings and attitudes that make the worker an intelligent and productive participant in economic life. To this end, most youth need supervised work experience as well as education in the skills and knowledge of their occupation.
2. All youth need to develop and maintain good health and physical fitness.
3. All youth need to understand the rights and duties of the citizens of a democratic society, and to be diligent and competent in the performance of their obligations as members of the community and citizens of the state and nation.
4. All youth need to understand the significance of the family for the individual and society and the conditions conducive to successful family life.
5. All youth need to know how to purchase and use goods and services intelligently, understanding both the values received by the consumer and the economic consequences of their acts.
6. All youth need to understand the methods of science, the influences of science on human life, and the main scientific facts concerning the nature of the world and man.
7. All youth need opportunities to develop their capacities to appreciate beauty in literature, art, music and nature.
8. All youth need to be able to use their leisure time well and to budget it wisely, balancing activities that yield satisfactions to the individual with those that are socially useful.
9. All youth need to develop respect for other persons, to grow in their insight into ethical values and principles, and to be able to live and work cooperatively with others.
10. All youth need to grow in their ability to think rationally, to express their thoughts clearly, and to read and listen with understanding.

The second example of state level goals, listed in Appendix C, is the "Goals for Elementary, Secondary, and Continuing Education in New York State." As the title implies, these goals are meant to guide not only K–12 curriculum planning, but also educational programs beyond high school. The other noteworthy point about these goals is that they include clarifying statements. Recognizing that the acquisition of the goals may be influenced by nonschool learning, the state specified the particular contribution that the school might make. In this way, the state also implied that its schools cannot be held solely responsible for achieving the goals.

American Association of School Administrators Institutional Goals (1966)

1. To make urban life rewarding and satisfying
2. To prepare people for the world of work
3. To discover and nurture creative talent
4. To strengthen the moral fabric of society
5. To deal constructively with psychological tensions
6. To keep democracy working
7. To make intelligent use of natural resources
8. To make the best use of leisure time
9. To work with other peoples of the world for human betterment

■ **Local District Level**

Like the various states, virtually all local school districts have goal statements. Their development stems not only from the idea that goals are useful in curriculum planning, but also from the fact that state and regional accrediting agencies normally require them. Local district goal statements are particularly important because at this level opportunities for participation and commitment are greatest. However, the local level is also the one at which special-interest groups may have the most power. For example, local groups may feel strongly that district goals should reflect local interests regardless of their relation to national or state values. For this reason, the local district development process must be particularly sensitive to the fact that one's citizenship responsibilities extend beyond the community to the state, national, and world levels.

One example of a local goal statement focuses on learner goals developed by the Attica, New York, school district. This statement, shown in Appendix D, is particularly interesting for three reasons. First, it was developed through a process much like the one previously described in this chapter. Second, it considers ideas from the foundation areas. Third, each goal statement includes clarifying statements to illustrate the goal.

A second local district example (Frame 4.5) was developed for the Pulaski Community Schools in Pulaski, Wisconsin. The goals themselves are institutional goals, and they are preceded by a philosophy statement that specifies views of learning and the learner. As is clear in the philosophy statement, these goals were largely influenced by the district's longstanding commitment to the community school concept.

Twelve Goals of Quality Education

(Pennsylvania State Board of Education, 1979)

Communication Goals	Quality education should help every student acquire communication skills of understanding, speaking, reading, and writing.
Mathematics	Quality education should help every student acquire skills in mathematics.
Self-Esteem	Quality education should help every student develop self-understanding and a feeling of self-worth.
Analytical Thinking	Quality education should help every student develop analytical thinking skills.
Understanding Others	Quality education should help every student acquire knowledge of different cultures and an appreciation of the worth of all people.
Citizenship	Quality education should help every student learn the history of the nation, understand its systems of government and economics, and acquire the values and attitudes necessary for responsible citizenship.
Arts and the Humanities	Quality education should help every student acquire knowledge, appreciation, and skills in the arts and humanities.
Science and Technology	Quality education should help every student acquire knowledge, understanding, skills, and appreciation of science and technology.
Work	Quality education should help every student acquire the knowledge, skills, and attitudes necessary to become a self-supporting member of society.
Family Living	Quality education should help every student acquire the knowledge, skills, and attitudes necessary for successful personal and family living.
Health	Quality education should help every student acquire knowledge and develop practices necessary to maintain physical and emotional well-being.
Environment	Quality education should help every student acquire the knowledge and attitudes necessary to maintain the quality of life in a balanced environment.

GOAL ANALYSIS

■ ■ No matter how carefully goals are developed, they should be open to continuous examination and analysis. By periodically reviewing goal statements, educators, citizens, and learners try to assure that the goals continue to represent worthwhile and appropriate educational purposes. Most school districts are subject to ten-year reviews by regional and/or state accrediting agencies. These events typically involve analysis of goals as one part of a more comprehensive evaluation. However, more frequent reviews may be undertaken by district curriculum councils, or as interested groups suggest the need to do so. This does not necessarily mean that goals are under constant revision. In fact, goals are critical enough that any change in them should result from clear evidence that change is called for. Furthermore, the process of revising goals should be as carefully constructed as that used in their initial formulation. In analyzing goals, whether for revision or simple review, several criteria can be used. In each case, application of any of the criteria may suggest deleting some goals, adding new ones, or revising those already in place.

1. *Does new information gleaned from the foundation areas suggest the need for goal revision?* A shift in philosophic views or emerging social trends may suggest the need to reconsider educational purposes. Given the pace of social and technological change, the latter may be a real possibility.
2. *Is the meaning of the goals clear?* As educators develop curriculum plans based upon goals, they may find that particular goal statements are ambiguous. Where this is the case, further work on the goals is called for since lack of clarity could lead to lack of their use in curriculum planning.
3. *Do various concerned groups continue to be committed to the goals?* Goals represent the fundamental purposes of education. As such, they ought to have the support of citizens, educators, and learners. If such support is not evident, reasons why should be determined. It may be that over time, new residents in a community are simply unaware of the goals. On the other hand, lack of commitment may mean the need to reconsider the goals.
4. *Are the goals timely?* As local communities and the society at large change, goals may gradually lose their relevance to the modern world. Thus curriculum plans based upon them may be out of step with the times. Where this is the case, a revision project may be needed to update the goals.
5. *Do the various goal statements have internal consistency?* Through some misunderstanding or oversight, particular goal statements may be in conflict with each other. For example, one may call for awareness of global interdependence while another limits understanding of political processes to those of a single nation. In such cases, those responsible for specific curriculum plans may be unsure of which goal to follow. Where

Pulaski School District Philosophy and Goals

■ **Philosophy**

We believe that a community's and a nation's greatest resource is its people, especially the students of our schools. At Pulaski Community Schools, the student is the nucleus of the school system and our educational decisions are guided by what we consider to be best for every student. We maintain that the student should be given every reasonable opportunity to realize his/her best self.

We are now, and should continue to be, a school offering students a second, third, and fourth chance. This means that every available alternative will be explored to help the student grow academically and in self-control. Each new opportunity in the area of discipline will be designed to encourage the students to accept responsibility for his/her actions. New alternatives in the area of academics will be explored, when necessary, to satisfy the student's needs and interests.

It is our belief that our curriculum should serve the needs, interests, and abilities of the student population and promote the mental and physical health of the student. It should instill a pride of heritage and a sense of responsibility, and provide the proper information, emphasis, and perspective for learning to live a successful life in our local community as well as the nation and the world.

Our educational system should help each student increase his/her knowledge, build greater understanding, and develop social attitudes and acceptable behavior to prepare him/her to be a contributing member of society. We feel that our curriculum must have a wide enough scope to prepare the college bound student, the vocationally oriented student, as well as the student who will seek a job upon graduation.

Our belief is that the Pulaski Community Schools should focus not only on its children, but it should also provide the adult members of the school district the facilities and services to continue their education. A school and community

this is the case, the goals in question must be reconsidered or clarified to establish internal consistency.

PUTTING GOALS INTO PRACTICE: A SPECIAL PROBLEM

■ ■ One of the consistent problems in education has been the gap between theory and practice. That is to say, we often do not practice what we preach. One prominent example of this gap has been the inconsistency between our goals and our specific curriculum plans. We have already discussed how this problem may arise from lack of clarity in goal statements. Hopefully, the addition of clarifying information and the formulation of general objectives will help in this regard.

that works closely together can use the students, faculty, and administrators to evaluate the assets, needs, and possibilities of the community and help provide direction for its growth. The community becomes a true learning laboratory.

We believe that the schools are the thread that binds the people of the community together. The name, Pulaski Community Schools, reflects the close ties between the schools and the people of its district. An active participation by the schools in the community, and the community in the schools, can help make education real and meaningful for all involved.

■ The Objectives of the Pulaski Community Schools

1. To aid students in acquiring and applying the fundamental skills necessary to learning.
2. To help each student understand, appreciate, and respect one's self.
3. To develop a sense of responsibility and instill a pride of heritage.
4. To help each individual maintain the basic physical and mental health necessary for optimum growth and development.
5. To equip students with thinking and problem solving skills so they become self-supportive members of a community.
6. To utilize community resources to teach students how to live productively and earn a living.
7. To stimulate active participation in school and community living by encouraging membership in a variety of organizations and interest groups.
8. To encourage all community members to continue their education as a life-long process.
9. To foster an appreciation of the fine arts.
10. To provide courses of study that give the proper information, emphasis, and perspective about the world around us.
11. To offer students every available opportunity to grow academically and learn to accept responsibility for his/her actions.

However, the goal-to-practice gap also involves an even more perplexing problem. As evidenced by the sample statements presented in this chapter, goals typically call for a wide range of knowledges, skills, attitudes, and behaviors. Further, they usually include aspects of personal and social development, problem-solving skills, and emphasis on contemporary and future social trends. Curriculum plans, however, often reflect a very different viewpoint. They tend to emphasize mastery of facts, teaching of subjects, and orientation to the past. In short, goals tend to be largely rooted in pragmatism, whereas specific curriculum plans more clearly approximate views suggested by realism, idealism, perennialism, and essentialism. Perhaps this problem arises from lack of a clear understanding of the philosophic foundations of curriculum. Perhaps it results from the possibility that we do not really believe in our goals. Or perhaps the goals are developed without careful thinking about their implications.

Goals derived from the foundation areas are the preferred primary screen for the development of curriculum plans at all levels. However, other factors may militate against the use of goals as described here. Such factors might include finances, vested interests, and ignorance. For example, a school district on an austerity budget might curtail or limit previously defined goals. Or a "back to basics" pressure group might force the restriction of an English literature curriculum designed to meet a particular goal. Even when goals are properly used, other elements become effective screens for further development and refinement of curriculum plans. Chapter 5 will treat this practice in specific detail.

Whatever the case, the gap between goals and practice represents a continuing problem in the curriculum field. It is an area that requires serious attention by those responsible for curriculum planning at all levels. Consistency between goals and practice is one topic that will be considered in our later chapter on curriculum evaluation. Until such consistency is achieved, however, we cannot expect to resolve some of the confusion that currently exists over what we do in schools. Furthermore, we cannot have a sound basis for examining the educational practices and programs that special-interest groups so frequently suggest be included in the curriculum.

GENERAL OBJECTIVES

■ ■   Goals represent the overall purpose toward which the whole school program leads. As a result, all the activities of the school should be related to those goals. However, because learning capacity varies from one developmental stage to another, different school levels or units contribute differently to learner attainment of broad goals. In other words, children, transescents, adolescents, and adults each pursue the goals based upon their different developmental characteristics.

General objectives define types of learning related to goals that may be expected at a particular developmental stage. For example, in developing citizenship skills, children may focus on awareness of their immediate relationships and their neighborhoods. Transescents might extend that awareness to peers and the local community. Adolescents and adults may focus on larger issues related to national and global awareness. In this way, each group of learners is concerned with citizenship, but at a level appropriate to their personal orientation and capacity to understand.

General objectives thus define two important aspects of the curriculum—scope and sequence. *Scope* represents the contribution made at a particular level, such as global citizenship during adolescence. *Sequence* reflects the flow of experience, in this case from the immediate environment in childhood to the global perspective in adolescence and adulthood. This does not necessarily mean that a particular aspect of citizenship is ignored at other stages. Rather, it suggests that appropriate emphasis be placed at each stage.

The advantage of including general objectives in comprehensive curriculum planning is that they provide guidelines for each level of schooling. Without them, teachers and other professionals may be confused about what they are expected to do. Consequently, expectations for learners may be unclear and inappropriate.

Finally, it should be noted that the procedures described for developing and analyzing goals apply also to general objectives. The latter should be developed in light of the foundation areas and through broad participation. They should include clarifying statements and they should be periodically reviewed. With this idea in mind, we will now examine illustrative general-objective statements for each developmental stage.

■ **Elementary School (Children)**

One of the most careful efforts to formulate general objectives at the elementary level was undertaken by the Mid-Century Committee on Outcomes in Elementary Education (Kearney, 1953). Through a systematic process, the group reached consensus on a set of statements that members viewed as "of sufficient importance to the individual pupil, or to society, to have an acknowledged place in the regular program of the school." The resulting recommendations included nine general objectives and suggestions for how these would be manifested at three levels—third, sixth, and ninth grades. Furthermore, illustrations of the "determining conditions" were made in the categories of knowledge and understanding, skill and competence, attitude and interest, and action pattern. For our purpose here, Frame 4.6 will include for each general objective only a summary of the clarifications listed for the end of third grade.

■ **Middle Level Education (Transescence)**

Since it is somewhat less widely understood than "children" or "adolescents," we should define the term "transescence" before we discuss this level of education. Perhaps the best statement was made by Donald H. Eichhorn in *The Middle School* (1966):

Third-Grade Clarifications for General Objectives Determined by the Mid-Century Committee on Outcomes in Elementary Education

1. Physical Development, Health, Body Care (health and safety, growth and development)
   Clarification: basic skills in physical health, hygiene and safety; physical skills, use of tools; knowledge of personal physical attributes, interest in growth and development.
2. Individual Social and Emotional Development (mental health, emotional stability, personality, self-concept)
   Clarification: understanding of personal strengths and weaknesses, assuming responsibility, sensitivity to others; independent work, humor; pride in contributions, hobbies, interests.
3. Ethical Behavior, Standards, Values (moral and civil law, ethics)
   Clarification: basic rules of ownership, rights of others, responsibility, fair play; expressing values, resolving simple conflicts; friendliness, lack of prejudice, respecting rights of others.
4. Social Relations (relationships with others)
   Clarification: understanding of others' behavior, familiarity with occupations, human relations; participation in group work, understanding how games are played, willingness to contribute, enjoyment of group activities.
5. The Social World (community, state, nation, world; civics, government)
   Clarification: understanding roles of others, facts about neighborhood and community, basic living modes; map-reading, getting from home to places in the community; developing attitudes toward institutions, interest in others.
6. The Physical World (natural environment, science)
   Clarification: basic knowledge about animals, natural resources, topography; map reading, using simple tools, observing nature; desire for information about nature and geography.
7. Esthetic Development (appreciation, expression, artistry)
   Clarification: conscious of color, form, arrangement, design; uses simple rhythm, draws, paints, sings; enjoys music, poetry, stories, art.
8. Communication (language arts)
   Clarification: reads, defines vocabulary, writes simple words; listens, speaks coherently; likes to use language arts.
9. Quantitative Relationships (numbers, measures, mathematics)
   Clarification: understands, reads and writes numbers, does simple calculations; understands quantity, simple proportions; can handle simple money, time calculations; respects usefulness of arithmetic.

. . . the stage of development which begins prior to the onset of puberty and extends through the early stages of adolescence. Since puberty does not occur for all precisely at the same chronological age in human development, the transescent designation is based upon the many physical, social, emotional, and intellectual changes in body chemistry that appear prior to the puberty cycle to the time in which the body gains a practical degree of stabilization over these complex pubescent changes. (p. 3)

During the past two decades, considerable attention has been given to middle level education. Most prominent in this regard has been the conversion of junior high schools to middle schools. Even where such reorganization has not taken place, middle level educators have given careful consideration to how the characteristics of transescents ought to influence the curriculum. As a result, the purposes of middle level education have been seriously reexamined. Virtually all statements of middle level purposes have taken the form of objectives for the school rather than learner outcomes. An exception to this is the suggestion by William Alexander and others (1968) that the middle school curriculum should provide learning opportunities in the following areas:

1. *Personal Development:* development of values, health and physical development, individual interests
2. *Skills for Continued Learning:* communications, generalizing from observation, evaluating opinion, problem-solving, planning
3. *Areas of Organized Knowledge:* studying basic concepts in subject areas, scientific method, humanities

Beyond this, one can conclude from school objective statements the kinds of learnings that are expected at this level. Such is the case in the following example adapted from the *Standards for Middle Childhood Educational Programs in West Virginia.* The general objectives here would appear to involve:

1. Development of reading, basic communications, and mathematics skills
2. Awareness and understanding of aesthetic, social, multicultural, and physiological areas of knowledge
3. Continuing the quest for self-identity and self-expression to assist in better decision making relating to education, career, and recreation
4. Development of attitudes and beliefs necessary to function effectively in a democratic and technological society

5. Acquisition of concepts, competencies, and attitudes needed to make a successful transition from the elementary to the secondary school and from childhood to adolescence
6. Development of skills in interpersonal relations among similar and other age groups

■ High School (Adolescents)

Since the high school is the level at which formal, compulsory education ends, it might seem reasonable simply to assume that the goals themselves represent general objectives. However, there is still a need to define how adolescent education will relate specifically to broader purposes.

Perhaps the most complete statement of general objectives for this level was developed by Will French and his associates in 1957. Using the 1938 Educational Policies Commission's four goals, French and his group developed illustrative behavioral outcomes for the high school level. Frame 4.7 contains selected illustrations of those statements. (See Appendix E for the full version of illustrative behaviors.)

Although the statement developed by French is noteworthy for its comprehensiveness, it is not the best known of general objectives for the high school level. That honor is reserved for what may, in fact, be the best known of all statements of educational purpose, "The Seven Cardinal Principles of Secondary Education." The reason for this is that it was the first widely recognized statement of educational purposes that did more than merely describe subjects which learners ought to study. Developed in 1918 by the Commission on the Reorganization of Secondary Education, the Cardinal Principles were prefaced by the following statement:

> The purpose of a democracy is so to organize society that each member may develop his personality primarily through activities designed for the well-being of his fellow members and of society as a whole. . . .
> Consequently, education in a democracy, both within and without the school, should develop in each individual the knowledge, interests, ideals, habits, and powers whereby he will find his place and use that place to shape both himself and society toward even nobler ends. (p. 9)

The commission then went on to list seven principles as the basic objectives of secondary education:

1. Health
2. Command of Fundamental Processes

Examples of "General Objectives for the High Schools"

French and Associates, 1957

1. Goal: Growing Toward Self-Realization
   1.1 General Objective: Developing Behaviors Indicative of Intellectual Self-realization
      1.12 Improving in His Ability to Communicate Ideas and to Recognize and Use Good Standards
         1.121 Commands and uses the basic skills of reading for information, ideas, opinions, stimulation, and leisure.
         1.122 Express his ideas in speech, writing, or in some artistic form with increasing clarity and correctness.
2. Goal: Growing in Ability to Maintain Desirable Small Group Relationships
   2.13 General Objective: Developing Behaviors Indicative of the Kinds of Competence Needed as a Member of Small Organized Groups
      2.131 Joins organized groups when their purposes relate to his tastes and interests, and develops the personal characteristics which contribute to successful small group membership.
3. Goal: Growing in the Ability to Maintain the Relationships Imposed by Membership in Large Organizations
   3.11 General Objective: Becoming Intellectually Able to Follow Developments on the World and National Levels and to Formulate Opinions About Proposed Solutions to Some of the Principal Problems and Issues
      3.111 Is developing an interest in, and understanding of, world events, conditions, and organizations.
      3.112 Endeavors to become well informed on the backgrounds of the larger problems of our nation and the world and to make an intelligent analysis of the issues involved.

3. Worthy Home Membership
4. Vocation
5. Citizenship
6. Worthy Use of Leisure Time
7. Ethical Character

All of the sample goals and general objectives described in this chapter were developed after the Seven Cardinal Principles of Secondary Education. Clearly this statement was an important step in viewing education as something more than studying subject areas. The fact that it described personal, social, and academic outcomes emphasized education of the learner as a total human being. This view influenced not only subsequent goal and general education statements, but those developed as specific instructional objectives as well. Even as recently as 1976, a National Education Association Commission reviewed the Seven Cardinal Principles and concluded that they were still highly worthy of consideration.

CHAPTER SUMMARY

Goals represent statements of purposes for the total educational program. They are thus different from general objectives that define purposes of units or levels of the school, and from specific objectives that are involved in teaching–learning situations. Nevertheless, each type should reflect the other two so that the various purposes of education are interrelated. Goals themselves are usually of two types: those intended for learners and those which specify institutional purposes.

Goals should be developed in light of three considerations. First, they should be developed on the basis of ideas gleaned from the foundation areas of philosophy, sociology, and psychology. Second, they should be developed through broad participation to ensure commitment. Third, since goals represent broad statements, they frequently require clarification to avoid ambiguity.

Over the years, goals have been developed at the national, state, and local levels. Included in this chapter were several examples of these statements. Since goals represent ideas and perceptions at the time they are developed, periodic reviews of their content are necessary. When this is done, criteria for analysis may include clarity, commitment, timeliness, internal consistency, and appropriateness to emerging ideas from the foundations areas.

One continuing problem in the curriculum field is the frequent gap between goals and practice. This gap may result from lack of goal clarity or lack of understanding of philosophic foundations. However, it may also result from a lack of professional commitment to the stated purposes of education. Whatever the case, the gap between goals and practice should be of concern to those responsible for curriculum planning.

General objectives are statements reflecting the purposes of a particular unit or level of the school program, such as the elementary, middle, or high school. As such, they clarify the contributions each level will make to helping learners attain goals. The development of general objectives is based upon the idea that learners at different developmental stages approach goals in various ways depending on their developmental characteristics. Thus, general objectives describe the scope of curriculum purposes. Taken together, however, general objectives also describe the sequence of those purposes. Finally, the development of general objectives is subject to the same ideas regarding clarification, participation, and evaluation as are broader goal statements.

Having read Chapter 4, you should be able to:

1. Differentiate types of educational purposes
2. Describe the purpose of broad goals
3. Describe the role of goals in curriculum planning
4. Identify examples of goal statements
5. Describe procedures for developing broad educational purposes
6. Describe procedures for analyzing broad educational purposes
7. Describe the purposes of general objectives
8. Identify examples of general objectives

SUGGESTED ACTIVITIES

1. Obtain a list of goal statements for one or more local school districts. Analyze the goal statements in light of the following questions:

   a. What philosophy or philosophies do the statements reflect?
   b. Is the meaning of the statements clear? Which, if any are ambiguous? How could they be clarified?
   c. Do the goals reflect the characteristics of contemporary society? Do they reflect forecasts of the future?
   d. What statements, if any, might be added to the list?

2. Develop a set of goals using a consensus decision-making technique. For example, first have each individual generate his or her own list. Then form pairs and have each pair generate a single list from their individual sets of goals. Pair the pairs, forming new groups, and have each group come up with a single list. Keep combining groups in this manner until the participants are divided into two large groups, and then use the single goal statements from each to reach consensus on one list for the whole group.

3. Using the list developed in activity 2, have the group establish priorities for the goals. One possible way is to use a cross-impact matrix—comparing each goal to every other goal. The following directions will explain the activity.

Directions for Cross-Impact Matrix
Each individual draws a chart similar to the one below. In the sample there would be five numbered goal statements. (A matrix can be drawn similarly for any number of goals.) Start in the upper left-hand cell by comparing goal 1 with goal 5 in terms of its importance. Continue across the top row, comparing goal 1 with each of the other goals. Then move to the next row and compare goal 2 with each of the other statements. (Note that no goal is compared with itself; hence the matrix is drawn as shown.) When all cells are filled in, count the number of 1's, 2's, and so on. The priority order is determined by the number of times each goal is chosen. To determine a group's priority ranking, obtain the total for each goal statement from each individual in the group.

	5	4	3	2
1	1*			
2				
3			
4		

*For example, goal 1 is here given more importance than goal 5.

TOTALS   1's ____   2's ____   3's ____

4's ____   5's ____

4. Using a goal statement resulting from activity 1 or 2, identify the degree to which the goal is being adequately addressed in local schools. To do this, use a needs-gap survey technique, such as the following.

Goal Statement	A How important is this goal?					B How well are schools doing on this goal?				
1. ____	5	4	3	2	1	5	4	3	2	1
2. ____	5	4	3	2	1	5	4	3	2	1
3. ____	5	4	3	2	1	5	4	3	2	1

Code:
5 = very important
4 = important
3 = no opinion
2 = not important
1 = of no value

Code:
5 = very well
4 = a good job
3 = okay
2 = poor
1 = terrible

Each person in the group should rate the goals according to the rankings indicated in columns A and B. Obtain the needs-gap index for each goal by subtracting the square of its average score in column B from the square of its average score in column A. (Note that the values are squared so that the relative value of each score is considered. Otherwise the gap for an average A-score = 5 and B-score = 3 would be the same as an average A-score = 3 and B-score = 1.) The formula is: Needs-gap = $(\overline{A})^2 - (\overline{B})^2$, where $(\overline{A})$ = mean of the group's ranking for a particular objective in column A.

The higher the needs gap, presumably the more attention the goal deserves. Remember that responses reflect perceptions only. For example, a value of 2 for any goal in column B does not necessarily mean that the schools are actually doing a poor job on that goal. Further data gathering might reveal whether this perception is true or false.

5. Using a goal statement resulting from activity 1 or 2, develop a list of general objectives for each level of education. Do this by dividing the whole group into small groups according to common levels at which individuals work. After the general objectives are developed, combine the statements into a comprehensive set of general objectives reflecting a sequence across school levels. Analyze the comprehensive statement in terms of how realistic it is for each level and in terms of any gaps that appear.

REFERENCES

Alexander, W.; Williams, E.; Compton, M.; Hines, V.; and Prescott, D. *The Emergent Middle School*. New York: Holt, Rinehart and Winston, 1968.

American Association of School Administrators. *Imperatives in Education*. Arlington, Va.: The Association, 1966.

Commission on the Reorganization of Secondary Education. *Cardinal Principles of Education*. Bulletin No. 35. Washington, D.C.: Government Printing Office, 1918.

Educational Policies Commission. *The Purposes of Education in American Democracy*. Washington, D.C.: National Educational Association, 1938.

———. *Education for All American Youth*. Washington, D.C.: National Education Society, 1944.

Eichhorn, D. *The Middle School*. New York: Center for Applied Research in Education, 1966.

French, W., and Associates. *Behavioral Goals for General Education in the High School*. New York: Russell Sage Foundation, 1957.

Kearney, N. *Elementary School Objectives*. New York: Russell Sage Foundation, 1953.

National Education Association. "The Seven Cardinal Principles Revisited. *Today's Education* 65, no. 3 (1976): 57–72.

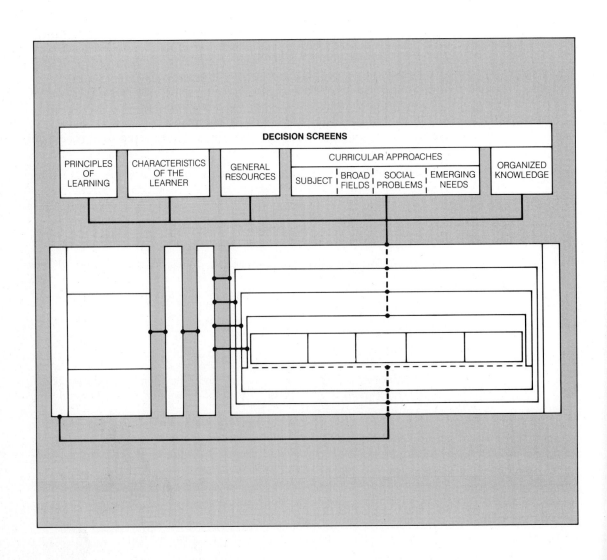

DECISION SCREENS

PRINCIPLES OF LEARNING

CHARACTERISTICS OF THE LEARNER

GENERAL RESOURCES

CURRICULAR APPROACHES

SUBJECT | BROAD FIELDS | SOCIAL PROBLEMS | EMERGING NEEDS

ORGANIZED KNOWLEDGE

5

Decision Screens for Developing Curriculum Plans

Up to this point we have considered several components that require attention in the process of curriculum planning. These have included the foundation areas, development of comprehensive goals, and clarification of general objectives. As stated earlier, goals derived from the foundation areas should be the primary screen for developing curriculum plans. We now turn to the issue of making the transition from those goals to plans for specific teaching–learning situations. At this stage, those responsible for curriculum planning should consider five other screens relating to the organization and effectiveness of their plans: characteristics of the learners for whom plans are intended, the nature of the learning process, the required resources for implementing plans, the curricular approaches around which plans may be organized, and the ways in which organized knowledge from specific disciplines may be used:

> As a result of reading Chapter 5, you should be able to:
>
> 1. Identify major theories about how learning takes place
> 2. Describe characteristics of children and youth that should be considered in developing curriculum plans
> 3. Identify general resources that should be considered in developing curriculum plans
> 3. Describe the appropriate use of several different curricular approaches
> 5. Describe the role of organized knowledge in developing teaching–learning situations.

PRINCIPLES OF LEARNING

■ ■ Educators need to recognize the importance of planning effective
teaching–learning activities upon sound principles of learning. "Learning" is loosely utilized to describe both the process and the outcome of
the learning activity. For example, the skills and processes needed to
understand long division would be essential to a student's "learning"
to do long division. At the same time, the student's mastery of long
division would also be considered as his or her "learning" long division.
Thus, both the process and the outcome of the activity planned by the
teacher are considered as "learning." In the experience of "learning,"
the learner is involved with the initial stimuli offered in the planned
learning activity, and then responds to them in particular fashions.
The change in, or reinforcement of, an existing behavior of the learner
is where the degree of learning is measured. Thomas Clayton (1965)
summarizes this in five helpful principles.

1. Learning is a process that involves behavior, sequences of events,
   and outcomes.
2. Learning results from experiencing. The learner must in some way
   act upon or react to a situation that impinges upon him.
3. Learning depends upon what the learner does. This involves how
   he perceives, how he thinks, how he feels and how he acts. There
   can be no learning unless he responds in some way.
4. The end result of the learning process is some change in the
   learner, demonstrable by a change in his behavior, potential or
   actual.
5. The change in the learner tends to be fixed in the consequences of
   his behavior in terms of his own motivational systems. (p. 45)

From this summary, we can see the elements of the stimulus (learning
activity), the organism (learner), and response (learner reaction) as
fundamental considerations for the planning of instruction, and teaching. There are variables within each of these three elements which are
important in curriculum planning.

The "S" or stimulation variables include those presentation and
practice concerns that the teacher can manipulate. It is important to
consider how individual learners will perceive those stimuli through
their own senses. The teacher must identify differences in how individual learners manipulate or process different kinds of stimuli. In
Education for What Is Real, Earl Kelley (1947) provides fascinating
data on how individuals differ in their perceptions. He reports a number
of experiments with mechanical devices that identify how diverse individual perceptions of a single stimulus can be. For example, the same
object was perceived as being of different sizes by different people
viewing it from the same distance. Such perceptions differed widely

among learners who all had normal vision. The influence of motion among arranged objects provided an amazing range of perceptions of individuals in a common viewing. Kelley points out that individuals get many different clues from a common stimulus, as they perceive the stimulus differently. Teachers, then, need to recognize how perceptions of a common stimulus will vary and need to understand that students will act on their perceptions differently. In planning instructional activities, teachers should not assume a "common experience will develop from a common stimulus." From this realization, the appropriate use of alternative or multiple stimuli for learning activities can be considered.

Clayton presents an excellent discussion of the "O" (learner) variables. The learner reflects his previous life experiences, perceptual skills, and a personal sense of reality in interacting with the stimuli. This constitutes the learner's individual "concept structure," which is his or her picture of the world. For example, self-concept is a variable that helps the learner find where he or she fits into that concept structure. Specifically, the clarity of the self-concept will influence the reality of how the learner sees himself or herself fitting into the surrounding world. The more clearly and accurately the learner can describe "self" through that conception, the more accurately he or she can interact with a given stimulus. Likewise, the learner's self-esteem deals with the positive or negative views the learner holds of himself or herself. Such feelings about self are a powerful influence upon a learner's confidence when interacting with any stimulus.

Other "O" (learner) variables important to consider include learner attitudes, needs, values, motives, goals, intelligence, previously learned skills and information, and previous life experiences. The more information that teachers have on these learner variables for individuals, the more their planned use of appropriate stimuli can result in more effectively responsive learning situations.

The "R" (response) variables are those that teachers can most readily identify. Response variables are usually taken to mean "what" has been learned or "how well" the learner has performed or succeeded. As Clayton observes, "learning depends upon what the learner does" (p. 42). The learner's response to the stimuli of the particular teaching–learning situation is what makes further change or learning possible. The learner's actions or reactions to that situation constitute "response variables" or observable behaviors. This response is based upon how well the learner has been able to interpret that learning activity. Not all stimuli are equally understood and interpreted by all students.

For example, one student may misunderstand the information put forth in one stimulus. Another might not have mastered skills needed to deal with the learning activity suggested by that same stimulus. A third student may make an error in processing the information that the stimulus puts forth. A range of "response variable" possibilities exists here. All three students *could* come to the same erroneous conclusion for different reasons. Each student might have different incorrect responses to the same stimulus. Any or all of the students might gain the correct response by guessing. It is important, therefore, that teachers examine the responses of individual learners to best identify "why" the response was made. The response itself, whether correct or incorrect, must be viewed within the interaction of S-O-R variables in that situation.

Whether positive or negative, learning will take place within this S-O-R interaction. Analysis of those individual interaction patterns will allow the teacher to identify differing needs for follow-up learning activities. Teachers should not anticipate mass outcomes among learners in response patterns. Some students will require follow-up activities, such as reteaching with alternate stimulus patterns. Whether in follow-up corrective activities or planning new units of learning after success has been achieved, the teacher can improve the quality of learning opportunities through study of the S-O-R variables in a specific situation. As teachers come to know the S and O variables of individuals and groups of learners, they can facilitate greater growth and success in learning at the R level. The understanding of the impact of these variables upon curriculum planning by the teacher is a most important contribution of learning psychology. Let us now briefly examine how different schools of learning psychology emphasize these variables.

■ The Specifists and Behaviorism Theory

Specifist learning theory places major emphasis on S (stimulus) and R (response) variables, with relatively little focus on the O (learner) areas. Specifist theory attempts to concentrate on the relationships of specific stimuli to specific responses. Rewards are used to reinforce "desired" responses once the desired stimulus–response (S–R) pattern has been established. That is to say, a kind of cause–effect pattern is developed. Early efforts with the specifist approach, such as the work of Edward Thorndike, led to highly controlled experimental settings that began with animal experimentations. Thorndike (1913) was attempting to identify the relationship of a stimulus and a response to improve motivation theory that could be utilized with students in educational settings. For example, Thorndike's work was concerned with the specific response of learners to stimuli and the use of reward and punishment. It was highly applicable to drill and habit formation in students. It also sought to help learners develop behavior which they would need to learn.

The connection between the specifist and behaviorist areas came from the work of J. B. Watson. Called the father of Behaviorist Psychology, Watson (1919) based his ideas upon Ivan Pavlov's notion of conditioning. Pavlov's work is best known for conditioning dogs to salivate at the sound of a bell—a conditioned response to a particular stimulus. Watson used the conditioned reflex data to help identify development of certain behavior as problems for study of learning. For example, Watson's work was based on the idea that the great majority of all behavior is learned and can be extended by pairing of stimuli and responses from infancy onward.

C. L. Hull (1951) took the existing work on S–R relationships to deductive studies in complicated mathematical settings. This led to further explanation of essential human behavior as patterns of S–R combinations. Hull introduced the idea that learners could develop specific drives to accomplish specific learnings (R), which would then reduce the specific area of drive or need. For example, the drive of hunger (S) would result in eating (R), which would reduce the hunger. This drive reduction provided the reinforcement of the need. Thus, Hull considered learning to be concerned with associating stimulus–response sequences that could be refined in situations where drive, reinforcement, and needs reduction are patterned. Analysis of these situations would then identify how learning took place.

B. F. Skinner (1953) refined this work by concentrating almost exclusively on the R variables. In producing the desired response, a stimulus is then used to reinforce the response. This "operant conditioning" approach of Skinner reverses the relationship into an R–S pattern. Skinner's work led to the broader use of certain aspects of programmed learning that can be used as curriculum materials in some teaching–learning situations. For example, teaching machines take advantage of this approach in breaking the information to be learned into a sequence of small units. As the learner makes the correct response, he or she can move on to the next unit. Learners can move at their own rate and get immediate reinforcement when their answer is correct. In the case of an incorrect response, the program or machine can take them to an alternate sequence to pursue the information to be learned in a different fashion.

The work of the Specifists and Behaviorists has supported the development of "prepackaged" curriculum programs. Such approaches are used by some teachers, while not particularly helpful to others. Teachers seeking to improve their own skills as curriculum builders will find that the two other categories of learning theory to be discussed may be more supportive of their needs. However, the Specifist–Behaviorist group provided an early learning theory base that served as the source for the development of differing points of view in learning theory and how learning takes place.

■ The Field Theorists

Another view of learning, Field Theory, stemmed from the disagreement of a group of German psychologists with the notions of Thorndike and Watson. Rather than an S–R emphasis, this group saw a need to consider all three variable components (S-O-R). They also saw a need to emphasize O (learner) variables more heavily than the other two categories. Field learning theory developed the position that behavior is more than the mere sum of the three S-O-R elements. The *Gestalt* group, as the early Field Theorists became known, sought to define the area of the O (learner) variables that the Specifists had largely ignored. The nature of the learner, as the Gestaltists saw it, had a great impact on how stimuli could be processed and a great deal of bearing on what the response might be. Their concern echoed the early arguments of John Dewey. Dewey was a psychologist before he became a philosopher, and he argued before the turn of this century with the S–R infatuations of the Specifists (1896). He spoke of the need to focus upon the "mediated experiences" of the learner himself as the learner bridged from the existing stage to where the teacher hoped the student could get in the "response" area. The Gestaltists' concerns built an area of learning theory that facilitated a much more holistic look at the three variables.

The Gestaltists developed concerns about perception and cognition in the learner from initial studies of visual perceptions. Their controlled experiments with vision and perception were moved into more naturalistic studies by Kurt Lewin. Working in real rather than laboratory environments, Lewin (1935) began to examine the cognitive field of a person. These were the first attempts to study the impact of an individual's perception on his or her cognition, or process of "knowing." For the first time, teachers now had a theoretical base to consider whether or not a stimulus in the form of a piece of information or subject matter is the same to the learner as it is to the teacher. In what different ways would different learners perceive a common learning stimulus? These concerns raised by the Gestaltists remain as important questions for the teacher as curriculum planner, since most learning experiences produce multiple outcomes.

Field Theory evolved from the Gestaltist concern with "life space," the view we all have of the external world. "Life space" deals with the assumption that we all exist and act in the same real world but have different perceptions of it. This concern with perception and focus on cognition, or knowing, helped Field Theory to become an effective means to examine the learning process. With Field and Gestalt Theory, comments F. J. McDonald, "cognition provided the ground for adaptive behavior. Reorganization of perceptions, understanding and insight became the central psychological events" (1964, p. 20). For example, modern concerns about the nature of individual differences in learners and the needs for teachers to plan differentiated learning activities have relied on these findings from Gestalt learning theory.

The impact of these concerns for curriculum planning have been foundational to the curriculum field. Whereas the planning of learning outcomes was stressed in the S–R findings of the Specifists and Behaviorists, the notion of curriculum or learning alternatives is largely due to the Field learning theorists. Because of the accomplishments of the Gestalt theorists, the planning of learning activities could use the O (learner) variables in mediating both the S (stimulus) and possible range of R (response) learning outcomes.

■ **The Personality Theorists**

The development of Personality Theory was not in disagreement with existing theory, as was Field Theory with the Specifists and Behaviorists. Personality Theory takes root in the work of Sigmund Freud. Freud caused psychology to develop an analytical look at personality structure. Indeed, Freud's greatest contribution to the education field may well be his influence on the later Personality Theorists rather than his own work. Lawrence Cremin observes "the really pervasive influence of Freudianism on pedagogy came rather indirectly through gradual public acceptance of the psychoanalytic image of the child" (1961, p. 214). Our contemporary acceptance of analysis of personality and behavior in learner (O) variables and in the learning process stems from Freud's influence. Personality Theory, then, has great implications for further spelling out Field Theory concerns with the learner in describing how children learn.

H. A. Murray (1938) organized a dimension of personality theory from the work of the Gestaltists. He defined concerns that he labels as "press" and "need." He identified an analytical emphasis from Freud's work that described a real setting for the learner in which "press" can create stimuli that can affect the organism (learner). For instance, Murray notes dangerous and threatening "presses" of childhood. These "presses" are defined by the child's personal experiences as well as observations of situations that might be harmful. This helped teachers become aware of such critical stimuli facing learners at different stages of childhood. They provided means to build positive learning situations in response to learner "press" concerns. In the matter of "needs," Murray took a descriptive approach identifying needs children have for affiliation, deference, nurturance, harm–avoidance, blame–avoidance, abasement, aggression, dominance, nonavoidance, achievement, recognition, and order. Murray was seeking a description of human motivation that could, from a psychoanalytical perspective, help teachers define more responsive learning activities to balance between "press" and "need."

Abraham Maslow (1954) saw a hierarchical order of needs for personal development that would facilitate the becoming and being of the learner. In ascending order, they were physiological needs, safety, love and belonging, esteem, and self-actualization. Maslow saw the satisfying of these needs as a means to remove deficiencies and find satisfactions for individual fulfillment. As teachers could provide learning experiences that achieved these ends, personality development would be enhanced. Other contemporary personality theorists who have influenced the curriculum field are Arthur Combs and Carl Rogers. Combs (1962) feels that learners can develop a sense of personal adequacy as they reduce drives by defining and maintaining their own needs. Thus, as learning experiences could help learners maintain and enhance their satisfaction of needs, their personality development would complement their growth in all learning situations. This is similar to Rogers's notion of a "fully functioning person" who develops personality in social and learning situations. Although Rogers is best known for his work in client-centered therapy (1951), his ideas are also of value to teachers concerned with using individual personality development as a basis for organizing learning activities.

No one theory of learning can satisfy a majority of teacher concerns in curriculum planning. The three areas described here all have specific areas of application as teachers work to develop responsible learning activities. The varying needs in particular situations with regard to S, O, and R variable categories will help the teacher examine ways in which information from Specifist, Behaviorist, Field, and Personality learning theories can be supportive in organizing teaching–learning activities. As teachers continue to identify the interrelationships of these elements, their effectiveness in planning specifically helpful learning activities will noticeably improve.

SOME PSYCHOLOGICAL CONCERNS IN CURRICULUM PLANNING

■ ■   Learning psychology offers a range of means that can be used by teachers to improve the quality of learning activities in the classroom. Some of these situations continue to persist in the curriculum field, and others are relatively new. All are recommended as critical concerns that must be addressed in planning learning activities at the school and classroom level.

■ **Transfer of Training**

Transfer of training is a major concern that persists as a challenge to the planning of learning activities. It refers to the idea that students can transfer what they learned in one situation to another. Teachers need to establish the degree to which transfer of training is possible in specific situations. They can then identify how to maximize transfer in specific situations. While there is general acceptance that transfer of training is possible in all psychological theories, the Gestaltists maintain that transfer occurs best when one teaches for transfer. Most simply stated, transfer can best occur when the teacher has consciously shown or taught learners how to do it. The teacher must consider the limits of transfer of a particular learning as well as where transfer may readily occur. Edward Krug (1957) observes:

> Learning to play a violin then will not only transfer more readily to other musical learnings than it will to other fields of endeavor, but it will also transfer more readily to playing a cello or viola than it will to the playing of a piano or horn. The study of physics will have more transfer value for the study of chemistry than it will for history. (p. 39)

Thorndike (1913) deals with the identical elements theory, in which transfer is seen as the relationship among the elements of two or more teaching–learning situations.

> . . . the real question is not, "does improvement of one function alter the others?" but, "to what extent, and how does it?"
>   The answer which I shall try to defend is that a change in one function alters any other only in so far as the two functions have as factors identical elements. To take a concrete example, improvement in addition will alter one's ability in multiplication because addition is absolutely identical with multiplication and because certain other processes—e.g., eye movements and the inhibition of all save arithmetical impulses—are in part common to the two functions. (pp. 358–359)

This use of the identical elements theory in the educational process was criticized by Pedro Orata (1928).

> If it is true that mental functions are independent of each other, it would be a waste of time, energy, and money to teach a child to deal with one situation in order that he might be prepared to meet another situation. Consequently, education consists in equipping the individual with those items of knowledge, skills, and ideals which he will be sure to use in his life's career. To put it differently, the emphasis in teaching must center upon the practical needs of life. (p. 146)

The identical elements concept is somewhat extended in the generalization theory. In generalization, transfer of training relies on the extent that the initial learning included general principles capable of wide application. C. H. Judd (1927) comments:

> Mental development consists not in storing the mind with knowledge nor in training the nervous system to perform with readiness particular habitual acts but rather in equipping the individual with the power to think abstractly and to form general ideas.
>
> When the ends thus described are attained, transfer of training, or formal discipline, has taken place because it is the very nature of generalization and abstraction that they extend beyond the particular experience in which they originate. (p. 441)

Teachers have to resolve these issues in terms of their own experiences with learners. Obviously, the nature of the learning that is to be transferred will affect the limits of transfer. If the learning dealt with process, as opposed to more factual content, the limits of transfer could be more easily identified. Teachers should take note of the limits and range in which transfer seems to occur with different kinds of learning. Against such observations and in light of information gathered, the principles of the positions on identical elements, educational process, and generalization may help the teacher find the best cue for anticipated transfer of specific learnings. It is through such thoughtful study by educators that the resolution of the role of transfer of training may be refined for improving the planning of teaching–learning situations. Curriculum planners must look to develop a base from which they can make best use of the range of psychology of learning positions on transfer of training.

■ Sample Application

One of the most interesting attempts to relate ideas about learning to curriculum was developed by J. Minor Gwynn and John B. Chase (1969). In their opinion, certain postulates about curriculum flow from basic beliefs about psychology and philosophy. Frame 5.1 includes only those postulates associated with the psychology of learning. Obviously this list and others like it represent the perspectives of those who developed them. As such, they serve well as examples that translate theories of learning into guiding principles for the curriculum planner. This bridge between theories of learning and other elements in curriculum planning is a critical issue. It is practically useless to develop plans without attention to how people learn. Learning theory must permeate the thinking of educators in designing the all-school program as well as specific curriculum plans for particular groups of learners.

Disregarding the practical implications of learning theory presents the ultimate risk that what ought to be learned may not be.

CHARACTERISTICS OF THE LEARNER

■ ■ The characteristics of learners for whom plans are intended constitute one of the most critical screens in curriculum planning. Even the most careful and creative thinking about curriculum plans will come to little effect if those plans are inappropriate for the learner. Fortunately, the research conducted by psychologists and sociologists provides guidance in this phase of curriculum planning. For our purposes, we will now review some of the ways in which one might identify and consider the characteristics of learners.

■ **Growth and Development in Domains of Learning**

As learners grow and develop, they experience noteworthy transitions. The developmental stages of early childhood, transescence, and adolescence are each defined by specific characteristics. One way of viewing learners, then, is to consider them in terms of the characteristics of each stage.

☐ *Intellectual Development*   The work of Jean Piaget is particularly important in defining cognitive development. Piaget (1958) described four stages of cognitive reasoning that appear at particular points in human development. (See Frame 5.2.) Infants and very young children (up to age 2) are characterized by a sensorimotor stage in which they experience and perceive their world through sensory interaction—touching, seeing, hearing, smelling, and tasting. In middle childhood (about ages 2 to 7), this way of viewing the world progresses to the preoperational stage. Now the child begins to see that symbols represent objects. This understanding allows the use of pictures, letters, and numbers to develop a basis for reading and more specific oral communication. In later childhood (about ages 7 to 11), achievement of the concrete operational stage allows the child to use elementary logic as a supplement to perception in organizing his or her environment. Such activities as classification, serial ordering, and numbering are supported by this level of reasoning. In transescence (about 11 to 14) and adolescence (14 to adulthood), the learner develops the final Piagetian stage of formal operations. This allows the individual to use abstract, hypothetical reasoning. Students can begin to analyze imagery and literature, and can begin to do formal problem-solving.

Piaget was frequently criticized for suggesting fairly definite ages

Basic Beliefs—Philosophical and Psychological

Gwynn and Chase, 1969

1. The nature of the learner is that of a choosing individual with responsibility for his choices.
2. Knowledge is meaning, and since the individual is an integrated whole, knowledge to be meaningful must be viewed as integrated.
3. The process of learning is the process of becoming through perceiving and behaving, based on one's field of perception at the time.
4. When students select or help select goals of real need or interest, and further, when they relate these goals to individual purposes, meaningful learning is more likely to occur. . . .
5. When students choose goals they are more likely to be responsible for fulfillment of these goals.
6. When units and instructional guides for learning provide alternative experiences, greater possibility for choice-making and effective learning occurs.
7. When a design is organized around ideas and experiences relevant to the individual and his experiences, greater opportunity for involvement is provided.
8. When teaching techniques are varied and are directed at development of the total individual—intellectual, spiritual, emotional, and social—personal responsibility for effective learning will more likely be realized.
9. Students learn best through concrete, relevant, and predominantly first-hand experiences that elicit critical thinking, discovery, and total involvement.
10. Students learn best when they are challenged within the range of their abilities and interest.
11. The more the individual needs and purposes become the focus for learning, the greater the depth of student involvement and commitment.
12. Any evaluation of behavioral change or student progress presupposes an ongoing diagnosis of student needs, interests, and ability for choice-making.
13. Self-evaluation is the most meaningful of all forms of student evaluation. . . .

at which each cognitive stage emerged. However, the recent work of biophysicist Herman Epstein now suggests that the appearance of each stage may be related to corresponding stages of brain development. Thus, Piaget's stages of cognitive development may correspond to biological development. It is important to note that the onset of each stage simply signals the potential capacity for a type of reasoning, but

14. Learning experiences become most desirable and meaningful when they enable students to fulfill present needs, interests, and goals. In this way these experiences are not something apart from the students, but rather an integral part of their daily lives.
15. The rate, depth, and intensity of learning varies according to individual abilities, drives, purposes, attitudes, and values in relation to felt needs for what is to be learned.
16. To discover meaning is to become involved in a situation; learning or knowledge as meaning is enhanced when there is a relevant relationship between classroom activities and problems of daily life.
17. When learning experiences attempt to prepare students for the challenges of tomorrow's problems, and further, when they critically examine the issues and problems of today, students become aware of the important role they must play and the responsibility toward society that is theirs. . . .
18. Students learn best that which they choose to learn.
19. The greater the alternatives in the choice of subject matter that satisfies student needs and purposes, the more effective the learning.
20. Students must be aware that subject matter embraces all media and data suitable for sensory and perceptual learning by the individual.
21. Selection and organization of materials should be based upon the nature of students' perceptual power, and the experiences necessary to enhance their feeling of success in learning.
22. The learning environment that demands self-government is that which is most conducive to self-learning and to an awareness of the needs and choice-rights of others.
23. The discovery of new knowledge and new meanings is more likely to occur when students have the opportunity to identify and explore problems that interest them and for which no obvious solution is foreseeable at the time.
24. When students are given the opportunity to act on that which they value, transfer of knowledge into behavior takes place.
25. The process of transferring knowledge and meaning into behavior is best begun in the classroom when students have opportunities to relate knowledge and meaning to unique situations, to unknown problems, and to areas of living.

not necessarily its use. Application or maturation of a particular level is learned through practice. From this work we can see that curriculum plans must be compatible with the cognitive stage of the learner and must also promote the transition from onset of any type of reasoning to its mature use. (These ideas will be discussed more fully in this chapter's section on "Neuropsychology and Learner Needs.") Individ-

Illustrative Behaviors for Piagetian Stages

■ **Sensorimotor (birth to 2 years)**

Infants experience the environment through the senses of taste, smell, touch, sight, and hearing. Newborn children "taste" all objects that can be put in their mouths. They call attention to their needs and wants by crying. Infants avoid things that are distasteful, smell odious, give pain, or sound or appear frightening. Their locomotion progressses through crawling to walking, and thus expands the environment that they can experience.

■ **Preoperational (about 2 to 7 years)**

Children begin to understand their environment through symbols. Colors, shapes, pictures, numbers, and letters are used to represent things in their lives. While not "logical" in this process, youngsters are perceptually oriented as they organize their environment. They develop a system of codified symbols for communication. As they learn numbers and alphabet, they complete readiness for reading and basic number functions.

■ **Concrete Operations (about 7 to 11 years)**

Children begin to perform elementary logical operations and expand upon their sole dependence upon perceptual judgments. They notice inconsistencies between thought and action. While they cannot formulate hypotheses, they do master the Piagetian tasks of reversability and conservation, and they can learn operations such as long division. These learners still accept the ethics and rules of parents and other authorities.

■ **Formal Operations (about 11 years and older)**

The developing adolescent begins to use more abstract hypothetico-deductive reasoning. At this stage, learners can perform logic and can control variables in experimentation. These learners need to know "why" something happens and also question "why" authorities require them to do specific things. Now the learner can reverse directions between reality and possibility, and test the viability of alternatives by experimentation.

---

uals will vary in the exact times at which they develop these reasoning capacities. Thus, educators should constantly remind themselves of Piaget's warning that children think like children, and no matter what we do, we cannot force them to reason like adults.

☐ *Social–Emotional Development*   Social development across the stages of growth may be characterized by certain broad trends. Among these are the gradual movements from dependence to independence and the expansion of orientation to others. Young children tend to be largely self-centered, concerned mainly with their own interests and feelings. Their awareness of others is generally limited to significant adults, particularly parents or guardians upon whom they depend for support and guidance. In middle and later childhood, children become more aware of others as they develop friendships with age-mates and adults other than their parents. They begin to be aware of how they affect these other people, and they widen the range of people upon whom they depend. Parents or guardians continue to be highly significant, but their influence may begin to lessen. During transescence, the orientation to others takes a dramatic turn as peers take on much greater significance. At this point the individual begins to depend on peers for feedback regarding behavior and beliefs.

Transescence also marks a major shift as seeking independence becomes a primary goal. Frequently, this results in conflict with adults who would prefer to retain their influence. The classic "identity crisis" described by Erik Erikson may begin during transescence and expand during adolescence. Compelling questions of "Who am I?," "What am I doing here?," and "Where am I going?" mark this critical point in the development of self-concept. Feedback from a range of significant others, including parents, friends, and heroes, and feedback from television and other media may also influence the view of self. Furthermore, the capacity for conceptual reasoning enables the individual to begin thinking of himself or herself as a member of a larger community, possibly with global citizenship. More mature relations based on sexual attraction also emerge as the capacity for intimacy develops. For all of these reasons, those responsible for curriculum development need to recognize that their plans should account for stages of orientation and dependency, and should support transition in these areas. Again, though, educators must remember that learners are who they are and cannot be expected to reflect social–emotional development beyond their developmental stages. As it becomes appropriate, curriculum plans should reflect the student's increasing capacity for independence and/ or the changing influence of peer orientation that occurs in various stages.

□ *Additional Characteristics*   In Chapter 7 we shall see how in selecting specific objectives, activities, resources, and measuring devices, those responsible for planning and implementing the curriculum must consider a wide variety of learner characteristics. In the final analysis, the effectiveness of teaching–learning situations depends not only upon the match between curriculum plans and the major factors discussed above, but also upon the following types of variables.

DEVELOPMENTAL TASKS   One way of viewing learners is to identify their emerging needs at each stage of growth and development. As we saw in Chapter 3, Robert Havighurst suggested that each stage of life is characterized by certain "developmental tasks." These tasks might well serve as a foundation for the statement of general objectives at each of those developmental levels.

INTEREST   We tend to work hardest on and most effectively at those things in which we are most interested. Thus the identification of and attention to learner interest in curriculum plans is a crucial task. Because of this, the more learning activities are related to student interests, the greater the probability that effective learning will take place.

LANGUAGE ARTS SKILL LEVELS   Regardless of curricular approach, a variety of instructional materials should be used. The effective use of materials depends upon language arts skills such as reading, writing, speaking, listening, viewing, observing, and so on. If the level of materials is inappropriate for the skill level of students, the materials may be of little use.

CHRONOLOGICAL AGE   Young people have different interests and capacities at different stages of development. An activity that is appropriate for young children may be inappropriate for transescents or adolescents. In like manner, adolescents may find meaning in a particular instructional material that makes little sense to children.

MENTAL AGE   Like chronological age, the ability to process ideas mentally varies from one stage to another. The clear relationship between mental age and stages of cognitive development makes this variable a particularly sensitive one. Furthermore, the frequent discrepancy between chronological age and mental age implies that teachers must carefully diagnose the latter.

PHYSICAL HANDICAPS   Obviously, conditions such as blindness or deafness among learners should influence the selection of activities and materials. The attention to special education in recent years has done much to facilitate the availability of suitable alternatives in this area.

SOCIOECONOMIC CLASS   We know from numerous research studies that the prior experiences of learners influence their receptivity to various activities and materials. It is also clear that prior experiences vary depending upon socioeconomic class. Therefore, curriculum planners must take this variable into account when developing assumptions about the readiness of learners for specific tasks.

SELF-CONCEPT/SELF-ESTEEM The degree to which learners feel capable and confident in taking on new learning opportunities is a crucial factor in success. Experts who deal with learning disabilities, for example, know that many young people so labeled are victims of learned helplessness; they believe that no matter how hard they try, they cannot succeed. On the other hand, those who have experienced success in some area can be expected to believe they can continue to succeed. The learner's self-concept and esteem in a particular area must, therefore, be considered in designing or selecting learning activities.

These variables do not exhaust all the possibilities that curriculum planners might take into account in designing teacher–learning situations. They do, however, represent several important possibilities that might be considered. Taken jointly with a knowledge of general characteristics of stages and of characteristics such as developmental tasks, they reflect the kind of focus that is given to the nature of the learner in curriculum planning. The ultimate test of these decision screens lies in the sensitivity of teachers to actual learners encountered in specific teaching–learning situations.

■ Neuropsychology and Learner Needs

Neurology is the study of the function of the central nervous system as controlled by the brain. The traditional separation of neurology and psychology is a problem since research shows that both are essential to learning. The growing separation of these areas is a major problem for responsible curriculum planning.

Psychology has been considered a foundation area in education because of its contributions in studying human learning. Child, adolescent, and, more recently, transescent or early adolescent psychology has given educators more appropriate information on the nature of learners at each of those levels. As the first section of this chapter outlined, the psychology of learning has sought to identify what learning is and how it takes place, and to develop alternate theories about that process. Because of this, educational psychology has been properly designated as a foundation area in the study of education. However, traditional learning theory, as we know it, is not interacting with the burgeoning base of neuroscience findings. In 1965, Clayton could write with confidence that

> an understanding of the physiology of brain functioning must eventually be achieved in order to have a completely satisfying theory of learning. The brain is much more active and complex than earlier theories would imply. Perception and memory are fundamental to learning theory and need continued exploration at the physiological level. Those interested in understanding learning must remain aware of developments in this area. (p. 80)

For instance, a quarter century ago, psychologists concurred that "nurture" in relationship was predominant over nature. That is to say, the role of environment was considered to be more powerful in child development than biologically determined factors. Some psychologists now admit the need to rethink that position. In a number of instances, neuroscience findings are indicating that a biological inevitability in the development of the brain and central nervous system reduces nurture to a subordinate influence. From the psychological perspective, Jerome Kagan's studies (1980, 1984) show that major intellectual and personality traits appear at similar ages in children reared in a wide range of cultural and anthropological settings.

Other areas of neurological findings indicate that the development of the brain will have a still greater impact upon the teaching–learning process. Educators concerned with curriculum planning cannot be expected to develop neurological backgrounds. Thus, there is a growing need for the neurosciences and learning psychology to become an interactive "neuropsychology" of learning. In this way, that area can remain a major educational foundation area. As Toepfer observes:

> The syncretism of learning psychology with neuropsychology based on careful study of the range of neuropsychological discoveries may well be the best way to improve school programs. This would allow the traditional interaction of curriculum designers and the neuropsychologically competent learning psychologists to work at responsive curriculum planning and improvement of instruction in the school setting. (1982, p. 3)

The development of such a neuropsychology of learning would provide an interface for teachers and other curriculum planners that is absolutely necessary to understand neuroscience findings. Included in these neuroscience findings are a number that have critical implications both for a neuropsychology of learning and for curriculum planning. Educators are already looking for ways to deal with findings such as the following.

□ *Brain Growth Periodization*   Brain growth periodization, based upon the research of Herman Epstein, is a subject of much interest in the curriculum area, and it has already furnished a basis for considering school program revisions. Epstein's data suggest that the human brain grows in a periodic or stagewise fashion in which growth "spurts" alternate with times of low growth. His findings indicate that intervals of greater brain growth occur somewhere between the ages of 3 to 10 months, 2 to 4 years, 6 to 8 years, 10 to 12 years, and 14 to 16 years. Periods of lesser growth in the brain are believed to occur somewhere between ages 10 months and 2, 4 and 6, 8 and 10, and 12 and 14 years

(Epstein, 1979). Findings identify that children can learn *facts* and *information* equally well during both brain growth spurt and low brain growth intervals. However, youngsters appear to have greater success in initiating *new and more difficult thinking skills* during the intervals of greater growth than during those of lesser brain growth.

This observation led to Epstein's interest in trying to match the learner's level of learning to the learning activities offered her or him (Epstein, 1981). Tests have been developed that allow educators to identify the cognitive levels of students during their years in school. These correlate with psychologist Jean Piaget's thinking stages, as follows.

Between birth and age 2, Piaget found, children develop "sensorimotor thinking" as they deal with the environment at perceptual levels. From 2 to 7 years, children develop "preoperational thinking" as they acquire symbolic thought. From 7 to 11 years,"concrete operational thinking" emerges as the child develops logical structures to deal with changing objects in the physical world. Piaget's final stage of development is "formal operational thinking," which appears between ages 11 and 15 years. At this time children can begin hypothetical–deductive reasoning of ideas or hypotheses (Piaget, 1969).

☐ *Cognitive Levels Matching* Cognitive levels matching is an attempt to plan and develop learning experiences that match the learner's developmental readiness at a particular time. As mentioned in our earlier discussion of Gordon's ideas, basic human needs for achievement, expression, participation, satisfaction, and status are accommodated when learning challenges do not frustrate one's readiness to learn.

Epstein (1981) recommended that neuropsychological information about the cognitive readiness of learners could be utilized for developing learning experiences that accurately respond to student cognitive levels as they change across the years of schooling. His work was the basis for the Shoreham–Wading River, New York, school district establishing an ongoing program to develop learning activities in this way (Brooks, Fusco, and Grennon, 1983). Their cognitive-levels-matching project has required continuing in-service and staff development activities to provide teachers with the abilities to identify cognitive levels in students (Brooks, 1984). Educators have gained the skill to develop learning activities that appropriately challenge this changing readiness of learners in the various subject-matter areas. The curriculum work at Shoreham has resulted in a model (Arlin, 1984a) that educators may wish to examine in considering how to deal with the readiness issue. Arlin's development of a standardized test (1984b) allows educators to identify readily whether a student is a concrete, transitional, or formal operational thinker.

In 1957, Piaget recommended that educators "construct" school experiences around the readiness of youngsters to function rather than expect them to be able to adapt to adult expectations. Cognitive levels matching has achieved a major step in this direction by taking such a constructivist approach to developing responsive learning experiences. The advantages of this approach in helping youngsters better meet school goals through experiences matched to their readiness has resulted in more effective satisfaction of their basic human needs. This is an important example of how educators can use neuropsychological data to develop school programs that more effectively respond to the readiness and basic human needs of youngsters.

☐ *Cerebral Lateralization and Hemispheric Dominance*   A second area of neuroscience findings of great interest to teachers and other curriculum planners is cerebral lateralization and hemispheric dominance. This area suggests that specific functions of the brain tend to reside respectively in the left and right hemispheres. This creates the need to understand so-called "split-brain" and "whole-brain" functions in learning. The left hemisphere tends to control linear and sequential skills, such as those needed to perform mathematical functions and deal with the structure of language. The right hemisphere tends to control visual, spatial, and holistic functions needed in dealing with shapes, images, and the like.

Some individuals have a dominance in one hemisphere or the other, and this has an impact on their individual way of learning. Others tend to be more bilateralized or more balanced in both their linear and visual–spatial abilities (Kinsbourne and Hiscock, 1978). The degree of balance also would have influence on how an individual would best be able to pursue her or his basic human needs. S. Levine (1984) discusses the child's ability to redirect hemispheric skills. Changes in an individual's handedness, dominance of eye, and the like serve as indications of dominance or balance of abilities in her or his brain hemispheres.

However, Jerre Levy (1982) cautions educators about making premature judgments over hemispheric difference and maintains that most children learn in a whole- or integrated-brain fashion. She points out that all subject matters engage specialties residing on both sides of the brain. Although educational and popular journals continue to present writings about split- and whole-brain learning, premature judgments about curriculum applications to specific learning situations could prove inaccurate.

In this instance, a neuropsychological clarification of the range of application of split- and whole-brain findings is necessary before sweeping approaches to teaching and learning are undertaken. With such clarification, the potential of what the whole- and the split-brain activities bring to learning could be a powerful means to improve the organization of learning activities across the years of schooling. Imagine how the teaching of facts, skills, and information could be enhanced if this area can refine our understanding of the way learning and processing of information actually occurs.

Whole- and split-brain findings can be expected to specify further the growing area of information dealing with learning styles. The work of Rita and Kenneth Dunn (1978) shows that individual learners have preferred styles of learning in a wide range of dimensions. Anthony Gregorc (1982) has developed means by which teachers can match intellectual modes of learning in individual students with their own preferred teaching styles. While the work already available to teachers in learning-styles inventories has proven helpful, any further speci- fication of why individual styles develop because of brain functioning would be important information for teachers.

Although a number of other areas dealing with neuroscience find- ings could be sketched, it remains for the interaction of neuroscientists and learning psychologists to define a neuropsychological basis for educational considerations before any final decisions are made (Stra- han and Toepfer, 1984). In the instances discussed here, we can begin to see what the application of a neuropsychology of learning may mean for our educational future. It is important for educators to recognize that neuropsychology holds great potential for identifying how indi- viduals differ in the ways they deal with basic human needs. The brain and central nervous system have an impact on individual differences that has yet to be fully understood. The situations described here have suggested how educators can deal with some of these differences. Their implications for curriculum workers, in terms of potential ways to improve learning activities in schools, may prove almost limitless.

■ Influence of the Out-of-School Curriculum

It is a mistake to assume that young people learn only from what is offered within the school. In fact, the school is only one source of learn- ing for them. In today's world, many traditional and emerging sources are available for information, skills, attitudes, and suggested behav- iors. William Schubert (1981, 1986) offers that the out-of-school curric- ulum has become so powerful that it is a requisite for a full understand- ing of learners. Some of the more obvious sources include the following.

- ■ Traditional agencies or groups, such as the family or church, which may heavily influence values and beliefs
- ■ Youth groups such as scouting, YMCA, YWCA, Jewish Youth Organizations, and the like, which offer various skill devel- opment programs
- ■ Media such as television, radio, newspapers, magazines, and movies that are directed toward youth audiences

- Home computers through which youth may supplement or even go beyond what is offered in the school
- Informal interaction with peers at playgrounds, malls, and other gathering places
- Visits to or participation in programs offered by libraries, museums, and other cultural institutions
- Travel to other areas, states, and countries

From these types of sources, young people may gain many experiences that can lead to their developing special interests or skills. As educators attempt to develop experience-centered or life-related plans, efforts must be made to identify and deal with such out-of-school learnings.

From some sources, such as rock music videos and movies, young people may also develop images of the school that are negative. These attitudes may in turn influence the behaviors they display in teaching–learning situations. Teachers, in particular, should try to be aware of this possibility and consider ways to counteract it. At the very least, they ought to sample pertinent music, videos, movies, and the like, to have some knowledge of what young people are experiencing.

Before leaving this brief discussion, we feel that one more point is important. Professional educators are supposed to be concerned with the healthy growth and development of young people. Since the out-of-school curriculum is a source of learning, its content should be examined by the profession in terms of its positive or negative impact on youth. Those persons who are responsible for out-of-school sources should be offered assistance in considering what and how they are teaching the young. In turn, they should be consulted about how they believe their work may interface with that of the school. Finally, where necessary, they should be advised if their influence on young people is perceived to be clearly negative. In other words, it is not enough simply to complain about the out-of-school curriculum and its influence on youth. Rather, it is our professional obligation to examine and monitor its content in the best interests of young people.

GENERAL RESOURCES

In order to implement curriculum plans effectively, teachers and learners need to have a variety of resources available to them. If the real world of schools operated according to educational theory, this aspect of curriculum planning would be easily handled. Whatever resources were needed would simply be made available. It is of course true that resources needed to support curriculum plans are often acquired when requested. However, in a great many cases teachers and learners must make the best possible use of what is already available. Sometimes these are sufficient; but at other times, plans must be revised to adjust for the lack of desired resources.

In this section we will consider several kinds of resources that influence the implementation of curriculum plans. These include facilities, money, materials, supplies, equipment, and community resources. In each case, we will note problems associated with the particular type of resource and efforts that have been made to overcome them. When developing curriculum plans, it is important to consider each area in light of questions such as the following:

- What resources will be needed to carry out the curriculum plans?
- What resources are currently available to provide needed support?
- Can the resources that are not currently available be acquired?
- If those needed cannot be acquired, how must the plans be modified?

■ Facilities, Equipment, and Supplies

A story is often told about John Dewey as principal of the celebrated University of Chicago Laboratory School in the early 1900s. Evidently he searched all over Chicago for furniture for the school and found nothing except the traditional school desks and chairs. Finally he remarked to one salesperson that he was dissatisfied because all of the furniture was made for listening rather than learning. Dewey's dilemma is still with us. Most often, facilities and equipment are in place before programs are designed.

Most schools are built in an "egg-crate" fashion—long corridors lined with standard-sized rooms in which teachers and learners are expected to carry out learning experiences. Such arrangements are certainly appropriate for those activities that call for groups of fixed size. With some modification, such as rearrangement of furniture, they may also be used for small-group activities. Double rooms with folding partitions allow for additional large-group experiences. Some schools have been designed on an open-space basis that theoretically permits many variations in group size and types of activities. While many teachers are pleased with this opportunity, others prefer to place bookcases and file cabinets strategically to create standard-sized learning areas. Other available facilities, such as physical education space, shops, kitchens, playgrounds, school-owned nature trails, and the like, also enter into or affect curriculum plans. The more variety there is in facilities, the greater the variety of activities that can be implemented;

the more limited the facilities, the more chance that learning activities will have to be modified.

Effective implementation of curriculum plans also depends upon the range of equipment available. Preferably, items like overhead projectors, film projectors, seminar tables, televisions, interactive video disks, and audio cassettes should be accessible to all teachers and learners. In the early 1980s, the most compelling issue concerning equipment was the availability of computers. No problem was more consuming than the obsessive rush to acquire the latest hardware. While there is no doubt that computers can and will continue to enhance learning, the necessary step of providing teachers with an understanding of how computers can be used in planning and teaching is frequently overlooked. Enlightened educators are carefully developing comprehensive plans for the acquisition of computers—plans that take into account the variety of learner characteristics, instructional techniques, and broad goals of their school programs. However, as in Dewey's furniture dilemma, some schools are acquiring computer hardware and then trying to determine its use. In other words, curriculum planning is done on the basis of what purchased computers can do rather than the reverse. In Chapter 3 we discussed the breadth of influence these computers may have on the school. In Chapters 7 and 10 we will consider this situation further, including a look at how computers may be used in curriculum planning itself.

Beyond facilities and equipment, curriculum planners must also be aware of available material resources. In Chapter 7 we will discuss the use of specific materials. Again, however, educators must be aware that computer and other communications technology may continue to change this area drastically. Whereas plans were previously hindered by the lack of available materials, it is most probable that schools will have access to centralized databases that will provide instant access to virtually all materials. The lack of a certain book or film will simply no longer be a problem. This actuality will certainly do much to enhance the quality of instruction, since all learners will have access to the best possible material resources.

■ **Finances**

Formal education costs money. The maintenance and improvement of schools require financial support for professional personnel, facilities, materials, energy resources, and a host of other fixed and variable costs. Most people teaching today have lived through two very different periods with regard to this issue. Until the 1970s, education was viewed as a growth enterprise. Enrollments were consistently increasing, more teachers were needed, and education seemed almost immune to swings in the larger public economy. In many ways the 1960s may be retrospectively viewed as the financial golden years in education. Following the launching of *Sputnik* in 1957, concern grew over the quality of curriculum, teaching, and learning. At local and state levels, citizens were willing to provide increasing money to improve the schools. The Federal Elementary and Secondary Education Act of 1965 contributed massive funding for curriculum development, instructional supplies, facilities, and preservice and inservice professional education. Education and the curriculum field were clearly on the upswing. Then, seemingly without warning, there was a sudden shift. Enrollments began to decline, taxpayers felt overburdened, and the cost of energy resources soared. These along with other issues confronted the schools with a problem not faced since the Great Depression. Financial support became scarce. Lower enrollments meant lower per-pupil support; budgets were defeated across the country, and more and more money was required to purchase energy supplies. This downswing affected the curriculum almost immediately. Professional salaries, energy, and other costs were fixed in budgets. One of the most obvious variable costs was curriculum development and implementation. Summer curriculum-development workshops disappeared, new instructional materials were put on hold, and federal, state, and local funding dwindled. Faced with budget cuts and school closings, curriculum took a back seat in financial thinking. Class sizes increased, materials became aged and worn, and curriculum innovation became a topic for nostalgia. Finally in the 1980s, federal officials and the general public became aware that such conditions had reached a point where the quality of education was threatened. Commission reports recommended the need for more financial support of schools and for a variety of ways to provide it.

Adjusting to a period of low growth was difficult for the schools and often disastrous to curriculum planning efforts. But during that period of adjustment, some new and innovative ideas did emerge. If commercial materials could not be purchased, local materials would have to be substituted. As a result, workshops focused on development of teacher-made materials. Some teachers found new and creative ways to use "junk" materials for curriculum implementation. These ranged from simple dittos to more innovative projects. For example, in one middle school near Boston, a team of teachers used scrap wood and rolls of wrapping paper to re-create the inside of an Egyptian tomb. In this and other cases, teachers found that such projects actually provided more concrete and effective learning for students.

A more conceptual idea that gained popularity involved the use of so-called Planning-Programming-Budgeting Systems (PPBS). Here the purpose was to make systematic decisions about the allocation of financial resources. Since the supply of money was limited, what was available needed to be more effectively used. The PPBS approach suggested that the budget be developed after program planning was done.

Thus the amount of financial support provided would depend upon what was really needed to carry out curriculum plans. From a theoretical standpoint, this approach made a good deal of sense. The amount of money allotted to a particular program should be determined after it is planned rather than expanding or cutting the program to fit the budget.

Despite these and other attempts to make do, those responsible for curriculum planning have learned to live with the fact that there is rarely enough money around to support their highest hopes. Certainly the emergence of the computer and other communications technology offers the potential for doing more with less. For teachers and learners, however, living within the budget is still the reality of everyday life in the school.

■ Community Resources

The community is frequently overlooked as an important resource for the school. If school and community are viewed in a cooperative relationship, we might imagine several patterns of resource use. One involves bringing community resources into the school to support and supplement those already available. Another has students leaving the school to engage in direct learning experiences in the community. A third alternative, and perhaps the most inviting one, is to envision the school without walls and to consider the entire community as a school, rich in both resources and opportunities for learning.

Consider the fact that communities include several types of resources that can be acquired for use in the school. Among these are both people and material resources. Virtually every community has numerous individuals who have special talents, interests, and experiences that can be shared with learners. These include government officials, artisans, scientists, writers, and many more. In addition, various businesses, industries, cultural institutions, and other agencies are usually willing to provide materials and sometimes even financial support for special projects. Since teachers cannot be expected to memorize all these possibilities, many school districts maintain and continuously update community resource files. These lists identify by topics various individuals or agency representatives who may be contacted for help. In using these kinds of community resources, however, two issues must be kept in mind. First, individuals may know a great deal about a particular topic, but little about teaching. Thus, before actually working with students, they need to be involved in planning sessions to consider how they will "teach." Second, many agencies slant free instructional materials to support their special interest. These resources need to be carefully scrutinized before they are used or distributed to students.

In addition to resources that may be brought into the school, communities contain many that can provide direct learning experiences outside the school. These might include agencies, institutions, industries, museums, art galleries, zoos, parks, and camps. They can also be cataloged in a community resource file so that learners can take advantage of them. Individuals or groups may leave the school to visit them on short field trips, for outdoor education trips, or for lengthy internships. Teachers must decide how these resources are to be utilized and must carefully integrate them into curriculum plans. One special issue related to community resources involves the nature of the area in which the school is located. Obviously, metropolitan school districts include great numbers of the kinds of agencies and institutions traditionally used for this purpose. However, small rural communities typically may not include museums, art galleries, and the like. Hence, such communities typically may be viewed as being at a disadvantage. On the other hand, small rural communities often provide more resources such as camps, parks, and environmental projects. The task here is not to bemoan what is not available, but rather to take advantage of what is. For example, one of the most enlightened uses of community resources on record is Eliot Wigginton's well-known Foxfire Project in rural southern Appalachia. The several published volumes in this undertaking represent an important contribution to the preservation of arts, crafts, and folklore of that region. It is unfortunate that the difficult economic times of the early 1980s seriously inhibited the opportunity, in many districts, for extended field trips through which metropolitan and rural youth could experience the benefits of each other's communities.

Lastly, educators should consider the possibility of viewing the school as an educational opportunity without walls. In this case, those involved in curriculum planning should try to imagine a natural interaction between school and community or region. One example of this is the development of community service programs in which learners, as part of the regular school program, engage in various projects to improve the community. These may include working in hospitals, nursing homes, or day-care centers, tutoring other youth or adults, improving recreation facilities, and so on. Another example involves exchange programs between urban and rural schools. Here students spend a few days or more living in a different type of community, sharing ideas, experiences, values, customs, and so on. A third and possibly the best-known example is the Parkway Program developed in Philadelphia in the 1960s. In this project the community became the school. In addition to the types of projects already mentioned, regular classes were decentralized around the community and held in storefronts, museums, businesses, government agencies, and other places.

The plain fact is that the school itself cannot be expected to provide all the resources necessary for the best possible learning. The community or region can do much to fill the gaps that exist in this regard. For this reason alone, it is essential to consider the community as a general resource in curriculum planning and implementation at various levels—from the district-wide to the specific teaching–learning situation.

CURRICULAR APPROACHES

■ ■   In Chapter 1 we presented several examples of teachers at work with learners. In each case the teaching–learning situation focused on some particular type of learning: mastery of subject matter, studying a social problem, and so on. The variation in how those situations were organized reflected the use of one or another curricular approach. *A curricular approach is defined as a pattern of organization used in making decisions about the various aspects of a teaching–learning situation.* There is, of course, a wide range of approaches that are used. However, these generally fall into four major categories: subjects, broad fields, problems of living, and emerging needs of learners. As we shall see, the selection of an approach reflects and influences the organizing center for the teaching–learning situation, the selection of objectives, and the use of subject matter or content.

■   **Subject-Area Approach**

One way to organize curriculum plans is around separate subject areas or disciplines of knowledge. For example, the program of the school might be divided into areas of English language arts, social studies, mathematics, science, art, music and so on. When this is done, learning objectives involve mastering subject matter and skills within a given subject. Subject matter is drawn from within the subject. The subject-area approach is the most popular method of curriculum organization. Surveys indicate that this approach is used in about 96 percent of U. S. high schools (Tubbs and Beane, 1981). Furthermore, increasing numbers of elementary schools are using this approach, particularly in the upper grades. Even teachers in self-contained elementary classrooms often organize the program in this way, dividing the day into time segments devoted to each subject. Because this approach defines important learning in terms of subject matter from existing disciplines of knowledge, it is particularly favored by proponents of the philosophy of realism described in Chapter 3.

■ **Broad-Fields Approach**

A second method of organizing the curriculum involves combining two or more subject areas into a broader field. For example, a unit may be developed in art history in which learners study art as it relates to specific historical periods. Literature, art, history, and music may be combined to form a humanities program. A unit on metrics may involve the simultaneous study of metric mathematics and its use in science. The broad-fields approach recognizes and uses individual subject areas, but it also attempts to show learners the correlations between various disciplines of knowledge. Advocates of the broad-fields approach cite such correlation as an advantage over the separate-subject approach. The emphasis on broad ideas and concepts from subject fields makes this approach popular among those who favor the philosophy of idealism discussed in Chapter 3.

■ **Social-Problems Approach**

A third way of organizing curriculum plans is around major problems in society. For example, units may be developed regarding environmental problems, technology, the future, racism, global interdependence, and so on. In this approach, learning objectives involve analyzing the problem or issue, and the subject matter is drawn from any source pertinent to the problem. If the unit topic were "Futures," learners might turn to social studies for information about government or population growth, to science for trends in technology, or to language arts for ideas regarding communications. However, little, if any, concern is shown for retaining the identity of separate subjects even when subject matter is derived from them. Complete focus is placed upon the problem under study. The major purpose of using this approach is to help learners develop awareness of crucial social issues and the skills that they might use in the future to help solve them. For this reason, the problems approach is particularly popular among proponents of the reconstructionist philosophy of education discussed in Chapter 3.

■ **Emerging-Needs Approach**

A fourth way to organize curriculum plans focuses on the personal and social needs that are emerging in learners' lives at the present time. For example, units for use with transescents may center on topics such as getting along with others, understanding physical changes associated with puberty, developing personal values, and understanding peer status. In this case, the issues under study are obviously pertinent to the learners' developmental stage. Here, as in the social-problems approach, information may be drawn from various subject areas, but there is no attempt to recognize distinct lines between disciplines of knowledge. The major purpose behind this approach is to help learners come to grips with issues in their present lives so as to be prepared for the present rather than the future. While topics or issues for study may be preplanned by teachers, others may emerge spontaneously from discussions among teachers and students about pressing problems in learners' lives. Obviously this approach has support from those who adhere to the pragmatic and existential philosophies discussed in Chapter 3.

Before leaving the topic of curricular approaches, it is important to consider several issues related to them. The first issue involves the relationship between curricular approaches and various instructional methods. For one reason or another, many educators have come to stereotype various ideas and roles in curriculum. The most common stereotype is the distinction between traditional and progressive approaches. In this case, traditionalists are described as advocates of the subject approach and proponents of methods such as lecture. Progressives, on the other hand, are seen as advocates of the social problems or emerging needs approaches and methods such as small-group discussion. Educational stereotypes tend to be largely destructive and, in this case, erroneous. One can easily imagine an English teacher developing a unit on short stories. During the unit, a community resource person visits the classroom to conduct a small-group discussion about character personalities in one or another story. It is possible also, in a different situation, that a teacher studying peer pressure with a group of learners might present a lecture on the reasons why status is assigned to various individuals. In other words, the activities are independent of the approach.

The other unfortunate aspect of stereotyping approaches is the idea that the subject and broad-fields approaches involve hard work and "real" learning while the social-problems and needs approaches are simply fun and games or on the "soft side" of the curriculum. Again, such a conception is erroneous and foolish. Trying to understand racial prejudice in our society involves just as much serious attention and hard work as learning about the elements in the periodic chart in chemistry. Whether or not curriculum topics are considered seriously depends on what teachers and learners are willing to do, not on the curricular approach being used.

A second issue involves the relationship between curricular approaches and various instructional organizations. Two popular ideas in contemporary schools are general education and interdisciplinary teaching. General education refers to that portion of the school program which is considered central and is required of all students. Interdisciplinary teaching has gained attention through the formation of teaching teams involving various subject areas, such as language arts, mathematics, social studies, science and sometimes others. In both cases, the problems of stereotyping and narrow definition have again emerged. In the late 1970s and early 1980s, many school curriculum committees devoted time to defining what ought to constitute the general education curriculum. Unfortunately, most of these efforts have resulted in a listing of required subject areas that all students must take. This definition of "general education" excludes the idea that all learners might also develop knowledge and skill related to social problems and emerging needs. On the other hand, many interdisciplinary teaming efforts have failed because teachers have been led to believe mistakenly that such teams must always fuse the various subject areas into a social-problems approach. Such a narrow definition excludes the idea that interdisciplinary teams might use all four curricular approaches, thus providing balance in the curriculum plans.

A third issue concerns the question of desirability of one or another of the curricular approaches. Very often educators will propose that one approach is better than the others. While it is certainly probable that individuals would favor or emphasize a particular approach, it is equally clear that all four have an appropriate place in the school program. Each serves a different and important purpose. Each addresses a different aspect of a comprehensive education and of curriculum plans to provide it. Thus the real issue in considering curriculum approaches is not which one is better, but how all can be used in the school. By addressing the issue in this way, educators would confront the question of how to provide balance in the curriculum.

Finally, it is worth noting that some research has been completed on the use and effects of curricular approaches. No study is more frequently referenced in the curriculum field than the Eight Year Study. Between 1932 and 1940, the Progressive Education Association sponsored a major study on the effects of various curricular approaches. The study dealt with two groups of 1,475 students in thirty U.S. high schools. One group was taught using the traditional subject approach, while the other group studied in the context of various other alternatives, including the problems and needs approaches. Student outcomes were measured at various points, with emphasis on measurement at the completion of high school and again at the end of college. Wilford Aiken (1941) reported that, compared with students taught through the subject approach, those in the experimental groups

1. earned a slightly higher total grade average;
2. earned higher grade averages in all subject fields except foreign languages;

3. specialized in the same academic fields as did the comparison students;
4. did not differ from the comparison group in the number of times they were placed on probation;
5. received slightly more academic honors each year;
6. were more often judged to possess a high degree of intellectual curiosity and drive;
7. were more often judged to be precise, systematic and objective in their thinking;
8. were more often judged to have developed clear and well-formulated ideas concerning the meaning of education—especially in the first two years of college;
9. more often demonstrated a high degree of resourcefulness in meeting new situations;
10. did not differ from the comparison group in ability to plan their time effectively;
11. had about the same problems of adjustment as the comparison group, but approached their solution with greater effectiveness;
12. participated somewhat more frequently, and often enjoyed appreciative experiences in the arts;
13. participated more frequently in all organized student groups except religious and service activities;
14. earned in each college year a higher percentage of nonacademic honors (officership in organizations, election to managerial societies, athletic insignia, leading roles in dramatic and musical presentations);
15. did not differ from the comparison group in the quality of their adjustment to contemporaries;
16. differed only slightly from the comparison group in the kinds of judgment about their schooling;
17. had a somewhat better orientation toward the choice of a vocation;
18. demonstrated a more active concern for what was going on in the world. (pp.110–112)

ORGANIZED KNOWLEDGE

■ ■ Regardless of the curricular approach or approaches being used, concepts or techniques specific to a particular subject area or formal discipline may provide necessary information in the design of specific teaching–learning situations. The discipline of mathematics, for example, in its most formal organization, would suggest what concepts would be needed prior to understanding a certain arithmetic operation that is required by students who wish to learn about weather. At a more sophisticated level, secondary students investigating psychological relationships between queues (waiting lines) and people's willingness to patronize a particular grocery store may have their studies greatly aided if the teachers involved are aware of relevant techniques from calculus. Different models of literary analysis may be more or less appropriate to gaining insight from a novel being read to shed light on a local community problem. And various theoretical paradigms from physics may hold different strengths for students trying to internalize the concept of interdependence of life forms.

It is important to note that in all the examples cited, knowledge is taken from the content-logical organization of a subject. This organization is accomplished by scholars in a field as they continually attempt to synthesize the old and new aspects of their chosen discipline. It is done within the perspective of an overview of the entire discipline, but it is not an orientation that is student-logical, nor is it normally an organization that parallels the historical development of the area. This fact is seldom explained to students who are asked to comprehend a "theoretically logical" outline of some particular subject. They may not realize that the false starts, redundancies, unneeded steps, and unclear reasoning that originally characterized the work have been removed through years and lives of effort. Such a realization might serve to reduce the number of instances where students, upon seeing a "finished and polished" product, decide summarily that they are not "bright enough" to work in that field. (Perhaps a major part of this problem stems from the common belief that knowledge, especially what is taught in schools, is certain. Quite to the contrary, history has taught us that knowledge is, if anything, uncertain: the earth is *not* flat; Columbus did *not* discover America; the model of the atom is *not* the same as a model of our solar system.)

In sum, however, our use of organized knowledge in this screen is not to force a subject-centered curricular approach. It is, rather, to increase teacher awareness of the broad spectrum of information that is available to learners as they pursue instructional objectives.

CHAPTER SUMMARY

In Chapter 5 we have explored five screens that must be considered in the development of curriculum plans for specific teaching–learning situations. The first, characteristics of learners, focuses on understanding the children or youth for whom plans were intended. The second screen, the nature of learning, involves understanding the ways in which learners might approach, undertake, and process the intended learning situation. The third screen, general resources, focuses on such areas as finances, time, equipment, facilities, and the community as support areas for curriculum plans. The fourth screen, curricular approaches, involves the selection of an organizational pattern around which to develop curriculum plans. Finally, the fifth screen, organized knowledge, provides specific concepts or techniques that teachers and learners may use as they pursue instructional objectives.

Each of these screens reflects a critical aspect of curriculum decision-making. For example, curriculum plans that are not based on learner characteristics may be unsuccessful either because they fail to challenge the learners or because they are beyond their capacity to learn. Failing to consider available resources may lead to frustration due to factors such as lack of time or money. In other words, the development of curriculum plans without consideration of decision screens may seriously inhibit effective implementation of those plans.

Having read Chapter 5, you should be able to:

1. Identify major theories about how learning takes place
2. Describe characteristics of children and youth that should be considered in developing curriculum plans
3. Identify general resources that should be considered in developing curriculum plans
4. Describe the appropriate use of several different curricular approaches
5. Describe the role of organized knowledge in developing teaching–learning situations

SUGGESTED ACTIVITIES

1. Identify the curricular approaches used by members of the group. Develop a chart showing the various unit topics, subjects, and so on used in each category by the various members. If all members teach in the same subject area, identify various topics or areas within the subject that could reflect each approach. Analyze either chart to determine whether the group's ideas show balance in curriculum organization. Where gaps are shown, add topics or problems to develop balance.

2. Form groups on the basis of similar levels taught: primary, elementary, middle level, and/or high school. Develop in each group a chart on which members identify physical, social, and intellectual characteristics of learners at that level. Combine the charts into a comprehensive list across levels. Each group may then explain their list to other groups. Compare and contrast characteristics across levels.

3. Using a list of learner characteristics (such as that developed in activity 2), identify areas of the curriculum or other school features that are either appropriate or inappropriate for the learner's charac-

teristics. Develop recommendations for changing those which are inappropriate.

4. Based upon observations and experiences of group members, identify the theories of learning that appear to be most prevalent in schools. Develop a list of examples for each theory.

5. Develop two charts showing categories of general resources, such as equipment, facilities, and community resources. Complete one chart by having members of the group consider what resources they have used during the current year in each category. Complete the second chart by considering what resources would have improved learning if they had been available. Where gaps exist, ask members of the group for suggestions regarding how or where desired resources might be acquired.

6. Divide the group into smaller groups based upon various areas such as business and industry, arts and crafts, environmental issues, government agencies, and so on. Have each group identify local or regional community resources in the area assigned. From the results of each small group, develop a community resource file including names of contact persons, description of specific interests, and concerns of various agencies or individuals and how they might be used.

7. Divide the large group into four smaller groups. Have each small group develop a case or argument for a particular curricular approach. The small groups should examine theory, research, and experience in building their case. Invite a panel of four or five outside individuals to act as a hearing panel in which each group presents the case for its approach in a formal structure of presentation, rebuttal, and summary. The hearing panel then hands down a decision regarding the use of various approaches, based upon the arguments. Note that panel members may include teachers, professors, lawyers, business personnel, and others. (This activity follows the legal-evaluation model described in Robert L. Wolf, "Trial by Jury: A New Evaluation Method," *Phi Delta Kappan,* November 1975, pp. 185–187.)

REFERENCES

Aiken, W. *The Story of the Eight Year Study*. New York: Harper & Row, 1941.

Arlin, P. "Cognitive Levels Matching: An Instructional Model and a Model of Teacher Change." In *A Child's Brain,* edited by M. Frank. New York: Haworth Press, 1984a, pp. 99–109.

———. *The Arlin Test of Formal Reasoning*. East Aurora, N.Y.: Slosson Educational Publications, 1984b.

Brooks, M. "A Constructivist Approach to Staff Development." *Educational Leadership* 42, no. 3 (1984): 23–27.

——, and Fusco, E. "Constructivism and Education: the Child's Point of View." In *A Child's Brain*, edited by M. Frank. New York: Haworth, Press, 1984, pp. 111–132.

——; Fusco, E.; and Grennon, J. "Cognitive Levels Matching." *Educational Leadership* 40, no. 8 (1983): 4–8.

Clayton, T. *Teaching and Learning: A Psychological Perspective*. Englewood Cliffs, N.J.: Prentice-Hall, 1965.

Combs, A. "A Perceptual View of the Adequate Personality." *Perceiving, Behaving, Becoming: A New Focus for Education*. The 1962 Yearbook of the Association for Supervision and Curriculum Development. A. Combs, Chairman. Washington, D.C.: The Association for Supervision and Curriculum Development, 1962.

Cremin, L. *The Transformation of the School*. New York: Alfred A. Knopf, 1961.

Dewey, J. "The Reflex Arc Concept in Psychology." In *Psychological Review III* (1896). (The reference is to the reprint in *Readings in the History of Psychology*, edited by W. Dennis. New York: Appleton-Century-Crofts, 1948, pp. 358–359).

——. *Experience and Education*. New York: Macmillan, 1938.

Dunn, R., and Dunn, K. *Teaching Students through Their Individual Teaching Styles: A Practical Approach*. Reston, Va.: Reston, 1978.

Epstein, H. "Correlated Brain and Intelligence Development in Humans." In *Development and Evolution of Brain Size: Behavorial Implications*, edited by M. Hahn, D. Jensen, and B. Dudek. New York: Academic Press, 1979.

——. "Learning How to Learn: Matching Instructional Levels." *The Principal*, May 1981, pp. 25–30.

Gordon, I. *Human Development from Birth through Adolescence*. New York: Harper & Row, 1969.

Gregorc, A. *Gregorc Style Delineator*. Maynard, Mass.: Gabriel Systems, 1982.

Grennon, J. "Making Sense of Student Thinking." *Educational Leadership* 42, no. 3 (1984): 11–16.

Gwynn, J. M., and Chase, J. *Curriculum Principles and Social Trends*. 4th ed. New York: Macmillan, 1969.

Havigurst, R. *Developmental Tasks and Education*. New York: Longmans, Green, 1950.

Hull, C. *Essentials of Behavior*. New Haven, Conn.: Yale University Press, 1951.

Judd, C. *Psychology of Secondary Education*. New York: Ginn and Company, 1927.

Kagan, J., with C. Minton. *Infancy. Its Place in Human Development*. Cambridge, Mass.: Harvard University Press, 1980.

——. *The Nature of the Child*. New York: Basic Books, 1984.

Kelley, E. *Education for What Is Real*. New York: Harper & Row, 1947.

Kinsbourne, M., and Hiscock, M. "Cerebral Lateralization and Cognitive Development." In *Education and the Brain*, Seventy-seventh Yearbook of the National Society for the Study of Education, Part II, edited by J. Chall and A. Mirsky. Chicago: University of Chicago Press, 1978.

Krug, E. *Curriculum Planning*. Rev. ed. New York: Harper & Row, 1957.

Levine, S. "Hemispheric Specialization and Functional Plasticity during Development." In *A Child's Brain,* edited by M. Frank. New York, Haworth Press, 1984.

Levy, J. "Children Think with Whole Brains: Myth and Reality." In *Student Learning Styles and Brain Behavior,* edited by J. Keefe. Reston, Va.: National Association of Secondary School Principals, 1982.

Lewin, K. *A Dynamic Theory of Personality.* New York: McGraw-Hill, 1935.

Maslow, A. *Motivation and Personality.* New York: Harper & Row, 1954.

McDonald, F. J. "The Influence of Learning Theories on Education (1900–1950)." In *Theories of Learning and Instruction,* Sixty-third Yearbook of the National Society for the Study of Education, Part I, edited by E.R. Hilgard. Chicago: University of Chicago Press, 1964.

Murray, H. *Explorations in Personality.* New York: Oxford University Press, 1938.

Orata, P. *The Theory of Identical Elements.* Columbus: Ohio State University Press, 1928.

Piaget, J. *The Psychology of Intelligence.* Trans. by M. Piercy and D. Berlyne. Totowa, N.J.: Littlefield, Adams, 1969.

———, and Inhelder, B. *The Growth of Logical Thinking from Childhood to Adolescence.* New York: Basic Books, 1958.

Rogers, C. *Client-Centered Therapy.* Boston: Houghton Mifflin, 1951.

Schubert, W. "Knowledge about Out-of-School Curriculum." *The Educational Forum* 45 (1981): 185–198.

——— . *Curriculum: Perspective, Paradigm, and Possibility.* New York: Macmillan, 1986.

Sigel, I. "A Constructivist Perspective for Teaching Thinking." *Educational Leadership* 42, no. 3 (1984): pp. 18–21.

Skinner, B.F. *Science and Human Behavior.* New York: Macmillan, 1953.

Strahan, D. and Toepfer, C. Jr. "The Impact of Brain Research on Education: Agents of Change." *A Child's Brain* edited by M. Frank. New York: Haworth Press, 1984, pp. 219–233.

Thorndike, E. *Educational Psychology, The Psychology of Learning.* Vol. 2. New York: Teachers College, Columbia University, 1913.

Toepfer, C. Jr. *Brain Growth Periodization Research: Curricular Implications for Nursery Through Grade 12 Learning.* ERIC Document Reproduction Service No. ED. 204 835 EA 031 727, 1981.

———. "Curriculum Design and Neuropsychological Development." *The Journal of Research and Development in Education* 15, no. 3 (1982): 1–11.

Tubbs, M., and Beane, J. "Curricular Trends and Practices in High Schools: A Second Look." *High School Journal* 65 (1981): 203–208.

Watson, J. *Psychology from the Standpoint of the Behaviorist.* Philadelphia: J.B. Lippincott, 1919.

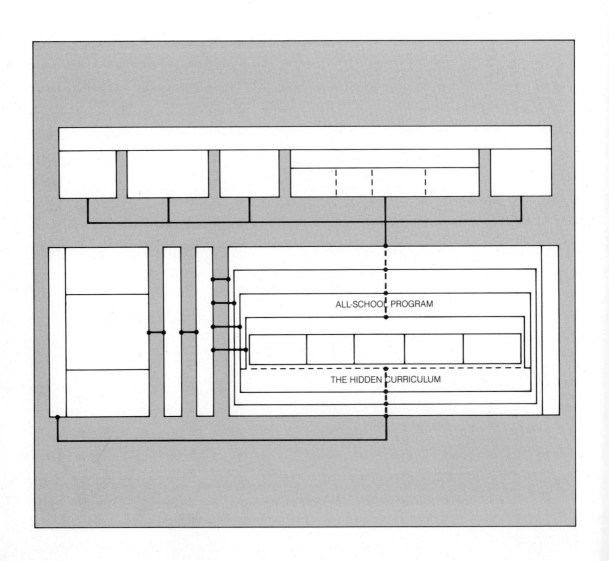

ALL-SCHOOL PROGRAM

THE HIDDEN CURRICULUM

6

Curriculum Issues in Organizing the All-School Program

The all-school program consists of all the learning opportunities offered under the auspices of the school. These may include formal and nonformal experiences in required and elective programs, general and specialized programs, and activities such as clubs and sports. Put together, these comprise all of the planned teaching–learning situations in the school. In this chapter we explore issues that address elements fundamental to organizing the program of the school. Procedures for organizing the curriculum are presented for use in a variety of circumstances by teachers and curriculum workers.

It is particularly important to note that the ideas for curriculum planning presented in Chapters 1 through 5 apply to every part of the all-school program, regardless of how it is organized. As new variations of the all-school program emerge, they are subject to the same basic principles and procedures of curriculum planning as were past and present organizations.

As a result of reading Chapter 6, you should be able to:

1. Identify critical questions related to organizing the all-school program
2. Describe patterns for defining the required portion of the all-school program
3. Identify the various types of electives that might be included in the all-school program
4. Identify ways of organizing the scope and sequence of the all-school program
5. Recognize the role of the hidden curriculum in the all-school program
6. Describe various patterns for organizing the professional staff to implement the all-school program

7. Describe patterns that may be used to group learners for various experiences within the all-school program
8. Identify methods of scheduling which support implementation of the all-school program
9. Describe various ways by which pupil personnel specialists can interact with faculty to articulate counseling and instructional services in the all-school program
10. Identify special need areas of exceptional students important in improving the all-school program
11. Identify ways to implement these issues in the all-school program in your school setting
12. Identify areas of support that library/media specialists can provide for planning school programs.

ORGANIZING THE GENERAL EDUCATION PROGRAM

■ ■   Once the many parts of the all-school program are defined, consideration must be given to identifying which learners will be involved in specific aspects of that program. At one level, this question calls for a decision about *required* versus *elective* portions of the program. As will be seen, it is more difficult to identify required than optional learning experiences.

The definition of required experiences rests on a very complex question: in light of the goals for education, what are the common needs of all learners? This single question has generated more debate in the curriculum field than any other. In fact, in the early 1980s, numerous groups and commissions issued reports calling for one or another set of requirements in the school program. These reports will be discussed in Chapter 10.

In practice, the definition of required experiences differs at various school levels. In the elementary school, requirements typically involve programs aimed at developing particular skills (such as communications and computation) as well as various subjects (such as social studies, science, art, music, and physical education). Furthermore, virtually all learners are required to participate in all programs and courses, and are required to attain specified levels of proficiency within them. For instance, major attention is usually given to the skill development areas of reading and computation. If remedial work is necessary, additional subjects may be deemphasized or completely ignored. Skills in reading and computation are thought to be required for even minimal achievement in later levels of schooling. Such a view, however, ignores the importance of knowledge and skills that may be gained in other areas. It also ignores the fact that those other areas may well offer an excellent functional context for the development and use of reading and computational skills.

Required experiences at the middle level are usually divided into two categories, academic and exploratory. The academic portion of the program includes courses in English language arts, social studies, science, and mathematics. Most often, the exploratory portion includes art, music, home economics, industrial arts, health, foreign language, and physical education. Academic courses typically involve the entire year and center on mastery of certain subject matter and skills. With the exception of physical education, exploratory courses usually last for one semester and are intended to introduce learners to the particular area so that they may determine if they have any interest or talent within it. Even though these latter experiences are exploratory, they are nonetheless required of all learners.

At the high school level, required experiences are usually limited to the same academic courses as the middle-level school (see Table 6.1). However, the requirements do vary from grade to grade, with English most often required in all years. The number and level of other required courses vary according to state and local requirements. It is important to note that high school requirements have varied little over the years, even though a number of proposals for change have been made. Although today's high schools are designed to serve a wide range of learner needs, the required portion of the program retains the characteristics of the college preparatory experience for which secondary schools were originally intended. In fact, most reports in the 1980s recommended an even greater emphasis on such courses, extending requirements to include four years of language arts, four years of social studies, three or four years of mathematics, three or four years of science, computer literacy, and mastery of a foreign language.

In sum, we can clearly see that schools have addressed the question of which aspects of the all-school program ought to be required of all learners, but the requirements center mostly on academic skills and courses. The range and number of required experiences differ at various school levels.

The idea of using academic courses and skills as the basis for required experiences is the most popular method, but by no means the only one. Other arrangements have also been proposed and, in some cases, implemented. Most prominent among these is the notion that the common needs of learners are most likely found not in academic disciplines, but in problems of living and in the emerging needs of children and youth. In Chapter 5, we discussed various curricular approaches, including subjects, broad fields, social problems, and emerging needs. Here we see that these organizing patterns may also serve as the basis for identifying the required portion of the all-school program. When the problems and needs approaches are so used, all learn-

TABLE 6.1   Percentage of High Schools Indicating a Subject or Course of Study as a Graduation Requirement in 1974 and 1979

Subject/Course of Study	1974	1979	% Change
English/Language Arts	99.1	100.0	+0.9
Social Studies	97.4	100.0	+2.6
Mathematics	92.6	96.9	+4.3
Physical Education	92.6	90.8	−1.7
Science	91.8	97.8	+6.0
Driver Education	23.7	18.6	−5.1
Economics	17.2	22.1	+4.9
Foreign Language	8.6	0.9	−6.7
Home Economics	8.2	5.6	−2.6
Reading	7.7	7.4	−0.3
Industrial Arts	6.0	4.3	−1.7
Business Education	4.7	3.5	−1.2
Vocational Education	4.7	3.5	−1.2
Environmental Studies	2.5	3.5	+1.0

ers are engaged in courses or units that reflect compelling personal and social topics. At any given level these may include such themes as getting along with others, living in the community, understanding the environment, exploring technology, understanding personal development, and so on. Skills such as those related to communications and computation are still emphasized, but the content or subject matter of required learnings shifts from academic disciplines to concepts more similar to Florence Stratemeyer's persistent life situations (see Chapter 7) or Robert Havighurst's developmental tasks (see Chapter 3).

The required portion of the all-school program has been identified by many terms over the years, including general education, basic education, common learnings, and core curriculum. Each of these was developed as a response to the persistent curriculum question, "What knowledge is of most worth?" Among these various program titles, perhaps none has given rise to more confusion than the so-called "core" curriculum. Originally intended to describe block-time programs centered on a problems or needs approach, "core" has also been used as a label for required subject areas. Harold and Elsie Alberty (1962) developed a classification for core programs that is also useful for describing the many variations in required learning experiences (see Frame 6.1). They further pointed out that "there is considerable evidence to support the conclusion that Core Types Three and Four (problem- and need-centered) have many advantages over Core Types One and Two (subject-centered), especially in the areas of attitudes and values" (p. 230).

The identification of the required portion of the all-school program is a crucial issue in curriculum planning. Whatever is chosen to be included will presumably be required of all students regardless of their

Types of Core Programs

Adapted from Alberty and Alberty, 1962

Type-One Core:	Based upon separate subjects taught as separate courses by one or more teachers.
Type-Two Core:	Based upon correlation to two or more subjects in an attempt to show relationships between them. The subjects are taught separately, but teachers plan together and point out correlations to students. For example, the American history and American literature teachers may correlate subject matter under the general heading of American studies.
Type-Three Core:	Based upon the fusion of two or more subjects. For example, a unit on colonial living may include learnings from a number of academic and exploratory courses such as language arts, social studies, science, math, home economics, industrial arts, and others.
Type-Four Core:	Based upon common problems, needs, and interests of learners within a framework of problem areas. This type breaks from subject-related studies in considering units such as school living, self-understanding, world peace, and finding values by which we live.
Type-Five Core:	Based on teacher–student planned activities without references to any formal structure. Units follow the interests of teachers and learners without preplanned topics or themes.

characteristics. There should be no room in general education for anything less than that which is genuinely important for all students to learn. Thus, in making decisions regarding general education, those responsible for curriculum policy must reflect upon the foundation areas discussed in Chapter 3. In doing so, they must ask such questions as:

- What experiences will most likely help learners to develop knowledge, skills, attitudes, and behaviors that would enhance the quality of their lives?
- What experiences will most likely help learners deal with the compelling issues in contemporary and future society?
- What experiences will most likely help learners to be able to meet their basic human needs?

By answering these kinds of questions, the general education program may truly be worth the time and effort of all learners.

ORGANIZING THE ELECTIVE PROGRAM

■ ■   If the required portion of the program is intended for the common needs of all learners, then the elective portion is designed to meet needs or interests that are shared by some, but not all, learners. As we have seen, the proportion of the all-school program that is required varies from one school level to another. Elementary education is basically a general education experience. Therefore, few elective programs are offered at that level. Middle level and high schools place increasing emphasis on specialization. Thus, the proportion of elective courses increases.

Electives may include a wide variety of activities in which learners can participate. Basically, these may be divided into four types.

■   General Education Extensions (Type-One)

Type-one electives are based upon the organization of the general education program. If the required portion of the program consists of certain general academic courses, the elective portion may include related advanced courses in those same areas. For example, all learners may be required to participate in general mathematics courses, while some may continue this work in probability, calculus, and so on. On the other hand, if the required portion of the program consists of courses or units based upon a problems or needs approach, the elective portion may include both basic and advanced academic or subject-centered courses.

■   Career Related (Type-Two)

Whether required experiences are centered on subjects or problems and needs, electives may be offered that are related to various vocations or occupations. These may include business or secretarial courses, trade and industrial preparation, and the like. Such electives may be offered by the home school or by a vocational education center serving several school districts. For example, in New York State many school districts offer occupational electives through a county-level Board of Cooperative Educational Services. Such arrangements are particularly helpful to small schools that could otherwise not afford this part of a comprehensive all-school program.

■   Advanced Exploratory (Type-Three)

Where required exploratory courses are offered as basic introductory experiences in some area, electives may be offered to learners with special interest or talent. For example, advanced work in art or music may be chosen by some learners as an extension of the general program in those areas. This type of elective is often offered at all levels of schooling, including elementary, and may include both group and individual instruction.

■ Activities (Type-Four)

Most schools offer a variety of activities beyond courses or classroom studies from which learners may choose on the basis of interest. These types of electives usually fall into two categories. The first includes organized activities that are subject-related. Examples of this category are foreign language clubs, yearbook, debate, band, orchestra, chorus, and intramural or interscholastic sports. The second category includes various service-oriented or social clubs. Like type-three electives, these are frequently offered at all three levels of schooling.

It is worth noting here that elective type four is often termed an extra-curricular or co-curricular program. However, we believe that these types of experiences play an integral part in the all-school program and involve important learnings. Some educators may view these activities as peripheral to the academic program, but for learners they represent an integral part of the comprehensive school experience. In fact, for some students, what they learn in electives may be more important than what they gain from required experiences. For example, attitudes and skills learned in service-oriented clubs may be more powerful in life than some remote piece of subject matter. Terms like "extra-curricular" and "co-curricular" simply do not do justice to the place of these elective activities in the all-school program.

Electives of all types serve the specialized needs and interests of learners beyond the common needs addressed in required experiences. Since important learnings are involved, electives deserve as much thought and planning as required courses.

Thus far in Chapter 6 we have discussed two aspects of the all-school program: required experiences, including both academic and exploratory, and types of electives. While each aspect may be individually identified and described, an effective program offers opportunities for integrating them in a comprehensive, balanced experience for learners. Figure 6.1 illustrates several ways in which the various aspects may interface with one another. The four areas of intersection in the figure can be explained in the following manner.

INTERSECTION A   Academic and exploratory experiences may interface through cooperative curriculum planning by teachers. For example, as learners undertake projects in academic courses, they may use skills developed in such programs as art, music, or industrial arts. Learning

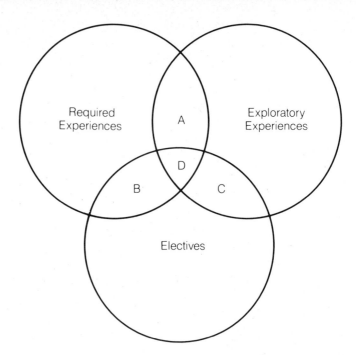

**FIGURE 6.1
Possibilities for
Integrating
Aspects of the All-
School Program**

about child development in home economics may be supplemented by the study of how perceptions and roles of children have varied throughout history. These kinds of interdisciplinary efforts are especially promoted when the use of the broad-fields and problems curricular approaches are purposely developed through careful curriculum planning.

INTERSECTION B   When the required portion of the program is developed around introductory academic courses, it may be extended through advanced courses (type-one electives). If the required portion consists of experiences related to a problems or needs approach, academic or subject-centered courses may be offered on an elective basis (again, type-one electives). In either case, various clubs or activities may be developed related to courses using a subject or problems approach. These may include, for example, language clubs, newspaper clubs, science clubs, and others (type-four electives).

INTERSECTION C   When exploratory courses consist of introductory experiences in art, music, physical education, home economics, industrial arts, and so on, electives may offer opportunities to extend them through more specialized learning activities. These may include courses directed toward vocational or occupational education, or activities such as sports, music groups, play productions, and others.

INTERSECTION D   This section of the figure represents the integration of all aspects of the program. Rather than considering intersection D within any particular course or activity, we prefer to think of it in terms of the learner's own experience. In other words, this section is developed by the individual learner as he or she integrates the various aspects of the all-school program into a unified whole that represents a personally meaningful educational experience. Where relationships between various courses, programs, units, and activities are planned and pointed out, the chances for meaningful synthesis by the learner are greatly enhanced.

ORGANIZING SCOPE AND SEQUENCE

In Chapters 4 and 5, we discussed possibilities for broad goals upon which curriculum plans may be based, and we discussed some of the decision screens that may influence those plans. With these in mind, we now turn to how the program of the school may be organized in terms of sequence (the order or flow of learning experiences) and scope (the depth and breadth at each level of experience). With these considerations, several decisions and issues enter into curriculum planning.

One decision involves program organization in various units in the school system. For example, when we review the general objectives for the elementary, middle level, or high school, what do they suggest about the program for that level? The answer to this question focuses on defining specific knowledges, skills, behaviors, and attitudes that will be addressed through the school program of learning opportunities. In defining these, attention must also be given to how the implied learning experiences will be organized. Several alternatives might be considered. One possibility involves developing a sequence of objectives or skills through which learners will move while in the school. In the area of mathematics, for instance, one might indicate that the sequence starts with recognizing numbers and proceeds through simple arithmetic computations (like adding and subtracting) to more complex operations using fractions and decimals. Once such a sequence is identified, specific plans may be developed for addressing each part.

A second alternative follows a model known as the "spiral curriculum." In this case a particular concept or skill is addressed repeatedly, but at each succeeding level it is given broader or deeper treatment depending upon increasing skill, maturity, and readiness of learners. As Figure 6.2 illustrates, a given issue like the view of "family" may appear at each stage in the growth process, but because of new insights and maturity, it takes on new meaning.

A third alternative involves a rotating schedule of courses or units

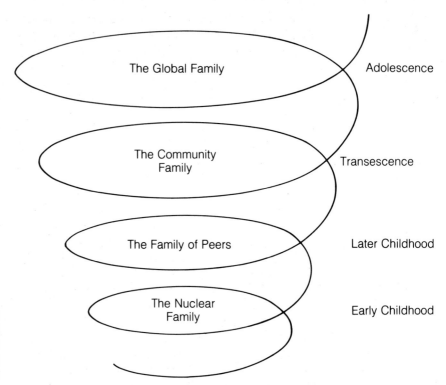

The Global Family — Adolescence

The Community Family — Transescence

The Family of Peers — Later Childhood

The Nuclear Family — Early Childhood

**FIGURE 6.2
A Spiral
Curriculum Based
upon Broadening
Concepts of Family**

that might be offered most appropriately at the high school level. For example, the social studies area may be organized around three broad concepts such as "Problems of Democracy," "American Studies," and "Global Issues." In any given year only one would be offered, and all learners would participate within it. In this way all learners would be exposed to all three concepts during the grade 10 through 12 sequence. This arrangement assumes that the concepts or skills to be learned are not sequential, and thus the order in which they are addressed is not important. In addition, it implies that learners who would otherwise be assigned to particular grade levels would now be mixed together in social studies courses.

In the case of the rotated course offerings, another type of decision is also implied. As noted, the rotating model mixes together learners of different ages in a *multigrade* pattern. Another version of this pattern, *continuous progress,* may be used where skills or concepts are developed on a sequential basis. Here learners begin with the first level of the sequence and proceed through the remaining parts at their own paces. This organization abandons the traditional grade-level structure of schools since one no longer need be concerned with getting students through particular skills or concepts in a given year. Instead, learners may proceed through the sequence as rapidly or slowly as they can. Both of these cases represent departures from the usual grade-level pattern. However, age-grade organization is still the most popular alternative used in schools. In this case, the sequence or spiral of skills and concepts is divided among the various grade levels in the school. Thus, in each grade, teachers and learners are expected to cover their allotted portion in such a way that learners are prepared for the next grade. The persistent question of whether to promote or retain particular learners at the end of any given year is evidence that such expectations are not always realistic for all learners. Some schools have chosen to combine continuous progress and grade level patterns. For example, reading and mathematics may be organized on the basis of the former, while others use the latter pattern.

Beyond decisions about sequencing and apportioning of learning experiences, there remain considerations regarding how the *scope* or horizontal aspects of the program will be organized. Whatever the sequence pattern, teachers and learners will eventually come together in some type of situation to pursue particular skills or concepts. Once again, several alternatives are possible. For example, intended learnings may be organized into courses of various lengths, grade-level arrangements taught by one or more teachers, required or elective experiences, and many other patterns. In Chapter 7 we will discuss these more fully. For the time being, however, it should be noted that eventually even these arrangements are typically divided again into *units of instruction* or *learning*. It is this unit phase that will serve as the major focus of the next chapter.

A *unit* is defined as a learning experience of moderate length (e.g., three to five weeks), organized around some theme, topic, problem, or issue, that focuses on several learning objectives. In this sense it is more specific than a long-term learning experience such as a course or grade level, but more general than a daily or weekly lesson plan that focuses on one or a few specific objectives. One way of viewing the unit is that combined with other units it makes up the long-term experience and, in turn, includes the shorter-term daily or weekly plans. In other words, it divides the year- or semester-length organization into manageable parts, and it provides unity and context for daily plans.

THE HIDDEN CURRICULUM

■ ■ One of the most important contributions to curriculum thinking in the last few decades has been clarification of what is known as the hidden curriculum. From a theoretical viewpoint, we may talk about the planned curriculum, which is the object of intentional and formal curriculum planning procedures, and the hidden curriculum, which is not ordinarily addressed through regular curriculum planning but which nevertheless influences what and how students learn.

The source of the hidden curriculum is found in the fact that the school is an institution concerned with the socialization of the young. For this purpose, it has rules and regulations that govern social conduct, organizational features that allow it to "manage" students within the context of the educational program, and a system of procedures that make it an acceptable institution in the larger society. This collection of institutional features communicates to learners a set of social values. What is learned from the subtle or hidden curriculum is frequently more powerful and lasting than that which is learned from the more obvious, planned curriculum.

For young people, school is a place in which they carry on a large portion of their lives. The way in which they do so is partly determined by their own social customs, but more largely influenced by the rules and regulations of the institution. Most schools have a comprehensive set of rules and regulations for behavior, and penalties for their violation. Rules indicate when students arrive and leave, when they may move around, when they may talk, when to use lavatories, how to move from one place to another, how to resolve conflict, when they may eat, how to behave toward adults, and more. Hardly any aspect of life in school is unregulated. Certainly the school has a custodial function, but many observers wonder what it is that students really learn from all of this. Philip Jackson (1969) suggested that:

> As he learns to live in school our student learns to subjugate his own desires to the will of the teacher and to subdue his own actions in the interest of the common good. He learns to be passive and to acquiesce to the network of rules, regulations and routines in which he is embedded. He learns to tolerate petty frustrations and accept plans and policies of higher authorities even when their rationale is unexplained and their meaning unclear. (p. 36)

The way in which students are governed is manifested in what Donald Willower, Terry Eidell, and Wayne Hoy (1967) describe as pupil control ideology—the perception of adults about how students should be treated. They described two types of school climate or environment. The first, *custodial,* places a premium on the maintenance of order, autocratic procedures, student stereotyping, punitive sanctions, and obedience. The second, *humanistic climate,* emphasizes democratic procedures, a high degree of interaction, personalness, individual dignity, self-discipline, flexibility, and participatory decision making. Not surprising is the fact that research indicates that students learn to behave according to the type of school climate they experience, and that they feel more self-actualized in the humanistic climate (Deibert and Hoy, 1977).

Besides learning social values from the educational structure of the school, students may learn about themselves and others. Two examples are noteworthy in this aspect of the hidden curriculum. The first is the system of grouping learners for instruction. Very often students are arranged according to ability or general achievement in groups with labels such as "advanced," "average," "slow," or "remedial." Unfortunately, educators frequently have biases that lead them to stereotype learners in each group. Whether individuals fit the description or not, they may be viewed as "fun, sharp, independent, interesting, and witty" at the one extreme, and "dull, boring, indifferent, careless, and malcontent" at the other. Often, students gradually tend to accept these expectations, and they may even change their self-concepts and behavior to fit them. In some cases, this kind of grouping is extended into a tracking system that involves keeping students of a particular ability or achievement level together for all courses or subjects, regardless of whether they are equally capable in each. Because these groups remain constant across the school day, they become de facto definitions of status and social mix (Rosenbaum, 1976). Thus, learners may be led to believe whom they ought to associate with and where they stand in the social order.

A second example of the educational structure as hidden curriculum might be found in the grading or marking system of the school. Despite research supporting cooperative work, students are usually made to compete for academic rewards (Slavin, 1980). For instance, the traditional "grading curve" suggests that some will succeed and others fail, regardless of effort. Sometimes those students placed in "slower" groups are limited to lower grades so that their work is not confused with that of advanced groups. Contests for class rank often pit one student against another in heated battles to maintain averages to the hundredth or thousandth decimal place. (Mathematicians are well aware that it is not possible to gain any more significance, in the statistical sense, than was in the original data. Most class ranking procedures are therefore totally invalid.) Such procedures clearly suggest that competition for rewards and awards is more important than what is to be learned. In a stinging analysis of higher education, Bensen Snyder (1973) concluded that competition is probably the most powerful learning in professional schools.

Another aspect of the hidden curriculum is the way in which the school portrays itself to the general society so as to maintain its acceptance. As J. Galen Saylor and William Alexander (1974) point out:

> We all know too well the images created by Ichabod Crane, "Our Miss Brooks," "Goodbye, Mr Chips," and "Mr. Peepers," and many more caricatures of school masters and teachers, and the images of the school portrayed by sports writers, television shows, movies, novels and all forms of communications. The impact of such images on the attitudes of students and parents toward teachers and the school is a significant factor in the effectiveness of the school. (pp. 272–273)

More recently, the school as an institution and educators as individuals have been portrayed in rock music videos (and even some movies) as objects of scorn and ridicule. From these images, students may bring to school perceptions and expectations that devalue its role and, ultimately, the larger concept of education. How the school is organized and how educators behave may either reinforce this view or dispel it. Since these sources of information are highly valued by some students, their outright rejection by educators is not an effective means for offsetting them. Only consistent behavior in other directions can convince students and others that our profession is worthy of respect. Furthermore, the extent to which negative images may be true in some schools ought to be a major concern of educators.

Finally, the planned curriculum itself may have unintended meanings that are a part of the hidden curriculum. For example, one of the compelling issues of our time is that of peace in a world threatened by war. Certainly the vast majority of educators would gladly go on record as favoring peace over war as a means of resolving conflict. However, the hidden curriculum in many schools seems to suggest otherwise to learners. For instance, history lessons often focus on wars and glorify those who are heroes of battle rather than those who are peacemakers. Furthermore, in cases of conflict between individuals and the school, the latter most often wins by virtue of its institutional power rather than its rational logic. Our sports programs frequently emphasize power, winning at all costs, and sometimes humiliation of opponents. Under these conditions, how can we claim to be promoting peace? What can we really say that our students are learning about conflict resolution? How will they think when presented with the issue of differences among nations of the world?

The hidden curriculum is just as much a part of the school program as any course or subject or unit that is offered. It is a powerful and pervasive source of learning. For this reason it should be subject to the same policies and procedures for curriculum planning as any other part of the program. In the cases of school governance, school climate, extracurricular programs, management procedures, and so on, educators ought to consider the same questions as they do in planning other aspects of the curriculum.

- What do we want students to learn?
- What are they currently learning from the hidden curriculum?
- How should sources of the hidden curriculum be structured to promote desired learning?

PATTERNS OF STAFF ORGANIZATION

■ ■ Implementing the all-school program requires a variety of skills and knowledges on the part of teachers. Needed skills include those related to working with large groups, small groups, and individuals to accomplish a wide range of cognitive, affective, and psychomotor objectives. In addition, teachers must have knowledge of the many concepts and understandings that learners are to acquire. Such skills and knowledges are usually present within the combined expertise of an entire faculty. In many cases, they may be possessed by a smaller group within the faculty, or even by individual teachers. In view of these possibilities, alternative patterns for staff organization may be considered.

■ The Self-Contained Classroom

Where a single teacher possesses the required knowledge and skill to work with a group of learners, it is possible to organize learning groups in self-contained classrooms. In this case an individual teacher spends all or most of the day with a single group of learners. Within the day, the curriculum may be organized around units involving specific skill development, various subjects, or problems and needs of youth.

The self-contained classroom is most often found at the elementary level, where teachers are presumed to have adequate knowledge to work with learners in a variety of areas. Where special skills are called for, exceptions to the self-contained pattern are frequently made by having separate teachers in art, music, and physical education provide the instruction. If the self-contained classrooms are heterogeneously grouped, teachers may also exchange particular learners for short periods in which achievement groups are constructed for reading instruction.

While self-contained classrooms are most often found at the elementary level, they are sometimes used in middle-level and even high schools. In these cases, a group of learners may spend two or more periods working with a single teacher in some type of core program. For example, language arts and social studies may be combined in a two-period block of time with the curriculum organized around units that correlate the two areas. The core teacher may also act as a homeroom or guidance teacher for the small group by including units related to the problems and needs of the learners. Block-time core arrangements are frequently used at the middle level to provide a transition from the self-contained elementary school to the fully departmentalized high school. Additionally, a self-contained classroom may be desirable when the need for a particular skill overrides the desire for a broader variety of backgrounds. Such a case may include special education, where the teacher's expertise in dealing with an extreme handicap or learning disability provides the primary rationale for a self-contained situation.

Proponents of the self-contained classroom suggest that it offers several advantages over the departmentalized or separate teacher pattern. Chief among these is the idea that in the larger time block, teachers may get to know learners better and thus be more sensitive to their needs, problems, interests, and characteristics. Amounts of time allotted for various tasks may be on a flexible basis as the need arises. Learners may also gain a greater sense of security and belonging as members of a small group working with an individual teacher.

Critics of the self-contained classroom argue that a single teacher cannot be expected to have the range of skill and knowledge required to teach a variety of subjects. Thus they believe that learner achievement is enhanced if teaching is done by specialists. However, research comparing learner achievement in self-contained and departmentalized settings at the elementary level suggests that the learners in the self-contained arrangement typically do just as well or better on academic measures, and consistently better on affective measures. Furthermore, research on block-time core programs at the middle and high school level generally indicates the same pattern of results.

■ **Team Arrangements**

A second pattern of staff organization is the arrangement of teachers into teams. In this case it is presumed that while a single teacher might not possess a desired range of knowledge and skill, a small group of teachers would. A teaching team may be defined as two or more teachers who plan and implement instructional programs together. Team arrangements tend to be of two types, subject teams and interdisciplinary teams.

During the 1960s, many educators recognized that effective instruction required the use of large-group, small-group, and independent work. Furthermore, it was held that single teachers were unlikely to have equalized skill at working with all three group sizes. As a result, individual departments, particularly at the high school level, organized teaching teams within various subjects. For example, learning experiences in chemistry might involve large-group lectures about important concepts, small-group seminars to discuss the concepts, and individual laboratory work. In this case, the team might involve five teachers, with one delivering the lectures, two working with seminar groups, and two supervising laboratory work. Teaching assignments were made on the basis of skill in carrying out each type of teaching. In addition, this type of team arrangement often involved two kinds of organizational structures. Vertical and hierarchical teams were arranged in such a way that one teacher was designated as master teacher (usually the lecturer), while the others were termed associate or assistant teachers. The master teacher then supervised the planning and teaching of the others. In horizontal team arrangements, all teachers had equal status, and teaching assignments were made simply on the basis of skill, or on a rotating basis. In general, those teachers who were willing to try team teaching also preferred the horizontal model since they believed that skill at working with one group size did not necessarily suggest superiority at teaching in general. Furthermore, they perceived that such arrangements promoted competition rather than cooperation among team members. Similar objections were heard to proposals in the early 1980s to designate master teachers and institute differentiated teacher pay based upon merit. Whatever the reason, subject teams declined in popularity. In 1974, 8 percent of high schools reported their use, while only 5 percent did so in 1979 (Tubbs and Beane, 1981).

Interdisciplinary teams involve representatives of two or more subject areas in a team-teaching arrangement. While this plan can be traced as far back as the high schools involved in the Eight Year study in the 1930s, its most common use today can be found in middle level schools where teachers from language arts, social studies, science, and mathematics work together with a common group of learners. In theory these teams are provided with a large block of instructional time that may be used with flexibility, as well as adequate team planning time. The team is expected to use various methods to correlate their subject areas, such as those suggested by Alberty and Alberty earlier in this chapter. Furthermore, they have the advantage of using various group sizes and grouping patterns for instructional purposes. Clearly, interdisciplinary team arrangements offer numerous possibilities for developing variety in curriculum and instruction. However, this kind of staff organization has suffered from three problems.

First, many teams have been hindered by lack of cooperation due to poor group dynamics within the team. Second, they have been plagued by limited vision or definition of the purposes of interdisciplinary teaming. The previously mentioned combination of four academic teachers has become the rule rather than a variation. Third, teachers frequently simply teach their subject areas, failing to take advantage of opportunities for correlation.

Actually, an interdisciplinary team may consist of as few as two teachers representing different subject areas, or as many teachers as desired to implement a unit—including exploratory teachers (see Frame 6.2). The team may use all four curricular approaches in developing units. Individual members may contribute as much or as little time or content to a unit as is appropriate. Two or more teachers may work together on an interdisciplinary unit while others simultaneously teach their separate subjects. In short, interdisciplinary team teaching offers teachers the chance to use a wide variety of curricular and instructional approaches.

Beyond the obvious curriculum possibilities, team teaching also offers the advantage of professional cooperation. One of the frustrating working conditions for many teachers is their isolation from colleagues. Team teaching provides a framework in which professional interaction may take place about curriculum planning, teaching, grouping, scheduling, and other issues in curriculum implementation. Such interaction promotes the idea of professionalism through important decision-making and provides for professional growth through exchange of ideas.

FRAME 6.2

Contributions of Various Subjects to an Interdisciplinary Unit on Colonial Living

Subject	Possible Contributions
Social Studies	Governmental Structures, Geography, History, Social Issues
Language Arts	Language Patterns, Communications, Literature
Science	Superstitions, Medicines, Scientific Inventions and Beliefs
Mathematics	Currency, Weights and Measures
Physical Education	Games, Leisure Activities
Home Economics	Family Structure, Clothing, Foods, Personal Values
Industrial Arts	Housing, Tools, Trades, Agriculture
Art	Period Art, Dyes, Architecture
Music	Songs, Dance, Music as Storytelling
Community Resources	Candlemaking, Sheep Shearing, Quilting Bees, etc.

■ **Departmentalized Arrangements**

The most common pattern of staff organization in secondary school is the departmentalized approach. Individual specialists are considered necessary to offer instruction in the variety of subject areas associated with departmentalization. The argument certainly seems appropriate if it is also accepted that the curriculum ought to be organized around separate subjects.

However, from a curriculum planning perspective, departmentalization has several disadvantages. Chief among these is that it hinders the possibility for correlation of subject areas as well as the use of the problems and needs approaches. Teachers usually see a large number of students in a series of class periods with little chance to get to know individuals. Learners are usually grouped in tracks and do not have the opportunity to interact with peers who are working at different levels in various subjects.

Despite these disadvantages, departmentalized patterns prevail almost universally in high schools and in the majority of middle level schools. In recent years, many elementary schools have also adopted departmentalization in the upper grades. Given the current emphasis on academic specialization, it is likely that this arrangement will retain its popularity in the foreseeable future.

GROUPING OF LEARNERS

■ ■ It has been said that the ideal school would be a log with a teacher at one end and a student at the other. However, since there are far more learners than teachers, totally individual instruction is simply not possible. It also might not be desirable.

Learners must be grouped in different ways for the various parts of the all-school program. The decision about how to group learners is a complex and important one. In theory, the decision follows from the nature of objectives and activities to be accomplished; that is, grouping decisions depend upon which learners are expected to deal with particular aspects of the program. As we shall see, this is not always the case in practice.

Grouping patterns tend to fall into two major schemes—heterogeneous and homogeneous. *Heterogeneous grouping* brings together groups of learners on a random basis, without regard for particular characteristics. *Homogeneous grouping* organizes groups on the basis of some characteristic that the learners supposedly have in common. We will now examine each of these grouping patterns and the circumstances under which they might be used.

■ **Heterogeneous Grouping**

There are several circumstances under which teachers may prefer working with a heterogeneous group. Among the many purposes of the schools is the promotion of democratic attitudes and skills. These are perhaps best pursued in settings that reflect the broad range of human diversity that characterizes a democracy. Thus where social issues or problems are explored, a group composed of learners with a variety of backgrounds, interests, attitudes, and other characteristics might be constructed. Such a group may be developed by randomly assigning learners or by purposefully selecting a diverse group of individuals. Interaction among group members would be like that which occurs in democratic problem-solving groups in the society at large.

In other cases, teachers may wish to take advantage of certain kinds of instructional techniques that require a heterogeneous group. For example, they may want to construct team learning or peer tutoring arrangements in which learners teach each other. These methods are highly successful in enhancing both academic and affective outcomes. If the group is composed of learners at similar achievement levels, the opportunities for peer teaching would be less obvious. Hence, a heterogeneous group is more appropriate.

In situations where a group is going to develop a project, heterogeneity might also be preferred. If learners plan to construct something, do a dramatic production, or develop a display, a number of skills or talents might be required. In this case, the teachers might purposefully assign learners who individually possess the variety of skills and talents required to carry out the project.

It is clear from these examples that heterogeneous grouping has an appropriate and desirable place in the all-school program. Of special importance is the idea that heterogeneous groups bring together learners of widely diverse backgrounds who might not have opportunities to work together in some more limited homogeneous arrangements. If the goals of democratic interaction and human relations are ever to be fully realized heterogeneous grouping will be a critical requirement. For this reason alone, its use in the all-school program is a curriculum imperative.

■ **Homogeneous Grouping**

In many situations, curriculum objectives and activities are designed for learners with particular characteristics or needs. In these cases, it is appropriate to construct groups composed of individuals who possess the pertinent characteristics. Such homogeneous groups may be of several types, depending upon curriculum variables.

1. In many cases, objectives in a particular skill area cover a wide range from simple to complex. For example, a mathematics course may involve a sequence of twenty or thirty objectives. In situations like this, learners may be grouped on the basis of which objectives they have already accomplished. Past achievement may place some nearer the beginning of the sequence, some in the middle, and others near the end. It would be inappropriate to approach all these learners simultaneously. Thus, three or more groups might be constructed on the basis of *achievement*. Grouping on the basis of achievement is also used in the case of advanced courses that follow general, required experiences and that call for high levels of previous achievement. By the same token, remedial courses are generally grouped on the basis of a lack of minimal achievement in general courses.

2. As noted earlier in this chapter, required exploratory courses are intended to introduce learners to various areas. These courses may well be grouped heterogeneously. However, advanced exploratory courses that require *special talent or skill* may be grouped on the basis of those variables. For example while all learners may participate in general music, those with special talent and skill may also choose to participate in band and choral groups.

3. Many teachers provide a variety of objectives, activities, and resources within units of instruction. Learners are then given the opportunity to form groups on the basis of *interest*. Needless to say, interest-centered grouping is also used in forming groups in many elective courses and activities.

4. Many units in physical education and health require that learners have reached certain levels of physical maturity. Those who have not would lack physical skill or need for the units. In these cases, groups may be formed on the basis of *physical development or maturity*.

5. Certain units in social studies and health call for characteristics associated with *social maturity*. For example, children who are concerned only with their immediate environment are not likely to take an interest as adolescents would in global interdependence. In like manner, young children who tend to be largely ego-centered would probably lack the social maturity of transescents who might be concerned with peer group interactions.

6. In adolescence, *life plans* become a basis for selecting various elective portions of the all-school program. Such plans may include those related to higher education, careers, or general

interests. Thus, the life plans of learners themselves may be a basis for constructing some groups. It should be noted that life plans rarely become clear until at least adolescence, and therefore their use in grouping at earlier levels is inappropriate.

7. The *learning styles* area deals with components of one's preferred and most effective styles and ways of learning. Research shows that a range of factors influence an individual's learning preferences and her or his ability to learn more effectively. These preferences include the following: greater ability in either randomly or sequentially organizing information and/or activities; greater ability in either linear or holistic ways of dealing with information; abstract or concrete thinking abilities; particular environmental circumstances (e.g., noise levels, temperature levels, time of day, intensity of light); and, working in individual or small-group settings. As schools plan and organize long- and short-term homogeneous grouping arrangements, teachers will find that information pertaining to the learning styles area will become more specifically helpful.

From these examples, it is clear that homogeneous grouping has an appropriate place in the all-school program. Variables used in constructing groups may include achievement, special talent or skill, interest, physical development, social maturity, life plans, and learning styles. There is one other variable used in grouping that needs to be mentioned here, namely, ability. Ability grouping on the basis of intelligence or IQ has been a widespread practice in schools. In some cases it has been extended into tracking systems in which groups of learners are assigned to all aspects of the school program on the basis of intelligence. In this arrangement, high-ability, average-ability, and low-ability learners are put in groups for virtually all of their studies. Ability groups and tracking have been the subject of a good deal of research, and evidence indicates that their use is largely inappropriate. Perhaps this point is summarized best by Dominick Esposito (1973), who condensed the findings of Warren Findley and Miriam Bryan (1971). Their findings were as follows:

1. Homogeneous ability grouping as currently practiced shows no consistent positive value for helping students generally, or particular groups of students, to achieve more scholastically or to experience more effective learning conditions. Among the studies showing significant effects, the slight gains favoring high ability students is more than offset by evidence of unfavorable effects on the learning of students of average and below average ability, particularly the latter.

2. The findings regarding the impact on homogeneous ability grouping on affective development are essentially unfavorable. Whatever the practice does to build or inflate the esteem of children in the

high ability groups is counterbalanced by evidence of unfavorable effects of stigmatizing those placed in average and below average ability groups as inferior and incapable of learning.

3. Homogeneous ability grouping, by design, is a separative educational policy, ostensibly according to students' test performance ability, but practically, according to students' socio-economic status and, to a lesser but observable degree, according to students' ethnic status.

4. In cases where homogeneous or heterogeneous ability grouping is related to improved scholastic performance, the curriculum is subject to substantial modification of teaching methods, materials, and other variables which are intrinsic to the teaching–learning process, and which, therefore, may well be the causative factors related to academic development wholly apart from ability grouping per se. Similarly, with respect to social development, there is evidence which points to variables other than ability grouping which tend to relate substantially to children's personal growth or lack of growth.

In other words, homogeneous grouping by ability does not improve academic achievement. Furthermore, tracking acts as a method of defining friends and social status in the school. Mobility between tracks, although possible, is unlikely. Once in an ability track, learners tend to remain there no matter what their achievement. Ability grouping also reinforces unfair teacher biases such as "Bright students are independent, but slow students cannot work alone." These biases become a part of teachers' expectations, which in turn may affect learners' achievements and self-concepts in negative ways. Again, research evidence does *not* support the belief by some educators that academic and affective growth are enhanced by ability grouping.

Decisions about the grouping of learners are obviously complex and difficult. However, the effectiveness of instruction partly depends upon the matching of appropriate learners with various curriculum objectives and activities. The number of alternative grouping patterns available is larger than those usually found in schools. Effective curriculum planning requires that all the possibilities discussed here be considered and used in implementing the all-school program.

TIME AND SCHEDULES

■ ■ The amount of time needed and available to implement curriculum plans is a crucial issue in their development. In general, the variable of time may be considered in two ways: first, in terms of the overall time needed, and second, in terms of daily or weekly needs.

The overall time needed to carry out curriculum plans may be either fixed or variable, depending upon other arrangements in the school. In most secondary schools, courses are offered for a semester or for a whole year. In some cases, mini-course or electives may be scheduled for shorter periods, such as six to ten weeks. Teachers know ahead of time how long the particular course will be offered and may plan accordingly. Full-year or full-semester courses may be broken up into a series of units, whereas mini-courses may involve only a single unit. In self-contained classrooms, typically found at the elementary level and in some flexibly scheduled secondary schools, teachers may choose to offer units of varying length. A given unit may last several weeks, depending upon what is needed and how much time is allotted daily to the particular topic. Perhaps the biggest problem related to overall available time is that teachers feel they are required to cover too many topics or units during a particular semester or year. An often-heard lament is, "I wish more time could be devoted to this unit, but there's too much to cover in my syllabus." Given the fact that the length of the school year is fixed, teachers do need to make decisions about how much overall time will be allotted for each topic. Differentiating between activities that are necessary and activities that are optional or less important is a key task for all teachers.

Since the needs of day-to-day life in the school are more immediate than long-term issues, teachers and learners are typically more concerned with time as a short-term problem. They are faced with concrete blocks of time in which to carry out specific activities, use particular resources, and so on. Most secondary and some elementary school schedules are arranged to allot specific time periods each day for each subject. The most common form of this arrangement is known as Carnegie scheduling.

In 1909, the Carnegie Foundation identified particular subjects that ought to be taught in the school and proposed a standard unit for measurement of high school credits. It soon became the standard quantitative measure used by colleges in their admission policies and was thereby imposed on high schools. A Carnegie unit was earned for completing a minimum of 120 hours in a subject during the school year, and sixteen units became required for high school graduation. As a result, the school day was divided into seven, eight, or nine periods of forty to fifty minutes each. Ellsworth Tompkins and Walter Gaumlitz (1954) noted that the Carnegie Unit caused schools to measure education in terms of time served, and to consider different subjects to be of the same worth if they met common time restrictions.

This scheduling persists today even though many teachers are frustrated with its limitations. Various activities require different lengths of time, and they lose their effectiveness if the available time is not sufficient. For example, if class periods are forty minutes in length, then a one-hour movie must be shown over two days. In another case, a group discussion might be just gaining momentum when the class period ends. Such activities tend to lose energy if interrupted.

Thus, the schedule interferes with effective learning; the "teachable moment" may be lost. Many teachers feel that curriculum planning is limited when the activities they design must be limited to the length of Carnegie-scheduled periods. In an attempt to overcome this problem, several scheduling variations have been developed. Two of the more common are block-time scheduling and flexible/modular scheduling.

In the block-time schedule, larger periods are set aside in which teachers and learners may vary the length of time for different activities. Thus, a discussion or project may continue for as little or as much time as is needed. In the 1950s, some junior high schools and a few high schools provided the equivalent of two or three standard periods in which a single teacher taught two or more subjects. They were either taught separately or integrated. Known as "unified studies" or "block-time (core) programs," these arrangements became preferred by those who used them. But they gained relatively little popularity in the schools because of the separate subject preparation of most teachers. As noted earlier, many middle-level schools have revived the idea of block-time scheduling to support interdisciplinary team teaching.

Another time format, flexible/modular scheduling, enjoyed some popularity in secondary schools during the 1960s and is still used in some schools. In this format, the length of daily time blocks assigned to various subjects varies from some fraction of a standard Carnegie period to some multiple of those periods. A single concept in mathematics may require only twenty minutes of teaching, but a project in home economics might require eighty. In their most sophisticated forms, flexible/modular schedules varied from one day or week to the next depending upon teacher requests in light of curriculum plans. The availability of computers in the 1960s made flexible schedules more possible than in the past, and the proliferation of computers today may well revive such arrangements. Figure 6.3 illustrates student versions of the four scheduling variations we have described. It should be noted that other kinds have also been developed. In the end, the possibility of scheduling designs is limited only by the imagination educators are willing to apply in considering the use of available time in the school day.

Before leaving this topic, it is worth noting that in the past few years a new concern has arisen over the use of time schedules. In 1973, Thomas Good and Jere Brophy completed a research project that indicated that a large portion of the school day was devoted to a myriad of noninstructional activities. The data in this study suggested that learners were "academically engaged" for relatively limited amounts of time. As a result, a series of additional studies was undertaken, and recommendations were made for the amount of time learners needed to be "academically engaged" to achieve certain skill levels, as well as for the gross amount of time that needed to be set aside to promote

FIGURE 6.3 Four Different Types of Schedules Used in Schools (Subjects offered in various time slots may vary from day to day, week to week, etc.)

Self-Contained Classroom	Carnegie Schedule	Block-Time Schedule	Modular Schedule
In classroom	Homeroom	In classroom with teaching team (Language Arts, Social Studies, Science, Math)	English / Language Arts
	English / Language Arts		
Art	Science		Science
Lunch	Lunch	Lunch	Lunch
In classroom	Math	Exploratory program (Art, Music, Industrial Arts, Home Economics, Physical Ed., etc.)	Math
Physical Education	Physical Education		Social Studies
In classroom	Social Studies		
	Foreign Language	Activities program (Interest groups)	Home Economics
	Homeroom		Music

the needed "engaged time." On the heels of these studies followed a series of national and state reports recommending the lengthening of the school day and year. Although many educators find fault with these reports, their appearance and the reactions to them demonstrate the recognition of time as a crucial aspect in curriculum planning and subsequent learning.

PUPIL PERSONNEL SUPPORT

■ ■ Pupil personnel services historically derived from the need to counsel high school students for matriculation to college, and later dealt with occupational counseling for non-college-bound students. The development of psychological counseling expanded that role to counseling students about their personal needs and interests. Today this is manifest in the total kindergarten-through-twelfth-grade all-school program, wherein pupil personnel staff provide a range of services to parents and students. School psychologists, consulting psychiatrists, social workers, school nurses and health specialists, and counselors are available in many situations to provide the specifics of this broad program of pupil personnel support.

Support for the personal needs of students remains the major concern of pupil personnel services. However, a growing interaction between curriculum and pupil personnel services has developed during the past three decades. This has evolved from a mutual recognition that teachers have a definite counseling role and that pupil personnel specialists can play a supportive role in teaching and learning. There are two levels at which pupil personnel services operate in the all-school program.

The classroom teacher is the student's primary adult contact in the all-school program. In addition to organizing instructional programs for students, teachers gain a daily perspective of students that may provide information to counselors and other pupil personnel staff. Teachers observe students' interactions with peers in class and other school settings, and teachers themselves interact regularly with students. But teachers likewise need to become aware of the two levels at which they can effectively use and interact with pupil personnel service resources.

■ Level I

For pupil personnel services, Level I operations deal with the traditional concerns to provide support for personal needs of students. The school offers regular opportunities for students to interact with guidance counselors. These include meetings and interviews for orientations and introductions to school programs and curriculum options. Special counseling opportunities are also available to help students deal with individual personal problems. Regularly scheduled conferences enable counselors to open lines of communication and develop rapport with students. Students can initiate contacts with pupil personnel services in order to discuss questions they may have on programs and services, or to deal with personal and special needs.

Counselors provide individual and group counseling programs as additional means for dealing with student needs as situations arise. These can be interfaced with other school programs such as homeroom, grade-level meetings with students, and other advisement activities provided by the school. Orientation programs for parents are offered to advise them of these pupil services and to encourage parents to initiate contact if they feel their child is having a problem.

It is important that teachers not view themselves as trained psychologists, counselors, or other pupil personnel specialists. However, the organization of learning and instruction does deal with psychological principles of learning, mental health, and the like. For example, Louis Raths (1972) presents a careful argument to show how unmet emotional needs related to achievement, belonging, and security may block a student's learning and development. A teacher is often the first adult in school whom students contact about problems. Although teachers should, and do, make referrals to the most appropriate pupil personnel specialists, they have the initial opportunity to provide an important counseling role as helpful, empathic adults. Most of us vividly recall individual teachers who were very helpful at some time in our own lives.

Teachers need to recognize the importance of this front-line or entry-level counseling role, but it is essential that they also apprise the appropriate pupil personnel specialists or make a referral in such circumstances. Teachers can likewise become more effective in their entry-level counseling activities through brief but specific inservice sessions led by the school counselors. As teachers establish such relationships with students, they gain a better understanding of instructional needs and of how the all-school program can become more supportive and effective.

■ Level II

Level II deals with integrating the activities of counselors and other pupil personnel specialists with teachers into the regular curriculum and program of the school. As discussed by Dorothy Rosenbaum and Conrad Toepfer (1966), the areas of instruction and pupil personnel traditionally worked separately from each other. This isolation resulted in problems of poor communication, lack of information by pupil personnel staff about student classroom performance, lack of the consideration of learning needs by both groups, and lack of awareness of the nature of particular developmental needs of students by many teachers. The interaction of both groups is essential to eliminate these problems.

Counselors assigned to particular groups or grade levels should meet with individual teachers or teacher planning teams to discuss pertinent information about the students involved. These meetings can be used to provide teachers with nonconfidential information about their students, review and interpret standardized and other tests given their students, and answer questions teachers may have about resources appropriate for their students. Counselors also may interact with teachers during their instructional planning time to discuss ways in which pupil personnel staff could serve as resources in particular classroom situations.

These possibilities can be best decided by the expertise of both counselors and teachers as they plan and work together. Level II expands the counseling role of teachers and increases possibilities for pupil personnel staff to become involved in instructional activities. Cooperative planning can identify means to develop such interaction through the following kinds of activities:

1. *Classroom visitation by counselors and other pupil personnel specialists*. This is not an observation of teachers, but an observation of program and how students perform and react in the classroom setting. The purpose here is to broaden the experience and understanding of the pupil personnel staff. This broadened experience is essential to follow-up interactions among teachers and pupil personnel staff to plan Level II activities.

2. *Workshops for teachers and pupil personnel staff*. These would provide opportunity for teachers and pupil personnel staff to interact after the visitation program. These workshops can facilitate common understandings of curriculum issues and needs. Also, teachers can better understand their counseling roles as well as identify possible ways to involve pupil personnel staff in instructional activities.

3. *Elementary, middle level, and high school workshops*. As a follow-up to general workshops promoting planning and discussion among teachers and pupil personnel staff, specific workshops can be organized at each of the three levels of the school system. These workshops would deal with specific concerns identified by staff, and would organize activities allowing teachers and pupil personnel staff to interact more effectively on program concerns. Topics included might be "Entry-Level Counseling Activities for Use by Teachers," "Advisor–Advisee Programs" (in which students meet on a regular, scheduled basis), and "Pupil Personnel Workshops for Students." Topics for individual and group counseling by pupil personnel staff could also be identified in these workshops.

4. *Unit planning*. The planning of instructional units can be enriched by utilizing the expertise of pupil personnel specialists. Teachers see the value of, but may not always feel confident to develop units in, areas such as "The Relation of Nutrition to Culture and Society," "Tobacco, Alcohol, and Other Drug Concerns," "An Experimental Approach to Democracy in the Classroom," and "Impact on Youth of Contemporary Change in Family Structure."

5. *Classroom consultation by pupil personnel staff*. This allows teachers to work directly with pupil personnel staff in the classroom setting. A counselor or psychologist might participate in the following kinds of instructional activities: discus-

sion of guilt and motivation in various literary works at different levels; discussion of the impact of self-concept and self-esteem concerns of historical figures upon events that shaped history; and discussion of animal behavioristic theories in science classes. Teachers and pupil personnel can develop unique approaches to basic subject matter though cooperative planning. Again, Rosenbaum and Toepfer (1966) present detailed descriptions of how a school district developed these approaches.

The advantages for planning more responsive curricula in Level II situations should be apparent. As schools develop this kind of interactive planning, the resultant learning experiences developed for students will be more specifically responsive to student needs. Such opportunities seldom are developed when these two areas of expertise remain isolated and focus on their separate concerns in the all-school program.

MEETING SPECIAL NEEDS OF EXCEPTIONAL CHILDREN

■ ■   American public schools have taken on the task of educating all of the children of all of the people at public expense to a degree which no other nation has attempted. This requires that schools be prepared to deal with the extremes of individual differences across the total spectrum of abilities. But school programs most generally reflect characteristics of the majority of students who cluster about the median. A far more difficult curriculum planning responsibility centers on developing and providing appropriate educational programs to accommodate the extremes of those exceptional differences above and below that median. The United States has demonstrated a greater historical concern and empathy for the economically, culturally, physically, emotionally, and intellectually disadvantaged than most others in the family of nations. Yet the road to providing responsively appropriate exceptional curricula and educational offerings for individuals representing such extremes has been long and difficult.

Exceptional education describes curricula and programs in those aspects of the all-school program developed for students who have educational needs apart from children whom people tend to consider "normal." More appropriately, exceptional education seeks to provide responsive experiences for youngsters with special problems or "inabilities" on the one hand, and those with special "talents" or high abilities on the other. One might say that it is a procedure for identifying, classifying, and grouping learners who fall into extremes above and below the vast majority of learners. The exceptional education population generally includes students who were historically identified as "bright," "slow," or "physically handicapped." The last decade has witnessed the development of specific approaches for the range of such exceptional learners, some of which have positive implications for curriculum organization.

■ Special Education—Mainstreaming

Learners with severely limited abilities have reflected the painful history of how most societies condescend to deal with such people. Children with severe special needs and handicaps were traditionally placed in isolated special school or care facilities. Such approaches denied these students access to the regular school program. These experiences of isolation were most often the prelude to an adult life in institutional or restricted environmental settings. The advent of homogeneous grouping by ability in the 1950s marked the beginning of increased efforts to identify and categorize different kinds of special needs conditions in children. Typically, these youngsters would receive a "watered-down" or lesser dose of the regular curriculum. Such programs were well intentioned but largely inappropriate and ineffective in terms of learners' special needs. Again, they sought to provide "places" in the school for low-challenge activities and had no real facets for students to share in the regular school program. While learner disabilities were generally recognized, their school programs were different in kind, rather than in degree, from the regular curriculum of the school. Nor were they specified in terms of special learning needs. The self-esteem of these youngsters was consistently negative with regard to school learning.

The early 1970s saw parents of special needs learners begin to coalesce and try to find alternatives that could provide specific, responsive education programs for their children. There was concern to find ways in which these special needs youngsters could have greater access to more aspects of the all-school program. In local community discussions, these parents came to recognize the range and complexities of these special needs. Categories such as EMR (educable mentally retarded), TMR (trainable mentally retarded), ED (emotionally disabled), LD (learning disabled), PH (physically handicapped), and MH (multiple handicapped) were used to identify and classify the different handicapping conditions with which youngsters had to cope in their efforts to learn within the school setting. Special needs arising from specific disabilities and the differing needs of single- and multiple-handicapped children led parents to involve psychologists and physicians in studying these problems. As a result, laypersons and educators concluded that major educational changes were necessary if special needs children were to achieve true success in their school experiences. Groups of parents, educators, psychologists, and physicians convened to diagnose the special educational needs of local populations of these learners. Local, state, and national organizations of parents of special needs children began to lobby to enact education legislation to institute conditions which would allow these children greater access to the all-school program.

This culminated in 1975 with the Ninety-fourth Congress passing Public Law 94-142, which required that each school district convene a special education committee for special needs learners. The committees identified and diagnosed the special needs and handicaps of learners and considered how the school could provide the most appropriate education for that child's special needs in the least restrictive environment. This prescription of a personalized curriculum plan is known as the child's Individual Educational Plan (IEP). The IEP includes objectives, content, materials, activities, and measuring devices responsive to the specialized learning needs of the individual student. This IEP is regularly reviewed to facilitate the development of "difference-of-kind" experiences that are as responsive as possible to the individual's educational needs. Public Law 94-142 led to the concept of mainstreaming and broke the virtual caste system that had effectively curtailed access of special needs youngsters to many aspects of the all-school program.

Mainstreaming has proven an effective means for these youngsters to gain access to the opportunities of the all-school program. It is based on the premise that exceptional children with disadvantaged and handicapping needs require special attention to enable them to be able to function in the mainstream of society. To the degree possible in terms of an individual's handicapping or special needs, he or she is put into regular classrooms with nonhandicapped/special needs learners where that student can experience meaningful and purposeful learning. In other portions of the school program in which a child's special needs preclude this mainstreaming, he or she is placed in a resource room. The resource room has special staff, equipment, and materials to deal with those learning areas in which that individual can only function successfully in a more restricted learning environment. This approach is consistent with the curriculum field's concern to meet individual differences. As youngsters demonstrate increasing readiness, they expand their involvement in the mainstreamed setting. Mainstreaming attempts to build the skills and capabilities of each special needs learner so that she or he can successfully participate in more mainstreamed classes and reduce the time necessary in the resource room. The goal is to help special needs youngsters gain greater involvement in the all-school program and maximize their capabilities to function as independent adults in the mainstream of society.

■ Gifted/Talented Education

The extreme of talent and superior ability has presented difficulties of another dimension as schools have attempted to develop curricula and programs for this exceptional population. Historically, brighter and more able children have been considered to learn faster than other age-mates. Current gifted and talented programs developed from earlier efforts to deal with the intellectually superior student population during the past forty years.

The concept of acceleration was initially manifested as students were allowed to skip a year or grade at certain points in school. While a few students might successfully skip an entire year in all content areas, many who skipped entire grades later found that large gaps in content and skill sequences created problems in their subsequent learning. In some cases, the decision to skip a grade was an ego issue or a point of pride for parents. Skipping was an either/or matter, and the decision was most frequently made upon a student's past performance. New or greater difficulties inherent in the grade to be skipped were seldom considered. Neither was there consideration of whether or not the new placement would require higher-level abilities beyond those demonstrated in earlier school years. This approach fails to recognize that students of all abilities follow developmental patterns. Decisions about whether or not students can accelerate an entire grade should be based on that child's synchrony of social, emotional, and intellectual readiness. David Elkind's research (1981) confirms the problems created in children's lives when they are accelerated without regard to their total readiness.

In the mid-1950s, tracking programs appeared that were based upon homogeneous grouping by ability. In theory, this would allow a student more able in given content areas to experience higher curriculum challenges in those areas only. Tracking had a potential advantage over the practice of skipping all curriculum areas in advancing an entire grade. However, it subdivided many aspects of the all-school program into tracks or subtracks. This often created scheduling limitations for a student needing some less-than-high tracks in particular subjects. As a result, most students were placed in high-ability or high-achievement tracks in all subjects.

Tracking decisions should consider the merits of elective opportunities for students while maintaining the context of the all-school program for the broadest base of students possible. Advanced placement courses proved to be an effective approach that preserved this balance far more than tracking. Students with high ability, achievement, or interest in a particular subject could elect an advanced placement course in that content area. They did not have to elect high-challenge courses in any other areas unless they had similar credentials in those subjects.

Gifted and talented educational approaches developed against this background of practice. No one disputes the need to help the most able students utilize their intellectual abilities for maximum achievement, but the same should hold true for all students. A major question deals with how the all-school program can assist the talented learner to maximize her or his abilities and to maintain healthy social–emotional development. C. Frederick (1978) notes that problems of suicide, suicide attempt, and emotional stress and illness are highest among very bright students. High-ability students and their parents could benefit from counseling and other interaction with pupil personnel staff. It is essential that these high-risk issues be understood and that information and support be provided as curriculum options are considered for these students.

Gifted and talented programs vary widely. Most radical are the elitist programs based on the philosophy that bright students should be largely segregated from less able students in the school setting. These programs have little concern with the all-school program, and they maintain that excellence comes in the separation of student groups by ability. Many gifted and talented programs are based on the acceleration model, which moves youngsters ahead as quickly as possible. Programs of this nature are strongly rooted in the subject approach to curriculum organization.

Other approaches operate from a commitment to enrichment. They try to provide students with the broadest possible learning experience in a content area before moving them to higher levels. One approach works from a largely heterogeneous base in which students move individually at their own rate but gain experience as tutors of other students. This is based on the premise that learning is reinforced by interaction with other students sharing common interests in an area of information. Another of these approaches phases students in and out of special programs on the premise that all youngsters have special abilities. This almost reverses the mainstreaming model. The gifted and talented program becomes a kind of "resource room" into which youngsters are cycled in terms of their talents, interests, and abilities from the mainstream of the more heterogeneous, above-average-ability population. These kinds of gifted and talented programs facilitate a broad involvement of students in the all-school program.

As schools deal with students at either extreme of the ability spectrum, curriculum planning for exceptional educational programs must pursue two objectives. First, specfic means must be planned that respond to and accommodate the special learning needs of those students. Second, approaches must be developed that allow optimal access for students of all abilities to the all-school program. An open society requires citizens who can live, work with, and respect the broad range of individuality of humanity.

LIBRARY/MEDIA/INFORMATION SERVICES

■ ■ This chapter began by describing the all-school program as all of the learning opportunities offered under the auspices of the school. The all-school program is therefore the curriculum in operation. It includes all of the comprehensive information, skills, processes, values, attitudes, appreciations, and understandings represented in learning experiences available in the school. Society today is acknowledging that we are leaving the industrial era and entering what is being called the information age. The technology we can observe now, and that which is rapidly emerging, is concerned with helping humankind manage, manipulate, and deal with information in ways never imagined until very recently.

The knowledge explosion in technology and information processing is occurring so rapidly that the state of the art in processing information changes almost before we can gain competency in the area. Schools have fared poorly in trying to keep current with these developments. This phenomenon has critical implication in the planning of educational experiences for today's children. Curriculum plans need to deal with developing skills for all learners that will enable them to function and gain future skills as citizens in the emerging information society. Unfortunately, schools are being expected to develop school technology programs involving skills and information which few educators possess themselves.

The library/media center is that part of the school which offers access to information in print and nonprint media. However, it has seldom been broadly utilized by teachers and other school professionals in carrying out the all-school program. We most often view and use the library/media center as a place to look for materials, information and audiovisual aids. However, this facility and its personnel offer perhaps the best resource that may assist educators in taking themselves and students into that information society. Thus, both in terms of process and content, curriculum planning faces a major challenge in identifying how it will deal with this transformation into the information society. Quite clearly, it is essential that educators involve library/media/computer personnel in planning how schools will enter into that transformation.

■ Utilizing the Library/Media Center and Specialists

Educators need to investigate ways in which district and school library information and media resources could be utilized in developing school programs in the areas discussed here. It will be a serious oversight to look at the resources of the library/media center as a place we utilize on demand. Library/media personnel have a rich background in planning and using media and other resources that is typically overlooked by educators. Most library/media specialists have teaching experience and offer group and individual lessons for students in library/media centers. In many cases, they come into regular classrooms and teach library/media information and skills.

Library/media specialists also plan instructional programs within their own centers. Many have graduate preparation in curriculum planning from colleges and schools of library and information science. These specialists can participate in developing inservice activities dealing with information science skills. Library and Information Science graduate programs also provide training with computers. As a result, library/media specialists increasingly use computers and other electronic media in organizing library/media collections and learning activities. They frequently have better information and word processing skills than other professionals in schools. Their perspective on dealing with information, skills in managing and processing data, and ways in which they utilize computers, can help educators define and deal with these emerging issues.

As an example, a major area of library/media specialist expertise deals with techniques for "accessing," "querying," and "sorting" relevant information from a wide spectrum of databases. Such skills provide a means of doing an almost instantaneous review of the literature and research when a staff is contemplating some program revision or change. Even more important, it means that students participating in a unit of study may have opportunities to "see" and "use" materials and resources far beyond those which are physically available in a single building. Ultimately, the skills of the library/media specialist, rather than the collections they manage, have brought us to a state where *every* library information center can be as extensive and comprehensive as *any* information center. The implications for curriculum planning, though mind-boggling, are both challenging and exciting.

Educators have to reverse their long-standing patterns of minimal interaction with library/media specialists. The need for interactive planning with these professionals is essential. It can enhance the chances of developing curriculum plans to help children function and succeed in the growing information society.

CHAPTER SUMMARY

In Chapter 6 we have considered a number of issues involved in implementing the all-school program. These included decisions about required and elective programs, the hidden curriculum, organizing the staff, the grouping of learners, scheduling, pupil personnel support, planning for exceptional children, and cooperating with library/media specialists. Each plays a critical role in supporting the many teaching–learning situations that comprise the ongoing activities of the school. (See Figure 6.4.)

Required learning experiences are those which reflect the common needs of all learners. Their components are embedded in the perennial curriculum question, "What knowledge is of most worth?" Several different positions have been taken on this issue, ranging from delineation of required academic courses to identification of compelling social problems and learner needs. Elective experiences are intended to meet the needs of some but not all learners. Electives may include advanced courses, vocational preparation, advanced exploratory experiences, and activities such as clubs and sports.

FIGURE 6.4   Decision Areas Related to the All-School Program

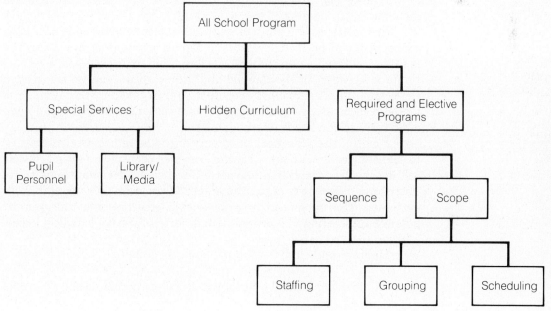

The organization of staff may be based upon several alternatives. Where one teacher possesses sufficient skill and knowledge to work with learners, self-contained classrooms may be used. Both subject and interdisciplinary teams offer opportunities to use skill and knowledge possessed by a small group of teachers. Departmentalized arrangements are generally associated with the subject-centered approach, although research has questioned their appropriateness. Each approach is widely used in schools, but their most common usage is found at elementary, middle, and high school levels, respectively.

Decisions about the grouping of learners are difficult and complex. Generally, learners are grouped either heterogeneously or homogeneously. The former approach involves groups either randomly or purposefully formed to include a wide variety of learner characteristics. The latter involves the formation of groups based upon such variables as achievement, interest, special talent or skill, physical development, social maturity, life plans, and learning styles. Homogeneous grouping by ability or intelligence has little support in research, whereas nongraded, continuous progress, and multi-age plans have received less support in practice than they deserve. Decisions about grouping should be made in terms of curriculum and learning goals and should organize students into the most appropriate groups for achieving those goals.

The scheduling of learning activities is an important factor in organizing effective instruction. Many school schedules are developed around traditional Carnegie period arrangements. However, other plans, such as block-time and modular scheduling, have proven more effective in providing the kind of flexibility related to the variety of activities included in curriculum plans.

Instructional and pupil personnel services need to coordinate both counseling and teaching services in the all-school program. Learning is best facilitated when the school's developmental programs and curricula are cooperatively planned and utilize all the special services in the school. Pupil personnel specialists, library/media specialists, and teachers cooperating together can organize programs that respond more effectively to the needs of students.

Finally, the all-school program cannot be effectively responsive to learner needs without a careful consideration of the special needs of the school's exceptional learners. Curriculum decisions need to reflect these differences in planning special programs for needs at both extremes. The all-school program should also promote the greatest possible interaction of learners with different kinds of learning needs.

Having read Chapter 6, you should be able to:

1. Identify critical questions related to organizing the all-school program

2. Describe patterns for defining the required portion of the all-school program
3. Identify the various types of electives that might be included in the all-school program
4. Identify ways of organizing the scope and sequence of the all-school program
5. Recognize the role of the hidden curriculum in the all-school program
6. Describe various patterns for organizing the professional staff to implement the all-school program
7. Describe patterns that may be used to group learners for various experiences within the all-school program
8. Identify methods of scheduling that support implementation of the all-school program
9. Describe various ways by which pupil personnel specialists can interact with faculty to articulate counseling and instructional services in the all-school program
10. Identify special need areas of exceptional students important in improving the all-school program
11. Identify ways to implement these issues in the all-school program in your school setting
12. Identify areas of support that library/media specialists can provide for planning school programs

SUGGESTED ACTIVITIES

1. Have the group identify a broad unit topic representing a problems or needs approach (e.g., Colonial Living, Futures, Life in School). Then illustrate the concept of interdisciplinary team teaching by brainstorming the contributions that each subject area might make to the unit. The discussion may be extended by asking representatives of various subject areas to speculate about how much time they might devote within such a unit, or what skills or concepts they feel would be addressed.

2. Divide the group into representatives from each level of schooling. Ask each group to specify requirements and electives at its level. Identify examples of instances where specific courses or experiences overlap the two categories. Also determine the approximate proportion of requirements to electives at each level. Summarize this latter analysis by examining how the proportion changes across school levels.

3. From state and/or local sources, secure lists of educational goals. (This may already have been done in conjunction with Chapter

4.) Next identify state and/or local requirements for high school graduation or basic competency tests. Do the requirements reflect the complete range of goals or a part of them? If only a part, what is left out
and what would have to be done to fill in gaps?

4. Assume that the group is a school faculty. Ask members of
the group to identify personal strengths in terms of teaching skills and
subject areas. Then analyze whether the group combines professional
competencies to address curriculum arrangements such as the following:

a. working with large groups, small groups, and individual
    learners
b. addressing concepts and skills reflected in curriculum goals
    (see Chapter 4)
c. providing counseling services for learners
d. working in self-contained, team, and departmentalized
    structures
e. working with parents and other community groups

Identify areas where additional skill would be needed. Would such
needs necessitate additional teachers or other professionals? What
learning needs or curriculum arrangements would have to be deemphasized if such personnel would not be available?

5. Proceed through a series of steps in which the group is subdivided by different grouping variables. Variables might include years
of teaching experience, number of graduate credits earned, certification
areas, or attributes such as color of hair, level of vision, etc. In each
case, ask individuals and groups to identify what advantages and disadvantages might be realized through such regrouping and how they
feel about the method of grouping. What does this suggest about grouping learners in school?

6. Ask members of the group to jot down a description of the
single best activity they have done with learners. After this, ask that
they note whether the time available for the activity was appropriate
and sufficient. Where the time available was not appropriate, identify
what would have been the ideal time arrangement. Select several of
the latter examples and consider the following questions.

a. What prevented the availability of appropriate time?
b. If appropriate time were available, how would other parts of
    school have been affected?
c. What objections would have been raised if such time had
    been requested?
d. Would any of the staffing/scheduling arrangements described
    in this chapter have facilitated better time arrangements for
    the activity in question?

7. Have each member of the group outline her or his teaching
schedule for any given day and identify curriculum problems encoun-

tered because of scheduling arrangements. In a large-group discussion, identify the similarities and differences in scheduling arrangements. Also, ask for suggestions for overcoming curriculum/scheduling problems, emphasizing those which can be gleaned from various practices described by members of the group.

8. Obtain a list of objectives and services of the pupil personnel program in your school. Identify some curriculum topics in your teaching activities similar to those discussed in the "Level II" section of this chapter. Share the results of these planning sessions with members of your department, team, or grade level to consider ways of facilitating broader interaction between pupil personnel staff and the instructional program in your area. In a class discussion, share the reactions and attitudes of participants' school colleagues to these proposals.

9. Read the objectives and program(s) serving gifted/talented and special needs youngsters in your school. Arrange a meeting with your colleagues who work in one of these programs. Consider the objectives of the program(s) in terms of the description of the all-school program presented in this chapter.

    a. To what degree do these programs address the unique needs of the specific population of students which they serve?

    b. To what degree do these programs address the needs of their specific population of students to have access to the all-school program and the total student community of your school?

Develop a set of goals for that program presenting directions that might be pursued to make the program more responsive to the two questions posed above in terms of the curriculum area that you teach. What were the similarities and differences in problems found by individuals who tried this activity? What major problems should teachers anticipate in their efforts to interrelate special needs programs with the all-school program?

10. Ask your school library/media specialists if you can meet together to discuss the resources in the center. In addition to identifying the print and nonprint media in the center, identify ways in which the library/media specialist could help you develop better information processing skills for your own teaching. Share the results of your investigation with colleagues, and see if you can identify ways that you can plan and interact with the library/media specialist.

REFERENCES

Alberty, H., and Alberty, E. *Reorganizing the High School Curriculum*. 3rd ed. New York: Macmillan, 1962.

Diebert, J., and Hoy, W. "Custodial High Schools and Self-Actualization of Students." *Education Review 2* (1977): 24–31.

Elkind, D. *The Hurried Child*. Reading, Mass.: Addison-Wesley, 1981.

Esposito, D. "Homogeneous and Heterogeneous Ability Grouping: Principal Findings and Implications for Evaluating and Designing More Effective Educational Environments." *Review of Educational Research* 43, no. 2 (1973): 163–180.

Findley, W., and Bryan, M. *Ability Grouping 1970: Status, Impact, and Alternatives*. Athens, Ga.: University of Georgia Center for Educational Improvement, 1971.

———. *The Pros and Cons of Ability Grouping*. Bloomington, Ind.: Phi Delta Kappa Foundation, 1975.

Frederick, C. "Current Trends in Suicidal Behavior in the United States," *American Journal of Psychotherapy* 2 (1978): 172–200.

Good, T., and Brophy, J. *Looking into Classrooms*. New York: Harper & Row, 1973.

Hipple, J., and Cimbolic, P. *The Counselor and Suicidal Crisis: Diagnosis and Intervention*. Los Angeles, Calif.: Western Psychological Services, 1984.

Jackson, P. *Life in Classrooms*. New York: Holt, Rinehart and Winston, 1969.

Overly, N. (ed.) *The Unstudied Curriculum: Its Impact on Children*. Washington, D.C.: Association for Supervision and Curriculum Development.

Raths, L. *Meeting the Needs of Children: Creating Trust and Security*. Columbus, Ohio: Charles E. Merrill, 1972.

Rosenbaum, D., and Toepfer, C. *School Psychology and Curriculum Planning: The Coordinated Approach*. Buffalo, N.Y.: Hertillon Press, 1966.

Rosenbaum, J. *Making Inequality: The Hidden Curriculum of High School Teaching*. New York: John Wiley & Sons, 1976.

Saylor, J. G., and Alexander, W. *Planning Curriculum for Schools*. New York: Holt, Rinehart and Winston, 1974.

Slavin, R. *Using Student Team Learning*. Rev ed. Baltimore, Md.: Johns Hopkins University, 1980.

Snyder, B. *The Hidden Curriculum*. Cambridge, Mass.: MIT Press, 1973.

Tompkins, E., and Gaumlitz, W. *The Carnegie Unit: Its Origin, Status, and Trends*. Washington, D.C.: U.S. Government Printing Office, 1954.

Tubbs, M., and Beane, J. "Curricular Trends and Practices in High Schools." *High School Journal* 655 (1981): 103–208.

Willower, D.J.; Eidel, T.L.; and Hoy, W.K. *The School and Pupil Control Ideology* (The Pennsylvania State University Studies No. 24). University Park, Penn: The Pennsylvania State University, 1967.

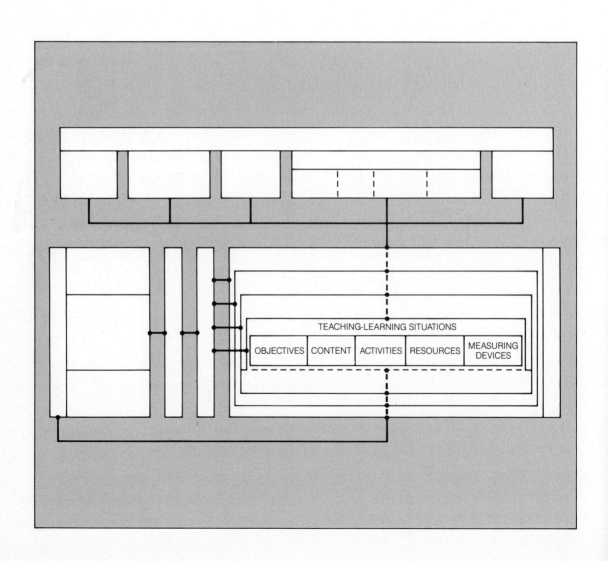

TEACHING-LEARNING SITUATIONS

| OBJECTIVES | CONTENT | ACTIVITIES | RESOURCES | MEASURING DEVICES |

7

Curriculum Planning for Specific Teaching–Learning Situations

The purpose of curriculum planning is to provide quality experiences for learners. For this reason, curriculum planning for specific teaching–learning situations is perhaps the most crucial stage in the process. In Chapter 7 we explore this important phase of our framework. Once again, we focus on the diversity of ideas that are available to those involved in curriculum planning. Here, more than anywhere else, educators must be aware that there is no "cookbook approach" that will satisfy all situations. What teachers and learners actually do together depends entirely upon what they want to accomplish, who they are, and how they want to learn.

The major portion of this chapter is devoted to discussing the several components of curriculum plans. To illustrate how these might appear and come together in a resource unit plan, we give examples of items in each component as they might appear in a unit on "Living in the Future." These examples appear in Frames 7.5, 7.7, 7.9, 7.11, and 7.12. In Appendix A to this book, the reader will find a complete listing of the unit and its components. In no case is our example intended to be an exhaustive list of possible items in any component. Many more might be added before the resource unit would actually be put to use. However, there are enough items in each list to illustrate sufficiently the form of a resource unit.

As a result of reading Chapter 7, you should be able to:

1. Describe the components of teaching–learning situations
2. Describe the relationships among the various components
3. Identify sources and appropriate uses of various organizing centers
4. Explain the meaning of and the choices related to
   a. objectives
   b. content

    c. activities

    d. resources

    e. measuring devices

5. Describe a process for constructing unit plans composed of a variety of alternatives within each component

6. Identify means for involving learners in curriculum planning

ORGANIZING CENTERS

■ ■   Effective teaching–learning situations focus on some topic, theme, problem, or issue. Initial curriculum planning for such situations involves identification of such an *organizing center*. Once the central idea is clarified, the components of specific curriculum plans can be developed in relation to it. Suppose, for example, that we have chosen the problem of environmental pollution as an organizing center. We may then ask such questions as: What knowledges, skills, attitudes, or behaviors would we like learners to acquire with regard to environmental pollution? What facts, principles, ideas, and understandings are related to environmental pollution? What activities might promote the acquisition of knowledge and skill related to environmental pollution? What resources may learners consult to obtain information about environmental pollution?

There are a variety of sources from which organizing centers might be identified. One is curriculum guides developed by agencies outside the school. Most states and school districts suggest particular topics or themes that ought to be addressed at various grade levels. By doing so, these groups hope to promote consistency of topics among various schools and thus to avoid the duplication of topics across grade levels. In other cases, commercial publishers may suggest organizing centers for particular subjects. For example, chapter titles are actually organizing centers within the subject of the textbook. Still another external source is recommendations from committees or groups of scholars sponsored by federal agencies or professional associations. This source was particularly popular in the 1960s, and in some cases it also contained suggestions for objectives, activities, resources, and measuring devices. Examples of these included the School Mathematics Study Group, Biological Sciences Curriculum Study, and "Man: A Course of Study," a unit developed by Jerome Bruner under the sponsorship of the Education Development Lab in Newton, Massachusetts. This particular unit was widely used in social studies classes but roundly criticized by many who felt that it was too "humanistic" and "progressive."

Florence Stratemeyer and her colleagues (1957) suggested that an important source of organizing centers is found in what they termed "persistent life situations." These are defined as "those situations that recur in the life of the individual in many different ways as he grows from infancy to maturity." The following excerpt illustrates two examples of how persistent life situations are manifested at particular stages of development. Those interested in this approach to curriculum development use specific situations as organizing centers, and then develop units according to how the situations appear at the developmental stage of particular learners.

■ **Examples of Persistent Life Situations (Stratemeyer et al., 1957)**

> *Achieving Status in Groups (Achieving Secure Relations with Others)*

Early Childhood	**Finding ways of contributing to group activities**—Sharing in family activities; sharing in class discussions; taking leadership responsibilities in games; finding ways of using special reading ability, artistic talent, musical ability in interest of group; sharing personal things, interests with group; locating smaller groups within class who have like interests . . .
Later Childhood	**Learning ways of taking appropriate responsibility in group situations**—Sharing in family activities and responsibilities; finding ways through which to make contribution to class activities; deciding what share to take in carrying out class project; taking leadership responsibilities in class group; sharing in club or "gang" activities; becoming part of group if physically much larger or smaller; making up for physical defects . . .
Youth	**Extending ability to use individual capacities to secure group status**—Sharing in responsibilities and decisions of family group; deciding whether to seek class office; finding means of participating in all-school activities; making constructive contribution to community groups; adjusting to social, economic, racial, religious, or other factors placing one in minority group; accepting and playing one's appropriate sex role; helping members of minority groups achieve status . . .
Adulthood	**Helping self and others to secure status in a variety of groups**—Playing satisfying role in family group; making constructive contribution to community group; finding status satisfactions in one's job;

adjusting and helping children adjust to minority group problems; helping colleagues or other group members achieve status needs; helping children find means through which to make positive contribution to family group, to school group, to church and social groups . . .

Solving Practical Problems (Using a Scientific Approach to the Study of Situations)

Early
Childhood

Applying simple tests in the solution of practical problems—Experimenting with methods of keeping paints and clay moist; testing to find which kind of paper is best for painting or drawing; finding when books or pictures can help solve a problem; finding that conclusions from firsthand experiences do not always agree—that one child may think dogs are fierce and another may think they are friendly; being helped to see when to withhold judgment until more information is secured; reasoning from several concrete experiences to simple generalization; giving concrete evidence rather than opinions as to why class plans did not work out, why an argument arose . . .

Later Childhood

Finding when and how to use simple research techniques—Finding how to test differences of opinion by experimentation—setting up experiments with animals, testing two methods of planting seeds; gathering needed facts to verify point of view, conclusion reached; making simple surveys—children using given street crossing, food wasted in school cafeteria; discussing why historical research might lead to conflicting dates or figures; discussing general procedures back of an important scientific discovery; discussing in general terms fact that individual behavior has to be interpreted in light of motives; deciding whether generalizations are based on sufficient evidence . . .

Youth

Extending ability to use scientific methods appropriate to situations—Finding how to use scientific tests to verify observations—quality of cloth, foods, tools and machines, others; following results of medical, other research; helping conduct school or community survey; using historical research methods to give needed perspective on problem; using logical reasoning to evaluate advice regarding a personal problem, to test logic of speaker or writer; deciding what steps are appropriate in resolving conflicting opinions; discovering importance of evaluating present generalizations in terms of new evidence; discovering influences that must be considered in analyzing personal behavior—realizing that illness, worry, fatigue, need for affection can influence actions . . .

Adulthood

Using a scientific approach effectively in the situations of daily living—Using appropriate methods to decide on selection of materials and equipment—testing new garden seeds, experimenting with new methods of insulation in housing, trying out new household or office equipment; making surveys needed as guides to business procedures; evaluating popular or professional articles quoting research; helping children resolve differences on basis of sound evidence; helping children arrive at sound generalizations; using generalizations about research techniques to evaluate new business and governmental proposals; supporting social and scientific experimentation; deciding when to encourage business firm to adopt new methods which are subject to experimentation; using case-study approaches in understanding problems of adjustment . . .

A third source of organizing centers is the interests of the learners themselves. Harold and Elsie Alberty (1962) characterized one type of the core curriculum organization as "based on the teacher–student planned activities without reference to any formal structure." In this statement they captured both the concept and the process of using centers of interest. The use of interest centers depends largely on active dialogue with learners, preferably in the form of teacher–student planning. From such discussions, teachers and students may identify particular topics, themes, problems, or issues that are of particular interest to the learners. Figure 7.1 illustrates a special use of the centers-of-interest concept. In this case, organizing centers are considered that are particularly relevant to the broad goal of enhancing self-concept, self-esteem, and values. Since such topics invite extensive and careful focus on self-perceptions, they are almost invariably of special interest to learners.

Finally, the identification of organizing centers is directly related to the choice of a curricular approach inasmuch as each approach serves as a source of possible topics. If one chose to use a subject approach in developing curriculum plans for English or language arts, one might then select organizing centers such as the short story, contemporary poetry, or developing a composition. A problems-of-living approach

FIGURE 7.1   Sources of Organizing Centers

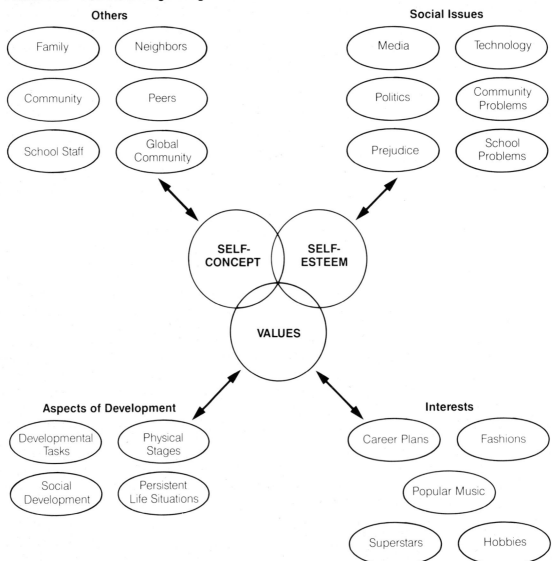

From James A. Beane and Richard P. Lipka, *Self-Concept, Self-Esteem, and the Curriculum* (Boston: Allyn and Bacon, 1984).

might suggest organizing centers such as the future of technology, contemporary lifestyles, or the impact of commercial media on our lives. Choosing an emerging needs approach may lead one to consider developmental stages of the learners and to select an organizing center that would add to knowledge or skill related to a particular developmental task.

The identification of organizing centers is a key phase of curriculum planning. They are, as the old children's game suggests, "the thread that runs so true" through all other aspects of the teaching–learning situation. Since they are broad topics, their study usually involves several weeks. Given the time and effort involved, organizing centers must be important, appropriate, and pertinent. Furthermore, no matter how exciting activities and resources may appear in plans, they will probably result in little effect if learners perceive the organizing centers as dull or meaningless.

OBJECTIVES

■ ■   Instructional objectives define the specific and immediate outcomes of particular teaching–learning situations. In curriculum plans, they ordinarily take form in a listing of statements describing the intended learnings for students. As such, instructional objectives serve three purposes in curriculum planning. First, they clarify for teacher and learner what is to be accomplished. Second, they serve as a guide for design or selection of meaningful content, activities, and resources. Third, they provide guidance for measuring learner progress.

During the 1930s, a curriculum trend that enjoyed some popularity was the so-called activity movement (Kilpatrick, 1934). Its major premise was that learners ought to be active rather than passive participants in learning. As a result, a premium was placed on engaging students in a wide variety of activities and projects. Some critics of the movement held that in many cases activities were carried on simply for their own sake rather than for some expressed purpose. Their concern was that many activities were thus aimless, leading nowhere in particular. Two decades later, Ralph Tyler (1950) described a curriculum rationale in which objectives played a crucial role in clarifying instructional purposes. Since that time, much attention has been given to the nature and design of instructional objectives. Understandably, then, there are a variety of ideas about what form objectives ought to take. Our idea is that the form is less important than the purpose. The form may vary from one situation to another, but what is really important is that teachers and learners have a mutual understanding of what is to be accomplished.

Specific instructional objectives may be drawn from three sources. One is the goals or general objectives for the total school program. For example, a goal indicating that learners should develop technological awareness suggests a specific objective having to do with gaining competence in the use of available computer programs. A second source of objectives is the organizing center or topic under study. A unit on news media analysis, for instance, might include a specific objective dealing with the analysis of laws pertaining to news reporting. A third source of objectives is the continuing development of skills for learning. For example, every teaching–learning situation might include attention to language arts objectives in areas such as speaking, listening, and observing. Although not a source like the three already mentioned, a fourth possibility, emerging objectives, should also be noted. Specific objectives are typically defined before undertaking a teaching–learning situation. As the situation unfolds, however, problems or questions not foreseen may emerge. If so, new objectives may be added to those initially defined, thereby expanding the breadth or depth of study.

■ Content and Process Objectives

One way to think about differences among objectives is to distinguish those having to do with content from others concerned with process. Content objectives focus on the acquisition of facts, principles, or concepts associated with the topic under study. Examples of content objectives may include the following:

- To identify the major causes of the American Revolution
- To describe reasons why air pollution is a threat to human health

Process objectives center on treatment of content or on action suggested by the topic at hand. Examples include the following:

- To evaluate the potential impact of computers on society
- To propose ways of improving community services to handicapped persons

■ Behavioral Objectives

Some educators hold that learning involves changing behavior or developing new ways of behaving. Furthermore, they suggest that only behavior can be measured. This implies that specific instructional objectives would need to specify some kind of behavior in order to represent actual learning and in order to be measurable. This trend has been typified by the work of Norman Gronlund in his book *Stating Objectives for Classroom Instruction* (1985). At issue was the specification of behaviors that would indicate whether learning had taken place. Examples of behavioral objectives include the following. (Note that the italicized words indicate a specific kind of behavior that the learner will demonstrate.)

- To *list* occupations, professions, and industries that have arisen in the twentieth century
- To *prepare* a brochure describing services and facilities of a town or local museum
- To *add* two three-digit numbers accurately
- To *predict* the consequences of acid rain on forests
- To *contribute* ideas to group projects

■ Performance Objectives

A variation on behavioral objectives is the development of performance objectives. In the 1960s and 1970s literally thousands of teachers attended workshops to learn how to write them. In this case, the objective is supposed to include four components: what is to be done, who is to do it, when is it to be done, and what level of proficiency is to be accepted. Examples of performance objectives include the following:

- By November 15, the student will be able to recite eight of the ten classifications in the Dewey Decimal System.
- By June 1, the student will have written three themes utilizing a word processing program on a microcomputer.

Proponents of performance objectives, such as Robert Mager (1962), believe that such statements offer the clearest and most useful form of specifying instructional purposes. However, critics maintain that performance objectives overdo the need for specificity and run the risk of limiting learning to the time and achievement level stated in the objective (see Frame 7.1).

■ Expressive Objectives

Some educators believe that behavior does not necessarily reveal all the feelings or attitudes that grow out of teaching–learning situations. Furthermore, they hold that learning is highly personal and thus what is actually learned may be as diverse and varied as the learners themselves. The leading proponent of this view, Eliot Eisner, recommends use of what he calls "expressive objectives" (1969). Here the learning activity is specified, but the actual outcome is left open-ended. Eisner illustrates expressive objectives as including the following:

- To visit the zoo and discuss what was of interest there
- To develop a three-dimensional form through the use of wire and wood

A Criticism of Performance Objectives
Gronlund, 1985

■ **Why Not Include Conditions and Standards?**

It is sometimes suggested that in addition to describing the desired *student performance,* an objective should include the *conditions* under which the performance is to be demonstrated and the *standard* of performance to be accepted. This method of stating objectives would result in a statement as follows (each element is identified to the left of the statement):

Condition   Given a drawing of a flower
Performance   The student will label in writing
Standard   At least 4 of the 5 parts shown

Statements such as this are especially useful for programmed instruction and for mastery testing in simple training programs. When used for regular classroom instruction, however, they result in long, cumbersome lists that restrict the freedom of the teacher. If we restated the above as "Identifies the parts of a given plant structure" it could be used with various units of study and the teacher would be free to use real plants, pictures, diagrams, slides, or other stimulus material. Also, the students could respond orally, in writing, or simply by pointing to a named part. The standard (in this case 80%) could be set at the time of testing, either for the whole test or separately for each part. Keeping the standard separate from the objective makes it possible to vary the standards as needed without rewriting the objectives. For example, we may want to set lower standards at the beginning of a unit of study and higher standards at the end. Similarly we may want to set higher standards for a gifted group and lower standards for a retarded group. Let's not waste time rewriting objectives to fit changing conditions.

Such statements have the ring of the activity movement mentioned earlier in that they do not seem to specify some definite purpose for learning. Yet as we come to appreciate more and more the diversity and the personal nature of learning, expressive objectives represent a means for providing a wide array of possible outcomes. They also encourage learners to find personal meanings in the activities provided in units.

■ **Domain-Referenced Objectives**

One way of thinking about learning is to imagine that it occurs in three areas or domains—cognitive, affective, and psychomotor. The cognitive domain refers to the acquisition and use of knowledge. The affective domain is concerned with values, feelings, attitudes, and emotions. The psychomotor domain focuses on the development of motoric or physical skills. The three domains are not mutually exclusive since virtually all learning activities involve more than one. For example, the development of values largely depends upon knowledge of alternative choices about what to prize or cherish. Learning to dance not only involves physical skill, but also knowledge of different types of music and, often, an emotional attachment to one's partner. Taken separately, however, the domains serve as valuable reference points for developing balance in the curriculum in terms of different areas of learning.

During the 1960s, a good deal of attention was given to identifying types of learning that take place within the various domains. This analysis resulted in the formulation of taxonomies or hierarchies of objectives for each domain. The following excerpt illustrates the taxonomies for each domain, with sample objectives for each point in the hierarchy. Opportunities to learn should be provided in all domains, and at the various levels within each.

■ Taxonomies of Objectives

Cognitive Domain (Bloom, 1956)

Level 1   Knowledge (memory of ideas or facts)
          • To list the capitals of each state

Level 2   Comprehension (understanding of information)
          • To paraphrase main ideas in the Declaration of Independence

Level 3   Application (applying knowledge to problem situations)
          • To demonstrate democratic principles in group work

Level 4   Analysis (identification of parts and their relationships)
          • To identify different computations needed to solve a complex mathematical problem

Level 5   Synthesis (combining parts to form a whole)
          • To develop a persuasive argument using several different supporting reasons

Level 6   Evaluation (developing judgments about value)
          • To identify the truth or fiction in beliefs about health

Affective Domain (Krathwhol, Bloom, and Masia, 1964)

Level 1   Receiving or attending (paying attention to phenomena and stimuli)
          • To listen attentively and with an open mind to the ideas of others

Level 2   Responding (reacting to or using that which is received)
          • To cooperate with others in group work

Level 3   Valuing (identifying and committing to particular beliefs)
           • To act in ways which enhance physical health

Level 4   Organization (establishing a set of values)
           • To suggest new or revised laws for improving society

Level 5   Characterization by a value or value complex (acting on and displaying values)
           • To campaign for human rights through communications to political leaders, speaking out at local forums, etc.

Psychomotor Domain (Simpson, 1972)

Level 1   Perception
           • To differentiate different foods by their odors

Level 2   Set
           • To demonstrate knowledge of rules of a sport

Level 3   Guided Response
           • To manipulate objects on the basis of directions

Level 4   Mechanism
           • To construct a model of a building

Level 5   Complex Overt Response
           • To demonstrate correct form in pole vaulting

Level 6   Adaptation
           • To change running form to gain more speed

Level 7   Origination
           • To develop an interpretive dance

The statement of objectives is a key ingredient in successful unit plans. If the items are clear, appropriate identification of other components will be greatly enhanced. Furthermore, they will provide learners with an understanding of what they are supposed to accomplish.

Frame 7.2 includes a list of objectives related to the topic "Living in the Future." This topic is the organizing center for the resource unit we have chosen to develop here for purposes of illustration.

CONTENT

The content component of teaching–learning situations refers to the important facts, principles, concepts, and understandings associated with objectives. In developing curriculum plans, this phase addresses the question, "What content will teachers and learners need to consider in order to accomplish the instructional objectives?" The placement of content identification at this stage is a departure from some ideas about curriculum planning. In many cases, curriculum planners believe that learning involves the mastery of content. As a result, they begin with

Objectives from the Resource Unit "Living in the Future"

1. To understand the concept of change
2. To identify and analyze present trends that may influence the future
3. To gather and interpret information about the future
4. To clarify personal images of the future
5. To clarify personal aspirations for the future
6. To develop skill in using future forecasting techniques
7. To identify issues that will confront people in the future
8. To develop forecasts for global futures
9. To determine aspects of the present that should be continued
10. To identify alternatives for the future in such areas as energy, communications, transportation, technology, medicine, and food
11. To design alternative educational futures
12. To analyze the role of religious/spiritual values in the future
13. To identify alternatives for leisure time use in the future (e.g., recreation, cultural activities, personal interests)
14. To analyze possible future lifestyles
15. To define common futures terminology
16. To differentiate between futures forecasting and predicting
17. To identify futures forecasts made in the past
18. To analyze future occupational/career alternatives
19. To analyze community resources in terms of future use
20. To identify the interrelationships among technology, politics, economics, and human needs

identification of content and then proceed to decide how mastery will be achieved. But as we have seen, mastery of content is the lowest level in the cognitive domain. So even though this kind of curriculum planning characterizes the subject approach used in most high schools, such a notion ignores not only other domains of learning, but the higher levels in the cognitive domain itself.

The identification of content in specific curriculum plans involves several issues. The first has to do with relating content to the organizing center and to the objectives. Here those responsible for curriculum development must make decisions about what knowledge is most appropriate and most pertinent. Certainly in studying any topic some facts and ideas are more important than others. Those objectives which are intended for the whole group presumably involve content of such importance that all learners should be aware of it. On the other hand, small-group and individual objectives may relate to content that is of lesser importance and that is of interest to some learners but not others.

Furthermore, the content should include what is necessary and sufficient for accomplishing the objectives at hand. As more and more content is added to a unit, there is a risk that trivial ideas will begin to appear—and also that emphasis will shift from accomplishing objectives to mastering content.

A second content issue is its relation to the lives of learners. Here we refer to John Dewey's idea of "psychologized" subject matter.

> The psychologized is of interest—that is, it is placed in the whole of conscious life so that it shares the worth of that life. But the externally presented material, conceived and generated in standpoints and attitudes remote from the child, and developed in motives alien to him, has no such place of its own. (1902)

The more pertinent content is to the needs and interests of the learner, the greater the likelihood that he or she will perceive its meaning and worth. As a result, there is a greater chance that the content will be learned and used. (The probable relationship between content and its mastery is illustrated in Figure 7.2.)

For example, in studying colonial living, learners may have an interest in learning about games their age-mates would have played at that time or about the similarity between parent–child conflict and the evolving stress in relationships between England and its colonies. Certainly not all important content can be directly related to learner needs and interests. However, some balance between remote and relevant content adds to the chance that the former will be given serious consideration by learners.

Yet a third issue in the identification of content focuses on its level or difficulty. In Chapter 5 we discussed Jean Piaget's stages of cognitive development. From those stages we can assume that appro-

FIGURE 7.2
Probable Learning as a Function of the Relationship Between Content and Learner Needs and Interests

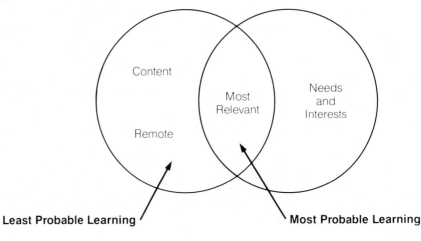

priateness of content depends partly on the capacity of learners to understand it. Children, for example, can address content and its application so long as it is concrete. Adolescents, on the other hand, can begin to address more abstract concepts. But when content is not congruent with the cognitive capacity of learners, they may feel as though they are trying to listen to or read an unfamiliar foreign language. Often, frustration sets in—with the result that students lose interest in the entire unit topic and all the objectives.

Frame 7.3 includes a list of content items related to the objectives in our illustrative unit plan, "Living in the Future." Along with each is a reference that teachers may consult for further information about the item.

ACTIVITIES

■ ■   As we have pointed out, during the past two decades a good deal of emphasis has been given to the preparation of objectives. In many cases, this emphasis arises from the viewpoint that the clear identification of purposes is the most crucial piece in curriculum development. However, one may also speculate that the most crucial moment in curriculum is the learning activity since it is the crux of the learner's everyday experience in the school. In this sense, activities are important not only in terms of their appropriateness to objectives, but also because they largely determine the learner's attitudes toward school. Whatever view is taken, the selection of activities is a very important part of curriculum planning.

Decisions about learning activities are based upon several criteria. These criteria are in the minds of curriculum planners when they select the activities and again in reviewing them before, during, and after the teaching–learning situation. Criteria for selection and review of activities include the following concerns:

1. Is the activity appropriate for the particular objective(s) of the teaching–learning situation?
2. Is the activity appropriate for the learners who will be involved? For example, is it congruent with past achievement, interests, age, developmental task level, handicapping conditions, and so on?
3. Is there enough variety in activities so that various learning styles are accounted for?
4. Can the activity be accomplished within available time frames?
5. Are sufficient and necessary resources available to support the activity?

Illustrative Content Items from "Living in the Future"

1. The history of humankind is a chronicle of change represented by increasing control over the environment, introduction of technological innovation, and growth in understanding of what it means to be human. Change is occurring at an increasingly rapid pace. As a result, we are often overwhelmed by the complexity of alternatives and by the consequences of change.

   Sources:
   Toffler, Alvin. *Future Shock.* New York: Random House, 1970.
   Toffler, Alvin. *The Third Wave.* New York: Bantam Books, 1981.
   Mesarovic, Mihajlo, and Pestel, Eduard. *Mankind at the Turning Point.* 2nd Report of the Club of Rome. New York: New American Library, 1974.

3. As a result of extrapolating future possibilities from present research and trends, futurists have constructed a body of subject matter about possible futures. Knowledge of these ideas is important in developing images of the future.

   Sources:
   McHale, John. *World Facts and Trends.* New York: Collier Books, 1972.
   Rosen, Stephen. *Future Facts.* New York: Simon and Schuster, 1976.
   Dickson, Paul. *The Future File.* New York: Rawson Associates, 1977.

6. To aid in thinking about the future, futurists use many techniques or

---

In addition to considering the criteria for selecting activities, attention must also be paid to other factors. These include the phase of instruction for which the activity is intended, the group size for the activity, the type of learner involvement, and the general effectiveness of the type of activity.

■ Some Noteworthy Types of Activities

A comprehensive description of activities for learning is beyond the scope of this book. However, we believe that there are a few general types of activities that are so promising and/or widely used that they deserve mention.

devices to generate and consider alternatives. These devices include extrapolation, scenarios, cross-impact matrices, and decision trees.

Sources:

Bright, James. *A Brief Introduction to Technology Forecasting.* Austin, Tex.: Pemafried Press, 1972.

Martino, Joseph. *An Introduction to Technological Forecasting.* New York: Gordon and Breach, 1972.

8. Much of the typical futures thinking has to do with our society and our nation. It is most probable that forming a preferable future will depend upon global thinking, which goes beyond national boundaries and ethnocentrism. Global futures involve thinking of ourselves as global citizens who recognize interdependence among people around the world.

Sources:

Clarke, Arthur C. *Profiles of the Future.* New York: Harper & Row, 1973.

Kahn, Herman. *The Next 200 Years.* Washington, D.C.: World Futures Society.

16. Predicting involves attempts to specify precise events, the time when they will take place, and their consequences. Prediction is as old as the seers in ancient times and as current as popular astrologers. Forecasting involves attempts to foresee possible alternatives and their consequences through systematic thinking about trends. Most futurists engage in forecasting and avoid efforts at precision in describing possible futures.

Source:

Glines, Don H. *Educational Futures,* vol. 1. Milville, Minn.: Anvil Press, 1978.

☐ *Cooperative Learning*   There is substantial evidence that learning is enhanced by the use of cooperative small-group arrangements in which learners work together and teach each other. Small-group work has been used for many years, with varying degrees of success. In the last decade, several educators have engaged in research and practice aimed at giving clearer form and structure to small-group, cooperative activities (Slavin, 1981). As a result, they have been able to provide specific suggestions for "cooperative learning." Their research has also demonstrated that these activities promote both cognitive and affective learning more effectively than do competitive structures.

☐ *Community Service Projects*   An old idea that has recently enjoyed renewed popularity is the involvement of learners in projects aimed at improving community life. For example, individuals or groups may work with elder or handicapped persons, assist in day-care centers, organize peer counseling programs, conduct citizen surveys, improve recreation programs, and so on. The purpose of the projects is to promote citizenship skills, develop feelings of self-worth, and encourage the idea of participation in community life. The success of this type of activity has been described in numerous sources that point to the need for its continuing use (Hedin and Conrad, 1980; Lipka, Beane, and O'Connell, 1985).

☐ *Mastery Learning* For those concerned with the achievement of basic academic skills and content, the inconsistent performance of learners has been a continuing problem. Teachers, in particular, are often perplexed as they meet with groups of learners whose individual members vary widely in their readiness to approach new objectives that depend upon previous achievement. Benjamin Bloom (1976) and others have devoted many years to researching and promoting a type of activity known as mastery learning. Under this plan, intended learnings are divided into a series of very specific performance objectives that build upon one another. Before proceeding to a new objective or level, learners are required to demonstrate an acceptable level of performance in the one preceding. Proponents of this plan also consider alternative methods for helping students to achieve the desired performance level. Critics of mastery learning point out that its use encourages teachers to limit objectives to basic or "low-level" skills and content. Nonetheless, research has shown that where these are the focus of instruction, mastery learning is a useful activity.

☐ *The Project Approach* Much of curriculum implementation and instruction today is based upon textbooks, workbooks, paper-and-pencil tests, and other content mastery devices. As we have seen, however, content and skills are really a means to some end or larger purpose. In 1918 William Kilpatrick published a short booklet entitled *The Project Method.* In it he proposed engaging students in various projects that would involve the application or functional use of content and skills. Since then, many teachers over the years have used projects as a culminating activity in units. For example, learners might devise time lines, build scale models, construct science displays, or dramatize stories. In one case to which we have already alluded, a group of sixth-grade students transformed a classroom into an Egyptian tomb, complete with sarcophagus, hieroglyphics, and related artifacts. Such projects bring the curriculum to life through concrete application. They have the added feature of giving learners a chance to have pride and ownership in their work.

☐ *Values/Moral Education Activities*   In an attempt to help learners develop in the affective domain, many units include activities aimed at
thinking about values and morals. Prompted largely through the works
of Dewey (1939), Louis Raths (1978), and Lawrence Kohlberg (1975),
educators have devised a number of ways to approach the affective
aspect of the curriculum. Activities may include values clarification,
moral dilemmas, role playing, and others. These methods also involve
self-esteem development, since self-images often depend upon one's
beliefs, attitudes, and opinions about others. The methods also promote
development of interpersonal skills through guided interaction among
learners. As we saw in Chapter 3, values/moral education is surrounded
by controversy as conservative groups have questioned the school's
right to work with young people in those areas. Other critics question
the idea that such activities ought to help learners develop their own
values, preferring instead to insist that they adopt some predetermined
set of beliefs. Another problem stems from the practice of using values/
moral development activities in short time blocks set aside for that
purpose. Critics of this approach maintain that such activities are only
a part of a larger program that ought to be integrated into the whole
curriculum. Thus, although values/moral education activities have frequently found a place in the school program, there is still much debate
about their purpose and preferred form in the curriculum.

■ Phase of Instruction

Teaching–learning situations are organized in three phases: introductory, developmental, and culminating. While a particular activity might
be appropriate for more than one phase, its actual use should depend
on the one for which it is best suited.

Introductory activities are intended to introduce learners to the
particular unit, topic, or problem that will be studied. Introductory
activities may include lectures, field trips, films, and other exploratory
events aimed at arousing learner interest and curiosity. In the introductory phase, teachers and learners may also engage in cooperative
planning to identify objectives, resources, and developmental and culminating activities.

Developmental activities constitute the main time frame of the
unit. They lead to the actual accomplishment of the objectives. Among
many others, developmental activities may consist of lectures, discussions, readings, field trips, surveys, and extensive research. The purpose of these activities is to encourage learners to gather data, and to
have experiences appropriate to the topic under study and the objectives to be accomplished.

Culminating activities conclude the teaching–learning situation. Specifically, they are intended to bring synthesis and closure to the situation, and to demonstrate accomplishment of objectives. Culminating activities may include projects, tests, reports, summary debates, presentation of data, self-evaluation, and unit evaluation.

■ Group Size

Different types of activities also suggest variations in the size of the group with which they will be used. For example, where the intention is simply to disseminate information, large-group activities are appropriate. These may include lectures, films, and the like. Where interaction is the purpose, small-group activities are appropriate. Small-group activities may focus on discussion, problem solving, and project work. In cases where objectives are of concern to individuals, activities are often of an independent type. These may include reading, interacting with a computer, and individual research.

The differences among these types of activities seem rather obvious. Yet in practice they have been somewhat confused in relation to the concept of individualization of instruction. We have heard many teachers claim to "individualize learning" and go on to explain that they usually have students work alone on activities. In doing so, they have confused the use of individual activities with the broader concept of individualization of instruction. Individualizing instruction refers to developing curriculum plans based upon the diverse characteristics of specific learners in a group. Such characteristics may include needs, problems, interests, previous experiences, and more. Since every group includes a variety of individual differences, the teacher who truly individualizes instruction plans for a variety of objectives, activities, resources, and measuring devices. When individual differences are accounted for in this way, instruction may be said to be individualized. This broad concept is of particular importance today since so much emphasis seems to be placed on individual work with computers, worksheets, and so on. While these activities certainly have an appropriate place in learning situations, they are not sufficient for all learning. Some objectives definitely call for large-group activities and for small-group interaction. Without these two types, the range of activities is almost certainly inadequate.

So in designing activities for particular teaching–learning situations, it is important to account for the variable of unit phase and group size. When statements of possible activities are completed, they may be classified using the grid shown in Figure 7.3. Where cells in the grid are empty, new activities might be considered or activities from other cells might be reclassified. When all cells are completed,

FIGURE 7.3 Grid for Classifying Activities by Unit Phase and by Group Size

UNIT PHASE	GROUP SIZE: Large Group	Small Group	Individual
Introductory	Conduct a survey of other students in the school to determine their future plans.	Small groups should try to reach consensus on and prioritize ten goals for themselves in the future.	Develop a personal time line from birth to present age and then extend it into a personally preferred future.
Developmental	Invite several elders to visit the class and discuss comparisons between the past and present.	Ask small groups to design a new sport or game that the whole group may try out.	Interview parents or other adults about their hopes for the future.
Culminating	Form teams and convene a debate on the choice between a technology-centered or person-centered society.	Build a scale model of a future community or city including a written or taped description.	Have individuals consult the pre- and post-unit inventory of attitudes toward the future to see if they have changed.

we may assume that each phase of the unit will offer activities for varying group sizes.

Frame 7.4 includes suggested activities from our illustrative unit plan, "Living in the Future."

RESOURCES

■ ■ The interactions learners have with resources deserve careful attention in curriculum planning. Ideas about learning resources are often limited to textbooks and audiovisual aids. A more useful view of resources includes any materials, places, or people that learners might use to pursue instructional objectives. This broader view allows teachers and learners to consider a much wider variety of possibilities for resources to support the teaching–learning process.

The first major type of resource is what are broadly termed "materials." Meredith Gall (1981) defines curriculum materials as "physical entities, representational in nature, used to facilitate the learning process." By this he means that such materials represent events, peo-

Illustrative Activities from "Living in the Future"

1. Form small groups around major future issues, such as the family, populations, the environment, world hunger, and education. Have each group develop a scenario of how they believe the issue may unfold in the next fifty years (in five-year increments). Check for cases where scenarios from different groups complement or contradict each other. Integrate the group scenarios into a comprehensive world futures scenario. Discuss whether the scenarios are possible, probable, preferable, etc. What major events or incidents might be introduced to change the scenarios (e.g., nuclear war)?

2. Develop a personal time line from your birth to your present age. Include important dates and events. Use pictures, and objects (e.g., party invitations, newspaper clippings, etc.) to illustrate events. Interview parents or other relatives for detailed information. Then extend the time line thirty to fifty years and fill in possible or desirable events.

3. Publish an issue of a newspaper for January 1, 2000. Include such items as front-page news, sports, comics, editorials, ads, and social events. In each item, the content should involve information based upon forecasts in such areas as lifestyles, scientific events, and world events.

4. Build a scale model of a future community or city. Consider possibilities related to transportation, construction, energy, recreation sources, weather control, and the like. Develop a written or taped description of the community and your reasons for designing it in particular ways.

5. Form small groups to design and build models that illustrate alternative

---

ple, things, and ideas related to objectives. Curriculum materials may thus include such items as the following:

Books and other printed matter
Computer software
Films and videotapes
Cassette tapes
Television and radio programs
Interactive videodisks

Because learners spend a great deal of time interacting with curriculum materials, the selection of these resources is particularly important. The process of analyzing and selecting materials is thus a energy resources for the future. Display these in an "Energy Fair" open to students, citizens, and others. Also convene a debate on the advantages and disadvantages of various energy resources. Have the debate judged by a panel including representatives from science, business, energy suppliers, citizens at large, and others.

6. Develop a dictionary addendum including words that could or should be added to our language. Begin by noting words or terms that have emerged recently, such as "hi-tech" and "punk rock." New words should be considered to denote futuristic products, foods, sports, vehicles, communications devices, etc.

7. Form small groups, and ask each to design a new sport or game. Alternatives might be based on present types or may be completely new. They may be competitive or noncompetitive. If possible, the whole group should try out various sports or games designed by the separate small groups.

8. Interview officials from local schools, businesses, and industries to determine present and future (planned) use of technology in the workplace. Determine the use of communications devices such as teleconferencing hardware and computers. Also investigate the possible impact of robots and other technologies.

9. Prepare a table of contents and brief narrative for a world history book written in the year 2000. Consider possible or probable major events in areas such as geopolitics, cultural values, environmental issues, war and peace, and world hunger.

10. Find copies of journals, magazines, and books written before 1950. Search for articles or ideas about what the future might be like. Develop a list of various forecasts and determine their accuracy (particularly those concerning the present time).

---

crucial aspect of curriculum planning. The excerpt below shows four major dimensions that Gall suggests for analyzing curriculum materials. Those responsible for selecting materials must make decisions in each of the four dimensions. For example, the "Instructional Properties" dimension, which is desirable for learning, may have to be considered in light of the "Publication and Cost" dimension. The cost of a particular commercially prepared material could put it beyond the instructional budget. This may lead to the decision to prepare local instructional material that seeks to provide the desired instructional properties. However, locally prepared materials, while meeting the "Content" dimension, may lack some desired "Physical Properties" of commercial publications. Thus, whether curriculum materials are purchased or developed locally, educators need to base their selection on all four of the dimensions suggested by Gall.

■   **Inventory of Dimensions for Analyzing Curriculum Materials (Gall, 1981)**

Publication and Cost

1. Authors
2. Cost
3. Development history
4. Edition
5. Publication date
6. Publisher
7. Purchase procedures
8. Quantity
9. Special requirements
10. Teacher training

Physical Properties

11. Aesthetic appeal
12. Components
13. Consumables
14. Durability
15. Media format
16. Quality
17. Safety

Content

18. Approach
19. Instructional objectives
20. Instructional objectives—types
21. Issues orientation
22. Multiculturalism
23. Scope and sequence
24. Sex roles
25. Time-boundedness

Instructional Properties

26. Assessment devices
27. Comprehensibility
28. Coordination with the curriculum
29. Individualization
30. Instructional effectiveness
31. Instructional patterns
32. Learner characteristics
33. Length
34. Management properties
35. Motivational properties
36. Prerequisites
37. Readability
38. Role of student
39. Role of teacher

The second major type of resource includes places that learners might visit to gather information and input. One of the most useful curriculum planning activities is the development of a directory of places to visit in communities surrounding a school. The directory may include businesses and industries, governmental and legal offices, recreational centers, cultural centers, and others. Teachers and learners may then use the directory as a resource to identify possibilities for group or individual field trips. The advantage of this type of resource is that it provides opportunities for learners to have direct rather than vicarious experiences. One of the most interesting attempts to build a community resource file was developed in the Philadelphia area. Called the *Yellow Pages for Learning,* the document described a wide range of community resources related to many different topics (Wurman, 1972).

The third major type of resource includes people with whom learners might interact. "People" resources may include teachers and other school personnel, other students, community resource persons, and so on. At present, the major interaction of this type is between a teacher and one or more learners. However, a good deal of evidence suggests that interaction with other students through peer tutoring or team activities holds much promise for enhancing learning. Additionally, many schools have reported favorable results from programs in which older persons teach, tutor, or simply talk with learners. In any event, the individual teacher cannot expect to provide the total quantity or quality of helpful interactions. Other learners, teachers, and community resource persons possess a wealth of information and ideas that may supplement those of the teacher. To ignore these resources is to risk severe limitation of opportunities to learn.

Frame 7.5 is a list of resources related to our illustrative unit plan, "Living in the Future." The list is limited to material resources since the availability of appropriate places and people would depend upon the local community in which the unit was implemented.

MEASURING DEVICES

■ ■ Teachers, learners, and others are concerned about whether learning has actually taken place. For this reason, specific curriculum plans include the identification of means to determine both quantity and quality of learning. Such means constitute measuring devices, the final component of plans for teaching–learning situations.

The measurement of learning is a complex task, and it has been the subject of much discussion and debate. If there is any phase of curriculum and instruction that educators shy away from, it is this one. The reasons for this are many. One is that purposes for learning as stated in objectives are often unclear and thus offer little guidance regarding how and what to measure. A second reason is that measuring devices are difficult to develop, even for experts in the field of instructional measurement. In addition, educators are often unsure about how to measure certain outcomes of learning, particularly those which involve the affective and higher-level cognitive domains. To alleviate these problems, many publishers market both actual measuring devices and sources of ideas for developing others. Many teachers find these useful; others prefer not to rely upon externally developed devices, feeling that they are not appropriate for local purposes.

In addition to those concerns, the issue of measurement is further clouded by the role of national and state assessment programs. These programs invariably involve standardized tests that compare one or more learners to others. A major purpose of these programs is to ex-

Resources from the Unit "Living in the Future"

Increased interest in the futures field has produced a growing list of resources. Journals, magazines, newspapers, films, and books have all been developed around the futures theme. Following are some examples.

■ **Magazines**

1. Probably the best ongoing source of information is *The Futurist,* journal of the World Futures Society, 4916 St. Elmo Avenue, Washington, D.C. 20014. Examples include:

   "How the Future May Surprise Us," April 1983
   "What May Happen in the Next 100 Years," October 1982
   "Crime in the Year 2000," April 1981
   "World Future Society Book Catalog," October 1983
   "Prospects for the Automobile," February 1980
   "Christianity in the Coming Decades," June 1979
   "The Computer Home," February 1982
   "Robots and the Economy," December 1984
   "Living on the Moon: Will Humans Develop an Unearthly Culture?" April 1985

2. Other magazines and newspapers include occasional articles, such as the following:

   "Prediction: Sunny Side Up," *Time,* September 19, 1983
   "21st Century Retirement May Be Easier," *USA Today,* August 1983
   "From a Textbook Written in 2001," *School Update,* April 1, 1983
   "What the Next 50 Years Will Bring," *US News and World Report,* May 9, 1983
   "Thinking about Education in the Year 2000," *Phi Delta Kappan,* May 1983

amine the quality of curriculum and teaching. This topic will be considered more fully in Chapter 8, which discusses curriculum evaluation. However, these programs are also important here since some do affect learners more directly. For example, the New York State Education Department annually administers Regents Examinations in a variety of subject areas to determine whether students will receive statewide diplomas upon high school graduation. Many states administer minimum competency tests to determine not only qualification for high school graduation, but movement from one grade to another and group

"Making It to the 21st Century," *Popular Science,* May 1982
"A Solar Home for a Sunless Climate," *Popular Science,* December 1983

■ **Films/Videotapes**

Films and videotapes typically available through county or regional clearinghouses include:

Future Shock: a documentary based on Toffler's book
Conserving Our Forests Today: how forest lands are protected and renewed for the future
Air Pollution: a discussion of long-range remedies
The Story of Our Money System: how our system evolved
Man Uses and Changes the Land: planning for the use of limited resources
Our Changing Cities: technology and cities
Planning Ahead—The Racer: planning to realize aspirations
People Need People: interdependency of workers
Make a Present for the Future: the making of a time capsule
Life beyond Earth: possibilities for extraterrestrial life

■ **Books**

Brenneman, Richard J. *Fuller's Earth: A Day with Bucky and the Kids.* New York: St. Martin's Press, 1984.
Clarke, Arthur C. *Profiles of the Future.* New York: Harper & Row, 1973.
Corn, Joseph J., and Horrigan, Brian. *Yesterday's Tomorrows: Past Visions of the American Future.* New York: Summit Books, 1984.
Dickson, Paul. *The Future File.* New York: Rawson Associates, 1977.
Kahn, Herman. *The Next 200 Years.* Washington, D.C.: World Futures Society.
Naisbitt, John. *Megatrends.* New York: Warner Books, 1982.
Glines, Don H. *Educational Futures.* Vols. 1–5. Millville, Minn.: Anvil Press, 1978–80.
Toffler, Alvin. *Future Shock.* New York: Random House, 1970.
———. *The Third Wave.* New York: Random House, 1981.

placement as well. The problem with these tests is that they often become "the tail that wags the dog." In other words, the content of the tests often determines curriculum objectives and content. In this case, rather than serving as means for assessing learning, measuring devices become determinants of the curriculum.

When identifying measuring devices for specific teaching–learning situations, it is important to remember two ideas. First, measuring devices should be appropriate for the objectives they are intended to measure. Second, there is a wide variety of measuring devices that can be used in teaching—learning situations. With these two ideas in mind, we will now examine several types of measuring devices.

■ Paper-and-Pencil Tests

Probably the most common type of measuring device is the paper-and-pencil test. These devices come in many forms and include multiple-choice, true—false, matching, and essay questions. Their most common and appropriate use is to assess mastery of subject-matter facts or concepts.

■ Observation

In many cases, teachers want to know whether learners are able to apply concepts in action. In this case, learning may be assessed through observation. The teacher may observe learners in small-group discussions, debates, laboratory experiments, and other hands-on activities. Such situations may be carried out as culminating activities, or as part of the developmental phase of a unit. The problem with observation is that its effectiveness depends on two concepts. First, objectives must be defined in such a way that they clearly suggest what behavior manifests their achievement. For example, when designing measuring devices for particular objectives, teachers might state that observers should look for "behaviors like these." Second, observation is often clouded by the observers' own biases or values. Thus, observers must be skilled in "watching." Also, they must remember that if no behavior is demonstrated, no conclusions about achievement may be drawn.

■ Self-Evaluation

Learning is a highly personal process. Often it is very difficult for one person to know accurately all that another has learned. For this reason, measuring devices ought to provide opportunities for learners to assess themselves. Some teachers ask learners to keep daily journals about what they have learned, what problems were encountered, and so on. Then, at the end of a unit, learners are invited to write two or three paragraphs in which they summarize their journals. This is followed by a discussion in which the teacher reacts to the self-evaluation by summarizing her or his thoughts on the learner's progress. The use of self-evaluation is an important aspect of learning since it helps learners develop the skills of self-analysis that are critical in clarifying self-concept.

■ **Analysis of Projects**

Learning units often culminate in the completion of some sort of project. This might involve building, dramatizing, writing, or similar activities. In this case, the learner is expected to apply concepts learned to the project. The teacher then analyzes the final project to determine whether the concepts are accurately applied. For example, a small group of learners may develop a mural depicting a local main street as it might have appeared in 1900. The mural itself is then analyzed for historical accuracy, authenticity, and so on. Project analysis is particularly useful when objectives are developed at the level of application or synthesis rather than simple knowledge.

■ **Unobtrusive Measures**

In some instances, teachers are aware that if learners know they are being evaluated, they often tend to act in desired ways. In other words, learners' behaviors or attitudes may be distorted for the teacher's sake. In order to get a more accurate view of what learners really think or know, the teacher looks for certain types of behavior without specifically alerting the learner. Such observations may be done in any of the settings described previously under "Observation." William Miller (1978) has described several examples of unobtrusive measures, such as "the number of situations in which students are voluntarily remaining after school to chat with teachers [or] carrying and/or using paperbacks which are not textbooks." (A more complete list appears in Chapter 8, Frame 8.1.) Unobtrusive measures are particularly valuable in assessing affective growth and development, since learners frequently feel compelled to follow the teacher's lead when expressing personal values or interests.

Frames 7.6 and 7.7 include some possible measuring devices and a self-evaluation that might be used in our illustrative unit, "Living in the Future."

DEVELOPING SPECIFIC CURRICULUM PLANS

■ ■ Before leaving this last phase of our curriculum planning framework, a further comment is necessary about the actual process of developing specific curriculum plans. In Chapter 2 we described various levels at which curriculum planning takes place. In this chapter we have explored the components of specific curriculum plans. Now the two may come together in the critical question, "How do individuals and groups proceed in putting actual plans together?"

Measuring Devices from the Unit "Living in the Future"

Following are some ideas for developing means to analyze learners' progress toward the objectives.

1. *Evaluation of Projects*
   As students devleop forecasts, models, etc., look for accuracy of present trend descriptions, reasonable use of time/change concepts, imaginative ideas, use of resources, and defensible arguments for forecasts.
2. *Oral and Written Reports*
   In addition to those items mentioned in (1) above, oral and written reports may be assessed in terms of manner of presentation.
3. *Pre- and Post-Unit Inventories*
   The teacher might construct a checklist of brief future facts or forecasts that learners might respond to at the beginning of the unit by assessing whether they see each item as possible or preferable. Given again at the end of the unit, the checklist may be analyzed for change of attitudes toward the future.
4. *Student Journals*
   See the "Self-Evaluation Activity" described immediately after this section.
5. *Paper-and-Pencil Tests*
   A variety of paper-and-pencil tests could be developed to assess knowledge of future facts and forecasts, futurists, and other subject matter.

The most frequently described format for specific curriculum plans is the resource unit. It may include the following components:

1. A unit title (i.e., organizing center)
2. A brief rationale statement clarifying the title and describing its importance
3. A brief statement describing the general characteristics of the learners for whom the plan is intended (age, grade, developmental stage, etc.)
4. A general description of where the particular unit fits in the scope and sequence of the total school program
5. A suggested time frame for the unit
6. A list of objectives
7. Statements of important content on which the teacher and learners will need to focus
8. A listing of activities in which learners may engage to approach the objectives

Self-Evaluation

In order for students to develop clear and accurate self-concepts, they need to learn the skills of self-evaluation. Following is a procedure that may be used in any subject, unit, or other learning experience.

1. At the beginning of a new unit or marking period, share with students the objectives that the class will undertake. Discuss these so that everyone understands what they mean. Also discuss planned activities and criteria for measuring objectives.
2. At the end of each class (or at least every other day), give the students a few minutes to record on paper their reactions to the class. What were they supposed to learn? What did they learn? Did they encounter problems? Was homework completed? Did anything interfere with learning, inside or outside of the class? Provide a storage space for students' folders, and have each day's log stored there.
3. At the end of each week, have students review their daily logs and write a summary for that week.
4. At the end of the unit or marking period, have students review their daily and weekly logs. Also review the objectives and criteria from (1) above. Then have students write a self-evaluation considering the questions in (2) above in relation to the objectives.
5. Review the written statements with each student. (This takes only a few minutes per student.) If you agree with what is written, cosign the statement. If not—and these cases should be few—write a brief statement of your views. Arrange to have the statements mailed to students' homes (perhaps with report cards). Be prepared for parent conference requests if there is a difference between what you and the student have written.
6. As a variation, you may ask students for permission to review their logs from time to time. You may want to write your own comments in them or to meet with individuals.

This self-evaluation procedure not only helps students develop self-analysis skills, but provides an anecdotal record for parents without requiring the teacher to write about each student. It also helps students to keep track of their progress and focus on their own learning. At the same time, if they review logs periodically, teachers may be alerted to emerging problems. Finally, the process encourages student involvement in planning and evaluation of learning.

9. A listing of possible resources that learners may consult
10. A listing of measuring devices that may indicate learner progress with regard to the objectives
11. Suggestions for evaluation of the unit plan or resource unit

There are two techniques that are frequently used to formulate parts 6–10 of the unit plan or resource unit format listed above. One way is to begin with a list of objectives and then develop the selected content, activities, resources, and measuring devices. The second method recognizes that this process does not necessarily have to be linear. In this instance, participants begin by developing possible activities, and then consider the types of objectives that those activities suggest. This method may run the risk of missing some important objectives. Nevertheless, teachers often think first in terms of exciting and worthwhile activities for learners, and thus they may prefer to begin with this component of their unit plans. The particular technique to be used is a decision that the curriculum planning participants themselves should make.

Earlier in this chapter we alluded to the idea of using a variety of activities, resources, and measuring devices. This idea suggests that effective curriculum plans do not merely include one activity and resource and measuring device for each objective. If this were the case, all learners would pursue objectives in the same way, thus ignoring the diversity of learner characteristics and learning styles. To be really useful, resource units ought to provide several possible ways of reaching and measuring objectives. In cooperatively planning for specific teaching–learning situations, teachers and learners may then select those items that they feel are most appropriate and meaningful. Robert Harnack (1983) has developed a means by which such unit plans may be stored and retrieved on microcomputers, complete with coding that interrelates the various components, and coding that relates each component to specific learner variables, interest centers, and various professional decisions. This idea promises to contribute greatly to curriculum planning, since resource units may be shared and added to by many teachers. Furthermore, since the plans consist of many alternative suggestions, they do not interfere with the professional autonomy of individual teachers, and they may be adapted for unique local purposes.

Finally, we should note that specific curriculum plans may be developed by individuals or by groups. In either case, the plans' effectiveness depends upon the imagination, experience, and thoughtfulness of those who prepare them. However, our experience suggests that small-group participation typically offers several advantages over individual efforts. First, a group represents several different points of view and thus provides balance in ideas. Second, a group is more likely to generate a wide variety of ideas and to refine the particular ideas of any individual. Third, curriculum planning need not be a completely solemn activity. When several individuals come together in a group, they may approach the activity with a sense of fun and camaraderie. This opportunity offers much by way of creating a lively atmosphere in which curriculum planning is viewed as an exciting process. In a time when educator morale tends to be low, such a professional environment is sorely needed.

Appendix A illustrates a sample resource unit plan developed by combining and expanding the parts noted in earlier frames within this chapter. As noted at the outset, this sample unit is not intended to include all the possible alternatives for each component. Certainly many others could be added. However, this illustration demonstrates how the theory involved in this chapter may be applied in practice.

INVOLVING LEARNERS IN CURRICULUM PLANNING

■ ■ In Chapter 2 we portrayed situations in which curriculum planning took place at several levels. The last three situations focused on a team of teachers planning a unit, an individual teacher planning for a group of learners, and a teacher and a group of learners planning together. The first two of these portrayed the obvious and well-known realistic role that teachers play in curriculum planning. The third reflects the possible, but less typical, role that learners may assume in that process.

Throughout the twentieth century, many curriculum thinkers have spoken of the need in curriculum planning to consider seriously the interests and concerns of learners. Within that larger group, some have strongly advocated a technique known as pupil–teacher or teacher–student planning (e.g., Krug, 1957; Waskin and Parrish, 1967). This method has been a matter of controversy, but it has also been used successfully over the years by thousands of teachers. The controversy stems from the viewpoint of some educators that learners either should have no say in curriculum planning or do not know enough to participate intelligently. The fact that teacher–student planning is used in many places indicates that other educators are convinced that learners can and should play a role in curriculum planning.

As we have said, teaching–learning situations, and hence unit plans, consist of several components: organizing centers, objectives, content, activities, resources, and measuring devices. As Figure 7.4 indicates, the components present possibilities for planning by teachers alone, students alone, or both cooperatively. We have described unit planning as the identification of a variety of possibilities within each component. In other words, teachers may define a range of objectives and any number of content items, activities, resources, and measuring devices related to them. Following this, students may be involved in selecting from any one or more of the possibilities in each component. For example, the teacher may select the objectives and resources but ask students to choose from the possible activities and/or measuring

FIGURE 7.4   Whether Students and Teachers Plan Together or Alone, Unit Development Involves All Components

	ORGANIZING CENTER	OBJECTIVES	CONTENT	ACTIVITIES	RESOURCES	MEASURING DEVICES
Teachers Planning Alone	●	●	●	●	●	●
Teacher–Student Planning	●	●	●	●	●	●
Students Planning Alone	●	●	●	●	●	●

devices. Or the teachers and learners might decide which objectives will be addressed by the whole group, which by small groups, and which by individuals.

Some teachers choose to open up the entire process to learners. In this case, the teacher may ask learners to identify and decide upon organizing centers and then to help plan the remaining components. The degree to which learners are involved in curriculum planning is a teacher decision based upon perceived student ability. However, since independent, self-directed learning is a goal of almost all schools, it would seem obvious that teacher–student planning would become increasingly evident as learners progress through school.

Some educators feel that teacher–student planning may be used in a few areas but not in others. But the fact is, it may be used in virtually any situation. At the extreme, consider the case of a high school calculus class, ordinarily perceived as a situation in which learners have no knowledge or experience. They are thus perceived to be unqualified as planning participants. In this case, the teacher may select the objectives and the resources. Learners, however, might choose from activities based upon teacher lectures, problems, small-group exercises, peer teaching, or other alternatives. Their conscious selection can then be a significant factor in their ultimate understanding of course concepts and techniques.

Teacher–student planning offers several important advantages as a classroom technique:

1. It provides a model of democratic living based on cooperative and participatory decision-making.

2. It supports mental health by providing opportunities to have a feeling of belonging.
3. It enhances teacher–student relations by the suggestion that learning is a mutual adventure.
4. It offers a chance for teachers to know what is important and interesting to learners.
5. It enhances social competence by offering opportunities to participate.
6. It offers learners a chance to express their own ideas and interests.

However, it is important to note that teacher–student planning is not just a technique. Rather, it represents a larger commitment to the idea of basing the school—and curriculum planning—on the principles of democratic participation.

CHAPTER SUMMARY

In this chapter we have discussed curriculum planning for specific teaching–learning situations. This phase of the overall framework involved six components, derived from the six aspects of effective teaching–learning situations. These included identification and sources of organizing centers, development of objectives, and development of related content, activities, resources, and measuring devices. In each case, we have continued the themes of diversity and choice that characterize curriculum thought. Having now finished considering the curriculum framework, we will turn in the next chapters to several other important issues in curriculum.

Having read Chapter 7, you should be able to:

1. Describe the components of teaching–learning situations
2. Describe the relationships among the various components
3. Identify sources and appropriate uses of various organizing centers
4. Explain the meaning of and the choices related to
   a. objectives
   b. content
   c. activities
   d. resources
   e. measuring devices
5. Describe a process for constructing unit plans composed of a variety of alternatives within each component
6. Identify means for involving learners in curriculum planning

SUGGESTED ACTIVITIES

1. Conduct a survey of several groups of learners at various grade levels. Focus the survey questions on identifying social issues and personal interests with which the learners are concerned. Collate the results from each level to identify possible organizing centers of interest for different developmental stages. Then compare results across stages.
   a. Which centers are of interest only at certain stages?
   b. Do any issues or interests represent broad themes that could be addressed at each stage, but in different ways?
   c. Which topics are typically addressed in school programs?
   d. Which are not addressed in school programs?
   e. How could they be addressed?

2. Select two organizing centers, one from a subject area and the other from a list of social issues or youth needs. For each organizing center, identify two objectives. Then identify related content, possible activities, resources, and measuring devices for each objective. Try to come up with at least three ideas for each component.

3. Identify an organizing center from a list of social issues. Make a list of all the subject areas offered in school programs. These may include academic, vocational, exploratory, and other subjects. Identify topics or activities that each subject might contribute to the unit. If desired, teachers of various subjects may then develop their contributions more fully. Collate these ideas in the form of an interdisciplinary resource unit. Keep in mind that the degree of contribution, including time, may vary from one subject to another.

4. Select an organizing center from some subject, or list of social issues, or list of youth needs. Using the "Unit Phase/Group Size" matrix shown in Figure 7.3, identify activities to fill each cell. In the culminating phase, try to focus on projects rather than tests.

5. Analyze a set of curriculum plans currently being used by one or more members of the group. Reorganize them using the resource unit format described in this chapter. Are there any gaps in the current plans? What types of objectives are emphasized? Is there variety in activities and resources? What types of measuring devices are used? What suggestions can be made to improve the current unit plan?

6. Carefully review the complete illustrative unit, "Living in the Future." (The unit is listed in Appendix A.) Choose one or two objectives, and examine the related items of content, activities, and resources. Use the various components to plan a series of specific teaching–learning situations for a group of students with whom you are working or with whom you may work. Consider such questions as the following.

a. Which activities might be used as introductory? developmental? culminating?
b. Which activities might be appropriate for large groups? small groups? individuals?
c. What other statements of content might you add that are related to the objective(s)?
d. What specific past achievement, interests, age, developmental task level, or learning styles might be required or supported by the activities?
e. To what additional resources that could be used with the unit do you have access?
f. What are two specific evaluation projects that you could suggest to assess learner progress toward the objectives selected? Suggestions can be shared with the entire group in order to increase the number of possibilities in each component of the unit. (Through use in specific teaching–learning situations, and with teacher–student planning, units can be continually expanded, updated, and revised. Teacher and student suggestions for additional items in each component increase the diversity and the value of any resource unit. They also serve to demonstrate that no resource unit is ever closed to improvement and modification.)

REFERENCES

Alberty, H., and Alberty, E. *Reorganizing the High School Curriculum*. 3rd ed. New York: Macmillan, 1962.

Beane, J., and Lipka, R. *Self-Concept, Self-Esteem, and the Curriculum*. Boston: Allyn and Bacon, 1984.

Bloom, B. (ed.) *Taxonomy of Educational Objectives, Handbook I: Cognitive Domain*. New York: Longmans, 1956.

Bloom, B. *Human Characteristics and School Learning*. New York: McGraw-Hill, 1976.

Dewey, J. *The Child and the Curriculum*. Chicago: University of Chicago Press, 1902.

———. *Theory of Valuation*. Chicago: University of Chicago Press, 1939.

Eisner, E. "Instructional and Expressive Educational Objectives: Their Formulation and Use in Curriculum." In *Instructional Objectives*, edited by W. J. Popham et al. AERA Monograph Series on Curriculum Evaluation. Chicago: Rand McNally, 1969.

Gall, M. D. *Handbook for Evaluating and Selecting Curriculum Materials*. Boston: Allyn and Bacon, 1981.

Gronlund, N. *Stating Objectives for Classroom Instruction*. 3rd ed. New York: Macmillan, 1985.

Harnack, R. *Developing and Using Micro-Computer-Based Resource Units*.

Amherst, N.Y.: Faculty of Educational Studies, State University of New York at Buffalo, 1983.

Hedin, D., and Conrad, D. "Study Proves Hypotheses and More." *Synergist* 9 (1980): 8–14.

Hopkins, L. T. *Interaction: The Democratic Process*. New York: D.C. Heath, 1941.

Kilpatrick, W. *The Project Method,* New York: Teachers College, Columbia University Press, 1918.

———. "The Essentials of the Activity Movement." *Progressive Education* 11:(1934) 346–359.

Kohlberg, L. "The Cognitive-Developmental Approach to Moral Education." *Phi Delta Kappan* 56 (1975): 670–677.

Krathwohl, D. R.; Bloom, B.; and Masia B. B. *Taxonomy of Educational Objectives, Handbook II: Affective Domain*. New York: Longmans, 1964.

Krug, E. *Curriculum Planning*. Rev. ed. New York: Harper & Row, 1957.

Lipka, R. P.; Beane, J. A.; and O'Connell, B. *Community Service Projects*. Bloomington, Ind.: Phi Delta Kappa Foundation, 1985.

Mager R. F. *Preparing Instructional Objectives*. Palo Alto, Calif.: Fearon, 1962.

Miller, W. "Unobtrusive Measures Can Help in Assessing Growth." *Educational Leadership* 35 (1978): 264–269.

Raths, L.; Harmin, M.; and Simon, S. *Values and Teaching*. 2nd ed. Columbus, Ohio: Charles E. Merrill, 1978.

Simpson, E. J. "The Classification of Educational Objectives in the Psycho-motor Domain." *The Psychomotor Domain*. Vol. 3. Washington, D.C.: Gryphon House, 1972.

Slavin, R. "Synthesis of Research on Cooperative Learning." *Educational Leadership* 38 (1981): 655–660.

Stratemeyer, F.; Forkner, H.; McKim, M.; and Passow, A. H. *Developing a Curriculum for Modern Living*. 2nd ed. New York: Bureau of Publications, Teachers College, Columbia University, 1957.

Tyler, R. *Basic Principles of Curriculum and Instruction*. Chicago: University of Chicago Press, 1950.

Waskin, Y., and Parrish, L. *Teacher–Pupil Planning for Better Classroom Learning*. New York: Pittman Press, 1967.

Wurman, R. (ed.) *Yellow Pages for Learning Resource*. Philadelphia: GEE! Group for Environmental Education, 1972.

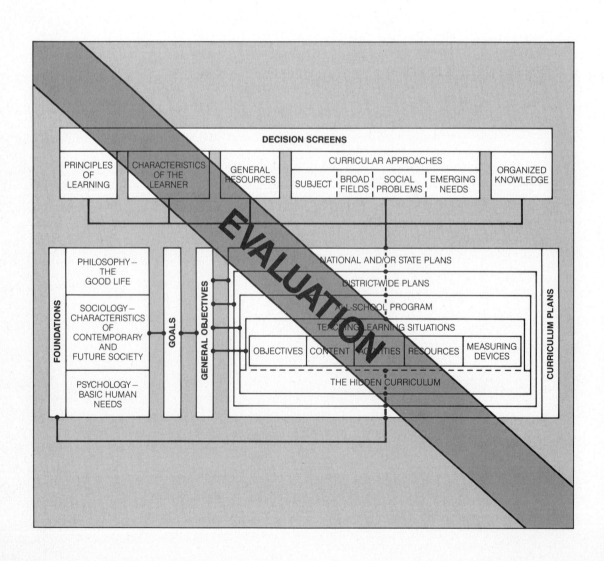

DECISION SCREENS

PRINCIPLES OF LEARNING

CHARACTERISTICS OF THE LEARNER

GENERAL RESOURCES

CURRICULAR APPROACHES

SUBJECT | BROAD FIELDS | SOCIAL PROBLEMS | EMERGING NEEDS

ORGANIZED KNOWLEDGE

FOUNDATIONS

PHILOSOPHY — THE GOOD LIFE

SOCIOLOGY — CHARACTERISTICS OF CONTEMPORARY AND FUTURE SOCIETY

PSYCHOLOGY — BASIC HUMAN NEEDS

GOALS

GENERAL OBJECTIVES

NATIONAL AND/OR STATE PLANS

DISTRICT-WIDE PLANS

ALL-SCHOOL PROGRAM

TEACHING-LEARNING SITUATIONS

OBJECTIVES | CONTENT | ACTIVITIES | RESOURCES | MEASURING DEVICES

THE HIDDEN CURRICULUM

CURRICULUM PLANS

EVALUATION

8

Evaluating the Curriculum

Without apparent planning, but with seemingly inexorable progress, two factors have had a major impact on curricular evaluation over the last fifteen years. The first has been a growing mystique linking evaluation to high-powered mathematical methods, advanced statistical designs, and computer analyses. The second has been a growing call for "accountability" and all of its attendant requirements for standardized tests, national norms, and comparative rankings. The result of both thrusts has been to distance the classroom teacher and the building principal from the evaluation process. More often than not, evaluation has come to be seen as the province of a specialist or a consultant—a ritual or special event to be endured periodically, suffered gracefully, and put aside until the next reminders appear to prepare for the start of a new cycle. (Without meaning to cast unnecessary aspersions, it appears that evaluation and visits to the dentist are regarded as similar experiences!)

Yet the first of the factors mentioned results from a confusion of evaluation and measurement. And the second of the factors emphasizes one particular set of objectives to the almost total exclusion of all others. Put together, these two factors have caused the most basic and the most critical role of evaluation to be relegated to an undeserved subservience. In fact, *evaluation has a role in every level of curricular decision-making*. Whether the question is one of accountability, accreditation, state regulations for required learnings, school board policies, district staff development, school program effectiveness in a particular content area, appropriate student grouping, instructional activities, or individual student progress, the answer must depend on evaluation.

Are students who complete my vocational education course in plumbing really ready to assume a job when they graduate?

Will my students be able to learn new skills and procedures as they change careers throughout their lives?

Will our school's computer education program really prepare our graduates to do computing in the world of work?

Do our students have the best possible preparation for college?

Does our health program really prepare students to cope with and survive against the growing drug and alcohol abuse problems in our society?

Do our students' SAT scores indicate their real readiness for higher education?

Why don't our students achieve as well in their high school mathematics course as they do in their middle school math course?

Is Lisa working up to her capacity?

Are Claire's teaching techniques the best choice for the learning styles of her students?

As a result of their education in our school, are the students less likely to commit suicide?

Is Geoff's enthusiasm for learning being strengthened or weakened by his participation in our enrichment program for gifted students?

Does Sarah's use of vocabulary in her writing compare favorably with the writing styles of other fourth graders?

These and hundreds of others are the kinds of questions which regularly occupy the concerns of educators at various levels. Rather than any mystique triggering insecure feelings about sophisticated statistics or complicated procedures, and rather than a too-narrow concern which centers only on how one group of students compares with another, the heart of evaluation really deals with finding answers to the myriad questions of which the above are examples.

As a result of reading Chapter 8, you should be able to:

1. Describe a working definition of evaluation as it relates to curriculum improvement
2. Describe the components of the evaluation process
3. Describe the uses of evaluation in the curriculum planning process
4. Describe important roles in the evaluation process
5. Understand some of the basic terminology and distinctions used in discussing evaluation, including "norms," "formative" and "summative" evaluation, "measurement," "testing," and "reporting"
6. Recognize the differences in several significant evaluation models dealing with curriculum improvement
7. Recognize several of the problem areas facing evaluation of curriculum plans and school programs

A WORKING DEFINITION OF EVALUATION

■ ■ Regardless of misapprehensions or mystiques, it is the fundamental definition of evaluation that must be uppermost in the curriculum planning process that we have been discussing. Expressed most simply, *evaluation is the process in which we decide how well we have done whatever it is we were trying to do.* But lest a false impression be formed that evaluation is only an after-the-fact operation, we must add that the definition could just as rightly be stated as "the process in which we decide how well we *are doing* whatever it is we *are trying* to do."

As simple as this definition is, it has several immediate consequences. *Evaluation cannot occur unless we know what we are trying to accomplish.* The goals of the school program, for example, or the objectives of the specific teaching–learning situation must be apparent and must be understood. Otherwise, evaluation is more than difficult; it is impossible. Additionally, *we (or someone) must be trying to achieve those goals or objectives, and we (or someone) must look at what is being attempted*—that is, observe the actions or happenings of the situation.

Then *a decision is required:* an answer to the "how well" phrase in our definition. *That decision, in turn, has to be made on the basis of some particular judgmental criterion*—a norm. When all aspects of the components are combined—awareness and understanding of the goal or objective; action addressed to achieving the goal or objective; observation of whatever is occurring; determination of an appropriate norm for analyzing the situation; and, finally, judgment—the evaluation process is complete. (See Figure 8.1.) Despite the simplicity of our working definition, however, each component of the process is necessary. Each component also requires careful consideration in and of itself.

COMPONENTS OF THE EVALUATION PROCESS

■ ■ **The What**

Chapters 4 and 7 dealt with the nature and roles of goals, general objectives, and specific objectives in curriculum planning. That discussion assumes special importance when one is preparing to evaluate curriculum or to assess the effectiveness of curriculum plans. Just as goals and general objectives must be clear and unambiguous in order to allow teachers to select organizing centers and determine specific instructional objectives, so also is clarity of all three of these "levels" necessary before one can begin an evaluation process. A goal of "helping the student become a good person" or an objective that seeks "to develop mathematical competence" is so nebulous that it provides no suggestions for an evaluative focus.

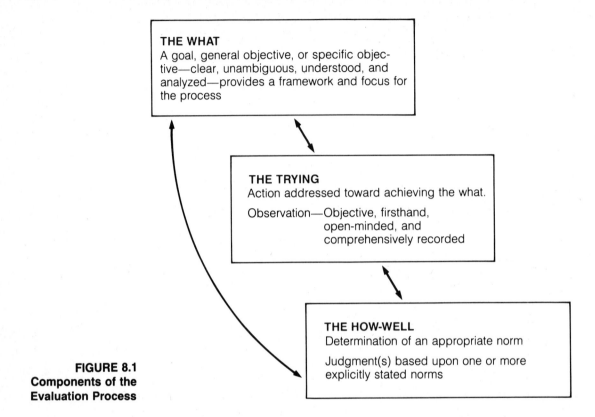

**FIGURE 8.1
Components of the
Evaluation Process**

It should also be apparent that even the best-written goals or objectives will have little impact on a school's program if the professional staff is not fully aware of those aims. All too often, it seems, a district's comprehensive and carefully planned goals, developed cooperatively by a professional or lay committee to satisfy some state requirement or some accreditation mandate, remain filed away and unused. *If goal documents are to become the foundations for planning the "real" curriculum in the district, then they must have wide distribution, ongoing discussion, and continual analysis.* The same strictures would apply to the general objectives of a particular school, and, similarly, to the specific objectives of an individual teacher. It is frequently the case that the skill, concept, knowledge, or understanding that a teacher has carefully identified in preplanning a unit or an activity goes unmentioned to the student. As a result, desired connections or interrelationships or transfers remain unrealized unless that same student struggles to discover the overriding links that provide cohesiveness.

Unambiguous, clearly understood goals and objectives provide "the what" of evaluation. Without them as a framework and a focus, the process cannot even begin.

■ **The Trying**

"The trying" component contains one more possibility that could cause the evaluation process to reach a quick termination. If no action or behavior can be identified that is aimed at achieving the goal or objective being considered, then evaluation ceases. But in any such case, a new question immediately arises: Is the goal or objective worth keeping? An affirmative response necessitates curriculum planning to select content, activities, and materials appropriate for new or modified teaching–learning situations. A negative response necessitates removing the goal or objective from any overall or specific statement of aims. (It might also suggest a serious examination of why the particular item was identified in the first place. Has it lost its importance or its relevance? Has it been superseded or subsumed by some new item? Was it incorrectly included right from the start? And, particularly if the object in question is a broad statement from an overall plan, is it time to reexamine all of the items to determine other gaps between goals and practice?)

Once confirmation of action addressed to achieving the goal or objective has occurred, it is time to begin observation. Presumably, the same techniques or activities that comprise the action also become the objects being evaluated. Careful observation, therefore, becomes a critical part of this component. Without that "care," this stage of the process can undermine everything that follows. (It is important to emphasize that the use of the term "observation" here does not merely refer to "observation of teaching" in the familiar supervisory sense. It deals, rather, with one's observation of any of the ways in which teaching–learning may be evidenced in support of the goals or objectives in a particular environment, of how data may demonstrate effectiveness of a particular instructional program, or of how well the comprehensive curriculum planning process is being implemented in a particular situation. Its use, therefore, is intended to convey the broadest possible perspective.)

Three potential "observation" problems are especially worth noting. It is often tempting to try to reduce effort by relying on someone else's version of what specific actions are occurring. But this acceptance of what is really no more than *hearsay* can result in a totally invalid final judgment—unless, of course, the person conveying information has been specifically trained in observation techniques. Equally problematic is the well-intentioned reliance on *memory*. A classroom teacher, building principal, district supervisor, or curriculum coordinator has an undeniably busy workday. It is often tempting to put off recording the results of an observation until more time is available, perhaps in an evening or during a weekend. Unfortunately, however, memories can quickly lose their objectivity and transform what was actually observed into what was expected to be observed. Again, the effect is to invalidate final judgment. Likewise, observations that are too narrow in their focus, too yielding to closedmindedness, will also admit a serious potential for errors in judgment. Unless the record of what is going on allows for a wide range of behaviors and accommodates a broad base of possibilities, it may overlook factors that have great significance in determining what has occurred.

(Again, it is important to point out that the "observation" in an evaluation process very often takes the form of specific testing. Even though it is an extremely common practice, testing requires an understanding of several key concepts and definitions before it can be used effectively in the evaluation process. Later in this chapter we shall address some of those concepts from a perspective that places testing squarely within the framework of our "working definition.")

In the final analysis, then, observation can dramatically affect the direction that an evaluation takes. Done with objectivity, firsthand contact, and open-mindedness, and comprehensively recorded in a manner that permits extended consideration and detailed examination, observation brings together a key segment of the data necessary to complete the evaluation process.

■ The How-Well

The third and last component of evaluation also has two phases—determination of an appropriate norm, and judgment. Final judgment, the answer to our question of "how well," depends on the norm or comparative standard being applied in the situation under consideration. To cite a frequently heard example, we might quote two typical "parents' night" statements.

> "Your daughter Kathy has done better than she ever did before, but she still isn't achieving as well as the rest of the class."

> "I know your son Mike did extremely well on all the tests, but he never turns in homework and he just isn't working up to capacity."

At issue here are conflicts in norms; at variance are the judgments that result. Individual capacity or potential is one possible norm to use in judging adequacy. But so is comparison with the performance of a peer group or a national sample of "similar" students. And so is actual performance on test questions designed to examine a particular skill or specialized knowledge. Yet each of these norms can result in a different judgment being made—all relative to the same situation or the same action being "observed." (We shall return to a discussion of norms later in this chapter.)

The point, then, is simple but critical. Different conclusions may very well be the result of different norms. Based upon those different norms, all of the conclusions may be equally valid. To avoid unnecessary conflict, or even a set of circumstances wherein decisions might be made to throw out the results of a crucial and careful evaluation, it is very important that the particular norm or standard being used to arrive at an evaluative judgment be clear and well understood. In some cases, the most appropriate course is to present more than one judgment—but to have each judgment carefully tied to an explicitly understood norm. But in every case, judgment expressed without reference to the norm being used is of little, if any, value.

Finally, to complete the interrelation of components, it must be stressed that an answer to the "how-well" without knowledge of "the what" is of no value. In other words, the statement "That's an outstanding program; it deserves to be continued" is worthless unless one knows the goals or objectives, is aware that there was considered action toward those goals, is confident that observation of the action was carefully competent, and accepts the norms used to arrive at the final decision.

THE USES OF EVALUATION

■ ■ When all the basics are said and done about the process itself, there are still four cases pertaining to the use of evaluation that require special mention before we go into any more detail about specific elements. The first involves those instances in curriculum planning (or teaching, or supervision, or inservice education) in which a decision is made not to do any evaluation. No matter what the reason for such a decision, it deserves only one, unequivocal response. *If something isn't worth evaluating, then it isn't worth doing.*

The second case involves those instances in which an evaluation (or at least the observation/testing component) is done, but the results aren't looked at by the parties actually doing "the trying." While this may at first seem an unlikely case, it is in fact quite frequent. Increasingly, students are required to take state or national competency or achievement tests. Schools that participate in such programs usually send the tests to that same state or national agency for scoring. In an all-too-typical instance, scores are returned to the district months later, and to the schools sometime after that. Students who are tested may have moved to new grades, new schools, or new districts. As a result of the untimely disclosure of results, no one bothers to look at them.

The third case is actually a variation of the one just presented. Observation/testing is done; results are quickly determined. Perhaps evaluation is even completed with appropriate consideration of norms and final judgments made about "how well" the "what" was done. But the judgments are ignored. The program or instructional activities remain unchanged—no matter what the outcome of the evaluation.

In the latter two cases, a fundamental use of evaluation is totally disregarded. *The results of evaluation must be used to improve future actions.* Otherwise, there is little sense in doing the evaluation in the first place. If judgments are not used to make decisions that have an impact on future actions in the instructional program or future actions by the learner, then the most valuable contribution of evaluation is overlooked. In fact, such occurrences might better be called "testing"; they should not be dignified with the more comprehensive connotations of "evaluation." Even one of the most commonly cited examples of evaluation is really no more than testing and reporting. Final examinations in a course are taken by most students, but those exams are seldom seen in a corrected version. Marks are reported, but errors are not discussed so that the student's future behavior or actions might change. Detailed analyses of group results are seldom conducted, so particular areas or skills being taught in the class are seldom identified as special problems. Therefore, unless the overall group results are so bad as to be blatant, the teacher's future behavior or actions do not change either. Neither of the key participants on whom the "evaluation" centers is influenced relative to future changes. What might have been a precious opportunity for learning and improvement becomes little more than a hurdle or a stressful situation.

In effect, this instance leads directly to the fourth case—and to the second major use of evaluation. When the prospect of evaluation is used to threaten the person attempting to learn or to do the action that may be evaluated, then a serious corruption of the process occurs. Once again, a few typical quotes may serve to suggest such situations.

"All right, class. Unless you quiet down immediately, we'll stop this and I'll give you a test."

"Jim, if you don't pay attention, you're not going to know this when the exam comes up."

"If all of you don't bring in homework tomorrow, we're going to have a full-period quiz."

"Those kids think they know everything. I'm going to give them a test that will really knock them down a peg or two."

"Jason, unless your students are better behaved (or do better on their exams), I'm going to have to ask your supervisor to come in and evaluate your teaching."

"John, we've had several complaints from parents about the program in your school. I think we should hire an outside consultant to come in and evaluate it."

Although the persons in the learner or student or actor role are different in several of these examples, in each case evaluation is used as a threat. Edward Krug (1957) states the case as follows:

> Evaluation has become too much a sort of punitive measure. In the minds of many students the entire process symbolizes a conflict between students and teachers. We need to help students see evaluation as a natural part of the learning process and to regard evaluation techniques as means by which they can judge their own growth and bring about further improvement. (p. 194)

In other words, when evaluation becomes a strain rather than a help, we destroy its second major use. *Evaluation should help the learner grow as he or she uses information gained during the process.* It should enhance self-esteem, not damage it.

What we have discussed so far, then, becomes our fundamental basis for considering evaluation in its relationship to curriculum planning. Within the context of our working definition, the key components of the process, and the major uses that make evaluation something more than testing and reporting, many additional subtleties, more complex understandings, terms, and techniques can be extremely helpful. But as we proceed to present some of these areas, it is worth reemphasizing that without our preliminary discussion as an ongoing and comprehensive framework, all of the more advanced or more technical notions dealing with evaluation are relatively worthless.

ROLES IN THE EVALUATION PROCESS

■ ■   Our discussion has already referred informally to various parts that people involved in evaluation might play. In his careful consideration of the evaluation process, Virgil Herrick (1962) identifies four roles that can be assumed by involved persons.

> The doer: the child, teacher, or person whose behavior is being evaluated.
> The observer: the person who is looking at what the learner is doing.
> The judger: the person who is taking the results of the observations and judging their value and adequacy.
> The actor: the individual who acts on the results of the evaluation. (p. 119)

These roles should be considered in terms of our working definition, the components of the evaluation process, and the various uses of evaluation. Two particular points, however, require special mention.

First, *the greater the degree of cooperation among persons serving in the four roles, the greater the likelihood that the evaluation will be used as a source of data for improving future actions.* When the roles are divided in some adversarial fashion, or used purely as a basis for exercising power, there is little chance that the "doer" (or learner) will view evaluation as a mechanism for personal growth or improvement.

Second, *one of the general objectives of education should be to assist the learner (or "doer") in gradually assuming all of the roles.* Only to the extent that an individual can learn to combine in his or her own person the evaluative roles of doer, observer, judger, and actor will the process of evaluation become a natural, ongoing framework for continual progress. The current concern for development of lifelong learning skills also points toward the central importance of continuous evaluation, with as many of the roles as possible played by the individual learner.

But becoming skilled in the overall process requires both careful teaching and extensive practice. The skill must be nurtured over a period of years, with the teacher (who in a given situation might be an outside consultant, a supervisor, a principal, or a classroom teacher) gradually relinquishing roles and the student (who in a given situation might also be any one of the persons mentioned) gradually assuming them. The transition must be a planned one, and it involves far more than asking a "student," "What grade do *you* think you should get?" or "How effective do *you* think the program is?"

Similarly, it is not sufficient to wait until the end of twelfth grade and then suddenly require a senior to design his or her own evaluation for a particular unit of study. Such actions generally meet the same fate as twelfth-grade independent study courses where for the first time in his or her school career a student is asked, "What do you want to do this semester?" The instructor is greeted by a blank look or a mumbled, "I don't know; you're the teacher." From that time on, whenever independent study is a topic for discussion, the teacher's reaction is liable to be: "I tried that once and it didn't work. The kids didn't want to do anything."

The similar response in evaluation is: "I tried that once. The kids all gave themselves A's." In both examples, what was overlooked is the necessary gradual nature of the transition and the necessary careful teaching and discussion of the process. At the program level, this might correspond to asking board members to approve or judge the worth of a new health education syllabus without providing any information about developmental characteristics of contemporary adolescents. Or it could involve asking principals to support a change to middle schools from junior high schools without providing any information about the philosophical rationale or about how the new schools would be appraised for effectiveness.

In order for anyone to play all the roles in the evaluation process, he or she must understand each of the components, their specialized techniques or concerns, and their interaction. This means knowing how to clarify goals or objectives, learning ways of observing and/or recording behavior, and knowing what norms may be appropriate for rendering judgment about how well that behavior is addressing the goals. When all this is understood, a single person can actively assume the four evaluation roles.

In writing on resources in education, Elsie Clapp (1952) presented the following absolutely critical observations about evaluation roles.

> These techniques will cause the learner to ask himself how he is doing, rather than cause the teacher to ask himself how the learner is doing. What the teacher thinks of the learner is of passing moment, but what the learner thinks of himself is of lasting import, because it is built into experience and modifies the organism from there on.
>
> We think evaluation is important because it seems absurd for anyone ever to do anything without asking himself how well he did, and whether what he did worked out in the light of his unique purposes. The only place where he does not do this automatically is in school, where he knows the teacher will do it for him. Of course he evaluates even then, but not what was supposed to be learned. If he started the course to get a grade in the book, he will ask himself how well he did in getting a good grade, not what he learned. (p. 85)

Only when the evaluation roles shift to the informed and understanding learner (whether that learner is a student, teacher, principal, central office staff person, board member, or individual going about the business of living) will the evaluation product shift to progress.

ADDITIONAL TERMINOLOGY

■ ■ Formative and Summative Evaluation

Although we have tried to minimize jargon so that evaluation might be seen as a straightforward, easily attainable process, there are some additional terms that can be used to provide a deeper understanding of some of the issues involved in this aspect of curriculum planning. One pair of terms, "formative" and "summative," suggests a way of classifying evaluation approaches. With respect to program evaluation, the terms are concisely summarized and described in the *Encyclopedia of Educational Research* (Mitzel, 1982).

Scriven (1967) classified evaluation into two types: formative and summative. Formative studies are those conducted during the planning and implementation phases of program development. The purpose of formative evaluation is to provide the developer with useful information for ongoing adjustments during program development. . . . Summative evaluation involves decisions about the worth of the program some time following the adjustment period. Although these distinctions prove helpful, they are not necessarily mutually exclusive. As Scriven himself recognizes, both types of evaluation do take place at various phases in a program's development, implementation, and final installation. During the formative phase of program evaluation, summative decisions are made about various parts of the program. At the conclusion of summative studies, the information is used to further modify programs. . . .

Alkin (1969) identified five types of program evaluations; the first three can be labeled "formative" and the last two "summative." Each evaluation is identified with a particular phase of a program's development. The first type, "systems assessment," is associated with the preplanning phase of a program's development, also called "needs assessment." It answers questions such as the following: Is there a need for a new program? What type of program? How will it be received? How will it fit into the ongoing education program? "Program planning," the second type of evaluation mentioned by Alkin, is concerned with designing the program; evaluation looks at the internal "fit" among the various components of the program. "Program implementation," the third type, is frequently referred to as "process evaluation" (Stufflebeam & Guba, 1970; Provus, 1971; Worthen & Sanders, 1973), although Stake (1967) uses the term "transactions." Evaluation of program implementation concerns the process of carrying out the program, and involves not only program activities but how an organization puts the program into action.

The two summative evaluation types are designated by Alkin as "program improvement" and "program certification." In the former, the focus of evaluation is upon program effects. Program comparison, compliance review, and audit studies would fall into the category of program certification. (p. 603)

With particular focus on student learning (which is, after all, one of the primary criteria used in judging program effectiveness), Benjamin Bloom, J. Thomas Hastings, and George Madaus (1971) also discuss the terms which we are considering.

The main purpose of formative observations (there are other useful ways of observing behavior besides testing) is to determine the degree of mastery of a given learning task and to pinpoint the part of the task not mastered. Perhaps a negative description will make it even clearer. The purpose is not to grade or certify the learner; it is to help both the learner and the teacher focus upon the particular learning necessary for movement toward mastery. On the other hand, summative evaluation is directed toward a much more general assessment of the degree to which the larger outcomes have been attained over the entire course or some substantial part of it. In fifth-grade arithmetic, for example, summative evaluation would have as its major purpose to determine the degree to which a student can translate word problems into quantitative solutions or his accuracy and rapidity in handling division. Further purposes would be to grade pupils and to report to parents or administrators. In formative evaluation the concern is with seeing whether a deficiency in translating word problems is due to vocabulary inadequacies or to inability to demonstrate arithmetic formulations; and the division question would focus on type of error. Here the purpose would be to direct both the student and the teacher to specific learnings needed for mastery. (p. 61)

Lest there be any misunderstanding, we should emphasize that it is the purpose or function of the evaluation, not the intended audience, that is the major determiner of whether that evaluation is formative or summative. In their ongoing discussion and delineation of the terms, Bloom and his colleagues make this point very clear. For our purposes, however, it seems that a recognition of the distinctions between "formative" and "summative" may help in considering the components, uses, and roles of evaluation in all levels of the curriculum planning process.

■ Measurement and Testing

Two other terms that deserve at least passing clarification are *measurement* and *testing*. Often, these are used as permissible synonyms for *evaluation*. They are not. Measurement and testing are used to gather information or data descriptive of "the trying" and its results. Sometimes, statistical methods may be used to organize test (or other) data and arrive at a particular measure. It is also apparent that in some situations advanced statistical techniques may enable data to be analyzed into more usable forms—even establishing causal or predictive relationships. But evaluation is a more inclusive term and requires some judgment of adequacy following determination of appropriate norms.

This is not a perfectly linear relationship. In practice, it may be that one first determines norms and then devises tests to measure achievement relative to those norms. On the other hand, one may simply gather as much test data as possible, organize and interpret that data into useful measures of various factors that may be significant, and then analyze the results in terms of as many different norms as can be determined to be appropriate. We are dealing here with the general "observation" that is central to "the trying" component of evaluation. Measurement and testing enable us to gather and organize data from that observation.

Examples of Unobtrusive Measures
Miller, 1978

Consider the number of situations in which students are:

Voluntarily remaining after school to chat with teachers
Making significant choices
Involved with realia
Involved with resource people
In active roles
Involved in planning learning activities
Involved in planning social events
Rewriting, rehearsing, and polishing their efforts
Making bulletin boards, displays, or models
Choosing what is to be studied
Reporting to the class
Clarifying values
Asking questions
Learning from other than the written word
Working independently
Attempting to understand themselves with teacher assistance
Learning in areas off the school site
Learning from other students
Learning salable skills
Evaluating their own progress with teacher assistance
Smiling
Laughing

In and of itself, the literature, research, and debates that deal with testing might serve to occupy a lifetime of study. All of the concerns and warnings relative to testing (e.g., are they valid, are they reliable, are they of significance, should they be standardized or personalized, are they of enhancing or dehumanizing effect, do they measure comprehensive growth or achievement in a student or a program?) are concerns and warnings which are important in the curriculum planning process as a whole. Similarly, discussions of what measures may best describe "the trying" in any particular curricular program are also important.

■ Unobtrusive Measures

One idea that must be mentioned is that in addition to the most direct data relating to the success of a specific program, certain "unobtrusive

Playing
Using supplementary instructional materials
Examining current topics or issues
Carrying and/or using paperbacks which are not textbooks
Using their own funds to buy books
In risk taking situations (that is, doing new things)
Using interest centers

Gather data about students that answers:

What percentage of students are participating in a school or community
service program
What percentage of students drop out each year
What percentage of students skip each day
What percentage of students are tardy each day
How many students have been arrested this school year
How many students know the principal's name
How many students don't return to class after a fire drill
How many students left school because of pregnancy the last school year
How many students were high or nodded off because of substance abuse
yesterday
What percentage of students participate in extracurricular activities
How many shakedowns of students by other students occurred last week
How many students attend optional school events
How many students have well thought through educational or vocational
plans for next steps after termination of their secondary education
What percentage of students eat cafeteria lunches
What percentage of students participate in more than one extracurricular
activity

measures" may also give critical input to a truly comprehensive evaluation. William Miller (1978) listed several examples of such unobtrusive but perhaps highly significant measures (see Frame 8.1).

While such data as how many students are happy, actively involved, or helping one another to learn may at first glance appear less relevant than what percentage of students scored above the national mean on SAT tests, a complete evaluation of program effectiveness must consider a wide variety of outcomes—depending, of course, on the goals, objectives, and scope of what is being appraised.

■ **Norms**

Several times in our discussion thus far we have referred to the importance of being aware of appropriate norms and of realizing that different norms can result in dramatically different judgments being

Sample Norms of Adequacy for Educational Evaluation

Herrick, 1962

■ **Norm of the Task Itself**

It is possible to identify some tasks which are sufficiently unitary to be completed on an all-or-none basis. With children a word is not spelled correctly until it is complete, a ball is not hit with a bat until the event actually happens, a step is not taken until it has occurred. With teachers, it is possible to say that a report is not handed in until it is received on the principal's desk or that discipline is not being maintained until all children are quiet when the teacher speaks. In this approach to adequacy, the task to be accomplished or essential aspects of the task are defined so as to include the conception of adequacy. The evaluation problem is merely to observe the behavior in such situations and to judge whether it is present or not.

■ **Norm of the Capacity of the Individual**

Another common position taken in determining adequacy is to judge the behavior as being adequate for a person in relation to his capacity to perform the task. Common measures of capacity in this sense are tests of mental maturity, appraisals of what is done now with what the individual has been able to do in the past, or estimates of the "task" potential or "ceiling" of the individual. These measures or estimates are used as a referent to compare present with past accomplishments and, on the basis of this norm, to judge them as to their adequacy.

■ **Norm of What Is Socially or Educationally Desirable**

Teachers, like all people, develop model patterns or expected behavior which they apply to the other teachers, the children, and the parents, and then make

made from the same database. Thus, determination of norms is perhaps the most critical aspect in evaluation. By definition, norms are arbitrary; but once they have been selected, they become standards for judgment—of individuals, processes, or programs. The norms become the comparative standards of quantitative or qualitative value—the value that is integral to *evalu*ation.

Probably the most frequently used norms in educational evaluation are what Herrick calls a "norm of the experience of others." These are based on comparisons to the performance of similar groups of people or to the operation/results of similar types of programs. So-called measures of central tendency, normal curves, means, medians, modes, and value judgments about these individuals on the basis of this conception. Whether this "model" is *right,* in the sense that it represents the most efficient pattern of behavior for accomplishing the work of a teacher or principal, is not the question.

The recognition of the role and function of this kind of norm in evaluating persons and activities in programs of in-service education is extremely important.

■ **Norm of Use**

Generalizations are derived from present and past experience and then used to plan and direct future activities. If things get worse, the generalizing and/or the applications of that generalizing probably were not good. If things get better, then there is some confidence that these processes are of value and that the program is on the right track.

In the use of this norm, it should be recognized that generalizations as to ideas, processes, and values are intermingled. Other norms need to be applied as well in making final value judgments. The value of this norm of use is that it permits this kind of multiple evaluation to take place and that it provides an opportunity for any level of sophistication in evaluation to develop.

■ **Norm of Ends**

Much of the previous discussion has to do with the evaluation of the goodness of means and the adequacy of development. It should also be recognized that the ends have to be appraised as to whether they are worth trying to achieve. The three common tests of ends have to do with their importance, their significance, and their cruciality.

The importance of an end is determined by its role and position in the program or field of knowledge that it represents.

standard deviations are most usually associated with this type of norm. Other norms, however, can be equally appropriate and can lend additional insight to the evaluation process. Herrick gives several examples, which we cite in Frame 8.2.

While it should be apparent, we again stress that no clear evaluative judgment can be made unless the norm or norms upon which that judgment is being made are completely understood. Failure to recognize or clarify norms can lead to potentially devastating misinterpretations of observed data. Consequences for the "actor" (and perhaps even the "judger") are too critical to overlook the absolute necessity of this key aspect in the evaluation process.

■ Reporting

Since the fundamental uses of evaluation require that results be used to improve future actions and that results to help the "learner" grow and improve in future behavior, it is obvious that those results must be reported to all involved persons in a manner that:

- ■ assures understanding;
- ■ conveys comprehensive findings and judgments; and
- ■ encourages compliance, continued investigation, or modified conduct as a result of the findings.

It should then be equally obvious that much of what passes for evaluative reporting is extraordinarily inadequate. What does a report card grade of 85 in American Studies signify? What were the norms used? What objectives were regarded as keystones for the evaluation? Of what did the observation of "trying" consist?

Similarly, what does a statement that "your new social studies curriculum has been evaluated as excellent" signify? Norms? Goals? Measures and observation?

Evaluation reporting must enable at least the three considerations cited above. Otherwise, the entire process—the complete evaluative enterprise—stands a risk of being worthless. As with other terms discussed in this section, "reporting" and "evaluation" are not synonymous. Reporting is but one aspect of the much broader process. But again, as with most of those aspects, its full and proper use is essential to the success of evaluation—and, by extension, essential to the success of comprehensive curriculum planning.

Before continuing, we wish to expand very briefly upon that last point: evaluation is essential to the success of comprehensive curriculum planning. We have purposely avoided presenting any list or chart of what part of the curriculum planning process and what components of the framework for curriculum planning might be evaluated. The answer to those questions is concise and simple. *Everything is subject to evaluation.*

ALTERNATIVE EVALUATION MODELS

■ ■ While our working definition (as adapted from Herrick) is intended as a straightforward means of placing participants squarely at the helm or center of the evaluation process, our approach must in no way be construed as the only possibility. We have suggested that evaluation must be ongoing in all aspects of comprehensive curriculum planning. This includes addressing:

1. Questions of worth or validity pertaining to goals and general objectives
2. Questions of whether the preplanned elements of the teaching–learning situation (specific objectives, content, activities, materials, and measuring devices) will offer the best opportunities for achieving those goals
3. Questions of whether those same elements are appropriate to the needs, interests, and characteristics of the learners for whom they were designed
4. Questions centering on the quality of interactions between and among learners and teachers (including the planning and evaluation processes themselves)
5. Questions addressing the performance of participants in the instructional process (both "teacher" and "learner")
6. Questions examining in the broadest sense whether a particular curriculum plan has met the purposes for which it was conceived

Some of the newer conceptions of evaluation remove the actual decision-making, the answering of questions, from the evaluation process. Perhaps the best-known example of this approach is the CIPP model described by Daniel Stufflebeam, chairperson of the Phi Delta Kappa National Study Committee on Evaluation (1971). His report limits the role of evaluation to the process of "delineating, obtaining, and providing useful information for judging decision alternatives" (p. 40). The CIPP model would delineate the need for information, the plan for obtaining information, and the plan for providing information in four categories: *C*ontext, *I*nput, *P*rocess, and *P*roduct. Data in the first category would permit "planning decisions" to be made, including the definition of objectives. The second area would permit the "structuring decisions" necessary for answering questions of program design. The third area enables "implementation decisions" regarding operation. And the fourth category gives data needed for "recycling decisions"—whether program accomplishments suggest continuation, modification, or abolition.

Another advocate of what might be termed process evaluation, Malcolm Provus, in his work with the Pittsburgh Public Schools, developed a Discrepancy Model of evaluation that he felt could be used for programs being planned, piloted, or continued. His approach examines design adequacy, installation fidelity, process adjustment, product assessment, and cost-benefit comparisons in a process that centers on "(1) defining program standards; (2) determining whether a discrepancy exists between some aspect of program performance and the standards governing that aspect of the program; and (3) using discrepancy information either to change performance or to change program standards" (1971, p. 183).

A different way of looking at discrepancies between what was intended and what is observed forms the basis for Robert Stake's Congruence–Contingency Model. Congruence indicates the degree of match between intended and observed; contingencies are relationships among variables (e.g., which activities or materials are causally related to student achievement, which teacher characteristics most affect communications flow, etc.). Stake argues that the worth of a program can be determined only if evaluation data are collected in three categories: *antecedents* (e.g., "student characteristics, teacher characteristics, curricular content, curricular context, instructional materials, physical plant, school organization, community context"); *transactions* (e.g., "communications flow, time allocation, sequence of events, reinforcement schedule, social climate"); and *outcomes* (e.g., "student achievement, student attitudes, student motor skills, effects on teachers, institutional effects") (1969, p. 16). When all of the relevant data are available, decisions can be made.

Yet an additional way of examining desired outcomes and "the learner's current status with respect to those outcomes" is suggested by the United States Office of Education (USOE) in its various discussions and definitions of "needs assessment." Basically, this is another term for an evaluative process that looks at particular goals or objectives, uses a broad base of data to determine the difference between current status (relative to those same goals or objectives) and desired status, and then examines those differences to assess which ones seem to present the greatest need for concentrated action toward improvement. It is evaluation with regard for establishing priorities of future effort, arising originally from a concern for using limited funds to address those areas of most critical need. Although the term has sometimes been associated with the administration of an easily answered questionnaire that can be tallied to indicate priorities, needs assessment that is done properly must pay attention to all of the concerns and techniques that we are discussing in this chapter. Even the USOE cautioned that deciding which educational objectives most needed to be accomplished in a given instructional situation would necessitate examining data in all areas of learning—not only the cognitive domain, but the affective and psychomotor as well.

For Elliot Eisner, the relevant data definitely include much more than carefully structured, objective information that can be "ticked off" on any grid or simple questionnaire. Although not the only evaluation model to do so, his Educational Connoisseurship and Educational Criticism approach employs a wide-ranging and descriptive process to gather and report data. The "observation" might include looking at curriculum concerns, student outcomes, and classroom processes, but looking with a breadth, depth, and intensity that are too often ignored. Examples of the questions upon which Eisner would focus are quoted in Frame 8.3.

Once observation has addressed the questions, results are

> described, interpreted, and appraised in written narrative . . .
> [similar to] the kind of writing that film, drama, and art critics create.
> The descriptive aspect of written educational criticism helps readers
> visualize what has transpired in classrooms. The descriptive language
> is rich, makes use of metaphor, attempts to render the spirit of the
> place. The interpretive aspect of educational criticism attempts to
> account for what has happened. It employs theory and concepts from
> the social sciences to explicate what has been described. It is intended
> to answer *why* what occurs has occurred, while the descriptive aspect
> attempts to provide a vivid account of the events themselves. Finally,
> the evaluative aspect of criticism renders some judgment of the
> educational value of what has been described and interpreted. It
> appraises the conditions and practices observed, described, and
> interpreted. The end in view is to help an audience grasp the
> educational meaning of what has taken place. . . . (p. 46)

Lastly, it should be noted that Eisner's report is written differently —depending upon who will be playing the roles of judger and/or actor. While this may at first seem inconsequential, it really reemphasizes what we have already discussed relative to the uses of evaluation. As Eisner states it: "This chameleon-like approach to reporting rests on a simple premise: the aim of evaluation is to be helpful. To be helpful, an evaluation must address the audience for whom it is prepared. The same message is not necessarily suitable for everyone" (p. 46).

Still another evaluation model that has received attention in recent years is the "trial by jury" approach. In this process, a program is literally put on trial before a hearing panel using appeals court procedures. A "prosecution" team argues the program's deficiencies, while a "defense" team argues its strengths. Either side may introduce a variety of evidence, ranging from statistical data to expert testimony. After hearing that evidence, the panel may recommend continuation of the program, termination, or revisions in various program aspects. This "legal evaluation" model provides a set of procedures and allows introduction of many types of data. Its use, however, must be carefully planned to ensure reliability and comprehensiveness of evidence—especially when a program's continued existence is at stake.

Finally, though they are not necessarily formal models, two major evaluation projects are so pervasive that their criteria and instruments are often used as a framework for local evaluation. First is the National Assessment of Educational Progress. Its test instruments, in particu-

Sample Questions for Using Professional Judgment in Evaluation

Eisner, 1981

■ **What Is the Purpose of the Evaluation?**

> Are we interested in evaluating the educational merits of what is taught?
> Do we want to evaluate the quality of the teaching taking place in the program?
> Is our purpose to provide feedback to teachers about how things are going in their classrooms?
> Do we want to know what the outcomes of curriculum and instruction are?

■ **Curriculum Concerns**

If the focus were upon the quality of the curriculum, we would appraise not only the quality of the ideas, concepts, and structures it makes available to students, but also the activities it employs to engage students so that these ideas are acquired and meaningful, and the relationship between what was planned and what was implemented. This might translate into the following more specific questions:

> What are the central ideas constituting the curriculum?
> What concepts are focused upon?
> What general theoretical structures are being offered to the students on which these concepts can be placed?
> How do students gain access to the ideas that are believed to be so important: by debate, through lecture, by viewing and discussing films, by reading?
> Are teachers actually using the curriculum materials in a way consistent with the program's aims?
> What are the teachers doing that is in fact better than what was planned, and what things are not being done as well as was hoped for?

■ **Student Outcomes**

If the focus was on what children have learned, then attention shifts to the process of classroom life and what students are doing in those classrooms. But the ques-

---

lar, have been generally regarded as excellent examples of well-constructed, criterion-referenced items. And its overall plan of comparing achievement in a variety of study areas (art, career and occupational development, citizenship, literature, mathematics, music, reading, science, social studies, and writing) is an ambitious and potentially useful

tions are much broader than whether the students are achieving course objectives. The following might be examples:

> What is the level of discourse children are using? To what extent are their comments relevant and insightful regarding the material they are studying?
>
> How do the products which they produced (essays, drawings, paintings, plays, etc.) compare with the products they had produced earlier?
>
> How do the products compare with those of other students, of similar SES, which have been appraised in past educational experience?
>
> In interviews with students, to what extent are they able to transfer and make connections between what they were taught in the course and issues pertaining to problems outside the school?
>
> What is their grasp of key concepts which were taught?
>
> What satisfaction and excitement did they experience in the course?
>
> To what extent did the course generate activities outside the school that had roots in the classroom?
>
> In open-ended programs, when diversity of outcome is educationally valuable, is there uniqueness and fresh interpretation in the student's treatment of an idea or product?
>
> Is the program raising in the minds of students the kinds of questions that will feed them intellectually through life?
>
> Do the students recognize the unique contributions that different art forms (art, music, literature) make to what they have come to know?
>
> Can students rise above the course content and appreciate the contents' more general functions?

■ Classroom Processes

If the evaluation focus is on quality of teaching, the following specific questions may be appropriate:

> How do the teachers relate to the students?
>
> What kind of interest or enthusiasm do they generate?
>
> What is the nature of the questions they ask?
>
> To what extent do teachers model the skills and attitudes the course wants students to acquire?
>
> What do teachers do in their teaching that is unique and valuable?
>
> What aspects of their teaching can be improved?

one, even though it focuses on broad groups of student populations in making its conclusions.

Second are all the various regional accreditation and registration processes, many of which function under the general direction of the National Study of School Evaluation. Rather than specific test instruments, their overall approach is what makes these particularly worth noting. In conducting school evaluations, member organizations base their (arbitrary) judgments of quality on an assessment that considers not only student achievement, but also philosophy and goals, curricula in eighteen subject fields, facilities, counseling services, student activities, performance and qualifications of staff and administrative personnel, attendance and dropout data, community relations, planning processes, and statements/discussions of self-evaluation.

All in all, the various models cited serve to introduce different terminology and/or different perspectives relating to curriculum evaluation. They are not meant to be exhaustive, but rather to serve as indicators of the rich variety of available frameworks or approaches. Any paradigm or suggestion of techniques that gives increased insight to those who are evaluating curriculum can only serve to improve the quality of decisions made in the process. In an admittedly basic and preliminary discussion, it may not be critical whether one chooses to include judgment under the scope of evaluation (as we do), or to limit evaluation to the gathering of data to enable such judgment (Stufflebeam), or to argue for some intermediate or semantic position in between. All of the different approaches ultimately result in determining "how well" the "trying" has addressed some type of "what"—whether the major focus is on program or person (learner or teacher).

It does, however, seem that regardless of the need for consultants or experts to provide advanced or technical assistance in gathering or analyzing certain data, it is absolutely crucial that evaluation involve the participants (planners, "teachers," "learners") in every phase. Only in this way can curriculum evaluation be viewed as the natural, necessary, ongoing part of comprehensive curriculum planning that it must be.

EVALUATION PITFALLS

■ ■ We should like to close this general consideration of the evaluation process by pointing out several recurring problems. Often a simple realization or awareness of potential pitfalls does more to aid in their avoidance than a detailed presentation of possible solutions. The following observations arise from a sharing of teacher/supervisor experiences and summarize many of the points raised already in this chapter.

1. Sometimes in our observations or in our testing, we ask questions to which the answers should be immediately obvious. It always seems that time for evaluation is at a premium, so this type of activity is a waste of valuable effort.

2. We often base our judgments on predetermined analyses developed from group results and group norms. It is very possible that

these analyses are inappropriate for a particular individual being evaluated. It is also possible that the descriptive group statistics being used
are locking us into a "no-win situation." Eldon Gran dealt with both
of these aspects in his article "If I Have But One Life to Live, Let Me
Live It above the Median" (1970).

> Having 50 percent of a population below the median is the kind
> of illness that has no cure. There cannot be 50 percent above the
> median unless there are 50 percent below it. We dreamed up the
> concept, coined the term—and it survives to haunt us at every turn.
> Of course, one way to eliminate the median is to make everybody
> exactly alike so that no median exists. The standardized curriculum,
> measured by the standardized test, thus far has not accomplished this.
> But we do keep on trying. We even have an A-B-C-D-F grading scale
> which is useful in reporting degrees of deviation from the standard. (p.
> 32)

(A similar situation occurs when a school district decides or is required
to publish comparative rankings of all its schools. No matter how well
the district may be doing in relation to national or statewide norms,
half of its schools will be below the district median. And no matter
how upset parents might become if their children are in schools that
rank in the bottom half, this is a problem that has no possible solution!)

3. Sometimes the norms used in evaluation are totally unrealistic
or, at least, irrelevant to the learner's real world. (We see this in our
society's norms as well—e.g., wristwatches prized for their ability to
function at depths of 100 fathoms. What percentage of the general
population do deep-sea divers represent?) If the norms used are inappropriate, then the evaluation will lose most (if not all) of its significance.

4. Often we have held to our beliefs in spite of evaluative knowledge or research to the contrary. This may be acceptable in an idealistic
or personal value situation, but not when it affects children for whose
education we have direct responsibility.

5. We may fall into the trap of using evaluation as a device to
impress or deceive "outsiders" rather than as a means of changing or
improving those directly involved in a particular teaching–learning
situation. Not only is this a relative waste of valuable effort, but it
has also been known to encourage misrepresentation of data and/or
withholding of specific (unfavorable) results. Evaluation without in-
tegrity is evaluation without substance or worth.

6. Evaluation has often been plagued by questions or techniques
that lack specificity. Fill-in-the-blank test questions such as "The sky
is ——" are of little value. Unplanned observations that have not been
preceded by a determination of program goals are generally destined
to be failures. Judgments made without a consideration of appropriate
norms may be little more than biased opinions.

7. It must be understood and remembered that different people may form different conclusions from the same observational data and information. This can be directly related to the norms being used and/or the goals being considered. It again emphasizes the need for the complete and careful reporting of evaluation results in order to prevent misunderstanding or misinterpretation.

8. Sometimes evaluation raises further questions. If we are being honest and thorough, we must seek to answer those questions, not merely ignore them.

9. Despite the encouragement of anyone to do otherwise, the process of evaluation must not be ignored. It is, very simply, fundamental to curriculum planning and to education. We must also be careful not to convince ourselves that evaluation is just too much trouble to be worth the effort. It may be that what we're really saying is that we don't want to know how well we're doing, because that might force us to change something in which we have already invested a great deal of thought, effort, and time. No instructional program or curriculum plan is incapable of improvement.

10. It is too common for evaluation decisions to be regarded as the sole province of the person or persons doing the evaluating. (Obviously this case only occurs when the evaluation roles are being played by more than one individual.) Just as teacher–student planning can provide synergistic benefits when applied to the teaching–learning situation, so can it enhance the evaluation process. Cooperative planning, analysis, and decisions can strengthen every component of the process, can assure positive interaction among the four roles, and can almost guarantee that the purposes and uses of evaluation will not be compromised. Applied to the evaluation of broad goals or programs, such cooperation can very profitably involve the lay community as well as professional educators.

11. There is no doubt that most teachers, administrators, or consultants are able to structure an evaluation so that the results are apparent even before the process is complete. (A cartoon of Ebenezer Scrooge on trial before a judge and jury composed entirely of Santa Clauses comes immediately to mind.) If anyone is going to do this, don't bother with the evaluation in the first place. Entering evaluation with anything less than an open and questioning attitude leads toward findings that were already predisposed and that may be seriously inaccurate. (In the evaluation of "student learning," a related concern would address test items. Tests with all "easy" questions are just as meaningless as tests with all "impossible" questions. And grading students *exactly* on test averages may mean that the tests weren't worth giving!)

12. Sometimes in evaluation we can give too much feedback at one time. The result may be discouragement instead of positive support, encouragement, or help. Although this may appear to be of relatively

small consequence, it can actually result in the disruption of any worth
arising from evaluation. Walt Whitman's thoughts seem particularly
apt in this case.

> When I heard the learn'd astronomer,
> When the proofs, the figures, were ranged in columns before me,
> When I was shown the charts and diagrams, to add, divide,
> and measure them,
> When I sitting heard the astronomer where he lectured with
> much applause in the lecture-room,
> How soon unaccountable I became tired and sick,
> Till rising and gliding out I wander'd off by myself,
> In the mystical moist night-air, and from time to time,
> Look'd up in perfect silence at the stars.

13. Evaluation is not a place for trick questions whose only purpose is to intimidate or punish the learner. Nor is it a place to ignore
creativity or to close out answers that may not have been foreseen but
that are perfectly valid possibilities.

14. Perhaps the most potentially damaging pitfall is that of allowing evaluation to become stressful rather than helpful. This is a
terribly dangerous corruption of the role of evaluation. Making evaluation truly cooperative would begin to change this problem. But we
should always keep in mind the sentiments of William Pharis, who,
as Executive Director of the National Association of Elementary School
Principals, spoke the following in regard to testing (and, by extension,
the complete evaluation process):

> . . . I argued then and I argue now that any experience, any activity,
> and program, should have a payoff for the learner. Damn the teacher
> and his grade level boost. Damn the principal and his ego. Damn the
> tester and his charts, means, medians, and standard deviations. Damn
> the Superintendent and the School Board and their months above or
> below the national norms. And damn the test manufacturers with
> their split-quarter correlations, normative referencing and other
> statistical masturbations. Did my son emerge from the testing better
> than when he went in? As a result of the test can you tell me more
> about him? Do you know what he can do, what he knows, what he
> cannot do, what he does not know? And are you—we—prepared to
> modify his program as a result of what we now know about him?

CHAPTER SUMMARY

In its most fundamental and critical sense, evaluation is an ongoing
part of the comprehensive curriculum planning process. It is the province not only of consultants or specialists, but, much more important,

of all those persons who are actively engaged in planning and implementing broad curricular programs and specific teaching–learning situations.

Basically, evaluation is the process in which we decide how well we are doing whatever it is we are trying to do. It must be conducted in light of clear and unambiguous goals and objectives, using objective and comprehensive observation, and with respect to carefully determined norms or standards of judgment. Its essential place in curriculum planning is to improve future actions and to help the learner grow as he or she uses information gained during the process.

Whether done within the framework of a specific model or within the natural interactions of the teaching–learning situation, evaluation should be a cooperative, enhancing experience for all parties involved. As a foundation of education, evaluation may be thought of quite simply, but profoundly, by considering the words of Louis Raths: "A great deal of learning takes place when we silently think about our lives and what we did and what we are doing."

Having read Chapter 8, you should be able to:

1. Describe a working definition of evaluation as it relates to curriculum improvement
2. Describe the components of the evaluation process
3. Describe the uses of evaluation in the curriculum planning process
4. Describe important roles in the evaluation process
5. Understand some of the basic terminology and distinctions used in discussing evaluation, including "norms," "formative," and "summative" evaluation, "measurement," "testing," and "reporting"
6. Recognize the differences in several significant evaluation models dealing with curriculum improvement
7. Recognize several of the problem areas facing evaluation of curriculum plans and school programs

SUGGESTED ACTIVITIES

1. Identify some program, course of study, or unit commonly used in schools (e.g., health program, calculus unit, or values curriculum). After stating examples of the kinds of objectives that might be used in the program, ask the group to define as many variables as possible that might be considered in an evaluation. For each variable, describe types of data that might be collected to assess its effectiveness, and discuss how those data might be acquired.

2. Select a school or university building in which classes frequently meet. Ask the group to form two-person teams to collect unobtrusive data within the building. Teams may record graffiti, messages on bulletin boards, notes on chalkboards, etc. Once the data are collected, discuss what they might suggest about student attitudes, teaching methods, preferred activities, school life, etc.

3. Select a controversial curriculum-related topic, such as homogeneous versus heterogeneous grouping, values education, or mainstreaming. Form the group into two teams, one to argue each of the opposing sides of the issue. Also form a panel to hear the arguments and make a detemination in the case. (Note: This activity is a simulation of the "legal education" model, and it may require two or more weeks for the teams to collect evidence to form their arguments. Also, participants should consult literature regarding the model in order to familiarize themselves with its procedures.)

4. Collect several examples of judgments about schools from local or national media. Analyze and discuss the examples, considering such concerns as data used to form the judgment, accuracy of opinions, possible opposing or conflicting data, and relevance of nationally based judgments to local schools.

5. Obtain a set of goals for a local district or a state. (Examples from Chapter 4 might be used.) Discuss how the goals might be the subject of two types of evaluation. First, how might the goals themselves be evaluated in terms of relevance, comprehensiveness, and clarity? Second, what types of data might be collected to assess student achievement of each goal?

6. Choose one of the evaluation models described in this chapter. Discuss how the model addresses the components of the evaluation process identified at the outset of the chapter. For example, how does the model provide for identification and analysis of "the what", "the trying", and "the how well" in a situation or setting to be evaluated?

7. Select a program or a course of study to be evaluated. After discussing procedures and possible data sources for the evaluation, identify roles that might be played in conducting it (e.g., by students, teachers, administrators, board members, citizens, external evaluators). In each case, describe the minimum and maximum limits for each role (assuming everybody will participate and no one group will do everything). Discuss problems or issues that might arise if each group assumed its maximum participation limit.

8. Select three or four of the evaluation pitfalls described in this chapter. In large or small groups, discuss how these pitfalls might be avoided. Also, consider what consequences might occur if the pitfalls are not overcome (e.g, unfair criticism or inaccurate media reporting).

Where possible, identify examples of evaluation in (or of) local schools where one or more pitfalls were present.

9. Consider the following description of the first two components of the evaluation process that has been discussed in this chapter.

Several years ago, Liminality School District developed and implemented a middle school. One of the primary purposes of the school was to provide an educational program based upon the characteristics of emerging adolescence. Now the middle school staff is interested in finding out whether and to what degree that purpose has been fulfilled. They plan an evaluation project and publish a preliminary outline.

I.   *The What.* The central focus is on the educational program of the middle school. In this case, "program" might be interpreted to mean such things as climate, courses of study, and other aspects of the all-school program.

II. *The Trying.* We shall look at aspects of the all-school program such as the following.
   A. Do general and specific objectives reflect cognitive, affective, and psychomotor development?
   B. Do learning activities emphasize concrete experience and direct involvement rather than abstract and passive experience?
   C. Are grouping procedures flexible? If homogeneous grouping is used, what variables are represented?
   D. Do learning resources reflect the interests, concerns, thinking styles, and skill levels of emerging adolescents?
   E. Are middle school personnel aware of the developmental characteristics of emerging adolescents?
   F. Does concern for personal/social issues of emerging adolescence permeate the program through individual and group counseling, teacher attitudes and behavior, and school activities and regulations?
   G. Is provision made for student involvement in curriculum planning so that their concerns and ideas may be expressed?
   H. Is the curriculum sufficiently varied to address both the common needs of all learners and the special interests of individuals and small groups?
   I. Does the all-school program include an activities component (e.g., sports, clubs) based upon learner interests? Does this component reflect the physical and emotional needs of emerging adolescence?
   J. Is the school schedule sufficiently flexible to allow for

teacher and student decisions regarding how much time is allotted for specific activities?

K. Does the student progress reporting system reflect individual growth based upon the learner's personal developmental level and characteristics?

Possible Data Sources. Curriculum plans; teacher attitude surveys; achievement test results; classroom observations; student interviews; discipline records; attendance records; records of participation in school activities; parent interviews and surveys; lists of rules and regulations; school general objectives; school schedule; master list of courses and activity offerings; examination of textbooks and library/media center resources.

■ Are there any suggestions you could make to clarify "the what" as it is expressed in the outline?

■ What additions might be made to the list of questions and data sources described in "the trying" section of the outline?

■ Construct a "how-well" section for the outline that includes possible norms that could be used in the evaluation. Are particular norms more appropriate for specific questions?

■ In small groups, select one of the listed questions and construct a small set of hypothetical data relating to it. Based on the data and on a specific norm, decide on a "how-well" answer. Now exchange your question and related data with another group, but do not disclose the norm. Repeat the "how-well" component for your new question and data. Compare your decisions to both questions with the decisions made by the other group. Discuss any differences that may have arisen because of different norms. Finally, based upon the decisions made in the "how-well" component, suggest a possible course of action related to each of the two questions with which you have been working.

REFERENCES

Bloom, B.; Hastings, J. T.; and Madaus, G. *Handbook on Formative and Summative Evaluation of Student Learning.* New York: McGraw-Hill, 1971.
Clapp, E. *The Use of Resources in Education.* New York: Harper & Row, 1952.
Eisner, E. "Using Professional Judgment." *Applied Strategies for Curriculum Evaluation,* edited by R. Brandt. Alexandria, Va.: Association for Supervision and Curriculum Development, 1970, pp. 41–47.
Gran, E. "If I Have But One Life to Live, Let Me Live It above the Median." *The Education Digest,* October 1970, pp. 32–33.
Krug, E. *Curriculum Planning.* Rev. ed. New York: Harper & Row, 1957.

Macdonald, J.; Andersen, D.; and May, F.; (eds.). *Strategies of Curriculum Development: Selected Writings of the Late Virgil E. Herrick.* Columbus, Ohio: Charles E. Merrill, 1965.

Miller, W. "Unobtrusive Measures Can Help in Assessing Growth." *Educational Leadership* 35 (1978): 264–269.

Mitzel, H. (ed.) *Encyclopedia of Educational Research.* 5th ed. New York: Free Press, 1982.

Provus, M. *Discrepancy Evaluation for Educational Program Improvement and Assessment.* Berkeley, Calif.: McCutchan, 1971.

Stake, R. "Language, Rationality, and Assessment." In *Improving Educational Assessment and an Inventory of Measures of Affective Behavior,* edited by W. Beatty. Washington, D.C.: ASCD Publications, 1969.

Stufflebeam, D., Chairman, Phi Delta Kappa National Study Committee on Evaluation. *Educational Evaluation and Decision Making.* Itasca, Ill.: F. E. Peacock, 1971.

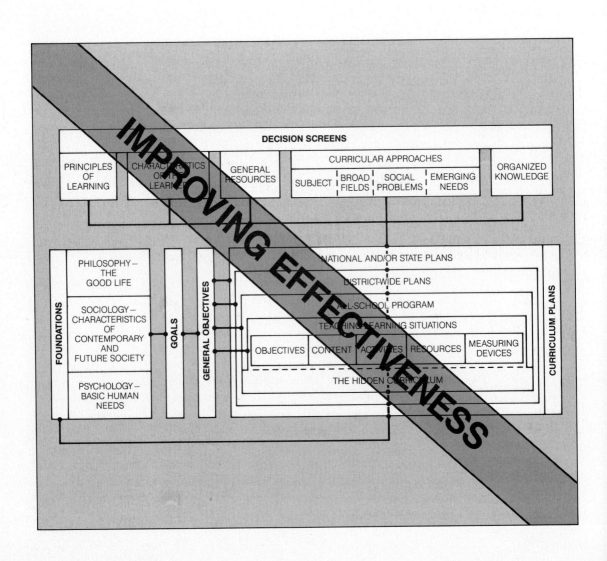

9

Toward More Effective Curriculum Planning

The first eight chapters of the book have attempted to provide the reader with understandings of the nature of the curriculum planning process, the foundations of curriculum, major roles for educators in curriculum planning, the components of curriculum planning, how to organize the all-school program, and approaches for evaluating the curriculum. With these understandings, educators should be able to consider ways in which they can participate in improving the curriculum planning program in their own professional environment. In Chapter 9 we explore means by which educators can improve curriculum planning. This chapter also identifies means through which the curriculum planning process can improve programs and identify curriculum issues requiring further study. Educators need to develop an understanding of means to participate effectively in curriculum planning activities in their educational environment.

As a result of reading Chapter 9, you should be able to:

1. Identify ways to improve the total curriculum planning program at the local level
2. Describe areas of lay concern in curriculum planning in which lay perspective is essential
3. Identify roles for lay participation in curriculum planning
4. Describe areas of concern in curriculum planning that require educational expertise for participation
5. Identify professional educator roles in curriculum planning
6. Identify ways in which professionals and laypersons can cooperatively work in the curriculum planning program
7. Identify staff development/inservice education roles in improving the curriculum planning program
8. Describe organizational structures essential to articulating

curriculum planning activities in the school—community
setting

9. Describe horizontal and vertical curriculum planning issues and how they relate to the district-wide curriculum
   planning program

10. Describe line and staff curriculum planning issues and how
    they must be supported to improve the district-wide curric-
    ulum planning program

11. Define and describe the concept of systemic curriculum
    planning as a means to provide ongoing curriculum
    improvement

PROFESSIONAL AND LAY CONCERNS IN IMPROVING CURRICULUM

■ ■ The local community is the setting in which the home and school strive
to nurture and educate children. Parents and laypersons respond to
many of the needs of children in home and community settings apart
from the school, while educators use their professional preparation to
deal with the educational needs of children in the schools. In this way
parents, laypersons, and educators serve particular needs of youth
through separate, noninteractive means. However, there are needs to
articulate both groups in particular aspects of the curriculum planning
process. Curriculum planning must strive to make appropriate use of
both professional expertise and parent/lay concerns in planning and
refining the all-school program.

Schools and their communities have largely failed to deal with
the major issues central to resolving lay and professional participation
in the curriculum planning process. The following concerns raised by
Edward Krug (1950) persist in most school districts today:

> The schools belong to the general public; citizens in general, therefore,
> should have much to say about the curriculum. On the other hand,
> professional educators have received special training for this work and
> should be expected to know more about it than anyone else. On what
> basis, then, can lay people participate in curriculum development
> programs? Where does their effective contribution lie? Wherein should
> school people defer to the fact that the schools belong not to them, but
> to the community as a whole? Wherein should lay people defer to the
> professional training and judgments of the teacher? (p. 16)

The "effective contribution" of both professionals and laypersons
in dealing with specific needs of children is increased when both plan
together to identify those areas which require cooperative interaction.
As these areas are defined, the issues and concerns best handled sep-

arately by each group can readily be sorted out. In that respect, it appears there is a sort of Gestalt at work and that the whole of this interaction does prove to be more than the sum of the parts. Let us consider some of the issues for each group in their involvement in cooperative curriculum planning activities.

■ Lay Concerns

The purpose of education is to maintain and improve society. Thus laypersons who make up that society have the predominant right to define what they want for their children. It is a fact that education is largely a state rather than a federal function, although specific state educational statutes may not violate federal laws. Likewise, local school district policies must not violate either state or federal regulations. But aside from any conflicts with federal or state laws, local educational regulations should reflect what laypersons see as broad goals and conditions for their public schools. Within this structure, local district educational policy reflects the goals and purposes that laypersons see as appropriate for school programs.

Krug (1950) identified a problem that schools today still must address to refine the effectiveness of lay participation in curriculum planning: "The major problem involved in lay participation, however, is not that of resolving conflicts, but of arousing lay interests. It is one of the responsibilities of local leadership to widen the base of community interest in educational objectives" (p. 6). Krug recommends the development of a local discussion guide that focuses upon key issues facing that school–community and directs attention to the important youth problems in the local setting. The number of districts that plan and develop such a guide is disappointingly small. The guide in itself is not as important as the lay and professional interaction that identifies the changing youth problems and issues that the school–community needs to address. Krug goes on to identify how such issues can be facilitated by state leadership groups that recognize similar concerns on regional or statewide bases. With or without such support, local districts must continually work to broaden the base and interest of lay involvement in the goals of their school programs. (See the final section of this chapter, "A Concept of Systemic Curriculum Planning," for suggestions as to how this may be accomplished.) Curriculum planning needs to increase lay participation in goal development and in the lesser but necessary role of advising on program decisions.

□ *Goals* Laypersons should be the primary determiners of educational goals (Toepfer, 1976). Problems arise when the community at large is not adequately represented in the formulation or revision of educational goals. When those participants represent only organized minorities, goals that are developed fail to represent the consensus of local parents and laypersons. Chapter 4 discussed how goals provide broad direction for the development and specification of curricula and educational programs. As laypersons agree on broad goals for the school, education professionals can translate those goals into general and specific objectives to which curriculum plans can respond.

Krug further observed: "Clearly, since schools belong to the people as a whole, the development of school programs should involve the participation of people as a whole. Conflicts should not occur between lay people and school people on basic educational purposes [goals]; when they do, the point of view of lay people should prevail" (p. 16). Professionals may be asked to provide advice to lay groups developing broad educational goals. However, the professionals need to understand that their role is only advisory to the lay group in this area. Schools should provide both leadership and support to efforts seeking to broaden the base of lay involvement in goal setting and assessment. As curriculum goals reflect consensus of the broad base of local citizens, school programs developed by the professional staff can become more responsive to those goals.

The failure of districts to develop and extend opportunities to laypersons for involvement in goal setting poses a major problem. Quite often, participation is considered appropriate only for parent groups. Although parents should have a major share in goal setting, other district lay constituencies should not be excluded. As senior citizen and other local groups become involved, broad educational and program goals will better represent the views of the community at large. Goals developed from such a base will provide direction for program decisions that should be more readily supported and financially underwritten by the local population. Therefore, professionals in the school should encourage the development of such a broad base of lay participation.

As an example, sex education remains a controversial area in school programming. Sex education programs are often the source of controversy and debate in many communities. Laypersons may question the rights of public schools to deal in value areas that some may see as conflicting with responsibilities properly belonging to the home and church. As long as federal and state statutes are not violated, the goals for local district or school sex education programs can reflect the consensus concerns of the community. If professionals disagree with these goals, they may pursue and exercise their opportunities to meet and have dialogue with lay groups to present their concerns and information. However, the final decision on the goal aspect of all program areas should arise from a consensus of laypersons. It is important that the local school district and community deal with Krug's basic tenet on this matter.

> If curriculum development involving the lay public is to become a genuine group process, we must get out of our system the idea that our [the professional] role is to instruct or to convert the public away from the error of their ways over to the righteousness of ours. For in a genuine group process, people work together on mutual goals according to their respective contributions. Nobody is there to instruct or convert. All views get modified as result of the planning and discussion involved. Communication between the professional group and the lay public must be a two-way process. Nor does this mean "giving the public what it wants" without evaluative study and criticism. Group process means interaction and careful study of issues. (1950, p. 249)

Despite the development of decision-making theory and public relations approaches in our society, the persistence of this problem in public school–communities for almost four decades since Krug's concise statement is appalling. Most school officials today have done little to institute the kinds of group process that Krug recommended to facilitate professional and lay involvement to deal with local educational needs. Again, let us go back to our example dealing with sex education programs.

It is true that some school–community sex education programs do not reflect consensus and agreement of the community as to the roles that school programs should serve and the broad goals upon which these programs should be organized. In such cases, program objectives may be either ambiguous or slanted toward the biases of organized pressure groups. This lack of broad community involvement in planning the objectives of these programs makes it difficult for educators to know how the local sex education program should respond. The same would be true of other curriculum and program areas, but most of those areas seldom draw as much public attention as this controversial topic does. Whenever educators develop a program based upon goals that do not represent the consensus of citizens' concerns, that program may not be effectively responsive to community interests. Furthermore, parents and other laypersons will often resist such programs because they do not readily see or agree with the purposes of that program. Effective curriculum planning requires the broad involvement of laypersons and the community in establishing and clarifying educational goals. This is essential if local educators are to gain an adequate basis for professional decision making when they develop curriculum plans and school programs that respond to local educational goals.

□ *Advising on Program Decisions* Advising on program decisions is a lesser but still essential area of lay participation in curriculum planning. As professionals develop curriculum plans, it is important that they have access to the opinion of representative, interested laypersons. As we will discuss in the next section, the primary professional role in curriculum planning deals with implementing program decisions that professionals have designed to meet the goals developed in the school–community setting. Professionals have expertise in designing and implementing programs. This is a competence separate and apart from laypersons. However, activities must be organized that provide educators with feedback on how projected programs are perceived by the laypersons who formulated the educational goals in that community. The following example deals with the development of an environmental education program based upon community-defined goals and needs.

As the school educators were developing a school environmental education program based upon local formulation of broad goals, it was helpful for them to meet periodically with representatives of the group that had developed those goals. Such interaction provided feedback and gave the educators perspective in finalizing specific curriculum plans. Lay participation in such interaction should be advisory and not perceived as the determining factor in developing curriculum plans. The educators developing this program were chosen because of their expertise in the subject-matter areas involved in the environmental education area. Advisory meetings with the lay group were established to allow ongoing interaction between both goal and program developers. These meetings provided perspective for both groups and made it possible for the program to respond as accurately as it could to goal issues dealing with local environmental education issues. In addition, the laypersons advising in this capacity had the opportunity to rethink and further develop environmental education goals based on the achievements of the curricula and school programs being planned and implemented.

Advising on school programs may also involve citizens in considering the degree to which a program does or does not meet broad goals. For example, let us assume that a community has developed goals in the area of education for better mental health. Let us further assume that the professional staff dealing with that program area feels an augmented sex education program is necessary to meet the mental health objectives developed by the community. The community does not retain the prerogative to decide whether or not such a program would be appropriate as a means to meet the mental health education goals developed by that community.

Discussion between laypersons and professionals here must be organized upon a careful definition of the lay and professional prerogatives in such a situation. The design and implementation of a school program is clearly a professional decision area, as long as the community agrees the particular program component is appropriate and consistent with the goals that the community has developed. If it does not, consideration must be given to the need to clarify the goal or revise the program. In either case, the appropriateness of a particular program as a means to achieve the appropriate goal requires lay–professional dialogue. However, the ultimate decision resides in lay agreement that the program is truly appropriate for achieving that goal. As the next section will discuss, once this is resolved, the design and implementation of that program become the prerogative of the professionals. Krug observed: "Teachers and administrators must be careful to maintain the discussion approach in working with lay people on educational purposes. Too often, the members of the professional group try to sell or interpret their philosophy to lay people. They devote their efforts to urging a point of view instead of raising important and critical questions" (1950, pp. 16–17). If those "critical questions" fail to persuade the community group, the professionals are obliged not to utilize that element in the school program. As this interaction develops, professionals can consider the perspective of laypersons more carefully in organizing school programs. A healthy advisory relationship can heighten the perceptions of both laypersons and professionals. Professionals develop a greater awareness of lay concerns and goals while laypersons become more sensitive to program needs in planning and formulating goals. This mutual consideration of goals and school programs is significant in improving the responsiveness of the all-school program to the needs of children.

■ Professional Concerns

Whereas the major curriculum planning role of laypersons is in the formulation of goals, the role of professional educators is to plan curriculum and develop school programs to meet those goals (Toepfer, 1976). Medical doctors and other health professionals have been educated and have developed the expertise necessary to deal with the needs of their profession. Likewise, educators have also been prepared to deal with the internal workings of education in terms of subject matter, or content, and methods, or pedagogy. Qualified physicians have the expertise to make professional decisions within the practice of medicine, and the same should hold true for educators in their profession.

Krug noted: "When agreement on purposes is reached, lay people should defer to professional judgment on specific techniques used in carrying out the purposes. Four of the major jobs of curriculum planning—setting up the all-school program, outlining the broad fields of instruction, providing aids for teachers and teaching—are therefore generally more the responsibilities of professional educators" (1950, p.

16). (Krug's fifth major job of curriculum planning, that of defining or identifying the goals or functions of the school, is classified as a lay responsibility, as discussed in the previous section.)

The public questions this proposition far less with physicians than with teachers. Indeed, it seems that many people consider themselves educational experts because they have experienced elementary and secondary schools as students and/or have dealt with their own children's schools and teachers. While laypersons may inwardly question medical doctors, they do not have the familiarity with the medical profession to the degree they have with schools.

One should not underestimate the complexities that this creates for the authority of professionals in curriculum planning. While most laypersons would not, for instance, consider questioning how the physician holds a scalpel during a surgical procedure, they would be far less hesitant to pass similar judgment on an educator's choice of departmentalized instruction as opposed to a self-contained classroom or a team teaching arrangement to deal with an instructional need. As it is important for educators to recognize that their involvement in broad goal setting should be only advisory, it is equally important that laypersons understand that once a program is judged appropriate to local goals, professional decision-making prerogatives also need to be recognized and carefully secured.

Although their preparation is perceived by the public as less glamorous than physicians'; educators do possess an impressive authority of professional expertise that laypersons need to understand and respect more fully. This authority of expertise includes undergraduate and graduate preparation in child and/or adolescent growth and development, subject-matter and content background, and methodological or pedagogic skills to plan, organize, and implement curriculum plans and school programs. It is essential that the public come to understand the kind and degree of qualifications that educators have gained to design, implement, and make professional decisions about school programs.

☐ *Professional Roles in Program Design and Decisions*   Chapters 5, 6, and 7 discussed details about the variety of skills involved in curriculum planning and program design. The curriculum field has long recommended that professionals be allowed to deal with such issues in the school setting. In the latest edition of their work, J. Galen Saylor and William Alexander again allude to this continuing professional need, as they did in 1954: "There must be time when proposals are sifted down to specific plans for organizing instruction in every classroom. It is at this point that the teaching personnel of the school who direct this program and instruction in these classrooms must make specific decisions to take specific actions" (p. 549).

The persisting nature of this professional need continues to be overlooked in many communities, particularly as recent "back to basics" efforts have often attempted to usurp such prerogatives from professional educators. It is important that the expertise of all professionals in the school be brought to bear on identifying and working to overcome learning needs and problems for which they have been professionally prepared.

As discussed in Chapter 7, pupil personnel resources provide important data that should be utilized in making both curriculum plans and classroom instructional decisions. Professionals should make this information available to parents to help them understand their children's needs and what the school plans to do in order to meet those needs. Likewise, educators can take information gained from discussion with parents to specify curriculum plans and design learning activities that respond appropriately to the individual children's educational needs. The professional preparation of teachers and other school professionals qualifies them to deal with the importance of such factors such as the following:

- The length of a child's attention span
- Individual learning style(s)
- Special learning needs
- The developmental levels at which the child can think and process information
- A child's skills in working individually and/or with other youngsters

Categorically, laypersons do not have the expertise to plan programs and implement classroom activities that properly utilize these kinds of information.

For example, a child may be encouraged by her or his parents to handle and look at books and children's stories. As a result of illustrations or from having heard the story read by someone, that child may be able to deduce the story line of a children's book. Early childhood teachers have the professional preparation to identify whether or not youngsters have actually developed sufficient readiness to enter a reading program. Unfortunately, in many cases parents would rather trust their own hunch about their child's ability than the teacher's professional judgments. This is especially true if the teacher identifies their child as not ready for the reading program at the time such programs are first available in the local school. Ego is a powerful force in many of these situations.

Parents should and do have the legal right to accept or reject the recommendations of either physicians or educators. Obviously, the courts can overrule parents in situations where it has been proved that a parent decision would be critically harmful to the child. However, parents continue to give higher credibility to physicians' recommendations about children than those made by educators. The professional qualifications of one to make recommendations in his or her appropriate area of expertise is no less valid than the other's, although, in the case of educators, public bias is to the contrary. This is largely so because the public clearly does not perceive educators to be professionals to the degree they do in regard to other professional groups.

Thus it must be recognized that the capacity of educators to utilize their expertise fully in professional decision making requires raising public opinion and awareness of education as a profession. Achieving this will have a positive impact upon educators' using their professional authority in making curriculum plans and designing school programs, organizing appropriate classroom learning activities, and getting parents to give greater credibility to their recommendations concerning children's learning needs.

□ *Advising on Formulation of Goals*   Advising on formulation of goals is a lesser but essential area of professional participation in curriculum planning. As discussed earlier, laypersons should be and are the primary determiners of educational goals. However, the professional expertise of educators is an important source of information as laypersons consider goal issues. It is likewise important that laypersons become familiar with current school programs dealing with areas in which they are considering present or new goals. As Krug comments: "It can be said that every teacher should take part in study and discussion of the objectives of education—in relation to problems that teachers recognize and consider important. Also, teachers should have every right to present their views of the all-school program and to take part in discussions of those problems" (1950, pp. 14–15).

This establishes the need for an advisory relationship of educators to lay groups dealing with goals. Educators can accurately present research information and descriptions of current school programs related to the lay group's concerns in goal formulation. This interaction can overcome hearsay opinions about what current school programs actually do and can provide an accurate basis for goal definition or assessment. Lay groups need accurate information about what the school currently offers before determining whether goals need to be stated or how they need to be restated.

For example, let us assume a lay group is planning local goals for an alcohol education program that will be required by the state's department of public instruction. Suppose the school's driver education program currently has a classroom unit about the impact of alcohol upon driving a car and that a middle grades science program also deals with the effects of alcohol upon bodily functions. In this situation the lay group could waste important time looking for information that science and driver education teachers could readily provide. Failure to identify what information is currently available through other school programs also can result in the unnecessary development of materials already available in different district curriculum areas. Yet this frequently occurs where educators are not involved in advisory relationships to lay groups studying and formulating goals. Educator advisement also would help lay groups dealing with goal issues gain a better understanding of the interrelated aspects of different curriculum areas and school programs within the district.

The time that laypersons give to goal formulation activities is important and should not be wasted in attempts to "reinvent the wheel." A clear understanding of the advisory role that district educators should provide is facilitated when the professionals function as information givers and respect the fact that goal formulation is primarily a lay group prerogative. As this interaction proves helpful to lay groups in goal formulation activities, they should better see the value from the input and feedback that professionals can provide. And appreciating the value could increase lay/professional interaction to study the interface between school programs and goals. Such efforts could identify important goal/program curriculum planning issues and extend the all-school program to better meet the local educational needs of children.

A CYCLIC MODEL FOR LAY AND PROFESSIONAL INTERACTION

■ ■ Issues discussed to this point have dealt with both lay and professional curriculum planning prerogatives. It is important that these prerogatives be considered neither in a linear relationship nor with one subordinate to the other. In terms of major and minor areas of responsibility, the prerogatives of both groups should be reciprocal in the school–community setting. Figure 9.1 illustrates that relationship.

The inner circle identifies the program concerns of both laypersons and professionals. It identifies the different emphasis of each group in the area of program concerns. The left and right halves of the entire figure designate the respective authority areas of each group. Authority for both groups increases outward from the center dividing line, but the major prerogative of each group also phases into the minor responsibility of the other. This indicates that the nature of each function is itself a continuum. The outer circle represents the sum of lay–professional responsibilities in curriculum planning. The directional arrows outside that circle suggest that (1) programs should develop in response to goals and (2) goals should be reassessed according to pro-

FIGURE 9.1   A Cyclic Model for Lay and Professional Interaction

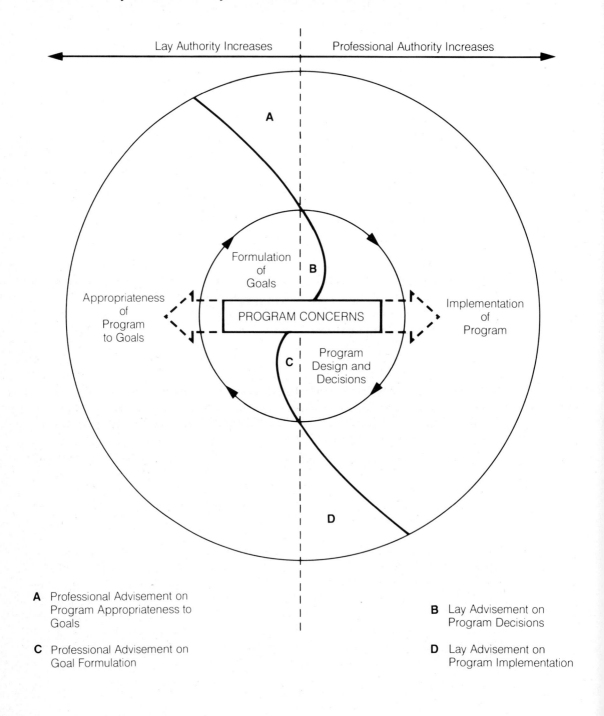

A   Professional Advisement on Program Appropriateness to Goals

B   Lay Advisement on Program Decisions

C   Professional Advisement on Goal Formulation

D   Lay Advisement on Program Implementation

gram needs. Maintaining this cyclic pattern of lay and professional interaction in curriculum planning is essential to extending the school–community's basis for ongoing improvement. This cyclic relationship will be considered further in later sections of this chapter.

■ Authority and Politics in Curriculum Planning

Figure 9.1 portrays the relationship between the roles of professionals and laypersons in making curriculum plans and developing school programs. Over the past few years there has been a populist movement in the United States that appears to serve as an important example of the implications discussed in that last section. This movement raises the need to address issues that are essential in considering bases of power and authority that professionals and laypersons require to function effectively in their appropriate curriculum planning responsibilities.

In 1974, Congress enacted the Hatch Act, designed to protect students' privacy in the school setting. Protection was afforded through the right of parents or guardians to review instructional materials used in research and experimental programs. This legislation was supported by a variety of professional education and citizen groups that were concerned with the wider issue of student rights and responsibilities.

In 1978, the Hatch Act was amended to include examination, testing, or treatment of students that might lead them to reveal information about political affiliations, psychological problems, illegal or antisocial behavior, family relationships, and other personal information. Then, in 1984, at the request of the Department of Education, Congress enacted regulations that could be used to clarify and/or implement the provisions of the 1978 Hatch Amendment. The new legislation reaffirms the rights of parents or guardians to review instructional materials, and it defines the terms "research or experimentation program or project," "psychiatric or psychological examination or test," and "psychiatric or psychological treatments."

Support for this final clarification came mainly from persons of fundamentalist Protestant Christian beliefs who allied with other traditional religious denominations. Their efforts centered on attempts to remove aspects of subject matter, curricular materials, teaching–learning activities, and school programs that they saw as being in conflict with their beliefs about what is essential to the moral and ethical development of youth. In growing instances this has resulted in what many see as an increasing erosion of the roles of professional decision making discussed in the previous section.

☐ *The Issue of Parents' Rights*   At the heart of this movement is the question of parents'/guardian's rights to control the educational programs in which their children are enrolled. The issue now has gone beyond the option of private education to meet those concerns and clearly is focusing upon the desire to gain such control of the curriculum and programs of public schools. This strategy poses a critical threat to the survival of the professional prerogative of educators to make professional decisions about public school programs. Figure 9.2 presents one of the best-known examples of how the group proceeded. This particular example was the widely circulated letter of the Maryland Coalition of Concerned Parents on Privacy Rights in Public Schools. It was distributed by Phyllis Schlafly and the Eagle Forum.

FIGURE 9.2   Letter of the Maryland Coalition of Concerned Parents

Dear   :
      I am the parent of _____
who attends/attend_____ .
      Under U.S. Law based on well-recognized legislation and court decisions, parents have the primary responsibility for their children's education, and pupils have certain rights which the schools may not deny. Parents have the right to assure that their children's beliefs and moral values are not undermined by the schools. Pupils have the right to have and to hold their values and moral standards without direct or indirect manipulation by the schools through curriculum, textbooks, audio-visual materials, or supplementary assignments.
      Accordingly, I hereby request that my child/children be involved in no school activities listed below unless I have first been given the opportunity to review all of the materials to be used and have given my written approval for their use:
   —Psychological and psychiatric examinations, tests, or surveys that
      are designed to elicit information about attitudes, habits, traits,
      opinions, beliefs, or feelings of an individual or group;
   —Psychological and psychiatric treatment that is designed to affect
      behavioral, emotional, or attitudinal characteristics of an
      individual or group;
   —Values clarification, including use of moral dilemmas, discussion
      of religious or moral standards, role playing of situations
      involving moral issues, open-ended discussions of moral issues,
      and survival games including life/death decision exercises;
   —Education pertaining to alcohol and drug abuse;
   —Death education, including abortion, euthanasia, suicide, and use
      of violence;
   —Instruction in nuclear war, nuclear policy, and nuclear classroom
      games;
   —Anti-nationalistic, one-world government or globalism
      curriculum;
   —Education in inter-personal relationships, including family life,
      discussions of attitudes toward parents, and parenting;

FIGURE 9.2   continued

—Education in human sexuality, including premarital sex, extramarital sex, contraception, abortion, homosexuality, group sex and marriages, prostitution, incest, masturbation, bestiality, divorce, population control, and roles of males and females;

—Pornography and any materials containing profanity and/or sexual explicitness;

—Guided fantasy techniques;

—Hypnotic techniques;

—Imagery and suggestology;

—Witchcraft and the occult, including horoscopes and zodiac signs;

—Organic evolution, including the idea that man has developed from previous or lower types of living things;

—Political affiliations and beliefs of student and family;

—Personal religious beliefs and practices;

—Mental and psychological problems potentially embarrassing to the student or family;

—Sex behavior and attitudes of student or family;

—Illegal, anti-social, self-incriminating and demeaning behavior;

—Critical appraisals of other individuals with whom the student has close family relationships;

—Legally recognized privileged and analogous relationships, such as those of lawyers, physicians, and ministers;

—Income, including the student's role in family activities and finances;

—Non-academic personality tests;

—Questionnaires on personal life, views, and family;

—Log books, diaries, personal journals, and autobiography assignments;

—Sociograms;

—Contrived incidents for self-revelation;

—Sensitivity training, including group encounter sessions, group contact sessions, talk-ins, magic circle techniques, self-evaluation and auto-criticism;

—Strategies specifically designed for self-disclosure, e.g., the zig-zag technique;

—Blindfold walks;

—Isolation techniques;

—Psychodrama;

—Sociodrama.

Many of the classroom practices and materials listed above are federally funded, in whole or in part, and are in use in schools throughout the United States. Such federally-funded activities are subject to newly-issued regulations for the Protection of Pupil Rights or so-called Hatch Amendment to the General Education Provisions Act, which became effective on November 12, 1984.

Under that law, no student shall be required as part of any

FIGURE 9.2 continued

program administered by the U.S. Department of Education to submit without prior written parental consent to psychiatric or psychological examination, testing, or treatment in which the primary purpose is to reveal information in specified sensitive areas. Full details of the new regulations are contained in the *Federal Register* for September 6, 1984.

These new federal regulations provide a procedure for the filing and reviewing of complaints. Alleged violations should first be filed by parents at the local and state levels. If the matter is not satisfactorily resolved there, then the complaint should be filed with the Family Educational Rights and Privacy Office, U.S. Department of Education, 400 Maryland Avenue, S.W., Washington, D.C. 20202. At the federal level, provisions are made first for a voluntary remedy. If that fails, federal funds will be withdrawn from a school system or other contractor determined to be in violation of the law.

The purpose of this letter is to preserve my parental responsibilities and my child's/children's rights under United States law based on legislation and court decisions. I respectfully ask you to provide me with a substantive response to this letter, notify the relevant teachers of my request for review and written permission procedures, and arrange to have a copy of this letter placed and kept in my child's/children's permanent file.

Thank you for your cooperation.

Sincerely,

□ *The Secular Humanism Issue*   Another goal that these same groups pursued was the elimination of secular humanism from the public schools. This effort, too, worked to erode the base of professional educators to make decisions about educational programs in the public schools. Even though the term "secular humanism" remained undefined in any strict legal sense, it still appeared in federal legislation as a prohibition for districts wishing to receive funding for magnet school programs. Furthermore, the Congress instructed the United States Office of Education not to define the term "secular humanism" but to allow local school districts to define the term as they see fit. The law deals with those school districts that have organized or may develop magnet schools to correct racial imbalance and facilitate racial integration. These programs are almost exclusively confined to urban communities that have large minority populations. Such schools must almost always apply for federal aid which may be available to support their implementation.

Yet now, parents as individuals or in groups could exert pressure on their local school boards and require their students to be exempted from programs that they considered to be secular humanist in nature.

The lack of federal guidelines to assist in defining what constitutes secular humanism posed increasing problems for existing curriculum and school programs, as well as effective limits for planning new ones.

These events presented serious danger to maintaining a balance of lay and professional prerogatives in planning curriculum and making decisions about school programs. The situations cited could potentially extend lay authority into areas of professional prerogative that would effectively restrict professional input in planning school programs to a point of ineffectiveness. This issue is as fundamental as the governance established in the United States Constitution. The explicit omission of education in the Constitution in effect defines education as a state rather than a federal function.

☐ *Extending Religious Power Bases into the Public Schools* The Constitution also provides for the separation of church and state in our nation. The Reverend Martin Marty, a leading authority on religion in the United States, provides an interpretation of this phenomenon that is important to understanding the shift of power. Efforts to safeguard professional bases of authority in curriculum planning and in decision making about school programs should consider Dr. Marty's points. (See Frame 9.1.)

Some religiously oriented groups interpreted the Hatch Act and its amendments as a justification for extending their authority and thereby eroding the base of professional decision-making prerogatives. This phenomenon has been viewed by some as reflecting the expressed goal of the Reverend Jerry Falwell of the Moral Majority. In his book *America Can Be Saved* (1979) he remarks: "I hope I live to see the day, when as in the early days of our country, we won't have any public schools. The churches will have taken them over again and Christians will be running them. What a happy day that will be" (p. 53).

☐ *Resolving the Issues* To resolve these issues school districts and school boards must define clearly the bases of authority essential to allowing professional educators to deal effectively with program design and implementation. At the same time, district and school board policy must fully describe the scope of authority for lay involvement and participation in formulating goals and deciding about the appropriateness of the relationship of school programs to goals. A written statement of the school system's goals, philosophy, and curriculum should be available to the community. These statements should carefully explain that professional decisions on content, materials, and activities are made to meet district and program goals. Any charges made against the school system should be addressed by the school board and administration, and any professionals involved in those charges should be apprised of such charges as soon as possible. The school board should

Rev. Martin Marty on Religion in Society

■ **"We've Screened Out the Reality of Religion in Society"**

Spiritual Forces in America's Consciousness

Every society tends to live by a small number of very broad ideas, about which most citizens may not even be conscious because they are so deeply embedded.

From the Bible, Americans down through the years have gotten several notions: That we are a nation under God, that God planned a mission for us. We also draw from the Bible the idea that God is concerned with a transcendent justice that holds sway over all causes, all parties, all nations, including our own.

A second spiritual force shaping our society comes from the founders of the nation—the religion of the Enlightenment. Most of the Founding Fathers didn't believe in a personal God—the God of the Bible—although they respected people who did, respected Jesus for His morals and were often church members. Theirs was a religion of Natural Rights, Natural Reason, Natural Law. They believed that any right-thinking, well-meaning person of conscience would come to see these universal truths—that all men are created equal and have the right to life, liberty and the pursuit of happiness.

"The Christian Right is Looking For Power"

The Founding Fathers did a very significant thing in separating the realms of church and state. This meant that churches would have to rely on persuasion to influence society, and time and again through our history church leaders have tried to affect social policies—from abolishing slavery to prohibiting liquor.

Episcopal, Presbyterian, Lutheran and other mainline Protestant churches, as well as Catholics and Jews, have regularly called upon their Biblical faith to influence American life. They reason that if one does not speak out publicly and relies solely on changing individuals, the culture can in the meantime become so corrupt and dominating that there's not much you can do. Recently, fundamentalists such as the Moral Majority have come to the same conclusion, which helps explain why a group that once considered activism sinful is now so vocal on such issues as family life, pornography, abortion.

never surrender its legal rights. Although laypersons and groups have a right to express their views to the board, their views should not dictate or take precedence over board policy.

The school board and district educational leaders need to work conscientiously toward maintaining a balance of effective lay and professional involvement in developing school goals and making curriculum plans. Two issues need to be considered. First, preserving a

Having seen blacks, Hispanics, women, homosexuals and other groups come to the fore in the '60s, the Christian right is looking for power. They see themselves as the custodians of the old American values. They have this nostalgic image of the America of the little red schoolhouse and the little white church. America, they feel, changed the textbooks to please blacks and Jews by taking out "Little Black Sambo" and "The Merchant of Venice" but was insensitive to what offended the fundamentalists.

Coercion Can Backfire

Every religious impulse can bring both good and bad. The Christian right struck a responsive chord in the wider society—including the intellectual community— about the importance of family, neighborhood and tradition. The activism of the Moral Majority or any other religious group becomes harmful, though, when it relies on coercion rather than persuasion to bring about change. This can invite a backlash against religion. Religious groups can also break down into tight factions that talk only to their own kind and have a theology that says, "You're really a full citizen only if you agree with us."

We tend to underestimate the power of religion in people's lives, because for many years in America religion had become a private affair. Thus, we were caught off guard by the Islamic revolution in Iran and by religious warfare in other nations. I do not believe in turning schools into churches, but our children would be well served by courses teaching about the role of religion in human life. Schools should teach reality, and media should cover reality; yet we've largely screened out the reality of religion in society. A youngster can watch 15 years of children's TV and learn about the mailperson and the grocer but never see a rabbi, monk or minister.

Young People: Religion's "Next Frontier"

The group I would regard as the next frontier for religion is that huge class of young adults—the high-rise, high-tech people—who devote tremendous energies to their careers and take the pressure off through a kind of hedonism. There are religious stirrings among them, yet few are attracted to established churches. This group and millions of other Americans are likely to pursue religion entirely privately, which can be a fine expression of personal freedom but a problem when it comes to reaching people and reforming society.

base of authority and power for both lay and professional input into such decision making is essential. This can be effectively accomplished only when adversarial relationships are replaced by complementary ones. Second, cooperative interaction must be utilized to broaden the base of involvement of the community in curriculum planning. At the same time, the effective use of professional expertise must be preserved.

We have previously cited George Counts's celebrated 1932 work which asked the question "Dare the Schools Build a New Social Order?" His concern was not that educators could or should define and build a new society through the schools in isolation from the wishes of the populace. Yet the controversy considered in this section could suggest that such worries may be at the heart of these efforts to extend lay authority in curriculum planning at the expense of professional educator prerogatives. It is important that this populist movement be channeled and articulated with professional concerns. If we are to better meet the needs of our youth, we must balance out a contemporary corollary to Counts's notion by considering, "Dare the social order build a new school?"

STAFF DEVELOPMENT/INSERVICE EDUCATION

■ ■ "Staff development" and "inservice education" are terms developed in the literature dealing with the theory and practice of curriculum planning. As Chapters 1 and 2 described, curriculum planning and development deal with the organization of the total program of the school. Within this broad context, a number of definitions of "curriculum" from the literature were supplied. The development of curriculum plans deals with objectives, content or subject matter, instructional activities, materials, and measuring devices. As components of the teaching–learning situation, these elements are the proper concern of educators in curriculum planning activities.

The concept of professional growth addresses the continuing development of any knowledge, skill, behavior, and attitude needed by educators. (See Figure 9.3.) Individuals and groups might participate in activities aimed at improving school climate, enhancing professional communications between administrators and teachers, improving teaching–learning situations, and so on. Improvement of teaching and learning is a major concern of the curriculum field. The professional growth of teachers may be necessary to implement such improvements. In this context, two possibilities may be considered. First, the very act of participating in curriculum planning can often lead to the development of new insights and skills as educators share ideas and experiences (point A in Figure 9.3). Second, the development of new or reorganized curriculum plans may necessitate that teachers develop new or improved teaching skills (point B in Figure 9.3). The latter takes place within the context of inservice education, which concerns itself with the skills of effective teaching. In particular situations, these might include developing skills such as teacher–student planning, structuring small instructional groups, or organizing individual projects. This specific aspect of inservice education, then, is concerned with giving teachers the skills necessary to implement successfully new programs and curriculum plans.

FIGURE 9.3   Relationship of Inservice Education to Curriculum Planning and Professional Growth

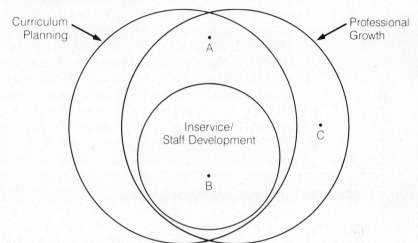

Curriculum
Planning

Professional
Growth

A

Inservice/
Staff Development

C

B

As was previously stated, some professional growth activities are incorrectly classified as inservice. (For example, a workshop on how to deal with stress and teacher "burnout" would be placed at point C on Figure 9.3.) Obviously, not all professional development activities should be construed as staff development/inservice activities that properly arise from curriculum planning. Even though "staff development" and "inservice" may be carelessly used to describe a broad range of professional growth programs, their more precise meanings were originally developed in the curriculum planning field and its literature. Vernon Anderson (1956), Krug (1950), and Saylor and Alexander (1954) describe the relationship among these components in the following way.

Curriculum planning is a macrocosm concerned with all activities used to improve instruction. This range includes the development of programs and the development or updating of skills necessary to implement those programs. In the curriculum field, staff development and inservice education refer to the specific means used to address development or updating of skills. Thus, staff development and inservice education are organized to prepare educators for implementing the outcomes of curriculum planning activities. Those curriculum planning activities deal with the development or improvement of programs, courses, syllabi, curriculum guides, course outlines, resource units, teaching units, or lesson plans. It is important, therefore, to understand that curriculum planning and staff development/inservice education are not one and the same. *The primary needs for staff development/ inservice activities are identified from the curriculum planning activities that organize new programs or improve existing ones.* Staff development/inservice needs should be specified as those new or refined skills which educators need to acquire in order to implement successfully the new or revised program(s) in question. Thus, there is a means–ends relationship between the development of new curricula and skills that educators seek to gain through staff development/inservice education activities. There will be other sources requiring staff development support. However, organizing staff development/inservice education programs that lack skill development purposes derived from curriculum planning needs will probably only result in irrelevant activities for participants. Educators have too many personally identified skill improvement concerns to be frustrated with "busy work" or boring speeches unrelated to those needs.

■ Guidelines for Staff Development and Inservice Education

J. Cecil Parker (1957) developed general guidelines that have proven invaluable in designing effective staff development/inservice programs. (See Frame 9.2.) Parker's guidelines deal specifically with helping participants develop ownership in the inservice activities. For this reason, the group that plans the staff development/inservice programs should represent the concerns of teachers, staff, and all who are to participate in those activities. Parker observed:

> The term "guideline" is used here to represent an operational principle or a criterion which may consistently direct or guide individual and group action in planning, organizing, and conducting inservice activities. (p. 103)

> It is important that no "sequential-step" significance be attached to the order in which the guidelines are presented. This is true for two reasons: First, it is impossible, as well as unsound, to derive useful guidelines that are mutually exclusive. This is to say, practically all of the actions indicated by these guidelines are involved when a group plans how to work. Second, no two individuals or groups should proceed with the actions indicated by the guidelines in an identical series of steps. (p. 103)

An entire faculty might be involved in a single staff development/inservice activity. However, such activities are likely to be more appropriate for particular groups of participants seeking to develop similar skills. A number of different activities for different purposes could be held at the same time. In this way, staff development/inservice activities can deal more responsively with group or individual needs. It should be recognized that all school professionals, including school administrators, counselors, teachers, and other staff members have

Parker's Guidelines for Inservice Education
Parker, 1957, pp. 127–128

Guideline I People work as individuals and as members of groups on problems that are significant to them.

Guideline II The same people who work on problems formulate goals and plan how they will work.

Guideline III Many opportunities are developed for people to relate themselves to each other.

Guideline IV Continuous attention is given to individual and to group problem-solving processes.

Guideline V Atmosphere is created that is conducive to building mutual respect, support, permissiveness and creativeness.

Guideline VI Multiple and rich resources are made available and used.

Guideline VII The simplest possible means are developed to move through decisions to action.

Guideline VIII Constant encouragement is present to test and to try ideas and plans in real situations.

Guideline IX Appraisal is made an integral part of inservice activities.

Guideline X Continuous attention is given to the interrelationship of different groups.

Guideline XI The facts of individual differences among members of each group are accepted and utilized.

Guideline XII Activities are related to pertinent aspects of the current educational, cultural, political and economic scene.

professional development needs in skill areas that could be accommodated through inservice education activities. Parker's Guidelines provide helpful direction in planning realistic and effective staff development/inservice activities.

■ Inservice Education in Practice

Implications of the perspectives on staff development/inservice education presented thus far may be shown best by an example. The following case demonstrates how educators can deal with specific curriculum planning concerns through inservice education.

In this situation, a middle level school faculty has decided to reorganize from departmentalized instruction to team teaching. This change was made after a year's study of the degree to which the school's teaching organization met its instructional goals. It was decided that departmentalized instruction limited the degree of interdisciplinary teaching and learning the faculty considered necessary for transescent students. The maturity levels of these students convinced the staff that while departmentalization was appropriate for mature adolescents in high school, it did not suit instructional needs in this middle level school. As the new program was planned, the faculty identified a range of skills that they would need to implement the new team teaching program successfully. These included skills for correlating and fusing different subject areas such as language arts and social studies or mathematics and science.

Teaming also required the development of specific planning and interpersonal skills necessary to work closely together in team settings. Interaction among team members facilitated the identification of both team and individual inservice needs. Inservice activities dealing with those needs differed from inservice activities offered at the building-wide level. There was a need for some general inservice activities to meet overall staff needs. This included updating staff awareness of the latest information about attention span and other learning capacities of transescents. However, more specific needs of the team or of individual team members were met by more personalized inservice activities. These included small-group activities for projected teaching and planning teams as well as some individualized inservice options. As prospective team members worked together, they were able to identify further inservice needs for their own groups and for the faculty at large. Skill needs of team groups were assessed against their preparedness to meet goals developed for the team teaching program. Teachers found that team organization provided a means to identify further and changing needs for inservice experiences.

The foregoing example illustrates how team teaching provides opportunities for teachers to help identify inservice needs of their team colleagues as well as gaining similar feedback on their own inservice needs. This interaction provides a means for ongoing consideration of skills necessary to implement new or revised programs. The collegiality of this interaction can build individual and collective ownership in staff development activities that respond to skill needs. Staff development/inservice activities generated in this fashion tend to be oriented to problem-solving activities rather than to the mere presentation of information. Team personnel with expertise in particular skill areas serve as presenters in staff development activities. As staff members observe particular skills among their colleagues, that expertise can be shared to meet similar needs of other team members.

☐ *Short- and Long-Range Inservice Concerns*   Staff development/inservice education is an aspect of the total curriculum planning process and proves to be most effective when considered within that context. As new or reorganized school programs are planned and developed, both short- and long-range implications of skills necessary to implement these programs must be clearly identified. Decisions need to be made regarding immediate and subsequent skills needed by teachers to implement newly developed curricula and school programs. If a new program is initiated before teachers develop skills necessary to implement that program, it cannot achieve its potential success. The fate of the core curriculum approach in many school districts in the 1950s was a notable example of this.

Core was a popular curricular program at that time in middle-level schools. Few colleges or universities, however, had preservice programs that provided teachers with the skills necessary to implement core programs. These skills included pupil–teacher planning, informal and formal correlation and fusion skills, and skills in the dynamics of instructional groups. The staff development/inservice experiences needed by teachers who were to implement core programs were not clearly recognized in most school districts. As a result, only a small percentage of districts with core programs organized staff development/inservice education programs to provide core teachers with those skills. Most districts assigned teachers with multiple subject-area backgrounds to core classes without providing them these skills. Core programs staffed by teachers lacking these skills fared poorly. Inevitably, core programs in such districts were dismissed as ineffective educational fads.

Sadly, the core program was not at fault. The problem stemmed from the ridiculous assumption that teachers lacking skills necessary to implement an educational concept could succeed without them. The failure of core programs in these schools was, in reality, a staff development/inservice education disaster. This fact was never broadly recognized, and core programs subsequently fell from favor across the nation. Schools must recognize that clarifying short- and long-range staff development/inservice education concerns is critical to successful implementation of new curricula and school programs.

☐ *Gaining Faculty Commitment*   Faculty participation in decision making about all aspects of staff development/inservice education is necessary to build teacher ownership in the program. The success or failure of staff development/inservice education programs often depends upon faculty enthusiasm about and belief in those activities. Their involvement in planning those activities helps significantly in establishing faculty perceptions of the need for specific staff development/inservice programs. Where these activities are initiated by administrative fiat, we all too frequently see teachers enter classrooms and continue to teach their "old ways." Although they have gone through specific inservice activities, they may not have fully understood the relationship of that activity to new school programs. In such cases, teachers are often unable to make effective use of the skills that the activity tried to develop.

This outcome will occur most frequently when there is minimal or no involvement of faculty in planning the staff development/inservice activity. Teachers should have the opportunity to recognize the need for acquiring skills. Second, they need to decide whether the new skill is better than their present skills. Without these decisions, it is almost impossible to develop personal motivation in approaching a staff development/inservice activity. As a result, teachers gain little from such inservice activities and have continuing problems when they later try to implement new programs with those skills.

The time taken to establish such faculty involvement is fundamental if teachers are to understand and develop ownership in an inservice activity. Staff ownership is necessary if teachers are to implement successfully new or revised curricula with the skills they gain from a staff development/inservice activity. The degree to which teachers believe that a program is "ours" rather than "theirs" will greatly enhance its chances of success. Teachers may then also approach the inservice skill development activities with personal objectives based upon their own classroom situations.

☐ *A Realistic Time Line for Change*   A realistic time frame must be allowed for the planning and presentation of essential staff development/inservice activities after the new or revised curriculum is planned, piloted, and refined. *Failure to identify the time needed for implementing effective change is a serious oversight.* More often than not, this failure results in only surface changes in program structure. It will not facilitate the development of teacher perceptions about skills needed to implement the new school programs. Providing adequate time for teachers to develop these skills is therefore essential to successful program improvement. Short- and long-range inservice concerns, as was discussed in an earlier section, require the consideration of how much time is necessary to develop skills needed to implement specific aspects of new school programs. It is an important principle in planning effective inservice activities that support program development needs. For that reason, it is foolish and inefficient to expect that all inservice needs can be accommodated during the time frame of a year or less. Three years may be a completely reasonable timeline for the successful implementation of a new program such as the reorganization of a school.

For example, let us consider two situations in which a school reorganizes from a junior high school to a middle school. In the first situation the change has been made for administrative rather than educational reasons. Changes in the district's enrollment made it expeditious to move from a grade 7–9 school to a grade 6–8 pattern. Sixth-grade elementary school teachers, along with seventh- and eighth-grade junior high staff, were assigned to the middle grades building, and the ninth-grade program and faculty were moved to the district's high school. The administration developed new policies and schedules for the new middle school. A nationally recognized middle school expert was secured to develop a one-day superintendent's conference program for the prospective middle school staff in May before the reorganization was implemented. This was followed by three half-day release-time programs for teachers to plan and organize schedules and activities for the next school year. This program neither prepared the staff to deal with the middle school concept nor provided them with any skills to implement the new program. Ownership of the staff in the program and enthusiasm and morale likewise were low. Predictably, the school soon ended up housing a sixth-grade elementary program and a seventh- and eighth-grade secondary program in a single building with virtually no interaction between the two elements.

In another district, the decision to move to a middle school was made after a year's study by the community and the school staff. Enrollment trends, student needs, and program efficiency were studied, and the goals developed recommended the organization of a middle school program. During the next year the staff studied curriculum plans and developed a middle school program to meet the goals that had been established. The second year concentrated on inservice activities designed to develop skills that the faculty felt were necessary to implement the middle school program. The third year, the middle school program was implemented and a number of programs were piloted and revised for the fourth year. The faculty members were prepared and confident. Their ownership in the program and their high morale contributed to the middle school program achieving its goals. Enrollment needs were met, and students benefited from the middle school program. The inservice program provided faculty with the skills necessary to implement the new program concept.

The first of these situations took less time and money but resulted in no significant educational progress or change. The second one involved an investment of money and time by the district and effort by the professional staff. However, realistic planning of inservice activities as means to achieve a particular school program resulted in effective change and educational progress. Thus, the planning of inservice programs must include realistic consideration of the time frame necessary for that particular program change or development.

■ Personalizing Staff Development/Inservice Education

We have already mentioned the phrase "personalized inservice." As we come to know more about individualizing instruction, interest-centered education, and personalizing the curriculum, the obvious need is to apply those same principles to staff development/inservice education. The fact is that we already know a great deal about such approaches, including the fact that their use in staff development/inservice education is likely, through demonstration, to influence the use of similar approaches in the classroom.

The following components (see Figure 9.4) represent seven central characteristics of the kind of personalized staff development/inservice education programs necessary to help professional teachers grow.

1. PARTICIPATORY PLANNING Personalized staff development/inservice education programs are organized and coordinated on a participatory basis. When themes for such activities are identified by administrators, supervisors, or consultants alone, the resulting programs often fail to deal with problems central to improving the professional competence of the teachers involved. To identify essential professional growth concerns more accurately, staff development/inservice education programs should be organized by a special committee of the district-wide curriculum planning organization. Such a committee should be composed of elected representatives of the professional staff and representatives of the curriculum or supervisory staff. Its

FIGURE 9.4 Components of Personalized Staff Development/Inservice Education Programs

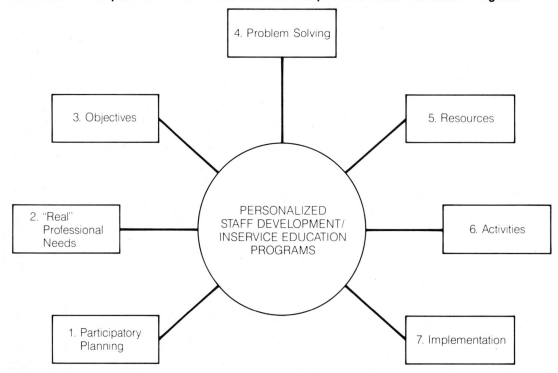

responsibilities should include identifying staff development/inservice needs, coordinating these professional growth activities, and evaluating these activities.

2. "REAL" PROFESSIONAL NEEDS   Personalized staff development/inservice education programs are organized around real teacher needs. Consequently, when such programs do not deal with teachers' essential professional growth needs, they may be of limited value to those teachers. In order to personalize these activities, teachers require the opportunity to identify needs that they feel should be met through staff development/inservice education programs. This input can be gained through survey instruments followed by in-depth planning by teachers and supervisors. The prior use of teacher self-evaluation techniques will further aid the specification of these needs. Such a needs assessment should result in staff development/inservice activities that gain stronger support of teachers because they have been planned to meet their real professional needs.

3. OBJECTIVES   Personalized staff development/inservice programs are organized around clearly and cooperatively defined objectives. Once general areas for staff development/inservice education are identified, specific objectives for participants must be defined. These objectives represent the actual purpose and interests of participants and give direction to both participants and supervisors or instructors. For example, within the area of interdisciplinary team teaching, concerns may include such specifics as understanding the philosophic rationale, building a resource unit, identifying problems of teaming, or effective use of time.

The identification of specific objectives must be done cooperatively. This means that supervisors or instructors and participants need to become involved in what amounts to pupil–teacher planning of staff development/inservice activities. In this way, the concerns of individuals, small groups, and large groups may be identified. Subsequent use of these grouping arrangements will enhance the possibilities that resultant staff development/inservice activities will meet a variety of important professional growth needs of staff members.

4. PROBLEM SOLVING   Personalized staff development/inservice education activities utilize problem-solving approaches. These activities should be responsive to real participant needs. Such needs are rarely met through mere acquisition of information. Although lectures and reading may be used as specific activities, major emphasis should be on assisting participants to solve actual problems. For example, teachers who perceive a need to increase student participation in curriculum

planning may develop and implement pupil–teacher planning techniques; some who are interested in new grouping patterns may carefully gather data on a number of student variables; and others entering a new middle-level school may study the psychology of emerging adolescence. In each situation, participants would be pursuing professional growth activities designed to help solve an instructional problem with which they need to deal. Obviously experimentation and action research should be as much a part of personalized staff development/inservice education as the use of consultants.

5. RESOURCES Personalized staff development/inservice education programs make intelligent use of resources in and out of the school. While the use of external consultants is an established practice, effort is rarely made to identify possible resources within the school or district staff for use in district professional growth activities. In many cases, teachers have experimented with particular techniques or have developed unique programs that they can share with colleagues. Others have done professional reading or investigation and can serve as sources of information. Using these kinds of internal resources not only builds cooperation but develops leadership as well. At the same time, the use of external resources in staff development/inservice programs should be more carefully planned. Typically, consultants or speakers are invited to deal only with a broad topic. They should be thoughtfully selected and then asked to deal with specific local professional growth needs related to a unique skill or knowledge that these experts have developed in a carefully defined area.

The development of resource units for staff development/inservice education activities is a promising new approach. With such a collection of objectives or skills related to suggested content, activities, and materials for dealing with professional growth needs, teachers could carry on their own staff development/inservice activities with supervisory support either individually or in groups. Where objectives are designed to match competencies, the use of resource units would contribute to the professionalization and personalization of competency-based programs.

6. ACTIVITIES Personalized staff development/inservice education programs make use of a wide variety of materials. The vast majority of such professional growth activities involve information dissemination and theoretical discussion through graduate courses, one-day programs, and local courses conducted by "experts." While these should not be excluded from staff development/inservice activities, other alternatives might include discussions of groups, independent reading,

community studies, analysis of student data, visitation to other schools, workshops, institutes, and development of action research projects. Such activities, of course, necessitate recognition that group sizes for these activities might range from the entire staff to a single teacher pursuing a unique problem.

7. IMPLEMENTATION Personalized staff development/inservice education programs lead to implementation of new skills, techniques, activities, and materials. One major cause of teacher skepticism about staff development/inservice programs has been the frustration they experience when new ideas developed in professional growth activities are ignored or quickly forgotten. As we have mentioned, research and experimentation are important professional growth activities. This stems from the notion that such activities, in the context of new idea or skill development, should lead to implementation. Supervisors and curriculum workers must not only encourage such development, but must also be prepared to provide both leadership and support for such implementation.

The seven characteristics of personalized staff development/inservice education programs described here are much like those found in effective instructional organization in classrooms. Their implementation in a school district not only enhances professional growth but also becomes a means to demonstrate effective teaching–learning situations. We have found that personalized staff development/inservice education programs also include an overall plan for continuous development.

Once new skills and ideas are implemented, opportunity must be made available for continued professional growth as refinements are made or new professional growth and development needs emerge. For this reason, the self-evaluation and supervisor–teacher consultation mentioned above must be carried on continuously. Aspects of these needs will be discussed further in the sections in this chapter considering Line and Staff curriculum planning concerns. In addition, the local committee for staff development/inservice education must keep in communication with the professional staff to maintain the input needed for continued development of responsive professional growth activities. The increasing sophistication of the total professional growth program becomes a predictable result of such efforts. Our own experiences in developing staff development/inservice programs cause us to suggest that professional growth best occurs when we involve professionals in developing their own professional growth activities. Personalizing staff development/inservice education programs as described here has produced such results.

ARTICULATING THE SCHOOL–COMMUNITY CURRICULUM PLANNING PROGRAM

■ ■   The elements of the curriculum planning process require articulation into a program that can deal effectively with program needs. The curriculum planning prerogatives of both laypersons and school professionals must be supported if school and community are to respond effectively to local educational needs. The goal here is to help school and community maximize the effectiveness of curriculum planning activities at the local level. Articulation of curriculum plans and school programs requires time and consideration. This section will consider four areas central in articulating the school–community curriculum program.

The first area deals with the need for school districts to consider organizational structures that can facilitate articulation of curriculum and school programs. Unless attention is given to developing structures to examine and deal with these issues, school programs can lose articulation and synchrony. Each school district also needs to deal with curriculum planning needs on an ongoing basis. *The second area involves horizontal and vertical curriculum articulation.* Horizontal concerns deal with subject matter, instructional activities, and materials across the grades of schools serving the same developmental levels (e.g., all the elementary schools in a district). Vertical articulation deals with similar concerns across the elementary, middle-level, and high school programs in the district. *The third area deals with the relationships and involvement of line and staff personnel in curriculum planning processes and activities.*

The fourth area discusses how all these elements and processes can best be utilized in developing systemic curriculum planning, an ongoing, self-renewing means to improve curriculum plans and school programs. The examples presented in this section illustrate the situations sketched in the seven scenes presented in Chapter 2. They indicate operational concerns with which educators need to deal in improving curriculum planning activities in their professional settings. Let us first consider how school districts can develop organizational structures to deal with curriculum planning issues and concerns.

■ Curriculum Planning Structures

The literature in the curriculum field presents specific organizational means to achieve the four areas just highlighted (Anderson, 1956; J. Minor Gwynn and John Chase, 1969; Krug, 1950, 1957; Saylor and Alexander, 1954; Glennys Unruh and Adolph Unruh, 1984; John Verduin, 1967). At the school district/community level, the board of education and the district's chief school officer should study this literature as well as school districts that have developed effective curriculum planning programs. Efforts to develop such programs at the local district/community level should grow from this first step of study and deliberation. This investigation should identify the kinds of curriculum planning organizations that could provide effective structures for improving curriculum planning within the district. Again, these structures must provide means to organize lay and professional involvement in a cyclic, interrelated fashion.

☐ *District-Wide Curriculum Planning Councils*   Organizationally, the first step is to establish a district-wide curriculum planning council (Verduin, 1967). The curriculum planning council should be advisory to the board of education and the chief school officer. Its membership should include representation from teachers, administrators, other school professionals, adult laypersons, and high school students. The issue of representation for younger students also requires consideration. It could be through individuals from middle level school student governance organizations. Council members should serve staggered terms to manage turnover and maintain continuity in the group's activities. Selection of professional members for the district-wide curriculum planning council is made by one of two means. Members may be either selected by the board of education or chosen by their respective professional constituencies. Lay members of the district-wide curriculum planning council are appointed by the board of education, whose members are themselves the elected representatives of the community.

The district-wide curriculum planning council works on curriculum issues referred to them for advisement by the board of education and chief school officer. Districts need to develop policies and procedures for such referrals. The district-wide council can also initiate curriculum study concerns and consider issues relevant to the objectives and scope of curriculum. The curriculum planning council serves as a forum to hear curriculum concerns of both laypersons and school professionals (Miel, 1946, pp. 78–82). It can also recommend convening ad hoc groups to study particular issues and problems further.

In some districts, the council is delegated responsibility to work with administrative and staff personnel assigned to curriculum planning roles and functions. Such personnel may include assistant superintendents for instruction, curriculum coordinators and/or directors, support service coordinators and/or directors, staff development/inservice education directors, principals and other school building administrators, subject-area coordinators, library/media/educational computing specialists, departmental chairpersons, research personnel assigned to curriculum and instruction areas, teachers assigned to curriculum planning responsibilities, and other professionals working in curriculum-related areas.

As previously stated, the curriculum planning council is always advisory to the board of education and chief school officer in all activities in which it becomes involved. Any decisions the curriculum planning council makes are recommendatory. It implements no decisions on policy or program, but may recommend possibilities for board of education consideration. The district-wide curriculum planning council is the organization central to studying curriculum issues and problems in the school district. Districts without a curriculum planning council do not have the advantage of systematic, representative lay and professional consideration of the district's curriculum planning concerns. The board of education benefits greatly from the advisement and recommendations provided by such a council.

□ *Individual School Curriculum Planning Councils*   The contributions of the district-wide curriculum planning council can be supported by developing a similar structure in the district's individual schools. In districts that have only a few schools, the district-wide curriculum planning council has maximum capacity to respond to the district's major curriculum planning concerns and issues. However, the district-wide curriculum planning council cannot provide as much help to these same needs in larger districts that have more individual schools. In larger districts, it takes longer for the curriculum concerns of individual schools to get before the district-wide curriculum planning council. Regardless of the district's size, the establishment of individual school curriculum planning councils can broaden and specify support for curriculum planning needs.

Even in smaller districts, laypersons and professionals find they deal most effectively with curriculum planning concerns and issues related to their own school–community setting. When all district schools develop building curriculum planning councils, there can be representative lay and professional interaction on concerns specific to each building. This facilitates the study of curriculum concerns, issues, and problems particular to the localized school–community environment. These curriculum planning councils are also advisory to the school's administration, staff, and community. The council can make recommendations to the district-wide curriculum planning council as well as convene ad hoc groups to study particular issues in greater detail.

School curriculum planning councils can study and develop advisory solutions on local curriculum concerns before they emerge as major problems at the district-wide council. The school curriculum planning council has the closest locus of control to curriculum issues and concerns arising in its own school–community environment. There is strong evidence that a school curriculum planning council's representative group of school educators and local community laypersons may be the most effective curriculum planning organization.

When school districts develop both district-wide and individual school curriculum planning councils, they provide means that can effectively respond to curriculum planning concerns at all levels throughout the school district. These organizations provide professionals and laypersons with necessary opportunities to interact, study, and recommend how curriculum planning issues can best be approached.

■ Horizontal and Vertical Curriculum Articulation

Learning experiences should be organized so that there is continuity of programs across the grades and from grade to grade across the vertical units within the school district. In Chapter 6 we introduced the ideas of scope and sequence in school programs. Scope refers to breadth and depth of the content, materials, and activities in programs, while sequence deals with ordering these components into learning activities that are logical and understandable to learners. There are both horizontal and vertical aspects of sequence. Horizontal sequence issues deal with the continuity of learning arrangements, materials, and activities on, or within, a particular level, grade, and so on. Vertical sequence deals with this continuity across levels, grades, school units, and the like. Hilda Taba (1962) considered these vertical aspects as sequence, but the horizontal aspects as integration. She commented: "The continuity of learning has two aspects: that of a vertical progress from one level to another, and that of a relationship between the learnings in various areas of the curriculum which take place at the same time. The first of these is associated with the term sequence, the other with the term integration" (p. 428–429).

Regardless of the terminology used, vertical and horizontal continuity continue to be persisting issues in the curriculum field. The spiral curriculum is another way to conceptualize and deal with both horizontal and vertical articulation aspects of scope and sequence issues. Jerome Bruner (1960) described the need to introduce basic ideas and then consider them in a spiraling fashion as the youngsters mature and develop higher thinking levels. He observed: "A curriculum as it develops should revisit these basic ideas repeatedly, building upon them until the student has grasped the full formal apparatus that goes with them" (p. 8).

John Dewey developed the notion of the spiral curriculum. To Dewey, growth depended upon the learner's use of intelligence to overcome difficulties arising in her or his own experience. This helped the learner understand the relationships among knowledge and information areas and the wider social applications of knowledge. Dewey (1938) observed that "the process is spiral" (p. 79) and maintained that the learner's experience is the essential point at which his or her spiraling of learning begins.

Taba (1962) also cautioned curriculum planners to consider the sequence of learning skills required for students to deal effectively with the spiral continuity in learning challenges. She observed:

> When the curriculum is viewed as a plan for learning and not merely a plan for exposition of content, additional considerations emerge regarding sequence. One is that of a sequence of learning experiences necessary to master the necessary behavior: to acquire an abstract concept, to develop a method of analyzing problems or an attitude of tolerance toward differences, to master a skill in analyzing data, or to learn a method of inquiry. Learning these behaviors is also a matter of sequence. (p. 293)

The concept of the spiral curriculum deals with building effective continuity in learning arrangements which respond to student maturation of learning capacities. Ronald Doll (1982) describes other approaches to deal with this aspect of sequencing. These include children's growing abilities to move from the simple to the complex, to develop upon prerequisite learnings, to progress from parts to the whole, and to experience concentric growth in ability to understand concepts. Let us consider some specific issues that deal with horizontal as well as vertical articulation curriculum planning concerns.

☐   *Horizontal Curriculum Planning Issues*   Problems of horizontal articulation may arise if schools at the same level in the district (i.e., elementary, middle level, or high schools) have differing instructional programs. Horizontal curriculum planning concerns are greater in districts that have more schools at each organizational level. For example, a district with eight elementary schools must pay greater attention to horizontal curriculum issues than a district with only two elementary schools. Identifying horizontal curriculum articulation problems and developing program solutions is very time-consuming. As a result, many districts spend time dealing with such issues only after they have become recognized as definite problems.

Schools will often select and develop alternative curriculum means to reach common goals and learning objectives. It is possible to develop such arrangements and still deal with horizontal curriculum articulation needs. Problems involving content or activities in a single grade throughout a district's schools would be other examples of horizontal curriculum planning concerns. Some schools create serious horizontal curriculum problems by selecting instructional materials and developing school programs without any regard to similar programs in other district schools serving the same level. This can result in situations where the school's program goes in directions that are virtually irreconcilable with subject matter and program goals. A student transferring into this school from another one in the district could have serious difficulties in adjusting to a totally different program. Horizontal curriculum articulation problems can be lessened if schools select subject materials and develop programs based upon both district and individual school goals and needs.

The following situation involved a school district with ten elementary schools that served a population having wide cultural and economic differences. The elementary schools selected several alternative reading and language arts programs to meet the varying needs of their students. The alternative programs and materials have responded well to the cultural and economic differences of the students from different communities. However, the district needed to develop a means—ends relationship between the range of programs offered in its ten elementary schools and its general objectives for elementary school reading and language arts. Failure to do this would have caused serious horizontal articulation problems.

A district-wide curriculum planning council offers a helpful means to identify horizontal articulation issues and to study and make recommendations for prevention or solution of those problems. The curriculum planning council could convene an ad hoc group representing the ten elementary schools to plan cooperative ways to address the problem. The ad hoc group could meet periodically with the entire curriculum planning council for discussion of possible solutions and further information. Attention could be given to ways in which the differentiation of the reading and language arts program can be reconciled and articulated with district program goals in those areas. Possibilities for making necessary changes in goal statements may also be considered. Study and resolution of such situations will be far more difficult without a district-wide curriculum planning council.

A district-wide planning council can also organize activities that can help prevent horizontal curriculum articulation problems. The council could work with school personnel to develop policies and guidelines for selecting new programs or materials. Educators from the grades and/or subject areas in which change is being considered could meet with the curriculum planning council. These meetings could examine potential articulation issues that need to be resolved. The district-wide council could also serve as a forum for resolving these concerns in selecting the programs or materials.

A district with both district-wide and individual school curriculum planning councils has far more responsive means available to deal with its needs. The previously mentioned ad hoc group could be convened from members of the ten elementary school curriculum planning councils. Each school curriculum planning council could examine the effectiveness of reading and language arts programs for its own school population. The ad hoc group would represent all ten schools and could relate its findings to the district-wide curriculum planning council as well. Findings of the individual schools, the school curriculum planning councils, and the ad hoc study group could readily be communicated to the district-wide curriculum planning council.

Horizontal curriculum planning issues can be addressed without the kinds of curriculum planning organizations described here. However, it will take far more time to convene a study group and deal with this problem if these organizations are not available in the district. The goal here is to maximize the time available to professionals and laypersons for improving curricula and school programs. District-wide and individual school curriculum planning councils offer effective means to involve educators and laypersons in dealing with horizontal curriculum planning issues. Curriculum planning councils can also develop possible solutions for these concerns.

☐ *Vertical Curriculum Planning Issues*   Problems of vertical articulation deal with program concerns involving at least two different grade levels. This may occur among consecutive grades in a single school, between the terminal grade in one school and the entry grade in the next one, and across all grades in the district (Koopman, 1966, p. 156). In the first case, any change in the seventh grade of a specific middle school's science program requires that this decision be made in cooperation with sixth- and eighth-grade science personnel. The vertical articulation issue would consider (1) the degree to which students entering the seventh-grade program would be prepared for its demands and (2) the degree to which the projected seventh-grade change would provide students with readiness to meet the demands of the eighth-grade program.

In the second case, the vertical articulation issue could involve a middle and a high school. If a grade 9–12 high school plans a change in its first-year mathematics program, two different vertical articulation issues need to be considered. One is similar to the last example involving the middle level science program. This would entail consideration of the implications of the projected ninth-grade changes for the school's tenth-grade mathematics program. Here, the vertical curriculum issue would involve determining sequence concerns of the projected change within the high school itself. The second issue concerns deliberations with the middle level schools that serve as feeder schools for that high school. It would be essential to determine that the change projected in the ninth-grade program would not create problems of gap and/or overlap with the eighth-grade programs in the middle level feeder schools.

Saylor and Alexander (1954) note that failure to ascertain the adequacy of sequence as changes are made in subject-matter programs between two school units creates the most serious problems of vertical curriculum articulation. Present practice would indicate that this problem continues to be a major articulation concern. Robert Zais (1976) and Peter Oliva (1982) present ways of studying sequence issues in more advanced notions of curriculum design.

In the third case, district curriculum planning organizations provide effective means to avoid vertical articulation problems across all grade levels. A district-wide curriculum planning council could recommend policy that would require that projected changes which involve vertical sequence be referred to the council for its consideration. The council would be able to convene an ad hoc study group from the grade levels and/or school units involved. As goal concerns are an issue, lay representatives from the curriculum planning councils can deal with them. Without policy and organization to monitor program, disruptions in vertical sequences can quickly become major problems. Quite often they continue to compound through further changes if there is no agency to monitor this process.

If the district had individual school curriculum planning councils, even more specific action could be facilitated. As individual schools considered internal vertical sequence changes, they could be handled by each school's curriculum planning council. Again, policy developed from the district-wide curriculum planning council could establish that such issues be cleared first through the curriculum planning councils of the individual schools involved. This would be particularly helpful in situations like the one involving a high school and its middle level feeder schools. Representatives from the individual school curriculum planning councils could meet to examine vertical articulation issues. If further study were necessary, a separate ad hoc group could also be convened.

Individual school curriculum planning councils constitute the most effective, strategic means for responding to vertical curriculum articulation at the individual school level. If the district has patterns of school "families" in which particular elementary, middle level, and high schools have defined feeder school relationships, the individual school curriculum planning councils can monitor all projected curriculum changes among the vertical family of schools. Developing policy that refers projected curriculum changes involving schools at different levels to their school curriculum planning councils can prevent most vertical articulation problems.

■ Line and Staff Concerns

Educators have either line or staff responsibilities that focus their professional activities. Line personnel deal with administration and management. They supervise and evaluate other personnel and also have major responsibility for managerial concerns in organizing curriculum planning activities. Staff personnel have collegial but not hierarchical relationships. They interact with other personnel and with students in the implementation of curriculum plans and school programs.

A major issue involves dealing with line versus staff concerns in the curriculum planning program. Staff personnel, as mentioned earlier, work on a collegial basis. Staff needs for discussion and facilitation can be hindered if a person holds both line and staff responsibilities. A teacher who is having a staff-level problem is less apt to discuss it with a person who will later rate him or her than with a person whose role is solely as a facilitator. For example, teachers will not readily reveal classroom problems to a principal who will have to observe them and develop dossiers that recommend decisions on awarding those teachers permanent contracts. Where this occurs, the staff member's problem usually does not gain the attention it requires.

Literature in the curriculum field (Anderson, 1956; Gwynn and Chase, 1969; Krug et al., 1956; Saylor and Alexander, 1954; Verduin, 1967) recommends that line and staff needs are best served by providing clearly separate channels to deal with such concerns. However, school districts have increasingly sought to deal with financial problems by curtailing positions. In many cases this has resulted in an individual's holding a position that combines both line and staff responsibilities. Business and industrial educational programs, on the other hand, have continued to give high priority to separating both functions through individuals and positions that clearly have either line or staff functions.

Professionalization of education depends on the degree to which personnel at all levels have input into the educational decision-making process. Robert Harnack (1968) feels that teachers will only become professionals when their decision-making roles are recognized and enhanced. He observes:

> Professional people, in order to grow, need to practice their profession. When professionals "practice," they use their knowledge to diagnose what is wrong in terms of a series of goals or ideals. They select a course of action which is relevant to those ideals and to the limitation of their knowledge. If a course of action cannot be reached, immediate steps are taken to identify the research problems which must be solved to find whatever knowledge is needed for reaching the goals. At the same time, the ideals themselves must be re-examined. It is this right to practice which enables professional people to define the needs for future professional knowledge. In education, this process of valuing, per se, must be philosophically protected in order that the teacher can work at his profession. Then the teacher practitioner can grow as a decision maker. (p. 142)

Extending the locus of control to teachers and other staff personnel most directly involved with those decisions is essential to their professionalization. It is the obligation of line personnel to provide the setting in which teachers and other staff personnel can improve their professional decision making in the way Harnack describes.

Supervision is another area with important line and staff considerations. Traditionally, supervision has been line supervision of staff personnel. However, clinical and other supervisory approaches now define staff roles and responsibilities in supervision and improvement of instruction. William Burton and Leo Brueckner (1955) foresaw these possibilities in describing supervision as "a social function." Kenneth Acheson and Meredith Gall (1980) contend that supervision needs to help educators develop ownership in establishing their goals for professional improvement as well as in developing specific means to accomplish those goals. Thus, curriculum planning articulation activities will increasingly require redefinition of supervision as a means to support professional growth of both line and staff personnel.

Ideas suggesting changes and refinements in curriculum plans and school programs can come from both line and staff levels. Effective curriculum planning needs to deal with both line and staff instructional concerns. Thus it is important that school districts study and develop means that accommodate both line and staff curriculum planning needs. Schools need to utilize the talents and responsibilities represented by the complete range of professionals employed within the district to respond adequately to program and instructional needs.

☐ *Line Curriculum Planning Concerns*   Line personnel have major responsibilities in areas of administration and management. Their relationship with and participation in curriculum planning activities also reflects these responsibilities. As the chief school officer's deputy, an associate or assistant superintendent for curriculum and instruction represents the highest vertical position charged with line curriculum planning concerns. Of necessity, this position also usually includes staff support responsibilities. Larger districts may have other line positions to articulate program at the various levels within the district. Directors for secondary, middle-level, and elementary education work with school building administrators in the administration of curriculum and program at those levels (Krug et al., 1956, pp. 62–87). A district may create other line positions such as directors of staff development/inservice education and curriculum. This occurs when a district perceives the need for positions to direct rather than coordinate program concerns. Other districts will develop coordinator positions to facilitate staff needs in particular curriculum areas. Coordinators interact with personnel on a staff basis. They recommend staff concerns to line personnel for managerial decisions.

Principals and school building administrators provide support and direction for faculty in their buildings. The principal is the building executive and the leader of the instructional personnel. Means to discharge those responsibilities through line leadership and staff support require careful deliberation. Schools may have department chairpersons who have some line responsibilities with colleagues in their subject area. If team teaching in the school is organized on a hierarchical basis, team leaders may also have some line responsibilities. The situations in which these individuals have line functions as opposed to their basic staff responsibilities must be clearly understood in determining the scope of line and staff curriculum planning responsibilities and how they are to operate within the school. Again, it is important that, to the greatest degree possible, schools separate line from staff functions by assigning individuals to one role or the other.

Some persons hold the belief that the staff's primary task is to implement rather than plan the curriculum. Those proponents would also see the planning function largely as belonging to line personnel. This is not accurate in terms of line curriculum planning concerns, and it ignores the role of the teacher as decision maker and curriculum planner (Harnack, 1968). Previous portions of this chapter have dealt with needs to broaden the base of persons interacting in curriculum planning activities. Again, the interaction between line and staff professionals needs to be cyclic in order to avoid linear, "top-to-bottom" curriculum planning arrangements. Personnel in line positions can be involved with either district-wide or individual school curriculum councils and generate their own input for consideration by groups studying both horizontal and vertical curriculum problems. Line personnel offer a resource that can provide administrative support in facilitating staff curriculum decisions. Thus, line involvement is essential in determining optimal conditions for curriculum change and improvement.

□ *Staff Curriculum Planning Concerns* Staff personnel have responsibility for planning teaching and learning based upon their experience at the classroom and other learning levels. The success of the curriculum depends upon staff abilities and skills to implement school programs as they have been planned. The district's curriculum planning activities should continually strive to improve the skills of making curriculum plans and developing school programs for those who work daily with children. Thus it is important to value the perspective of those who work in classrooms with children in the curriculum planning process.

Daniel and Laurel Tanner (1980) detail areas in which teacher and staff curriculum planning functions are essential. They see three levels of involvement as imitative-maintenance, mediative, and creative-generative. The first deals with traditional adaptive decision areas, the second with integrating curriculum content with emergent conditions, and the third with curriculum decisions in "an aggregate" or "macrocurricular" approach to horizontal and vertical concerns. Line personnel should not make such decisions alone. Staff personnel also need to be involved to provide bases that will help curriculum decisions impact positively upon school programs (pp. 636–639).

Staff curriculum planning positions were identified in the discussion of differences between specific kinds of line and staff positions. As opposed to directors, coordinator positions seek to provide staff persons with advanced levels of skill that can be used in collegial, non-hierarchical settings. A staff curriculum or subject-area coordinator is a resource who can share her or his skills and background in an invitational manner. Such persons are not involved in line decisions on tenure or promotion and the like. This allows staff members to develop confidential, professional relationships with coordinators.

Coordinators are more likely to be invited to visit a teacher's classes to observe situations related to instructional problems. The coordinator would continue to work with the teacher to develop skills and means to overcome the area(s) of difficulty and might even refer the staff person to other sources of information or help. For example, a teacher might bring up an instructional problem that he or she has personally recognized, or one identified through experience with a line supervisor. Teachers are more inclined to seek out coordinators for help because they are staff persons and not involved in supervisory decisions or other line relationships. As much as possible, line decisions involving a staff member should not infringe upon coordinators' capacities to function with staff members in the manner just described.

It is also important to develop channels that provide staff with access to curriculum planning organizations where they can present concerns directly. These should not have to be filtered through an intermediate decision-making mechanism. This point is raised here because the day-to-day experiences of individual staff members often are not given the immediate attention they require. This situation can be corrected when staff members have access to coordinators in the fashion just described. The coordinator can help the staff member confirm a specific concern, investigate it with the staff member, or refer to other situations that indicate that need or concern exists.

Another staff issue deals with involving students in decision-making. This is separate and apart from such organizational structures as student councils or other student governmental forums. Most commonly referred to as teacher–student or pupil–teacher planning, this process enables staff to involve students in decision making on aspects of program and/or regulations under which students must function. Krug (1950) raised the importance of identifying the needs of a school's real clients when he wrote, "After all, education is carried on to help children and youth. How can we involve their participation in arriving at ways of helping them?" (p. 19). Later he notes:

The everyday details of working and living together make the real curriculum, and it is on these matters that youth participation becomes vital and important. At its most significant level, the participation of children and youth in curriculum planning becomes one and the same thing with student–teacher planning in classroom instruction, in the total life of the school, and in school-community relations. (p. 20)

Yvonne Waskin and Louise Parrish (1967, pp. 90–96) synthesize ways to articulate student concerns in curriculum planning that respond to their expressed needs and concerns. Staff interact most closely with students on a daily basis and therefore have the primary opportunity to initiate student–teacher planning experiences. Krug (1957) further observed: "Teacher–student planning is aimed directly at helping students learn the understandings and skills of the planning process; it is only in a secondary sense a 'method' designed to facilitate the attainment of other objectives" (p. 185).

Krug also dealt with the "what, why, how, when, whom, and where" issues (1957, pp. 184–188) of teacher–student planning. Teachers need to consider these issues in preplanning before initiating student participation in planning. Preplanning is necessary to develop successful means to implement teacher–student planning activities throughout the school system. In terms of curriculum planning goals, teacher–student planning can develop skills that students will use in later educational experiences, for their adult planning needs, and someday perhaps even in lay curriculum planning roles.

The staff concerns presented here are important as school districts consider ways to improve articulation of their curriculum planning program. They represent essential functions with which staff personnel can best deal and provide balance to the line concerns presented earlier. Together, both areas offer means for school districts to develop broad and specifically responsive curriculum planning programs.

■ A Concept of Systemic Curriculum Planning

This chapter has considered elements essential for organizing systematic curriculum planning and ways in which school districts can move toward more effective curriculum planning on a district-wide basis. Study of districts with very effective curriculum planning programs reveals them to practice what Krug considered as the "four C's" in his "Guiding Principles for Future Curriculum Planning" (1950, pp. 288–290). He concluded that effective curriculum planning should be comprehensive, cooperative, continuous, and concrete.

Curriculum planning activities increase effectiveness as they consider the comprehensive needs of the all-school program in the community setting. In extending cooperative interaction among all segments of the public and school professionals, broad goals and school programs become more representative of all constituencies in the school—community setting. A continuous process of planning and development better serves the needs of the all-school program in the school community setting than an unrelated series of curriculum planning activities. Concrete rather than abstract issues serve as a focus for defining program issues from curriculum goals. Written curriculum plans facilitate identification of tasks important to improving specific features of school programs. Written plans also provide means for identifying concrete and definite progress toward goals.

Krug (1950) was concerned that "the democratic ideology should, of course, provide us with our major guiding criteria . . . what more significant conception do we have, then, to provide the basis for our future in curriculum development?" (pp. 288–289).

Curriculum planning becomes more effective as it develops school programs that respond to broad goals in the school—community setting. Broadening the base of both laypersons and professionals as described earlier in this chapter should be a central priority. School districts that experience success in this important dimension realize markedly higher achievement than other districts in attaining what is defined here as "systemic curriculum planning."

□ *Systemic Curriculum Planning Capability*   Science tells us that living creatures or plants can develop a systemic capacity to maintain normal, internal, physiological stability and equilibrium. This systemic capacity is known as homeostasis. It means that an organic system develops the capacity to compensate automatically for environmental changes. The capacity of the school—community to develop ongoing, curriculum planning processes that formulate goals, plan curricula and develop school programs to achieve those goals, and then evaluate program and goals in light of subsequent changes within that school—community setting, is seen as such a systemic or homeostatic capability. Schools pursuing means to improve systematic curriculum planning activities on a district-wide basis have long sought to improve the problem-solving abilities of laypersons and school professionals. Systemic curriculum planning likewise has improved problem-solving skills as a goal, but also adds other dimensions. These focus on extending a broader base of lay involvement and on developing more sophisticated planning skills of professionals. These capacities will serve as means to identify and deal with potential problems on a proactive rather than a reactive basis.

In achieving the regenerative aspect of systemic curriculum planning, schools will have to continue to solve problems. However, broader lay involvement and more sophisticated professional planning skills will facilitate the notion that *prevention* is one of the stabilizing characteristics of systemic curriculum planning. As stated earlier, this ability to stabilize and maintain equilibrium in a changing environment is a characteristic of systemic capacity and adds a powerful dimension to the district curriculum planning program.

A majority of school districts experience difficulties that preclude achievement of the continuous, cooperative, comprehensive, and concrete curriculum planning programs that Krug recommended. While many school districts approach the attainment of these characteristics in their curriculum planning activities and procedures, few finally achieve full, systemic capacity. Let us consider the following situation.

A school district had worked long and hard to broaden the base of lay participation in goal-setting activities. It had also developed structures and procedures that organized an extended, responsive curriculum planning program for district educators. As the program grew in effectiveness, less attention was given to monitoring these processes. Although some might see this as growing complacency or overconfidence, the curriculum planning activities continued to be responsive to district needs. For a variety of reasons there was a turnover in much of the professional staff during a two-year period. At the same time, a major local employer closed its local facilities and many residents transferred to plants in different communities. Another industry moved to town and opened a large plant that employed some area residents but also brought many managerial and other employees with it. The result was major turnover in both the local population and school personnel within a two-year period.

The reader will probably not be surprised that this district's curriculum planning program soon became relatively ineffective. Parts of the program were altered and others eliminated. In this unusual case, an effective, functioning curriculum planning program was not sufficiently systemic to monitor and extend process so that it could survive these traumatic shocks to both its lay and professional components. Most situations with programs established as well as this could have survived one or the other of the upheavals described and still have regenerated a functional, curriculum planning program. However, many districts have had curriculum planning programs collapse from far less than this critical combination of events.

☐ *Essential Systemic Planning Concerns* The reasons why most districts do not achieve full, systemic capacity are twofold, but both deal with the problems of population change and turnover. The first deals with continuous efforts to broaden the district's base of lay participation. As we discussed earlier, it is a serious error to concentrate only upon parents of schoolchildren in determining the lay participation base. This practice excludes many other publics who need to be involved in understanding school concerns if they are to support them. Broadening this base to include the community at large also prepares for changes among the district's parent population. Flux and dynamics in school parent populations must be anticipated much in the way one views a river: while the river is always there, the water is constantly changing. Numbers of parents will enter and leave the district. Even among those who stay, their children eventually complete and leave the district's schools. Other laypersons, in turn, become parents and send their children to school. This turnover problem will persist. However, curriculum planning programs can best deal with lay participation concerns by working continuously to extend the local base of lay participation.

The second area of concern deals with the need to institutionalize ongoing professional curriculum planning processes. Process needs must be continuously monitored to deal with emerging changes of kind and degree in order to generate systemic capacity. Dealing with the dynamics of the curriculum planning process is central to meeting changing professional curriculum planning needs. As district staff gain longevity, more sophisticated process needs will need to be addressed. At the same time, process must deal with turnover and orient incoming staff to the district's curriculum planning program. This initiating process must also allow new staff input into the system and utilize their professional experience and perspective.

Specific outcomes of the school–community curriculum planning program are important as means to attain district goals. However, the development of a systemic curriculum planning program requires an equal priority for process development. Careful attention to Krug's "four C's" will help curriculum planning programs to develop the regenerative, systemic capacity discussed here. Achievement of that capacity enhances a program's potential to endure and refine its capacity to develop curriculum plans and school programs which respond to changes in local school–community goals.

☐ *Inviting Community Involvement*   The elements and processes discussed in this chapter offer proven means to increase substantially the effectiveness of school district curriculum planning programs. The articulation of lay and professional involvement in these activities should not be limited to activities within the confines of the school. Many districts have responsively implemented the procedures discussed in this chapter, but have not achieved the broad results anticipated. In such cases, confinement of these activities to school settings appears to be a limiting factor.

The school–community setting is not regarded as a singular entity. In a territorial sense, there is often divisive perception of the community "turf" and the school "turf." Too frequently, the fence around the school is much more than a picturesque border. It can be the visual demarcation that signifies where community ends and school begins. Many citizens are not comfortable about going into schools. Parents may react to a telephone call from school with an involuntary "What's wrong?" knee-jerk reaction. A separation often exists even when both groups do interact. Professionals need to give high priority to making citizens comfortable with contacts from and visits to the school. A feeling of ease in dealing with school and local educators is prerequisite to increasing lay participation in curriculum planning activities. It is not sufficient that the schools belong to the community. Professionals have to make citizens feel comfortable about interaction with their schools and feel no qualms about interactions with educators in school settings.

This can be facilitated by the district aggressively developing means to encourage community groups from the range of lay publics to use school facilities during after-school hours and, when available, during the school day. Extending adult and continuing education programs, developing opportunities for evening and weekend family swimming and recreational programs, and making provisions which allow individual citizens to use school facilities for avocational interests are examples of ways to achieve this goal. Citizens could even be encouraged to enroll as students in regular daytime school programs. Schools should not underestimate the importance of extending citizens' sense of ownership in schools and feeling of comfort in coming to and using the schools. Laypersons who feel at ease in the school are more willing to support general educational needs within the district.

At the same time, educators may feel ill at ease in dealing with community members, especially when the latter are in the majority. Schools are the educational workplace, and educators usually hold meetings with parents and citizens there. Also, it is always more comfortable to deal with "outsiders" on your home "turf." Thus, there is a real need to overcome the uneasiness of both laypersons and professionals to come and work together. This development of ease and comfort in both groups is needed to improve articulation of lay and professional curriculum planning. This is essential if a district hopes to develop the systemic curriculum planning capability described earlier.

☐ *Extending Activities into the Local Community* Professionals must seize the initiative in developing this climate of ease by extending activities into the local community. Often an important meeting is scheduled for a school facility and is poorly attended. This dismays professionals who lament the lack of lay interest in a crucial area. It is impossible to identify whether a lack of interest or a lack of comfort in entering the school for the meeting was the major problem unless further efforts are undertaken. Educators can overcome this problem only as they plan alternative means to consider the agendas of such meetings. This requires the bold step of taking the school meeting(s) out of the schools and into the community's "turf." Although the prospect may initially be uncomfortable for school professionals, taking this step would demonstrate an attitude that can extend citizens' confidence to work with educators in pursuing the substance of the agendas needing attention.

Educators need to identify those organizations which constitute the inward or actual local power structure of that school–community. The objective is to gain permission to hold meetings that were poorly attended in schools in a setting where citizens feel more comfortable. Bringing school-related meetings out of the school turf will make it possible to identify whether lack of interest or lack of comfort is at issue. Community facilities such as fire halls, church halls, Granges, VFW posts, labor halls, and fraternal organizations are the home bases of community organizations that may reflect your school–community's inward power structure.

A broad range of community contacts can be built by using the facilities of different groups to hold a series of such meetings. Another approach is to get places on the programs of regular meetings of community service organizations to discuss school and curriculum planning concerns. Organizations such as Rotary, Kiwanis, Lions, JayCees, Masons, Knights of Columbus, Shriners, Eastern Star, Oddfellows, and Optimists involve representative groups of citizens interested in community needs.

The outreach approaches suggested here can do much to encourage citizens to increase their discussions of school-related matters with educators. Having met and dealt with educators in settings outside of school, more citizens may feel sufficiently comfortable to come into schools for other meetings. It is, however, a good idea to keep some meetings in community settings outside of the schools. When these approaches are paralleled by efforts described earlier to open and encourage lay utilization of school facilities for adult/community programs offered there, the chances of extending lay involvement in curriculum planning activities are greatly increased. The confidence of educators in working with citizens in the community at large likewise contributes to the creation of a singular school–community mentality that replaces the separate, divisive notions of school and community turf. The impact of these new relationships greatly enhances the district attaining a systemic capacity in its school–community curriculum planning program.

CHAPTER SUMMARY

In Chapter 9 we have considered the elements and processes necessary for curriculum planning to define broad goals and improve school programs in an optimal fashion. The discussion included a definition of major roles for lay participation in goal formulation and professional participation in program development, as well as minor areas of responsibility for both groups. Examples were provided to illustrate means by which both groups can articulate community needs and goals with curricula and school programs that respond effectively to those goals. The importance of a cyclic rather than linear relationship between lay and professional curriculum planning was illustrated. Examples were given that identified the necessity to provide ongoing, cyclic interaction of goals with program.

Staff development/inservice education issues were presented with examples that illustrated the relationship of these areas to the broad scope of curriculum planning. Guidelines for establishing staff development/inservice programs dealt with areas important in organizing inservice activities to meet the skill needs of school personnel. This discussion concluded that professionals require specific skills to implement new curricula and school programs successfully.

The purposes and functions of organizational curriculum structures that facilitate district curriculum planning activities were described. Operational roles of district-wide and individual school curriculum planning councils were related to curriculum planning procedures at several levels. These included horizontal and vertical curriculum planning issues and line and staff curriculum planning concerns. Examples of both horizontal and vertical articulation needs illustrated ways that lay and professional resources could be utilized to improve articulation of content and activities in such situations.

Curriculum planning issues specific to either line or staff dealt with ways that both these levels of personnel are essential to refining curriculum plans and school programs. Examples identified the kinds of concerns most appropriate to either line or staff curriculum planning activities. They also identified the kinds of organization and support required in line as opposed to staff curriculum planning settings.

Finally, the concept of systemic curriculum planning was considered as a means to develop curriculum planning processes that can regenerate and respond to changing needs and conditions in the school–community setting. The process characteristics of systemic planning were identified, and conditions were specified that need to be considered in developing such a capacity. Roles for school personnel to develop the extended base of lay participation necessary to achieve systemic curriculum planning were discussed. Examples were given of ways in which districts can overcome divisive concerns that view school and community as separate, noninteracting entities.

Having read Chapter 9, you should be able to:

1. Identify ways to improve the total curriculum planning program at the local level
2. Describe areas of lay concern in curriculum planning in which lay perspective is essential
3. Identify roles for lay participation in curriculum planning
4. Describe areas of concern in curriculum planning that require educational expertise for participation
5. Identify professional educator roles in curriculum planning
6. Identify ways in which professionals and laypersons can cooperatively work in the curriculum planning program
7. Identify staff development/inservice education roles in improving the curriculum planning program
8. Describe organizational structures essential to articulating curriculum planning activities in the school–community setting
9. Describe horizontal and vertical curriculum planning issues and how they relate to the district-wide curriculum planning program
10. Describe line and staff curriculum planning issues and how they must be supported to improve the district-wide curriculum planning program
11. Define and describe the concept of systemic curriculum planning as a means to provide ongoing curriculum improvement

SUGGESTED ACTIVITIES

1. Obtain a description of the curriculum planning program in your school district and examine it in light of the following questions.
   a. To what degree does it specify prerogative and roles for laypersons?
   b. How are professional decision-making prerogatives organized for interaction with those of the layperson group(s)?
   c. What provisions are made to consider the ongoing relationships of goals to school programs?
   d. In terms of the information presented in this chapter, what areas require attention in your district's lay and professional curriculum planning activities?

e. Identify what kind of model, if any, your school district uses to deal with the relationship of goal formulation to program development. Compare your information with that of other members of the class, and identify whether linear or cyclic models are most frequently used. What do these districts identify as advantages of the model or approach which they utilize?

2. Interview a person with major responsibility for staff development/inservice education in your school district to identify the following areas of concern.

a. How are staff development/inservice education needs identified in your district, and to what degree do individual schools or school levels have separate means to identify their needs?

b. Is staff development/inservice only concerned with general professional growth needs and interests, or can it deal with the skill needs of staff essential to implementing new or revised programs?

c. To what degree do staff personnel have input in defining specific staff development/inservice offered in the district or schools?

d. What kind of guidelines does the district use to organize staff development/inservice activities?

List the strengths and weaknesses of your district's staff/development/inservice program as it responds to skill needs of staff. Discuss this with colleagues and identify ways in which the program could become more responsive to skill needs of teachers.

3. Obtain the program for a system-wide inservice day in your district. Refer back to Figure 9.3 and classify each session or activity on that program as being most appropriately placed at point A, point B, or point C.

4. Select a specific inservice program in your district or school that was developed to address the skill needs of teachers. In light of this chapter's discussion, determine how the situation you have selected dealt with one of the following: short- and long-range concerns, gaining faculty commitment, and developing a realistic time line for change, *or* ways in which that situation utilized Parker's "Guidelines for Inservice Education" (Frame 9.3).

5. Identify the organizational structures that your school district uses to monitor and articulate district curriculum planning activities. Identify the objectives your district has for these organizations. Form groups of three and compare differences in the information from the different districts. Compare differences in how these districts organize structures to study and deal with curriculum planning needs. Develop

a statement of need that identifies major shortcomings in each district's organizational curriculum planning structures.

6. Divide the class into two equal groups. Individuals in group 1 will work in pairs to describe an actual problem situation involving horizontal curriculum articulation in their school district. Individuals in group 2 will work in pairs and do the same with an actual vertical curriculum articulation problem. Each pair is to: (a) describe how that problem was actually handled and/or resolved; (b) identify whether there were any continuing difficulties posed by the way that problem was handled; and (c) develop an alternative solution utilizing information from the chapter that might have resolved or handled the problem more efficiently. Convene new pairs of a person from group 1 and a person from group 2 to discuss the problems they identified.

7. Organize discussion groups of five class members. Have them review the section of the chapter dealing with line and staff curriculum planning concerns. What do group members consider the most serious staff curriculum planning needs in their own school districts? In what ways do the districts represented deal with these staff curriculum planning needs? Convene the groups and identify the consensus staff curriculum planning needs among class members. What are the consensus means by which districts deal with staff curriculum planning needs?

8. Have each class member develop a written statement identifying the kinds of things her or his school district needs to do in order to achieve a systemic capability in its present curriculum planning program. Conduct a class discussion and identify current curriculum planning procedures that districts use in working toward systemic capability. What are the consensus problems in the districts represented that preclude achieving systemic curriculum planning capability?

REFERENCES

Acheson, K., and Gall, M. *Techniques in the Clinical Supervision of Teachers.* New York: Longmans, 1980.

Anderson, V. *Principles and Procedures for Curriculum Improvement.* New York: Ronald Press, 1956.

Bruner, J. *The Process of Education.* Cambridge, Mass.: Harvard University Press, 1960.

Burton, W., and Brueckner, L. *Supervision: A Social Process.* 3rd ed. New York: Appleton-Century-Crofts, 1955.

Counts, G. *Dare the Schools Build a New Social Order?* New York: John Day, 1932.

Dewey, J. *Experience and Education.* New York: Macmillan, 1938.

Doll, R. *Curriculum Improvement: Decision-Making and Process.* 5th ed. Boston: Allyn and Bacon, 1982.

Falwell, J. *America Can Be Saved.* Murfeesboro, Tenn.: Sword of the Lord, 1979.

Gwynn, J., and Chase, J. *Curriculum Principles and Social Trends.* 4th ed. New York: Macmillan, 1969.

Harnack, R. *The Teacher: Decision Maker and Curriculum Planner.* Scranton, Pa.: International Textbook, 1968.

Koopman, R. *Curriculum Development.* New York: Center for Applied Research in Education, 1966.

Krug, E. *Curriculum Planning.* New York: Harper & Row, 1950.

———. *Curriculum Planning.* 2nd ed. New York: Harper & Row, 1957.

———; Babcock, C.; Fowkes, J.; and James, H. *Administering Curriculum Planning.* New York: Harper & Row, 1956.

Miel, A. *Changing the Curriculum.* New York: Appleton-Century-Crofts, 1946.

Oliva, P. *Developing the Curriculum.* Boston: Little, Brown, 1982.

Parker, J. *In-Service Education for Teachers, Supervisors and Administrators.* Fifty-sixth Yearbook of the National Society for the Study of Education, part 1. Chicago: University of Chicago Press, 1957.

Saylor, J., and Alexander, W. *Curriculum Planning for Better Teaching and Learning.* New York: Rinehart, 1954.

Taba, H. *Curriculum Development: Theory and Practice.* New York: Harcourt Brace Jovanovich, 1962.

Tanner, D., and Tanner, L. *Curriculum Development: Theory into Practice.* 2nd ed. New York: Macmillan, 1980.

Toepfer, C. "Will the Real Curriculum Players Step Forth?" *Educational Leadership* 34, no. 1 (1976): 12–16.

Unruh, G., and Unruh, A. *Curriculum Development: Problems, Processes and Progress.* Berkeley, Calif.: McCutchan, 1984.

Verduin, J. *Cooperative Curriculum Improvement.* Englewood Cliffs, N.J.: Prentice-Hall, 1967.

Waskin, Y., and Parrish, L. *Teacher–Pupil Planning for Better Classroom Learning.* New York: Pitman Publishing, 1967.

Zais, R. *Curriculum: Principles and Foundations.* New York: Thomas Y. Crowell, 1976.

Postulates for Curriculum Improvement

Throughout the preceding chapters, we have sought to clarify many ideas related to a comprehensive framework for curriculum planning and development. Our initial goal was to describe the variety of alternatives available to those concerned with curriculum improvement. In most cases, the discussion avoided supporting any particular alternative since curriculum decisions ultimately must be made through cooperative problem solving in the school–community setting. However, if the kind of systemic curriculum planning described in the previous chapter is to become a reality, certain basic principles are essential as guides to curriculum thinking. These *postulates* may be formulated within four general areas fundamental to effective curriculum work. The first area involves an understanding of the curriculum field itself. The second focuses on curriculum planning, the comprehensive process through which curriculum decisions are made. The third area is curriculum development, or the selection and organization of curriculum plans for teaching–learning situations. The fourth area involves aspects of curriculum leadership necessary to support ongoing curriculum planning and development. (See Summary Figure.) We believe that if thse postulates characterize curriculum work, it has a high probability of success. On the other hand, if they are ignored, the schools risk repeating many of the same mistakes that have detracted from educational quality in the past.

CURRICULUM

■ ■ Curriculum planning and development should be based upon general ideas about curriculum that derive from the interaction between theory and practice. The curriculum field, which contains these ideas, is concerned with both the process and content of education. Its concepts and skills are applicable to the whole range of learning activities in schools, business and industry, and other agencies that

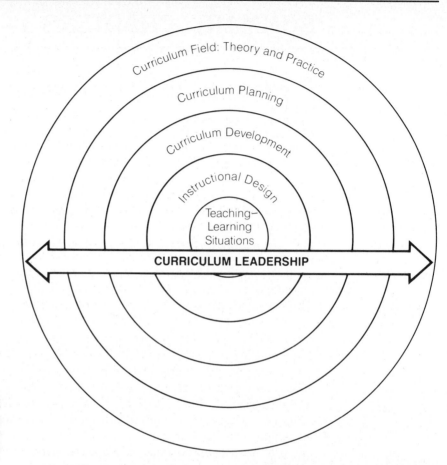

SUMMARY FIGURE
Relationship Among
Elements in the
Curriculum Field

provide educational programs. Growing interest in and concern with the curriculum field have been a particular characteristic of the twentieth century. One problematic feature of this development has been a wide diversity of opinion about the many aspects of the field, including the definition of curriculum itself. As a result, curriculum thinking is sometimes plagued by ambivalence, but more often enriched by continuing dialogue about even its most fundamental concerns. Although such debates are not likely to be resolved in the near future, there is a need to define basic principles that educators need to pursue curriculum improvement on behalf of learners. The following postulates about curriculum reflect crucial ideas that must be considered as curriculum work proceeds.

1. The curriculum field is a general area of study concerned with developing and implementing the goals and objectives of education and the means for achieving them. It is a synergism of theory and practice, both elements playing an integral part.

2. Study and practice in the curriculum field requires a broad understanding of foundation areas. These areas provide the philosophical, social, and psychological context within which curriculum activities take place.
3. In practice, the curriculum field includes planning, development, instructional design, research, theorizing, evaluation, and the leadership necessary to support and promote them.
4. Learning experiences result from both the intended or planned curriculum and the hidden curriculum. Those learnings related to the hidden curriculum are frequently more powerful since our actions in the everyday life of the school reflect our actual values and beliefs about young people and their world.
5. The curriculum field and decision making related to it involve a complex array of alternatives. Planning without knowledge and consideration of many alternatives is likely to limit opportunities for learning.
6. The curriculum field is interdisciplinary in that it brings together ideas from other educational fields in formulating the ends and means of school programs.
7. All activities in the curriculum field should derive from an ultimate concern with specific teaching–learning situations. It is the experience of learners in these settings that provides the only valid reason for schools to exist.

CURRICULUM PLANNING

■ ■ Curriculum planning is the comprehensive process by which the ends and means of learning are identified. It encompasses both broad and specific curriculum development, as well as other activities related to curriculum decision making (e.g., goal development and program evaluation). Without systematic curriculum planning, learning experiences may well be unconnected, disjointed, fragmented, and aimless. Put another way, careful curriculum planning is necessary to develop and maintain a continuous flow of educative experiences through which learners may successfully pursue both individual and societal purposes. As a process, curriculum planning coordinates those broad goals with the everyday activities meant to achieve them. It is an essential ingredient in the continuing search for excellence in education, but its systematic implementation in educational organizations remains an elusive goal. This is not to say that curriculum planning does not take place in such settings. In fact, all kinds of curriculum planning activities occur at all levels of the educational enterprise from the national to the classroom level.

However, too many of them are carried out without reference to a comprehensive and coordinated framework of ideas and action. To achieve the reality of systemic curriculum planning, a number of principles must support the process itself. Following are some curriculum planning postulates that must guide our efforts in the field.

1. Curriculum planning must be based upon a clear conception of what makes for a good life, the characteristics of contemporary and future society, and the basic needs of human beings. The omission of one or more of these foundations isolates the curriculum from the real world, the society in which we live, and the qualities of humanness that people have in common.

2. Curriculum planning must be done in light of a comprehensive framework that considers and coordinates the essential elements of effective teaching and learning. An inadequate or incomplete framework jeopardizes the effectiveness of teaching and the quality of learning.

3. Curriculum planning must be both reactive and anticipatory. On the one hand, education must be responsive to the present needs of society and individuals in order to help individuals lead worthwhile lives under current conditions. On the other hand, young learners will spend the majority of their lives in the next century. This factor necessitates the anticipation of future conditions insofar as that is possible, so that youth are prepared to meet them.

4. Educational goals should address a broad range of needs, interests, and concerns of both the individual and society. Schools are maintained to serve a variety of purposes, and this fact should be reflected in their goals.

5. Broad statements of educational goals should be clarified with concrete illustrations so that they may be useful in guiding the development of specific curriculum plans. The lack of such clarification contributes to the perception of goals as meaningless and to the contradictions between educational purposes and day-to-day activities.

6. The community at large has the right and responsibility to identify what it wants for its children through statements of educational goals. However, educators must inform citizens about the foundational areas so that goal decisions are based upon enlightened opinion.

7. Educators must guide the goal development and analysis process to ensure that goals evolve from broad-based community opinion while reflecting the concerns of responsible special-interest groups.

8. By virtue of their professional expertise, educators have the right and responsibility to identify programs that will most likely guide learners toward the attainment of educational goals. Citizens may and, where appropriate, should advise educators on school programs, but the professionals should make final decisions about them.

9. Curriculum planning and development are most effectively done in cooperative settings. Adequate consideration of the complex and varied elements in curriculum planning requires a broad range of expertise, typically best achieved through the combined knowledge and skill of several individuals.

10. Curriculum planning should address the articulation of school programs and learners across grade and school levels. The curriculum should consist of an integrated set of experiences rather than a disjointed conglomeration of activities.

11. School programs should be planned to coordinate all the elements in a total educational framework. A fragmented collection of unrelated programs hinders learners' chances of integrating their experiences.

12. Local school districts and individual schools should develop and refine an organizational structure that facilitates the study of curriculum problems and the sponsorship of curriculum improvement activities. Structured groups such as curriculum planning councils are a key ingredient in actualizing the concept of systemic curriculum planning.

13. Action research and ongoing evaluation are necessary to provide for the continuous revitalization of curriculum plans and programs. Lacking such provisions, they are liable to stagnate.

14. Cooperative participation should permeate curriculum planning activities. The range of such participation should include a span from citizen involvement in goal identification to learner involvement in planning specific teaching–learning situations.

15. The teacher is the key decision maker in the curriculum planning process. This individual is ultimately responsible for implementation of curriculum plans and also has the consistent contact with learners necessary to observe continuously their characteristics and needs.

16. Curriculum planning must provide for continuous evaluation of all aspects of curriculum decision making. This should include analysis of both the process and content of curriculum-related activities.

17. The only reason for having different levels of schools (elementary, middle level, high school) is to respond to and accommodate changes in the growth and development of youth. Thus, different levels should reflect organizational and procedural variations which respond to those learner characteristics.

CURRICULUM DEVELOPMENT

■ ■ Curriculum development is the curriculum planning process that results in broad and specific curriculum plans. It involves selecting and organizing the components of teaching–learning situations through such activities as the determination of curriculum organizing centers and the specification of suggested objectives, subject matter, activities, resources, and measuring devices. Curriculum development leads to the creation of resource units, unit plans, course outlines, and other curriculum guides that teachers and learners may use to facilitate the learning process. To carry out curriculum development effectively, educators must be familiar with a range of alternatives for each component of teaching–learning situations as well as the preplanning screens that influence them. Of all curriculum planning activities, curriculum development may be the most crucial since it basically defines the nature of the learner's day-to-day life in the school. Following are some crucial postulates which must guide curriculum development.

1. Curriculum plans should be developed in light of clearly defined goals and general objectives. One of the major purposes of curriculum plans is to identify the means by which goals may most probably be attained. Thus, they must be consistent with those goals.
2. Any program or activity carried out under the auspices of the school should be considered part of the curriculum and planned according to recognized procedures for curriculum development. Clubs and sports programs, for example, should be designed with reference to goals, objectives, measuring devices, and so on. This condition is necessary to ensure that such activities are educationally sound.
3. Curriculum plans have the highest probability of leading to worthwhile learning when they are related to the felt needs, problems, interests, and concerns of learners. When learners perceive personal meaning and worth in school programs, they are most likely to pursue them with interest, effort, and success.

4. Curriculum plans should recognize and encourage diversity among learners. Learning is most likely when curriculum plans provide a variety of means for learners to pursue objectives and the possibility for them to discover personal meaning in the activities and resources of the school.

5. Curriculum plans must make provisions for all aspects of teaching–learning situations. They should include, for example, suggested objectives, content, activities, resources, and measuring devices as well as recommendations of scheduling, facilities, and other supporting arrangements. Lacking such provisions, curriculum plans are less helpful to teachers and learners than they should be.

6. Curriculum plans should be developed in light of characteristics of the learners for whom they are intended. Those engaged in curriculum development must have a clear idea of learners' cognitive stages, developmental needs, learning styles, previous achievement, self-concepts as learners, and other critical variables.

7. The subject-area approach to curriculum organization is overused in schools. The use of other approaches within the all-school program is needed to provide the kind of balance necessary to meet the broad range of goals for education and the diversity of needs among learners.

8. Curriculum plans must provide flexibility to allow for teacher–student planning. Pupil–teacher planning provides opportunities for students to learn the skills of planning, as well as assuring that their characteristics and concerns are reflected in the curriculum planning process.

9. Curriculum plans must provide flexibility to allow for the infusion of spontaneous ideas which emerge during the interaction of students and teachers in specific learning situations.

10. Curriculum plans should reflect a balance among cognitive, affective, and psychomotor needs of learners. Components of plans should include provisions for reflective thinking, values and valuing, enhancement of self-concept and self-esteem, and improvement of physical capacities and health.

CURRICULUM LEADERSHIP

■ ■ Curriculum planning and development involve ongoing human enterprise to define effective learning opportunities. Because of this, they require supporting organizational structures that facilitate the best possible professional decision making as well as a continuous

flow of new information and ideas. These elements do not typically
emerge from educational agencies on a spontaneous basis. Instead
they result from effective leadership concerned with, skilled in, and
knowledgeable about curriculum improvement. Lacking leadership,
curriculum planning and development may be haphazard at best
and nonexistent at worst. Like other areas in the educational arena,
curriculum planning has been observed to suffer from a crisis in
leadership. This perception arises from two problems. The first has
to do with whether educators possess comprehensive knowledge of
content and processes in the curriculum field. The second problem
involves the declining number of school districts that employ professionals in positions specifically designated for curriculum leadership,
such as curriculum coordinator, supervisor of curriculum, and the
like. Effective curriculum planning and development require influential leadership guided by postulates such as the following.

1. Curriculum leadership may emerge from any category of
   professional personnel. Depending upon the situation, teachers, counselors, supervisors, and administrators all may assume leadership roles in curriculum improvement.
2. School districts have a responsibility to employ support personnel who have specialized knowledge and skill in curriculum planning and development, research and evaluation,
   and professional growth. Such personnel should be expected
   to provide leadership for ongoing curriculum improvement
   through work with teachers, school officials, and citizens.
3. The major responsibility of administrative and supervisory
   personnel should be to provide leadership and assistance in
   curriculum development and implementation. Other aspects
   of their work, such as budget development, grant writing,
   and interaction with school boards, should be carried out in
   such a way as to facilitate curriculum planning.
4. Educators have an obligation to study and comment on the
   out-of-school curriculum as part of their overall professional
   responsibility. Young people learn a great deal from experiences outside the school. Therefore, educators should be actively concerned about the nature of these learnings.
5. Advanced training of professional educators must include
   development of sophisticated knowledge and skill in curriculum planning. The continuous improvement of curriculum
   depends partly on the ability of educators to understand and
   employ continuously improving knowledge and techniques
   in curriculum planning.
6. School districts have a responsibility to provide educators
   with ongoing opportunities to grow professionally, including

staff development/inservice education. Such opportunities include workshops, conferences, study groups, and other means of professional interaction, as well as resources and scheduling arrangements to support them.

7. Administrative and supervisory personnel have a responsibility to provide the best possible conditions for teaching–learning situations. They must develop the means to implement flexible staffing, scheduling, and facilities arrangements necessary to support effective teaching.

8. Leadership for curriculum improvement requires knowledge and skill in organizational development, human relations, group dynamics, decision making, and planning. It is not enough to know about the curriculum field. Rather, the leader must also know how to work with others to make it come to life in educational organizations.

CONCLUSION

In this brief section we have synthesized ideas from Chapters 1–9 in a statement of postulates that should guide curriculum planning and development. The postulates reflect basic principles in four areas of concern: the curriculum field and its underlying concepts, curriculum planning, curriculum development, and curriculum leadership. The postulates listed above certainly do not include all of the possibilities within this realm. However, they do illustrate the essential ingredients for the process of curriculum improvement. We believe that if educators heed these postulates, curriculum planning and development will more closely approach its ultimate purpose of improving the quality of educational experiences available to learners. If these and similar ideas are ignored, curriculum work will continue to be threatened by ineffectiveness from the start. If we are truly concerned with the present and future lives of learners, the choice between these two alternatives is indeed clear.

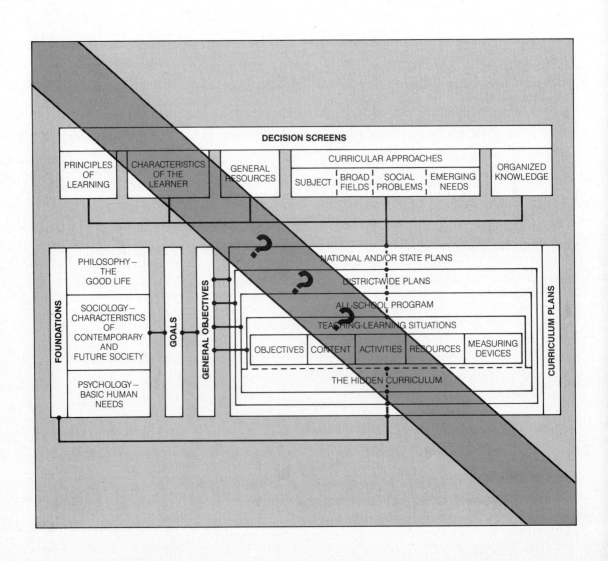

DECISION SCREENS

PRINCIPLES OF LEARNING	CHARACTERISTICS OF THE LEARNER	GENERAL RESOURCES	CURRICULAR APPROACHES				ORGANIZED KNOWLEDGE
			SUBJECT	BROAD FIELDS	SOCIAL PROBLEMS	EMERGING NEEDS	

FOUNDATIONS

PHILOSOPHY — THE GOOD LIFE

SOCIOLOGY — CHARACTERISTICS OF CONTEMPORARY AND FUTURE SOCIETY

PSYCHOLOGY — BASIC HUMAN NEEDS

GOALS

GENERAL OBJECTIVES

CURRICULUM PLANS

NATIONAL AND/OR STATE PLANS

DISTRICT-WIDE PLANS

ALL-SCHOOL PROGRAM

TEACHING-LEARNING SITUATIONS

OBJECTIVES	CONTENT	ACTIVITIES	RESOURCES	MEASURING DEVICES

THE HIDDEN CURRICULUM

10

Curriculum Planning Toward the Third Millennium: An Agenda for Educational Realities

> If past history can be used as any indication of what may happen in the future, the existing national and international crisis will improve our school curriculum. National emergencies of all sorts have furthered the cause of education in the United States. After the emergency has been met, an educational residue of some type has resulted in each instance; this residue has improved the curriculum and has advanced the schools a little further in their educational program. This has been true regardless of whether the emergency has been of an international or national nature, whether it has involved a war or merely a business depression. "Sweet are the uses of adversity."

The foregoing quotation sounds like much of the rhetoric we hear today about how schools will deal with contemporary educational problems. It is actually from the 1960 work of J. Minor Gwynn and John Chase. Their comments accurately reflect how schools traditionally went about change in the nineteenth and the first half of the twentieth century. However, we believe that both the rapidity and the acceleration of change in today's world make such a reactive posture ineffective in planning educational responses to maintain and improve present and future society.

This book opened with the observation that "the purpose of planning is to bring the future into the present to make decisions about that future now." We submit that the transformation from the industrial society at the time of Gwynn and Chase's observation to today's emerging information society makes it essential that schools assume a proactive posture if they are to remain in the mainstream of social change. Chapters 1 through 9 have provided background and understanding to implement the concepts, skills, and processes of curriculum planning in professional circumstances. The "Summary of Chapters 1–9" drew together essential postulates for curriculum improvement from the information we have presented in this volume. In this chapter we will consider some of the central issues to which these postulates can be applied in taking our schools into the future.

As a result of reading Chapter 10, you should be able to:

1. Identify major change issues facing curriculum planning
2. Identify the basic issues behind current criticism of schools
3. Identify major school, community, and youth issues that must be considered in shaping the future of schools

FROM TODAY INTO TOMORROW: SCHOOL AND COMMUNITY ISSUES

■ ■ Children who entered kindergarten in the fall of 1985 will graduate from high school in 1998 and from college in the year 2002. Can we be so myopic as to believe that merely increasing the quantity of traditional information that schools present to children will prepare them for the information society? *It is essential that educators and laypersons (1) identify and agree on the qualitative changes necessary in planning curricula before increasing the quantity of information taught in traditional areas and (2) identify appropriate methodological and process changes necessary to present and deal with that information in the all-school program.*

■ The Information Explosion

Today, the database of most technology-related areas is changing and doubling every five years, and it is predicted to double every two years by 1995. As an example, engineers graduating from a major university in 1985 were told at their commencement that the skills and information learned in their undergraduate program would be functional for about six years. The speaker concluded that much of what they would need to know as engineers by 1990 would largely be discovered between now and then. Those of us over age forty were educated to believe that the quantity of information learned in our schooling made us "educated persons" and that this information base would largely serve our future needs. As our society moves toward the third millennium, it is absolutely essential that laypersons and educators give up this antiquated perspective as they establish educational goals, make curriculum plans, and design school programs for the remainder of this century.

Both laypersons and educators may better see this dilemma in the following examples. Until 1954, high school students studying chemistry used virtually the same periodic chart of the elements as students had for thirty years previously. The minimal changes in that chart reflected the pace at which knowledge was changing during those years, even in scientific areas. However, the considerable changes in the periodic chart today, as opposed to the one that students studied only ten years ago, illustrates the growing educational implications of the information explosion issue. In another situation, students taking tenth-grade high school biology in 1977 found major changes when they took college biology as sophomores in 1981. Laypersons and educators must understand that these changes in databases will only continue to accelerate in the coming years.

We have said that persons in past times prized their education on the basis of what they had memorized and "learned." In the future, information in mathematical, scientific, and technological areas will increasingly be learned as short-term memory or recall. Computers will "memorize" and store such short-lived, temporary databases and update their memories as databases change. More and more, the mark of educated students and adults of the future will be how well they can think, process, and make accurate decisions with information that can be called up for any problem or situation.

Educators need to understand how the role of information will change in its relationship to making curriculum plans and developing school programs. Curriculum planning will have to assess the degree to which skills and information need to be considered either as temporary bases or as essential knowledge needed to function in the information society.

☐ *The Information Society* The information society is not just a future idea but a present reality. Futurist John Naisbitt (1982) states that this started in 1956 with the beginning of major efforts to refine the computer as a practical tool for electonic data, or information, processing. The launching of *Sputnik* by the Russians and the growth in the United States space program precipitated the development of sophisticated computers, which then became available for utilization in other areas. Beyond any previously known technologies, computers now provide the means for storing, manipulating, changing, and even generating and creating new knowledge.

Traditional knowledge will continue to be a part of our lives and minds. The joy of Shakespeare's words will remain a timeless description of basic human hopes, ambitions, and questions. Baroque music will not disappear in favor of newer musical idioms. However, people will need to know how to think and process information as never before. For instance, it is reputed that Benjamin Franklin may have been the last person who supposedly "knew everything." It is true that at the time Dr. Franklin lived it was possible for a "genius" to learn most of the important information from the knowledge in Western culture. But Dr. Franklin did not have to cope with a doubling of knowledge in specific fields every five years! The field of modern science is so recent that, even by conservative estimates, over 70 percent of all the scientists who ever lived are still alive today. There is no doubt that Benjamin Franklin was a superior thinker. He would probably have been as eminent today as he was over two hundred years ago. However, the level of thinking and information processing skills that will be required of persons in the next millennium certainly surpasses that needed by Dr. Franklin's contemporaries and will go far beyond those skills needed in the 1980s!

In the information society, all the present and past knowledge will be available and perhaps utilized better through new ways of organizing and processing that data. The "New Wealth," as Naisbitt calls it, will be "know-how" information, understanding process rather than mere rote memorization. This strategic information will be basic to learning and achieving. Basic skills as we know them today will still help persons deal with manuals and directions for implementing but not necessarily understanding technological tasks. Quality of life in terms of level of sustenance and employment possibilities will increasingly depend on one's attainment of thinking and information processing skills as soon as possible.

For this reason, school districts need to identify how school goals and objectives need to change to deal with the impact of such "New Wealth" and "know-how" information in the local and regional communities. This should serve as a major unifying theme for citizens and educators in curriculum planning activities.

☐   *The Need to Harness Computers*   Computers play a rapidly increasing role in our lives. Educators have not examined their own needs to develop computer literacy or the skills to use them significantly in other than school managerial operations. Only about one million computers were manufactured up to 1980, and that figure is now growing by factors of four and more each year. A half-million personal computers were sold in 1980, and the increase in annual sales since then has grown geometrically. To what degree do educators have access and skills to use microcomputers both at home and at school? To what degree are educators defining ways to use computers to plan and organize teaching–learning activities?

Gerald Rottier (1982) reports the following comments of futurist Earl Joseph. Joseph observed: "If educators wait three to ten years to use computers in the educational process, public schools will be out of business" (p. 31). Joseph further indicated that major corporations have already budgeted significant funds to replace public education!

Educators need training and access to computer hardware and software to make curriculum plans and to develop school programs. While some school districts have undertaken to provide these skills for teachers, most have only dealt with elementary programming and word processing. Sales in home computers with word processing capacity continue to increase dramatically. Conduct a brief, anonymous written survey of students to find out how many of them have access to microcomputers outside of school and how many of them have word processing skills. Results of such inquiries typically reveal that for the first time in American educational history, students, parents, and laypersons are developing a major educational skill beyond that achieved by many educators.

Educators need to acquire these skills as soon as possible and enter into curriculum planning activities to formulate ways in which school programs can move into the information age. This move offers an excellent opportunity for cooperative planning between laypersons and educators. It is important that every local school and school district formulate approaches to deal with this issue. Most communities probably have a significant number of laypersons with expertise that is important to formulating broad goals for developing school programs dealing with computers. These people could also serve as resources for educators planning staff development/inservice activities to develop skills necessary for implementing school programs in this area.

■ Educational Criticisms of the 1980s

Educators have endured criticism in and out of all kinds of contexts, since *A Nation at Risk* exploded on the public conscience on April 23, 1983. Any competent educator knows our profession has critical problems and needs. However, the public has largely failed to see many of the real problems confronting our schools and our society. We need to ask what good this bombardment of rhetoric has done for education. Both educators and laypersons need to realize that the traditional educational "business as usual" will not return to our schools. We feel that the national attention drawn to education through these criticisms demonstrates the differences faced by curriculum planners today. The degree to which we reshape education to meet emerging and future needs will require a proactive posture. We do not believe, as Gwynn and Chase observed in 1960, that education will be internally improved by the external residue of these latest criticisms.

Even the best of these reports have not substantially sketched their recommendations with an image of, or vision for, the future. Any critique of today's schools should clearly frame its recommendations within a projection of the demands that future life and a future world may make on today's students. Yet critiques fail almost universally in this dimension. (John Goodlad's *A Place Called School* [1983] was somewhat of an exception.)

While acknowledging a role for computers in the future, the recommendations in these reports are clearly based upon the industrial society of our immediate past rather than the information society that is already unfolding. These reports fail to address the need to harness computers for planning and implementing instruction in any of the directions discussed in this book. Instead, the reports, commissions, and panels seem to hold an almost naive sort of faith that education will be able to make our society succeed again in a kind of 1950s milieu. These reports have recommended increasing the quantity of factual information in content areas and lengthening the school day and year as primary solutions to educational shortcomings. Such silly thinking completely overlooks the need to consider qualitative changes in the school experience in responding to the fundamental questions, *"How much of what kind of learning is required to get where?"*

☐ *Illusions of Elitism*   Curriculum planners need to examine the data-bases upon which the national reports make their generalized conclusions. Charges of the general failure of secondary education in the United States are poorly founded. Our nation educates the children of all its people at public expense to a greater degree than any other nation in the world. While more than 75 percent of Americans graduate from secondary school, nations such as the United Kingdom, West Germany, Italy, and France graduate between 15 and 20 percent of their students from secondary school. Do we want to move to such a selective model? And by what means do we determine success? Fowler (1983) states that the United States has a 98.2 percent literacy rate, highest among the Western developed nations. Examination of the Nobel Prize laureates in the past decade shows that the United States has more winners than all of the nations of all the world combined. In addition, twenty-eight of the last twenty-nine U.S. Nobel Prize winners were graduates of the public schools of our nation. Also, twenty-three of the last twenty-five U.S. astronauts have been public school graduates.

☐ *A Question of Money*   The general public has accepted the ridiculous notion that our nation can improve the educational effectiveness of its schools without increasing expenditures. While the current national administration tells us we need more money to improve defense, we are to accept that we can improve education by cutting school budgets.

Basically, our nation tries to educate all of the children of all the people at public expense. We send the vast majority of our youth on to high school and graduate most. Nations such as Belgium, France, Italy, the Netherlands, Norway, Portugal, Spain, Sweden, Switzerland,

and West Germany keep only between 15 and 20 percent of their youngsters in school in the middle-level and high school years. Despite that, they spend a significantly larger portion of their Gross National Product on public education with considerably higher per-pupil expenditures than the United States does. In fact, the United States spends less of its Gross National Product on the public education of its children than any other developed Western nation in the world! Toepfer (1984) reports that the United States spends only 3 percent of its Gross National Product on its public education system. The least amount spent by any of the other previously cited nations is 12 percent. France, for instance, spends 16 percent of its Gross National Product on its public education system.

To emulate the expenditure of these other nations, we would have to at least quadruple our national expenditure on public education. Even then, we would be spreading out that money to educate virtually all our children through high school. These other developed nations, however, use their secondary-education money for less than one-fourth of their national budgets on defense. Despite this disparity in financial States spends a major portion of its federal budget on defense-related expenditures and, in effect, finances defense for these nations and much of the free world. This allows other Western developed nations to allocate more of their resources to education and other internal needs. As a result, these other nations spend between only 5 and 12 percent of their national budgets on defense. Despite this disparity in financial support, Daniel Tanner (1984) observes that the top 9 percent of post–elementary school students from the United States still perform as well as, or better than, the top 9 percent from the other developed Western nations.

Another unnoticed mark of the success of our nation's teachers is that in the other developed Western nations mentioned, teachers work with far fewer students each day than do U.S. teachers. Teachers of mathematics, science, or social studies in most of those countries teach no more than 75 students per school day in their programs that contain the top 25 percent, or less, of students still in school. Yet middle level and high school teachers in the United States routinely deal each instructional day with somewhere between 120 and 150 students from across the complete ability and achievement spectrum. It is fascinating to consider how well these teachers could do if they had only to deal with seventy-five individual students each day. While it would cost more to improve our nation's schools, let us not overlook the magnificence of the achievement of our mass public educational system. The combination of facts cited above show why the effectiveness of U.S. public education is truly the envy of the modern world. Clearly, no nation in the world has come close to these accomplishments, and yet critics have led the public to believe that poor education is endangering the American destiny. As will be discussed later, efforts are under way to legislate sweeping changes in the regulations of schooling in our individual states under the assumption that our schools are highly ineffective.

☐   *The College Preparation Issue*   The role of college preparation must be carefully studied in every state of the nation. The national panels, commissions, and reports all concur that technological preparation and college education are desirable goals for more and more American students. However, the emphasis that these reports put on technological education for employability has nothing more than a speculative base. Harold Howe and his colleagues (1984) in the "Symposium on the Year of the Reports" carefully refute the unsubstantiated allegations the national reports make on the technology education issue. All students need some technology education and to develop an awareness of how technology will increasingly impact on our culture and lives. This low-technology education needs to become a general education concern. However, critics of our schools are making an unfounded quantum leap in assuming that high-technology education will be a key to employment of most youth in the future. In studying the relation of high technology to education or employability, Eleanor Duckworth (1984) reports the contrary:

> The Bureau of Labor Standards . . . presents quite a different picture of the demands for highly educated young people in the next ten years. By 1990 the four fastest-growing high technology jobs together will create a total of 382,000 new jobs. The number of fast-food workers alone will increase by 400,000, and seven other kinds of work are above them on the list. (Secretaries top the list at 700,000; nurses' aides/orderlies are next at 508,000, followed by janitors, sales clerks, and cashiers.)
>
> The current crisis could be seen quite differently from the way these [the national educational] reports suggest. One could instead propose that it is the economy which is in crisis, and that young people know that perfectly well. When the prospect is for work in a fast-food restaurant, if you're lucky, what economic incentive is there to invest in education? Nor is the state of the economy the only grim element on the horizon for young people. Many of them are convinced that there will be no world left for them, anyway, ten years from now. *Action for Excellence* [Task Force on Education for Economic Growth, Denver: Education Commission of the States, 1983] nonetheless, stalwartly points out as one reason for being concerned about education that, in the armed forces, sophisticated weapons require more sophisticated skills. (p. 16)

In support of Duckworth's argument, the May 27, 1984, issue of the *Miami Herald* reported that students are not electing to pursue the skill development center programs in Florida's effort to prepare increased numbers of students for high-tech postsecondary education. Students cite boredom, hard work that does not relate to their interests, and better employment opportunities in non-high-tech areas as major reasons for not selecting the skill center programs. As a result, some Florida State Education Department officials have commented that no further changes in the state's programs should be made until there is time to judge the effectiveness of changes already made since *A Nation at Risk* appeared.

Let us remember the reason why exploration has been a major function of middle level education. Transescents between ten and fourteen years of age need to clarify who they are and what they would like to become. To decrease this function in the name of making the middle level school an integral part of the college preparatory system would be counterproductive to their educational needs.

Many of the recent national reports have attempted to build a rationale to make middle level education part of the college-preparatory cycle. Although middle level schools always had academic objectives for high school preparation, this focus cannot subsume other critical developmental needs of emerging adolescents. Responsible middle level education leaders from the days of early junior high school have worked steadfastly to keep inappropriate high school emphases out of middle level schools. We need to recall James M. Glass's observation of some sixty years ago: "There can be only one college preparatory unit in the public school system. This has been the senior high school and this school must continue to be the sole agency responsible for accrediting pupils to the higher institutions" (1924, p. 15). However, today legislators are pursuing that change in many states, despite data substantiating that this is contrary to the educational interests of early adolescents in middle level schools. As a matter of fact, there is great danger in considering college preparation to be the sole or major educational purpose at any school level. Even at the high school level, how many youngsters know what specialized preparation for postsecondary school they want and are able to pursue? Duckworth's data and the Florida problem suggest that perhaps even the high schools need to rethink the readiness of adolescents to make such decisions. Middle level educators must live up to their obligation of protective custody and maintain what we know to be the essential personal, social, emotional, and intellectual tasks for transescent youngsters.

Curriculum planning at the district level needs to consider what the major goals and emphases are for children in each unit of the school system. This deliberation can identify the necessary balance between developmental needs of youth and vocational and college preparation concerns. Similar planning needs to be done at regional and state levels to provide better guidelines to assist local districts in these efforts.

☐ *Elementary Education Concerns*   To this point, the national reports have suggested relatively little direction for change in early childhood education. Perhaps conventional wisdom has established a national understanding of the educational needs of young children beyond that achieved at either middle grades or high school levels. It may be that the elementary school setting in which teachers deal with a single class of students during most of the school day has been fundamental in this accomplishment. However, in postelementary schools teachers routinely deal with from 100 to 180 students daily. This could preclude the development of a similarly clear sensitivity to the central educational needs at those levels. For this reason, educators and laypersons need to keep abreast of increasing interests in departmentalizing upper elementary grades and beginning serious intellectual activities earlier in elementary schools. David Elkind (1981) has identified the dangers of accelerating the development of children beyond their readiness of mind and psyche. Therefore, schools and their communities must insist on hard data to substantiate that any such efforts would be neither futile, abortive, nor harmful to young children.

Curriculum planners have the obligation to stabilize this issue by providing lay curriculum planning groups with accurate information for child development research findings. Those data identify how learning capacities of young children, transescents, and adolescents specifically differ from one another. It is essential to counteract growing acceptance of the simplistic notion that there are no limits to which advanced learning demands can be introduced earlier in children's school experience.

■ Curriculum Planning versus Curriculum Legislation

The issues considered thus far in this chapter indicate that the choices educators make within the next few years will, in large measure, have an impact on how education will be organized by the early years of the next millennium. One of the scenarios presented in the introduction to this book saw education becoming a monolithic, national system, and a second one envisioned education being delivered through a technological system utilizing means that are currently nontraditional. The issues considered in this chapter indicate the likelihood that aspects of both these alternatives may come to pass.

Chapter 9 discussed ways to define and articulate lay and professional roles in curriculum planning activities at the school and district level. The consideration of present and emerging issues facing our schools requires that laypersons and professionals plan around these possibilities. Failure to do so is alarming in view of the growing trend of state legislatures assuming professional prerogatives in planning educational change. Traditionally, school boards have dealt with issues of policy and the establishment of goals. However, the past decade has witnessed a gradual extension of school board authority into the area of program implementation. This has eroded the base of prerogatives of school professionals. The resulting shift in the balance of policy-making between the chief school officer and the school board means that school superintendents and other professionals have more limited possibilities to plan with school boards today than in earlier times. This fact threatens to destroy the balance between lay and professional input in decision making about educational policy that is recommended for effective curriculum planning.

This phenomenon at the school district level is paralleled by a new perspective at the state legislative level. For the first time in U.S. educational history, state legislatures are now attempting to "legislate learning." While naively simplistic, the notion that academic achievement can be increased by passing laws requiring standards of performance is a growing trend. At least one state has gone so far as to legislate certification and teacher tenure requirements that virtually eliminate the need for professional educational preparation. This decision has been made by legislators who themselves are not professional educators. It will, however, have an impact upon the entrance of non–professionally prepared individuals into teaching and other educational positions in the schools. Extension of this trend may mean that education could become a "nonprofession." In that state, if a person can simply pass qualifying examinations, he or she can qualify for entrance into teaching.

Chapter 9 dealt with the issues involved in staff development/inservice education and the professional growth of teachers. The idea of "deprofessionalizing" teacher preparation also has serious implications for staff development/inservice education and the qualifications of those who plan this vital function. One state has suggested that colleges of education may not be needed in either the preservice or continuing inservice education of teachers. They project that school staff members will provide on-the-job training for both liberal arts graduates and persons making career switches to teaching. Some see these populations as our greatest source of future teachers. These issues are policy and political concerns, but we should not overlook their implications for curriculum planning activities at the local district level.

We believe that these legislative efforts will be no more effective than earlier attempts to legislate national temperance through the Volstead Act or contemporary efforts to reduce youth alcohol abuse by raising the minimum legal drinking age. Such problems involve changing both values and behaviors and have implications for learning, valuing, and counseling. Legislation is an attempt to control by fiat, whereas education requires planning to identify ways in which people can learn desired skills and information related to particular goals. Few would agree that children will walk at twelve months of age and read at four years and ten months of age simply because states pass laws that require it. However, there appears to be a growing belief that the passing of laws requiring higher achievement and professional competency will bring those things to pass. The quarrel is not necessarily with the goals of many of these efforts. However, we disagree that legislation is the means that will effect such changes. Also, the planning of goals for change necessitates the interaction of laypersons and professional educators for effective curriculum planning. This step needs to be restored if we hope to plan and develop realistic educational futures that will prepare youth to function in terms of the demands of the future. Instead, legislatures are assuming this function in an increasing number of states in our nation. Interactive curriculum planning between educators and laypersons at the district level is recommended as an effective way to build an understanding that such approaches cannot succeed.

This chapter began with Gwynn and Chase's observation that the residue left after meeting national emergencies always "has improved the curriculum and has advanced the schools a little further in their educational program." We submit that this use of the past can no longer be expected to refine education in our schools. Gwynn and Chase described a phenomenon that was characteristic of the industrial society. That "catch-up or spillover" effect does not appear to work any more. *The transition to the information society is fast changing our lives today and makes it essential that we take interactive and proactive postures to plan alternative educational futures.* Failure of educators to assume this responsibility will mean that educational futures will be planned without central input from professionals. The increasing attempts of nonprofessionals to legislate educational futures is an ominous portent of this shift. Recall that this book began with the observation that "the purpose of planning is to bring the context of the future into the present and make decisions about that future now." Our actions in the next few years will decide whether or not educators are allowed to retain an effective role in this process.

☐ *Previous Attempts at Educational Reform*   In considering how we may address this growing reality through curriculum planning, we must clarify the reason for this shift. In past eras of criticism of schools, the legislative route was not taken. Instead, efforts at curriculum reform were made. It may well be that because the curriculum reforms of the post-*Sputnik* era in the 1960s largely did not succeed, there has been a loss of confidence in curriculum reform efforts as a viable means to improve education. Perhaps this perception has contributed to the decision to attempt to legislate educational standards, achievements, and requirements. The current move is also evidence that groups with power will attempt to control the selection of alternative futures. It is therefore imperative that educators coalesce with laypersons to articulate the potential of the power base available through curriculum planning at the local district and school level. This process may then have an impact upon regional and state decision making as well. Failure to seize this available channel will result in greater centralization of such decisions at state legislative levels.

It is important to correct the misconception that the curriculum reforms of the 1960s were actually curriculum planning reforms. On the contrary, they were largely the development of curriculum content packages supported by resources of the National Educational Defense Act. The context of these efforts was based neither upon goals defined by educators and laypersons nor upon information from child development experts as to how schoolchildren learn at different ages. Yet the public mistakenly believed that these projects were representative of what improvements could be made in education through curriculum planning activities.

The post-*Sputnik* furor blamed education for the Russians beating the United States into space, and the fault was attributed to mathematics and science programs in our schools. As an aside, it is interesting to observe the recurrence of this theme in the opening lines of *A Nation at Risk* (Gardner, 1983). Both eras of criticism attributed the decline of U.S. international leadership as a fault of the schools. In the present situation it may be a Japan Toyota achievement that spurred criticism. However, could this "problem" not possibly relate to the issues discussed in this chapter's section on "A Question of Money"? The post-*Sputnik* solution was to have Nobel Prize laureates and other luminaries in areas such as biology, chemistry, mathematics, and physics develop content programs organizing the latest developments in their areas into school curriculum packages. It is interesting that most of the projects in modern mathematics and the sciences developed in this fashion did not succeed.

While falsely attributed to educators, the failure of these efforts was actually due to errors made by the content-area luminaries. There was inadequate involvement of curriculum planners or experts in child development to monitor and correct the conditions that doomed most of these subject-matter projects. For instance, one highly publicized national biology project for the middle grades was an immediate failure despite its organization of the most current advancements in the biology field into a fine, logical sequence. The program was written on a twelfth-grade reading level and required that learners be able to function at abstract, formal operational thinking levels. The science luminaries who designed and developed the program were not aware that middle grades youngsters need materials with a fourth- through ninth-grade readability level. Likewise, the developers lacked the knowledge that most of these learners function at the concrete operational thinking level and cannot yet do formal, abstract thinking as the program required. Involvement of curriculum planners and child development experts in this project could have corrected this terrible oversight.

Today's school mathematics programs use few of the modern math programs fashioned in similar ways during that era. Contemporary school mathematics programs are effectively synthesizing parts of those developments with more traditional mathematics teaching approaches into programs which are more intelligible to learners. As Archie LaPointe (1984) reports, these efforts are resulting in improved mathematics achievement. These successes are being achieved through curriculum planning activities that involve professional educators who know how children think and learn at different ages during their school years. However, the post-*Sputnik* critics thought professional educational expertise was not essential in efforts to catch up with the Russian achievement. Interestingly enough, when U.S. astronaut Neil Armstrong set foot on the moon, no retraction of earlier indictments of our schools was made. Likewise, no attention was drawn to the fact that this achievement was formulated by a generation whose education was through programs of pre-*Sputnik* schools. Did anyone consider that the quality of U.S. education was a contributing factor to this spectacular achievement?

□ *Unrecognized Current Educational Achievements* Some projects of the 1960s did combine professional educational expertise with that of content specialists to develop new school programs. Those did succeed and continue to be refined and used in American schools today. Oddly enough, these were among some of the programs viewed by *A Nation at Risk* as contributing to declines in U.S. educational achievement. A recent major international study validates that significant educational gains in science achievement were actually due to this maligned "process" approach. The Second International Science Study compared U.S. students with those from other nations in a follow-up to the First International Science Study completed in 1970. Rodney Doran and Willard Jacobson (1985) coordinated the American portion of the study, which revealed that U.S. ninth-grade students grew 5.2 percent in overall science achievement over students tested in the First International Science Study. These ninth-graders knew more about biology and physical science than their counterparts did ten years ago.

While *A Nation at Risk* concluded there was need for heavier doses in science, Professor Doran indicated that "that conclusion was based on testing conducted on American children ten years ago." American students participating in the Second International Science Study did much better on process questions that required them to classify, calculate, and analyze data rather than merely recall memorized facts. Irene Jennings (1984) reported Doran's observation that "the preliminary results of our study indicate that there has been some long-term, positive impact of the process approach to learning science begun in the mid and late 1960's" (p. B-1). This strongly contradicts the opinion of many national commissions, panels, and reports that educational innovations in the 1960s resulted in poorer student achievement.

The interaction of expertise of professionals on child and human development, curriculum planning, and teaching is essential to planning effective alternative educational futures. Present efforts to legislate change planned without sufficient professional educational input likewise offer little hope for developing viable solutions to the educational needs of children. Interactive planning among these constituencies holds an exciting potential for planning, developing, and selecting educational futures that could take us into the next millennium with greater chances for success than anything yet achieved in human history. The processes and organizations for defining and establishing lay and professional interaction in curriculum planning require the careful attention of those seeking to build educational reform and plan educational futures. The rethinking of lay and professional roles and prerogatives in this process at local, regional, state, and national levels is a central task. The possibilities of educators increasing their impact upon regional, state, and national decisions about alternative futures can best be achieved as local districts develop the purposeful involvement of professionals and laypersons in curriculum planning. The locus of control in such interaction within the school–community setting could be the ultimate key to the power base that is central to turning attention to the educational needs of youth.

THE YOUTH SURVIVAL ISSUE

■ ■ The ways in which educators deal with the issues just considered will in large measure determine the effectiveness with which education will function in the future. However, the ways in which educators make curriculum plans and develop school programs must pay equal attention to the needs and problems of youth in our society. In concluding *In Defense of Youth,* Earl Kelley (1962) made a strong case for giving higher priority to the needs of youth than society did in 1962. The issues in his summary persist today and are even perhaps more critical in terms of the continued growth of youth problems to the present time. Kelley observed:

I have heard people who are good friends of youth say that we simply cannot afford the burden of good schools. This is nonsense. The people in the richest country in the world buy what they want. It is only a question as to what they value. I believe that we in education should not concede that American people cannot afford a well educated teacher and an attractive classroom for each twenty-five of our own young. We just have to care more about that than something else.

I have mentioned the above items only because it seems to me that they are growing symptoms of an increase in the rejection of our own young, and will make the "youth problem," which is really an adult problem, worse instead of better. We can go on, of course, making our society more hostile and more rejecting of our young, but at an awful price. The price will be in more delinquency, more youth violence, more mental hospitals, more police, more juvenile courts. To summarize, I hold that we adults must keep these points in mind:

1. Our culture is in jeopardy unless we can adequately care for our young.
2. Our young people are all right when we get them. If all is not well with them, it is due to what has happened to them in an adult-managed world.
3. If youth have not been too badly damaged by the life that has been thrust upon them, they enjoy and desire a good society as much as we do.
4. In urban society, our young live under more difficult circumstances than they used to.
5. The amount of juvenile delinquency in any community is a measure of that community's lack of concern for its young.
6. There is really no valid, responsible place in our urban communities for youth. They are a displaced segment of our society.
7. A place must be made for them, and it seems to me that the only feasible place is the school.

Since nearly everybody believes that the "youth problem" is getting worse as the years go by (and this certainly seems to me to be so) it should be logical to admit that we must be doing something wrong, or neglecting something we should do. Let us try something different, something which seems dictated by the findings of researchers. Let us try:

Acceptance of all of our young as worthy, valuable, uniquely blessed with some gifts.
Making the school a real youth institution.
Involving youth in what is to be undertaken.
Choices for youth, for the development of free, creative minds.
Cooperation and democracy in the place of authoritarianism.
The human approach, rather than stressing those things which lie outside the learner.

Love, to replace alientation of so many of our own flesh and blood.
(pp. 144–145)

Kelley wrote these words in a time when society's recrimination of education also posed difficulties to curriculum planners in their efforts to respond to the needs of youth and society. Today, we again face similar problems in responding to the criticisms educators have experienced since 1983. Contemporary problems of youth survival can be seen in the growing numbers of our young who find increasing difficulty in reaching their adulthood psychologically and emotionally whole. As we approach the third millennium, youth problems today appear to differ in degree rather than kind from what Kelley observed in 1962. The problems of urban life have intensified but, because of increased mobility in our society, they are also more readily observable in both suburban and rural settings. Let us consider some of the critical aspects of the youth survival issue.

■ What the National Reports Failed to Consider

The appearance of *A Nation at Risk* set the mood of the nation to "get tough and shape up education." This mood produced a set of national reports that focus upon "excellence in education" with regard to intellectual growth and academic achievement alone. This infatuation with improving performance in these areas overlooks the need to address equally the critical affective, self-concept, and self-esteem needs of youth. *The literature of the national reports has lost contact with concern for the wholeness of the developmental needs of children, transescents, and adolescents.* Such emphases are almost categorically absent in the literature that has mushroomed since the appearance of *A Nation at Risk.* Should not "excellence" deal with these fundamental concerns in human development as well? *The fact is that schools do not create youth problems such as dissolution of personality, loneliness, lack of interaction with adults, and the "latch-key-syndrome." Youngsters bring those problems from their lives in society into the school.*

What is the school–community's obligation to balance a commitment to "excellence" and reverse these sad conditions among our youth?

We know that one's adolescent-adult value frame is largely influenced by the age ten to fourteen life experience. If a youngster does not survive her or his life psychologically and emotionally whole and "alive," does that student's academic performance really matter at all? State legislatures continue to pass changes in educational regulations that will bring learning challenges formerly required of high school adolescents down into the middle level school grades. The demands of these changes will be highly stressful for many young adolescents in middle level schools.

To what degree are these decisions being based upon careful consideration of the degree to which students can deal with the stress of more demands and accelerated changes in their young lives? We cannot legislate a reversal of the erosion of family and adult support for children. No laws can reverse the decline in the stability of marriage. Today, only 48 percent of thirteen-year-olds still live with both of their original parents. We can, however, make certain that in the simplistic zest to improve school achievement by merely increasing the difficulty of learning activities, we do not overchallenge large numbers of children prematurely and drive them into frustration and depression and over the brink to tragedy.

A recent obituary of a middle level student suicide noted her membership in the National Junior High Honor Society. How meaningful was that achievement in view of her inability to deal successfully with the problems that caused her to end her life? Each youth suicide also indicates the inability of adults to recognize danger signals and provide the support that might have helped that youngster solve her or his problems—and survive.

■ Youth Suicide: Problem and Response

To this point we have presented, in broad terms, a number of problems and concerns that call for a curriculum planning response. We have selected one problem for elaboration as an example of such a need, namely youth suicide. This issue is perhaps the most compelling since, if the young choose to end their lives, all the efforts of the school and community come to naught.

Educators and laypersons across the nation continue to witness the impact of youth suicide but do relatively little about it. We behave like the peasants in Bram Stoker's novel *Dracula* as they tried to avoid the ravages of the vampire. Most of them merely hoped this terror would not enter their lives. They spoke of this horror only in private circumstances, and they publicly pretended that it did not exist. This behavior tragically parallels lay and educator reactions to the specter of youth suicide in the United States today.

In an age when gathering and accessing information through electronic data processing is forging our technocracy ahead at blinding speed, we cannot seem to really document the incidence of this growing problem in our school–communities. Likewise, there is little sharing and communication of programs and efforts to deal with this problem from one school–community to another. We can readily observe the lack of networking among and within educator, psychiatric–psychological–mental health personnel, and lay constituencies in responding to the youth suicide problem. It is absolutely vital that educators and laypersons study the realities of this problem locally and plan ways to deal with it through programs in both the school and community. Such planning action is necessary to develop articulated courses of action that will address this problem more effectively than present efforts.

As of 1984, 1,000 American teenagers attempted suicide and 100 of them "succeeded" (Paul Mauceri, 1985). Reported suicides in the United States per 100,000 persons in the age range of 15–24 years increased by more than 100 percent from 5.2 percent to 12.3 percent between 1960 and 1980. Data on suicide in younger children are only beginning to be clarified. We have to look at that increase as it relates to suicide among older adolescents and young adults. Michael Peck (1982) reported that suicide in the age range of 10–14 years increased by 33 percent between 1968 and 1976 (p. 38). Data gathered from 1976–1983 indicated that the increase during this period was as great as 41 percent during that seven-year interval. Increases in suicide among children under 10 years of age appeared to be far less than in either the 10–14- or 15–24-year-old populations. However, any increase at all in early childhood suicide is horrifying. John Langone (1984) reported that as of 1981, suicide rose to the eighth leading cause of death among our 5–14-year-old population. Mauceri (1985) cited statistics documenting a 25 percent increase in suicides in the 12–19-year-old population in Massachusetts in 1983. From the extent of suicide data, the middle school grades constitute a crucial target area for consideration of efforts to deal with this critical issue.

In many states, a death does not have to be reported as a suicide unless a note has been left. Carl Frederick's work (1982) deals with the fact that many automobile fatalities in which the driver is the single occupant of the vehicle are really suicides. If no suicide note is left, these fatalities can be reported as accidental deaths. Medical doctors say that a decision to report suicide as an accidental death may be an effort to help the family survive the tragedy. For many reasons, suicidologists estimate that the increase in actual suicides may be considerably higher than reported because of the way these statistics are gathered and categorized. Despite this, it is essential that accurate reporting of suicides be made if we are to fully document the true scope of the youth suicide problem.

Other sources report a high incidence of drugs and other substances involved in many youth suicides. This information should not be simplistically construed to mean that drugs and substances caused that youngster to commit suicide. Youngsters may turn to these substances as an escape or an attempt to fill a critical void in the human support and interaction needs in their lives. A suicide involving drugs or alcohol may only mean that individual found no solution to her or his problems in those substances and could find no other way to deal with those problems before the decision to end life. Drugs, alcohol, and eating disorders (e.g., anorexia nervosa and bulimia) can cause atypical reactions to problems that might lead to potential suicidal behaviors (Harold Bruch, 1978, 1979). Anorexia and bulimia very often develop during a youngster's middle level school years. It would seem that these youngsters may fear leaving the known security of childhood and seek to stop the pubescent transition by malnourishing their bodies. When such symptoms appear, a psychiatric examination is essential to assess both the medical and psychological issues in the youngster's behavior. The psychiatrist can then refer that person to the most appropriate kinds of help.

In addition to the increasing rate of change and other stress-producing episodes as youngsters enter their early adolescent years, another factor that will continue to bring potential suicidal issues to transescent youngsters seems beyond our control. This is the slow, continued lowering of the chronological age at which pubescence occurs. The problems of postpubescent adjustment to unrequited love and to disillusionment with formerly stable elements in one's earlier years can bring about depression. As a person experiences growing inability to cope with and bring an end to a "normal" experience of depression, adjustment problems develop that could lead to potential suicide.

K. Ishi (1982) suggests that this continuing lowering of the age of puberty will bring more of the tasks experienced in years past during ages 14–18 into the middle level school years. The earlier physical maturation of youth has not been paralleled by an equally earlier achievement of social and emotional maturation. Indeed, the emotional and social maturity levels of today's transescents have not appreciably changed from those of students ten years ago. When adults are struck by the physically more mature appearance of many youngsters today, they should not assume that these youngsters have equally precocious social and emotional maturity. In fact, the adjustment problems of physically precocious transescents may signal a need for special understanding and help by adults. Adolescents and adults may mistakenly assume that these "bigger" individuals are ready for physical, social, emotional, and intellectual task situations that are appropriate for adolescents some two or more years older. In assuming a maturity and readiness belied by their physical precocity and the thin veneer of sophistication acquired from media, music, and pop culture, we may unfortunately be casting them adrift from the adult interaction, support, and guidance they need.

Sociologists and curriculum scholars need to reexamine Robert Havighurst's research of over thirty-five years ago on developmental tasks (1950). To what degree can it be substantiated that (1) developmental tasks of adolescents from that era are increasingly observable in middle level transescents today and (2) developmental tasks of early adolescence from that era increasingly observable in younger children today?

The frightening lyrics of a song popularized in the early 1970s by Peggy Lee, "Is That All There Is?," may best describe what unhappy, disillusioned, and lonely youth anticipate in contemplating suicide. The song deals with one person's disillusionment since childhood in searching for happiness and fulfillment in life. The final verse questions death as a means to find out whether there could be happiness and fulfillment beyond life or whether death will be only another disappointment. This kind of unhappiness is most often the cause of suicide. Our youth need interactions with adults that will develop their capacity to actualize their life though coping with and positively solving the problems in their young lives. Adults in the home, community, and school must give high priority to such interaction with youth. Suicide prevention requires our attention, study, and action in school–communities across the nation.

As understanding of this problem is increased, we can effectively work to raise local awareness of this issue and possible ways to pursue it in the school–community setting. Networking can develop more effective approaches to preventing suicide and dealing with that tragedy when it occurs. Curriculum planning activities involving both laypersons and professionals need to be formulated at the school district and building level. Steps to organize suicide crisis procedures and school–community education programs on a school district-wide and regional basis must be systematically planned. Ralph Smith and Paul Mauceri (1982) have organized an excellent suicide prevention and intervention program. Mauceri (1985) subsequently developed an effective model for school–communities that discusses tasks and steps for establishing such critically important procedures.

Identifying the scope of the youth suicide problem in the school–community setting is of primary importance. The development of information networking and crises approaches will facilitate greater success in dealing with this problem at each school level. This networking should involve local psychiatrists, physicians, psychologists, social workers, and mental health agency personnel. The involvement of the school board, district and building curriculum planning groups, and parent and parent–teacher organizations is essential in deciding how laypersons and school professionals can best be informed of the local realities of this problem.

Following the establishment of these strategic activities, schools need to develop specific support activities to deal with such concerns. These include (1) planning curriculum considerations of this issue, (2) developing means to identify students with potential problems, (3) developing means to communicate, work with, and support the family, and (4) getting these students to appropriate sources of help as soon as possible. We should not play amateur psychologist. School counselors, psychiatrists, psychologists, family physicians, or community health agency personnel can make referrals to sources of appropriate help as necessary. It is best to identify the source of these behaviors and deal with them as early as possible.

This is probably a new and uncomfortable area of consideration for most of us. Clearly, there is no other area in greater need of school–community study and support. The increase in potentially suicidal problems in the lives of children and youth cannot be underestimated. Developing means to identify the actual scope of this problem and approaches that responsively extend the capacities of youth to cope with and resolve their problems toward surviving their school years is a frightening and awesome concern. Unfortunately, probably not all youth suicides are preventable. However, continued failure to pursue the youth suicide problem will only contribute to further increases in its incidence.

■ An Agenda for Youth–Adult Interaction

In the sense of Kelley's concerns (1962), have we not long passed the point at which parents, educators, and community need to coalesce and intervene in the seduction of youth by the commercial and industrial sector? At what point do we give back the value of genuine, caring relationships with youth, the erosion of which has made them seek values in the motivationally advertised products of the cosmetics, fashion, entertainment, and other industries? Today's youth need more, rather than less, positive interaction with adults. In this interaction, we have to recognize that many of our students need greater support from adults as they attempt to deal with these difficult problems which, in earlier decades, were largely experienced by only older and more mature adolescents and young adults.

Youth are the future of each one of us, and in them reside the dreams and hopes of the society, our species, and perhaps of the universe. Not to involve them in our planning is even more ludicrous than it seemed to Earl Kelley in his time. Yet it remains for educators to do this through curriculum planning, for it seems that this reality escapes other adults. This chapter has dwelled at length on the pandemic nature of problems threatening youth survival today. We can readily observe the continued erosion of the traditional nurturing bases that most of us knew in our own youth. As a result, guidance, direction, and support of youth in their journey toward adulthood were never more needed and, in most cases, wanted. To deal with the complexities of today's and the emerging world, children are far more in need of models than critics. The increase in numbers of students who seize every opportunity to "hang around" particular teachers, counselors, administrators, school secretaries, and custodians is readily observable. This is often a poignant indication that school adults may be the best models of caring, responsible adult behavior that the youngster sees in her or his waking hours.

As educators, let us model patient, caring, and consistent behavior in our dealings with youth. Let us identify the degree to which this makes a difference in their dealings with us and others, and in their progress toward the goals of school and society. Let us put aside the ridiculous notion that there is something "old-fashioned" about authority and respect for it. Let us help students understand authority and facilitate their growth in the ability to handle successfully the increases in authority we gradually make available to them. As they grow in this ability, let us help them take pride as they prove to themselves and others their increasing capacity to handle that authority responsibly. While we often admonish that "authority goes with responsibility" we also must not overlook its corollary that "responsibility goes with authority." In truth, no one can be responsible in a situation unless some amount of authority for her or his actions is delegated to that person.

We have to decide how, when, and in what situations a youngster can responsibly handle increased authority. This should be discussed and planned with youth so that they understand the nature of the authority that may be delegated to them. They need to let us know if they feel ready and able to deal with such increased responsibility. When accord is reached, there is a far better chance that youngsters can succeed in that situation and demonstrate to themselves and us that they have the growing ability needed to handle that authority responsibly and well. If there are slip-ups, and there will be, let us remember Louis Raths's words that "the process of growing up is the process of making mistakes." Let us handle and discuss those situations and give that youngster an experience of growth as we plan and discuss ways that might resolve conditions positively. Let us find with that youngster a way in which growth toward trying that situation out again can be accomplished in a secure and caring rather than a punitive way. Let us also consider our own complicity in that unsuccessful situation. To what degree, perhaps, did we extend more authority than that youngster could handle? We, too, can grow from that situation and become more effective in this process with other youth. Let us remember that as youth grow up and enter more demanding situations, they benefit from an invitational posture on our part, since we are the hosts to adulthood. As youth increasingly develop their capacities, they do become our younger peers in adulthood. Let us work to help both adults and youth understand the narrowing of the line between us as youngsters grow toward adulthood. Let us not be threatened by the competencies of their youthful bodies, intimidated by their boundless energy, suspicious of their lesser cynicism, insensitive to their love of laughter and loudness, nor resentful of their possession of what we jealously observe we lose in our own aging. Let us shoulder the adult responsibility to set limits for youth. Let us make this a loving and positive experience as we work to help them to understand these limits and to grow and be able to extend those limits with success and maturing confidence in their abilities.

CHAPTER SUMMARY

In Chapter 10 we have considered a number of major factors in curriculum planning. The changing conditions accompanying our leaving the industrial society are bringing differences of both kind and degree to the curriculum planning issues facing schools at this time. Schools will have to deal with the implications of the current information explosion in defining how knowledge will be organized for effective education of youth. The coming information society will extend this need even further and will require schools to define appropriate ways to harness and use computers to manage this growth of information. Curriculum planners will have to identify ways that effectively assist educators in processing information toward solving schools' and society's emerging and future needs.

The nature, accuracy, and helpfulness of the reports and criticisms of American education in the first half of this decade were considered as they could help curriculum planners identify the realities, strengths, and needs facing education in the future. The issues facing education into the third millennium involve questions about maintaining a public educational system at public expense and needs for an adequate system for underwriting the cost of public education in the future. Future implications for the college preparation of youth will require a redefinition of general educational demands. These will include moral/ethical concerns and needs for both low- and high-tech preparation of young people. Needs to provide proper support for planning education for future needs as opposed to the mere legislation of requirements will continue to require study and scrutiny.

The persisting problems of youth were described with emphasis upon the growing need for attention to affective issues. An analysis of the increasing youth suicide problem focused on how schools might address this area. This was tied to a consideration of both broad and specific concerns involved in achieving excellence in educating our youth. The chapter concluded with a lengthy agenda for adult–youth interaction as we approach the third millennium.

Having read Chapter 10, you should be able to:

1. Identify major change issues facing curriculum planning
2. Identify the basic issues behind current criticism of schools
3. Identify major school, community, and youth issues that must be considered in shaping the future of schools

SUGGESTED ACTIVITIES

1. Have members of the class obtain samples of their school's curriculum guides, course outlines, and other curriculum materials used for teaching about computers. Determine the number of microcomputers capable of word processing that are available to students and the number of students in your school. In your discussion, analyze the information that class members obtained in terms of the issues presented in this chapter.

2. Ask interested members of the class to administer the following anonymous questionnaire to their own students.
   a. Do you have access to a microcomputer or word processor outside of school?
   b. If so, what kind of computer is it and where is it located?
   c. Who taught you how to use the computer?
   d. For what do you use the computer beside games and entertainment?
   e. Do other members of your family use the computer for other things than games or entertainment?
   f. In what ways do you use computers in school?

Have individuals present their findings and discuss the degree to which students in their schools are using computers outside of school and the degree to which schools do or do not utilize the skills.

3. Ask members of the class to find out how many microcomputers are available for teacher use in their school. Select interested members of the class to ask educators in their school to complete the following anonymous questionnaire.
   a. In what ways do you use computers in your professional activities?
   b. Briefly describe the computer skills you have developed.
   c. Do you have access to a computer outside of school?
   d. If so, what kind of computer is it?
   e. Briefly describe the kind of computer skills you feel you still need to extend your professional use of computers.
   f. How do you feel the school needs to better utilize computers in the instructional program?

g. Do you feel that this school is adequately preparing students for life in the information society?

h. In what ways could the school better prepare students to use computers in their own lives?

Organize a class presentation and discussion of the findings from these investigations. Ask the class to draw conclusions as to how well teachers have developed the computer skills necessary to use them with students in school. What areas do educators see as most critical to their using computers more effectively in school? In what ways does the group feel they need to develop more skills for using computers in their teaching?

4. Organize the class into three groups according to their background and interests in elementary, middle level, or high school. Members of each group should interview teachers and other professionals in their school on the following items.

a. What are some primary examples of the information explosion that you view as important at this level of education?

b. What changes, if any, do you see occurring in what and how we are teaching youngsters at this school level as opposed to what we did a decade ago?

c. To what degree do any changes you observe reflect an attempt to deal with any of the information explosion areas? Or do they appear to be retrenching and moving back to earlier school practices at this level?

d. Give some examples of instances that prompted your answer to the last question.

e. Do you feel that curriculum at this level of education is making any significant changes that respond to the information explosion issue and will prepare learners to deal with that condition in later life?

f. Give some examples of these changes and how you feel they will or will not benefit students in their later years.

g. What areas do you recommend as needing change to deal realistically with the information explosion issue which presently are not being considered in your school's program?

Have each group present its findings. Discuss the similarities and differences of the responses from each of the three levels. What do these findings suggest about ways in which school programs could deal more effectively with information explosion issues? What do the interview responses suggest as important futures concerns for schools?

5. Conduct a discussion about the ways in which the school-communities represented by class members have responded to the criticisms of education by the national reports since the appearance of *A Nation at Risk* on April 23, 1983. Identify how many situations have

taken a proactive stance supporting the accomplishments of schools not accounted in these criticisms. How many situations have largely endorsed the criticisms of contemporary education in the United States? What kinds of goals are the school–communities represented adopting to guide educational developments during the next five, ten, and fifteen years? What percentage of the school–communities represented are doing any long range planning beyond a three-year period?

6. Ask interested members of the class to identify, where possible, the SAT and ACT scores achieved by students in their district and compare them with scores of students at the present time. Have them compare the scores of the top 12 percent of students taking those tests now against the scores gathered from twenty years ago. This is the actual basis that the public needs to see. Twenty years ago only the top 17 percent of students took those tests, whereas today as many as 80 percent of students are taking them. Naturally the average of the majority of students taking those tests today will not match the average of the select population who took them two decades ago. It is therefore important to show the inequitable basis upon which this criticism of contemporary schools is being made.

7. Ask interested members of the class to gather data on their district's financial expenditures on educational programs over the past twenty years. They should be able to secure this information from district school board records since such documents are legally classified as public records. Including local, state, and other financial support, what are the increases in per-pupil expenditures in each district studied? Discuss the degree to which these expenditures reflect inflationary and cost-of-living increases in each locality during the same period. To what degree have schools budgeted to make advancements in educational quality beyond keeping up with fixed costs, mandated expenditures, and inflationary realities?

8. Conduct a discussion of the kinds of changes in college preparation programs being made or considered in local school communities. To what degree are major changes being considered or made in the middle level as opposed to the high school? In what ways, if any, are holistic concerns for student development in middle level schools being deemphasized to accommodate more academic or college-preparatory program demands?

9. Ask interested members of the class to identify the increases in time, numbers of classes, activities, and other requirements that will be added to school demands toward "strengthening" the curriculum of a particular school program level in their district. Can information be gathered about the degree to which these changes are based on the developmental capacities of students to handle these demands; or are

these efforts to merely accelerate program components into lower grades and units of the district? What efforts, if any, are being made to identify overload and stress factors these changes may create for students?

10. Ask interested members of the class to identify the degree to which your state's legislature is attempting to "legislate educational change" by raising standards and demands of schools and educators. To what degree is there professional input in these efforts? Organize a class discussion around their findings. What appear to be the major implications of such activities in your state?

11. Organize a panel of representatives from social and community organizations that deal with youth problems in your region. Ask them for information on the incidence and increase of youth problems related to juvenile delinquency, divorce, single families, "blended" families, the runaway syndrome, alcoholism and other addiction problems, and youth violence and crime. What do they think about the nature and adequacy of services to deal with these problems? In what ways should schools interact with agencies in dealing with these problems?

12. Ask interested members of the class to select and study a particular youth problem related to juvenile delinquency, divorce, single-parent families, "blended" families, the runaway syndrome, youth alcoholism and other addiction problems, and youth violence and crime. Have them try to identify what their school–community does to deal with those problems. To what degree are school–community curriculum planning activities concerned with these issues? To what degree are they involved in identifying better school–community approaches to dealing with these issues? Discuss the results of these investigations in class, and send summaries of the findings to all community and social agencies and boards of education of the school districts in your region.

13. Invite a panel of local mental health agency personnel to discuss the incidence and increase in youth suicide in your region. Identify any particular local or regional aspects to this problem as they may differ from national data. What do the panelists see as growing concerns about this problem in your area? What kinds of prevention, intervention, and crisis programs are available through these agencies? How directly are they involved with school–communities in cooperative efforts to deal with the youth suicide problem? What do they suggest as measures that could and need to be taken by and with school–communities to deal more effectively with this issue?

14. Ask interested members of the class to identify the degree in their own school district to which there are any (a) kinds of records and information maintained on suicides and suicide attempts, (b) kinds

of suicide prevention, intervention, and crises programs, (c) kinds of interaction established with local mental health agencies, (d) involvements of any other organizations to deal with the youth suicide problem, (e) kinds of networking activities carried on with other school–communities in dealing with the youth suicide problem, and (f) kinds of curriculum planning and program activities to help laypersons and/or professionals understand and deal with this problem.

REFERENCES

Bruch, H. *Eating Disorders*. New York: Basic Books, 1979.

——. *The Golden Cage: The Enigma of Anorexia Nervosa*. Cambridge, Mass.: Harvard University Press, 1978.

Doran, R., and Jacobson, W. "The Second International Science Study: U.S. Results." *Phi Delta Kappan* 66, no. 6 (1985): 414–417.

Duckworth, E. "What Teachers Know: The Best Knowledge Base." In "Symposium on the Year of the Reports: Response from the Educational Community," edited by H. Howe II. *Harvard Educational Review* 54, no. 1 (1984): 15–19.

Elkind, D. *The Hurried Child*. Reading, Mass.: Addison-Wesley, 1981.

Fowler, C. "Only a Masochist Could Accept the Findings of the Excellence Commission." *American School Board Journal* 170, no. 9 (1983): 43, 46, 49.

Frederick, C. "Current Trends in Suicidal Behavior in the United States." *American Journal of Psychotherapy* 32 (1982): 172–200.

Gardner, D., Chairman, *A Nation at Risk: the Imperative for Educational Reform*. Washington, D.C.: U.S. Office of Education, 1983.

Glass, J. *Curriculum Practices in the Junior High School and Grades Five and Six*. Supplementary Studies No. 25. Chicago: University of Chicago Press, 1924.

Goodlad, J. *A Place Called School: Prospects for the Future*. New York: McGraw-Hill, 1983.

Gwynn, J., and Chase, J. *Curriculum Principles and Social Trends*. 3rd ed. New York: Macmillan, 1960.

Havighurst, R. *Developmental Tasks and Education*. New York: Longmans, 1950.

Howe, H. II, et al. "Symposium on the Year of the Reports: Responses from the Educational Community." *Harvard Educational Review* 54, no. 1 (1984): 1–31.

Hunt, J. *Action for Excellence: A Comprehensive Plan to Improve our Nation's Schools*. Denver: Education Commission of the States, 1983.

Ishi, K. "Adolescent Self-Destructive Behaviors and Crisis Intervention." *Journal of Suicide and Life Threatening Behavior*, 1982 (Japan).

Jennings, I. "University of Buffalo Researcher Finds Science on the Upswing in United States Schools." *The Buffalo News*, June 18, 1984, p. B-1.

Kelley, E. *In Defense of Youth*. Englewood Cliffs, N.J.: Prentice-Hall, 1962.

Langone, J. "Too Weary to Go On." *In Human Development 84/85,* edited by H. Fitzgerald and M. Walraven. Guilford, Conn.: Dushkin Publishing Group, 1984.

LaPointe, A. "The Good News about American Education." *Phi Delta Kappan* 65, no. 10 (1984): 663–668.

Leonard, G. "The Great School Reform Hoax: What's Really Needed to Improve Public Education?" *Esquire,* April 1984, pp. 47–55.

Mauceri, P. "The Youth Suicide Epidemic." *Dissemination Services on the Middle Grades* 15, no. 5 (1985): 1–6.

The Miami Herald, May 27, 1984, p. B-2.

Naisbitt, J. *Megatrends: Ten New Directions Transforming Our Lives.* New York: Warner Books, 1982.

Peck, M. "Youth Suicide." *Death Education Journal* 6 (1982): 29–47.

Raths, L. "The Power of Groups" Presentation at State University of New York at Buffalo, February 16, 1978. Cited by R. Lipka in "Research Column," *Impact on Instructional Improvement* 31, no. 3 (1977): 26.

Rottier, G. "Computer Corner." *Middle School Journal* 13, no. 3 (1982): 30–31.

Smith, R., and Mauceri, P. "Suicide—The Ultimate Middle School Trauma." *Middle School Journal* 13, no. 2 (1982): 21–24.

Tanner, D. "The American High School at the Crossroads." *Educational Leadership* 41, no. 6 (1984): 4–13.

Toepfer, C. "Accentuate the Positive: What Is Really Effective in Today's Education?" In *The Search for Excellence,* edited by J. Lounsbury. Columbus, Ohio: The National Middle School Association, 1984, pp. 14–23.

EPILOGUE

Into the Future

This book began with three scenarios on possible educational futures, each one suggesting how present trends in school and society might take different curriculum paths over the next twenty years. Then in Chapter 2 we discussed how characteristics of contemporary society and forecasts about its future should serve as foundation areas in curriculum thinking. In Chapter 7 we illustrated the components of a resource unit using the topic "Living in the Future." The point of this recurring theme rests in our belief that educators must take a proactive rather than a reactive stance toward futures issues in developing curriculum plans for today's learners.

IDENTIFYING FUTURES ISSUES

■ ■ Children entering kindergarten in 1986 will live the majority of their lives in the twenty-first century, and some, if medical research persists at its present rate, will no doubt personally experience the beginnings of the twenty-second century. If curriculum plans are based only upon the present state of our world and society, they might justly be regarded as educationally unfair to children and youth. In taking a proactive stance about the future, curriculum planners should consider the following kinds of questions.

■ What are some of the broad, global futures issues in our world and society that will likely influence or confront tomorrow's world?
■ How might these issues influence the nature of education and learning as well as the form of schooling?
■ What forecasts or "visions" of the future might be formed from thinking about futures issues?
■ How might today's curriculum plans lead to awareness of the future, future-oriented decision making, and the creation of new agendas in school and society?

In reaching the present time, humankind has gone through several phases. At the earliest, human survival was almost dependent upon the whims of nature, geography, and chance. From this stage emerged the agricultural way of life which was marked by efforts to control the environment so that survival was more likely. This was a beginning effort to plan for the future. In a third stage, an industrial society developed in which people not only used early technology to improve their way of life but also increasingly came together in larger communities. Along with the rapid evolution of machinery and other technology, there arose a scientific view of the world and of human nature and behavior. It might justly be said that the past few centuries have been almost altogether rooted in science and the technology that it produces. Now, as the second millennium nears its end, we find ourselves at a new junction in civilization.

The industrial age is breaking up and giving way to a new phase based not only on the tremendous advances that the industrial age brought, but also upon our reactions to them. Since its true nature is as yet undefined, perhaps the safest way to characterize this new stage is as the "postindustrial society." In forecasting possible trends, various futurists have also used labels such as "the information society," "the person-centered society," "the technological society," and others, depending upon their view of those trends.

Whatever the label, most futurists seem to agree that while the industrial age brought many benefits, it also gave rise to enormous problems. The same technology that has brought power and convenience to industry and society has also led to the overconsumption of scarce resources such as water, soil, energy, and living space. The harnessing of nuclear power has also produced the threat of nuclear war and problems with nuclear waste. Higher standards of living among some groups in certain regions have been based upon the inequitable distribution of wealth, power, and resources. The convenience of technology in most parts of society has also produced serious threats to ecological balance, such as acid rain. Advances in medical technology have led to moral–political dilemmas associated with genetic engineering, biochemical manipulation, euthanasia, and distribution of donor transplant organs. It should be clear that our world has already paid and will continue to pay a price for the fruits of the industrial age.

The industrial phase of our development has also produced a myriad of social and political problems. The centralization of power and decision making has alienated and disenfranchised large segments of the population. Third World issues and the problems of developing nations typify these concerns. The emphasis on the work ethic is so deeply rooted in our thinking that unemployment is perhaps more a psychological than an economic problem. The drive to maintain affluence has led to tensions related to heart disease, substance abuse, alcoholism, crime, poor mental health, and suicide. This rapid pace of change has been paralleled by the emergence of a sometimes bewildering array of lifestyle values that often contradict long-standing customs and traditions.

In light of all this, today's youth are faced with two major problems. One is that *they are the first generation in which most will have little chance of exceeding the standard of living achieved by their parents.* Second, *their very survival in adulthood may well depend upon their success in solving the environmental, social, political, and economic problems created by previous generations.*

FOCUSING ON THE NEW AGE

■ ■ Futurists themselves are not certain how the new age will take shape. Some believe in what is called "techni-fix," the idea that new technology, as yet undiscovered, will be invented to solve problems such as resource scarcity, environmental pollution, and world hunger. Others believe that in order to survive we must go through a transformation of values that will shift our social and personal priorities. A few feel that our world has passed the point of survival capacity and that its future, if there is one, will depend mostly on pure chance.

At present, the majority of our own society seems tied to a combined version of the first and second views. As daily reports of technological advances are announced, most people appear optimistic about some degree of "techni-fix," at least with regard to environmental, resource, and medical problems. On the other hand, many are disturbed by the moral and values dilemmas that permeate our world. They have become increasingly skeptical of the purely scientific or mechanistic view. Some have reacted by forming small communes based on a common set of values that are counter to what they see as those held by the larger society. These range from survivalist groups opposed to governmental intervention to homestead communities searching for more basic values not tied to technology. Still others have sought refuge in fundamentalist religious groups that offer "right or wrong" beliefs in a society that otherwise seems without answers. Others, such as the "Yuppies," have sought a balance between an economically successful work life and a personally gratifying social life. Whatever the variation, it is clear that large segments of the population are aware of the dissonance and ambiguity in our society and, while they may not fully understand it, have nonetheless attempted a personally acceptable way of resolving it.

Our view is that while technology will surely provide many benefits, the development of a safe, sane, and desirable future depends to a large degree on three basic possibilities:

- The realization that we face many serious problems in our world
- The willingness to initiate and accept shifts in our values that will produce a livable and humane world
- The acceptance of responsibility for promoting those values, especially among powerful nations and institutions, including schools

Awareness of future-oriented problems will represent an important step toward improving the quality of life as we move into the postindustrial society. However, new values must also emerge from this awareness. Our final frame illustrates some examples of the shift from industrial to "new age values." Early stages of these shifts can already be observed in changing interests and beliefs among various groups in our society. Others reside only in "visions" of a desirable future. Likewise, some may be pursued with relatively little conflict, while others represent fundamental changes in our way of life. Several basic concepts underlie these value shifts.

- People are more important than institutions, and therefore political, social, and economic institutions ought to serve human needs rather than direct them.
- Isolationism within and across local, regional, and national boundaries contradicts the obvious interdependence among peoples of the world.
- Centralization and inequitable distribution of wealth, power, and resources debilitates the essential right to human dignity.
- Overemphasizing linear, convergent thinking impedes the development of intuitive, creative solutions to human problems.
- Contemporary overdependence on technology and unlimited growth threatens delicate balances in ecological systems.
- The future can be created in a desirable form rather than simply occurring by chance.

The acceptance of these concepts and related values, although they may be disruptive to our present belief systems, is a critical need if we are to resolve the issues that will confront us in the foreseeable future.

Shifting Values Toward a New Age

■ **Industrial Age Values to New Age Values**

Reactive planning	Proactive planning
Present gratification	Concern for the future
Competition	Cooperation
Individual isolation	Interdependence
Competitive distribution of wealth, power, and resources	Equitable distribution of wealth, power, and resources
Acquisition of information	Use of information for the social good
Conspicuous consumption	"Enoughness" consumption
Specialization of occupations	Generalist roles
Hierarchical power	Problem-solving networks
Centralization of power	Participatory consensus
Linear thinking	Systemic thinking
Conformity to norms	Promotion of diversity
Emphasis on science	Balance among science, art, perception, and intuition
Dependence on technology	Selective use of technology for human purpose
Unlimited growth goals	Selective, planned growth

As the designated educative institution in our society, schools have a responsibility to inform both learners and the community about compelling issues, including those which have implications for the future. Curriculum plans ought to reveal and address such problems as the interdependency of world populations; the threat of nuclear destruction; the inequitable distribution of wealth, power, and justice; world hunger; dysfunctional ecological systems; the hazards of disproportionate affluence among nations; the depletion of resources; and the moral issue of technological infusion. In examining more regional local life, such issues would further include problems connected with the aging of people, changing roles for women and minority groups, the cultural and political exclusion of particular population segments, the shift from a manufacturing to an information-rich society, the impact of media on belief systems and self-esteem, the psychological impact of nonemployment, the long-term effects of nutritional deficiency, and the causes of crime and other antisocial behavior.

CHANGING THE POSTURE OF SCHOOLS

■ ■   By emphasizing the existence of these problems, the school would
begin to assume a responsible role in developing awareness among
both young and older learners. Beyond this, however, the school
must consider how its own institutional form will respond to these
issues. In so doing, the following ideas represent some possible responsive actions for schools.

1. *The curriculum must become "futures-loaded" through direct
   units organized around futures issues.* Also, we must consider how such issues may permeate other parts of the curriculum, such as the literature we read, the themes of our
   essays and poetry, the content of our mathematics word
   problems, the content of our science activities, the topics of
   our social studies units, the problems in our home economics
   and industrial arts projects, and so on.
2. *The sequence of learning opportunities must be viewed in
   lifelong terms rather than in terms of early childhood
   through completion of adolescence.* As population age increases and work time decreases, people will seek opportunities to learn across the lifespan. The information-rich society
   with its technological access will make such learning a way
   of life. We will need what Harold Shane termed a "seamless
   curriculum," which abandons the limits of age and grade in
   school forms in favor of an open, accessible, and continuing
   approach to education.
3. *Among other basic skills, the school must consider teaching
   how to use decision-making approaches commonly employed
   by futurists in problem analysis.* These would inlcude delphi
   techniques, consensus decision methods, scenario development, cross-impact matrices, simulation gaming, time series
   extrapolation, brainstorming, and the like. These approaches
   should be used persistently in considering topical problems
   and in making decisions about curriculum and school-related concerns.
4. *The form of the school as an institution should represent or
   illustrate a preferred form of society.* This means that governance would be based upon participatory decision making.
   Institutional expedience would be secondary to human
   needs. Emphasis should be placed on high levels of interaction, cooperation, and interdependence. Systematic attempts
   would be made to remove vestiges of racism, sexism, and
   other forms of injustice. Diversity would be prized over conformity. Rules and regulations would promote individual

dignity and social responsibility rather than focus on petty or mundane issues. Such arrangements as grouping and scheduling would be used to support learning rather than merely to sort, label, and process groups of learners. Evaluation would emphasize self-assessment rather than external judgment alone.

5. *The schools must assume a more responsible role in helping communities deal with local needs and problems.* The material and technological resources of the school should be available to individual citizens and groups involved in problem-solving. Community service project programs should involve youth and educators in volunteer efforts to improve the quality of community life. Barriers to school–community cooperation such as bureaucratic convenience, institutional arrogance, and poor communications need to be replaced by attitudes of openness and interdependence.

These shifts in institutional and curriculum aspects of the school represent a fundamental reconceptualization of the values that it portrays and promotes. However, these shifts parallel the values and concepts that will be necessary if humankind is to move toward a new age in which we overcome the problems that emerged in the industrial age. As such, they are also necessary if we are to equip young people with the knowledge, skills, and values they will need to live satisfying lives in the next century. To engage in this reconceptualization is to create a school that assumes a responsible role in realizing a compelling and worthwhile vision of the future. To suggest that such a school is unrealistic is to suggest that the school as an institution should not or cannot contribute to the long-range quality of life in our society and world.

■ Futures Goals for Schools

Schools are not the only social institution charged with the responsibility for educating the young. Howver, the dissipating influence of other agenciesdoes not justify avoidance of the school's distinctive social function in society. Rather, it makes the school's role even more important since it may be the last institution in which concern for the young is a persistent goal. Even if that were not the case, it is still necessary to consider the place of the school in preparing young people to face the realities of their present and future lives. While the exact nature of the future is impossible to predict, it is most probable that the mix of emerging technological, political, social, and economic factors will require thinking and information processing skills more than the mere acquisition of knowledge. These cognitive skills will be necessary if people are to deal adequately with the growing affective concerns in our world.

In light of these considerations we believe that both citizens and professionals must carefully deliberate about the nature of curriculum planning toward the future. We also believe that such deliberations must identify important issues that may suggest direction for goals and curriculum plans. At the very least, a curriculum agenda for the future should focus on priorities such as those which follow here. In other words, schools should help young people achieve knowledge, skills, attitudes, and behaviors which will allow them:

1. *To consider intelligently the complex issues that affect daily living in our society.* Such issues include the essential need for world peace, the political, social, and economic aspects of class politics, energy resource depletion, global interrelationships, personal alienation, futures forecasts, and the like. Lacking comprehension of these problems, people are likely to experience frustration that results in aggression, apathy, and submission.

2. *To formulate value/moral systems that will promote responsible and thoughtful responses to personal and social issues.* The absence of such systems is likely to allow amoral hedonism, confusion, and moral barbarism.

3. *To secure a sense of belonging and self-worth.* Such perceptions begin in small groups and eventually extend through larger settings in the community, nation, and the world. The lack of personal security leads to alienation and negative self-esteem.

4. *To develop a sense of "enoughness" in the context of personal life-style and standard of living.* It is unlikely that succeeding generations can sustain even our present standard of living without depriving other people in the world of basic necessities and without exhausting natural resources.

5. *To maintain a reasonable balance between technological convenience and human needs.* For example, immersion in the media threatens human interaction, and "junk" foods jeopardize our nutritional needs. We stand in jeopardy of developing and using technology to limit rather than benefit and extend our human capacities.

6. *To organize and use information intelligently.* We are on the verge of obviating the need for the personal accumulation of information because of technologies that organize, integrate, and use knowledge for us. As new knowledge is

produced and people have instant access to what is known,
skills associated with information use will become increasingly important.

7. *To develop a sense of global interdependence.* What happens
   in one place in our world increasingly affects aspects of living for others. Isolationist thinking threatens world peace.
   To sustain a liveable planet, people must transcend the
   ideological and geographic boundaries that came to characterize and then permeated the industrial age.

8. *To develop an optimistic and creative attitude toward living
   and learning.* Negative images of aging are unproductive
   and debilitating, especially as lifespans increase. In the information society, continuous learning will be necessary to
   maintain positive self-esteem.

9. *To develop skills and predispositions associated with democratic living.* At all levels of human relationships, the democratic way of life still offers the best hope for empowering
   people. Cooperation must replace competition, and equity
   must supersede elitism. The absence of such conditions
   leads to alienation, disenfranchisement, and inequality.

10. *To formulate visions of the future toward which personal
    and social action may be directed.* The compelling question
    of our times should not be "What will the future be like?"
    but rather "What do we want the future to be?" We are
    still a society of individuals, but the quality of our future
    depends upon a collective and compelling image of its
    shape. Thus personal images must also be integrated into a
    common sense of values upon which our world might be
    brought to a worthwhile and desirable form.

THE HORIZON APPROACHES

■ ■ In summary, we should consider that futurists say our planet has
now passed the point at which we can expect to find solutions for the
problems of the future in the world's past experiences and knowledge. Rather, we need to define and find solutions from the study of
future conditions. Our society, species, and planet must deal with
problems of a kind and degree which we have never before faced.
Prior to 1985, human survival was measured by the degree to which
people could overcome problems created by nature. The high school
graduating class of 1985 is estimated to have been the first that will
concentrate their lives on trying to overcome this legacy of problems
created by past generations. In the past, predictable cycles have occurred and we could "pull back" during times of retrenchment and

wait for a propitious event to recycle a time of resurgence. Now it is less likely that history will recycle and allow us to make such use of the past.

Humankind's naive and imprudent use of our growing knowledge of science and continually advancing technologies has brought about the negative aspects of the problems previously discussed. Society's need at this "watershed" time is to respond and work at solving the problems facing today's and subsequent graduating classes. The survival and prosperity of our planet and its inhabitants into the third millennium will depend on our success in educating the next generation. *Can we educate youth to utilize the knowledge of science and the potential of technologies toward solving this residue of problems created by and inherited from previous generations? Can we help youth define values that they may use to build and sustain a more humane world?* We believe that curriculum planning has the key role in designing educational responses to these issues.

In past times, schools would "dodge the bullets" of critics and wait for the disaster to subside. We suggest that such an educational posture is now definitely obsolete. Such an approach will neither allow schools to survive nor orchestrate the resources that could develop educational programs to take us to unimagined positive realities.

We recommend the best proactive and interactive strategy is to develop the capacity for systemic curriculum planning. We are certainly not being overcritical or unjust in our analysis of schools. Quite to the contrary, our suggestions reflect the belief that schools can make a difference. Most important is that educators need not develop a totally new set of processes for transforming their roles and the nature of schools. Eighty years of curriculum thinking have produced a substantial reservoir of ideas for curriculum planning and development. The task is finally to put these into action as we plan toward the third millennium. Let us get on with the process.

Appendices

APPENDIX A
An Illustrative Interdisciplinary Resource Unit: Living in the Future

The sample resource unit that follows contains sections titled:

Rationale Statement
Objectives
Content (related to each objective) and Specific Resources
(Chart of) Relationship of Activities to Objectives
Activities
Resources
Measuring Devices
  (Description of a technique for) Self-Evaluation
(Description of a technique for) Cooperative Learning—The Jigsaw
  Method

RATIONALE STATEMENT

■ ■ Young people attending schools today will live most of their lives in
the twenty-first century. Given the rapid pace of change, it is most
probable that the world they experience will be much different from
ours. Certainly unimagined technological changes will emerge to enhance greatly the quality of living. However, many problems will also
arise, requiring imaginative solutions. Those people who are aware of
future possibilities and problems will be less likely to experience the
sense of alienation and powerlessness related to "future shock."

The purpose of this unit is to suggest ideas that teachers might
use in helping young people look down the road toward the future. In
using these suggestions, learners may be introduced to futures issues,
may be encouraged to develop personal visions of the future, and may
be made aware of some of the techniques used by futurists in forecasting
probable, possible, and preferable futures.

In developing this resource unit, several problems in the futures
field were addressed. First, the ideas are essentially value-free in the
sense that they promote neither an optimistic nor a pessimistic view

of the future. They favor neither "doomsday" forecasts nor "technolog-ical wonder" forecasts. Second, activities and resources address con-cepts and skills from a variety of subject areas. Finally, the emphasis is on forecasting rather than predicting. No attempt is made to specify particular dates for possible events. Rather, the focus is on developing a sense of general possibilities for the future.

OBJECTIVES

1. To understand the concept of change
2. To identify and analyze present trends that may influence the future
3. To gather and interpret information about the future
4. To clarify personal images of the future
5. To clarify personal aspirations for the future
6. To develop skill in using future forecasting techniques
7. To identify issues that will confront people in the future
8. To develop forecasts for global futures
9. To determine aspects of the present that should be continued
10. To identify alternatives for the future in such areas as energy, communications, transportation, technology, medicine, and food
11. To design alternative educational futures
12. To analyze the role of religious/spiritual values in the future
13. To identify alternatives for leisure time use in the future (e.g., recreation, cultural activities, personal interests)
14. To analyze possible future lifestyles
15. To define common futures terminology
16. To differentiate between futures forecasting and predicting
17. To identify futures forecasts made in the past
18. To analyze future occupational/career alternatives
19. To analyze community resources in terms of future use
20. To identify the interrelationships among technology, politics, economics, and human needs

CONTENT

This section notes important concepts and principles related to each objective and lists noteworthy resources dealing with the concepts wherever it is appropriate. Obviously, there are many more resource materials (films, books, articles, speakers, etc.) that can easily be iden-tified for each topic mentioned.

The number preceding each item is the number of the related *objective*.

1. The history of humankind is a chronicle of change represented by increasing control over the environment, introduction of technological innovation, and growth in understanding of what it means to be human. Change is occurring at an increasingly rapid pace. As a result, we are often overwhelmed by the complexity of alternatives and by the consequences of change.

   Sources:
   Toffler, Alvin. *Future Shock*. New York: Random House, 1970.
   Toffler, Alvin. *The Third Wave*. New York: Bantam Books, 1981.
   Mesarovic, Mihajlo, and Pestel, Eduard. *Mankind at the Turning Point*. 2nd Report of the Club of Rome. New York: New American Library, 1974.

2. One technique used for constructing future forecasts is extrapolation of present trends into images of possible, probable (or likely), and preferable futures. This process of imagining alternative futures is critical in both planning and considering consequences of present actions.

   Sources:
   Naisbitt, John. *Megatrends*. New York: Warner Books, 1982.
   Clarke, Arthur C. *Profiles of the Future*. New York: Harper and Row, 1973.

3. As a result of extrapolating future possibilities from present research and trends, futurists have constructed a body of subject matter about possible futures. Knowledge of these ideas is important in developing images of the future.

   Sources:
   McHale, John. *World Facts and Trends*. New York: Collier Books, 1972.
   Rosen, Stephen. *Future Facts*. New York: Simon and Schuster, 1976.
   Dickson, Paul. *The Future File*. New York: Rawson Associates, 1977.

4. If our society is to develop a positively perceived future, individuals must develop images of preferable alternatives. Such images are also important in helping individuals cope with the rapid changes that are taking place in the world. Personal

images consist of visions of possible and preferable alternatives for our future.

5. One aspect of learning about the future is identification of personal plans. Such plans serve as a guide in sorting out choices and making decisions about present actions. Clarity of personal aspirations also enhances the sense of self-esteem.

6. To aid in thinking about the future, futurists use many techniques or devices to generate and consider alternatives. These devices include extrapolation, scenarios, cross-impact matrices, and decision trees.

Sources:

Bright, James. *A Brief Introduction to Technology Forecasting*. Austin, Tex. Pemafried Press, 1972.

Martino, Joseph. *An Introduction to Technological Forecasting*. New York: Gordon and Breach, 1972.

7. As technology and social thinking evolve, we will be presented with numerous possibilities for dramatically changing ourselves and our world. However, these alternatives will involve value and moral as well as environmental dilemmas.

8. Much of typical futures thinking has to do with our society and our nation. It is most probable that forming a preferable future will depend upon global thinking, which goes beyond national boundaries and ethnocentrism. Global futures involve thinking of ourselves as global citizens who recognize interdependence among people around the world.

Sources:

Clarke, Arthur C. *Profiles of the Future*. New York: Harper & Row, 1973.

Kahn, Herman. *The Next 200 Years*. Washington, D.C.: World Futures Society.

9. In designing a preferable future, it is not neccessary to reject all aspects of the present. Rather, it is crucial to determine those values, customs, ideas, technologies, and so on, which are worth continuing in the future.

10. Virtually every area of living will be open to change in the future. Specialists in various fields have forecast numerous alternatives in areas of living. It is important not only to know about these, but also to consider the ways in which alternatives in one area may affect those in another.

Sources:

Clarke, Arthur C. *Profiles of the Future*. New York: Harper & Row, 1973.

Kahn, Herman. *The Next 200 Years*. Washington, D.C.: World
  Futures Society.

11. With advances in technology and changes in various areas
    of living, there are many new possibilities for education and
    learning. As lifelong learning opportunities expand in the
    "information age," people will be offered a wide variety of
    alternatives in the educational arena.

    Sources:
    Shane, Harold G. *The Educational Significance of the Future*.
      Bloomington, Ind.: Phi Delta Kappa, 1973.
    Toffler, Alvin. *Learning for Tomorrow*. New York: Random
      House, 1974.
    Naisbitt, John. *Megatrends*. New York: Warner Books, 1982.
    Glines, Don H. *Educational Futures*. Vols. 1–5. Milville,
      Minn.: Anvil Press, 1978–1980.

12. Recent statistics indicate that there has been a revival of
    religion in our society. Such thinking is related to a number
    of factors, including the larger movement to find personal
    meaning in life. In many cases, people are finding such mean-
    ing in nontraditional religious groups.

    Source:
    Winn, Ira Joy. "The Future of Religion in a Post-Industrial
      Society." *The Futurist,* October 1980.

13. As technology advances, people find they have increased time
    for leisure activities and more alternatives for using that
    time. Defining these alternatives is a part of clarifying per-
    sonal images and aspirations for the future.
14. Lifestyles encompass a variety of variables, including family
    structures, careers, leisure activities, nutrition, mobility, re-
    lationships, and so on. The present variety of lifestyles is
    expected to continue in the future, with the probability for
    an even wider range of alternatives.

    Source:
    Naisbitt, John. *Megatrends*. New York: Warner Books, 1982.

15. Futures terminology includes words and phrases invented to
    define new events, as well as variations on current language.
    Examples include "hi-tech," "forecasting," "J-curve," and
    "holography."

    Source:
    Jennings, Lane. "Brave New Words." *The Futurist,* June 1981.

16. Predicting involves attempts to specify precise events, the time when they will take place, and their consequences. Prediction is as old as the seers of ancient times and as current as popular astrologists. Forecasting involves attempts to foresee possible alternatives and their consequences through systematic thinking about trends. Most futurists engage in forecasting and avoid efforts at precision in describing possible futures.

    Source:
    Glines, Don H. *Educational Futures*. Vol 1. Milville, Minn.: Anvil Press, 1978.

17. Futuring is by no means a new activity, although the description of a futures field is relatively recent. Throughout history, one can find forecasts in the work of scientists (Galileo), novelists (Jules Verne), and others. Identifying past forecasts helps people understand the problems in speculation as well as the possibilities for foreseeing possible events.

    Source:
    Watkins, John Elfreth Jr. "What May Be Next." *Ladies Home Journal,* December 1900. Reprinted in *The Futurist,* October 1982.

18. Many jobs and careers currently available will change drastically, while others will become obsolete. The major influence on this change is technology, although changing human needs and interests also play their roles. In the foreseeable future, it is also probable that many new occupations will emerge.

    Source:
    Contact the U.S. Bureau of Labor Statistics, Washington, D.C., for information regarding occupational forecasts.

19. Future events and changing human needs will probably continue to have an impact on life at the local community level. Many of life's activities will probably also continue to focus on interactions at this level. Thus, people need to examine alternatives in the context of their own communities. Such understanding will also enhance the possibility of understanding interrelationships at the global level.

20. Actions and changes in one or another area of living do not occur in a vacuum. Rather, they affect those in other areas as well. For example, political events affect availability of energy resources, which in turn affect lifestyles.

Sources:
Naisbitt, John. *Megatrends*. New York: Warner Books, 1982.
Toffler, Alvin. *The Third Wave*. New York: Bantam Books, 1981.

ACTIVITIES

1. Small groups should try to reach consensus on about ten goals they have for themselves in the future. Individuals should then complete a cross-impact matrix to determine personal future priorities. Tabulate results to identify priorities for the entire group. Discuss reasons for choices and probabilities for reaching them.
2. Identify personal aspirations in occupational/career areas. Compare these with current projections about job trends, new occupations, and job obsolescence. In particular, determine how technology might affect any career area in the future.
3. Form small groups around major future issues such as the family, populations, the environment, world hunger, and education. Have each group develop a scenario of how they believe the issue may unfold in the next fifty years (in five-year increments). Check for cases where scenarios from dif-

Relationship of Activities to Objectives

Objective	Related Activities
1.	2, 3, 4, 5, 17, 45
2.	3, 7, 14, 16, 18, 19, 22, 25, 26, 31, 43
3.	19, 21, 26, 34, 44, 45
4.	1, 2, 4, 5, 6, 9, 10, 11, 12, 13, 14, 18, 19, 20, 21, 23, 27, 31, 32, 33
5.	2, 4, 5, 6, 19, 22, 24, 28, 34, 40, 42
6.	1, 3, 4, 25, 26, 29, 36, 43, 45
7.	1, 3, 8, 13, 16, 19, 22, 23, 24, 25, 26, 29, 33, 35, 40, 43, 45
8.	3, 7, 15, 25, 26, 30, 39, 42, 43
9.	11, 17, 19, 23, 29
10.	3, 10, 11, 12, 13, 14, 15, 18, 20, 21, 22, 23, 27, 31, 33, 38, 40
11.	38, 40, 41, 45
12.	16, 23, 24, 43
13.	3, 9, 10, 11, 19, 21, 29, 32
14.	1, 8, 10, 12, 14, 17, 19, 27, 29, 33, 36, 37
15.	16, 17, 23, 30, 39
16.	3, 4, 7, 19, 25, 26, 39
17.	6, 17, 44
18.	2, 4, 12, 34, 36
19.	37, 45
20.	3, 16, 26, 29, 33

ferent groups complement or contradict each other. Integrate the group scenarios into a comprehensive world futures scenario. Discuss whether the scenarios are possible, probable, preferable, etc. What major events or incidents might be introduced to change the scenarios (e.g., nuclear war)?

4. Develop a personal time line from birth to your present age. Include important dates and events. Use pictures and objects (e.g., party invitations, newspaper clippings, etc.) to illustrate events. Interview parents or other relatives for detailed information. Then extend the time line thirty to fifty years and fill in possible or desirable events.

5. Write an autobiography entitled "Chapters of My Life." Begin with pertinent factors about your past, including important events, past interests, and significant persons in your life. Then describe the same factors in your present life. In the final section, predict how these things will appear in your early, middle, and late adulthood.

6. Conduct an interview with your parents or guardians focusing on their hopes for you and other children. Ask how they formed these ideas and what they think you will have to do to fulfill their hopes.

7. Publish an issue of a newspaper for January 1, 2000. Include such items as front-page news, sports, comics, editorials, ads, and social events. In each item, the content should involve information based upon forecasts in such areas lifestyles, scientific events, and world events.

8. Write a short play based upon life during a day in the future. Consider scenes such as a family meal, a school event, and a work environment. Try to include flashbacks or references to events that led to life as it is portrayed in the play.

9. Develop and tape a television or radio show that you predict might take place in the future. The script might involve a news show or a situation comedy.

10. Build a model of a home technology center you would consider likely and/or preferable in the future. Include items related to communications, entertainment, exercise, food, and the like. Develop a written or taped explanation for each item.

11. Build a scale model of a future community or city. Consider possibilities related to transportation, construction, energy, recreation sources, weather control, and the like. Develop a written or taped description of the community and your reasons for designing it in particular ways.

12. Build a model of an office interior that you would consider likely in the future. Consider such concepts as occupational futures, technology, and worker environment/satisfaction.

Develop a written or taped rationale and description for various aspects of the model.

13. Build a solar greenhouse on school or community property. In doing so, consider scientific, biological, and construction aspects. Use the greenhouse to experiment with growing a variety of food resources that might be used to deal with food needs in the future.

14. Design and build models of future modes of transportation. In doing so, consider possibilities of technological advances and lifestyle needs. Develop a written or taped discussion of each model, including rationale, uses, design aspects, and the like.

15. Explore the possible effects of future food technology. Consider world hunger, nutrition, food types, technological advances, and so on. Then design a supermarket for the future. Plan for contents, construction, arrangement, delivery systems, and any other applicable aspects.

16. Form teams and convene a debate on the choice between a technology-centered society and a person-centered society. Form a panel to hear the debate. Include representatives from science, business, education, government, etc.

17. Invite several elder persons to visit the class. Ask them to describe life in the past as compared with the present. Focus on communications, medicine, economics, food, recreation, transportation, family styles, and other areas of living. Try to determine past-to-present trends that might suggest future possibilities in these areas.

18. Form small groups to design and build models that illustrate alternative energy resources for the future. Display these in an "Energy Fair" open to students, citizens, and others. Also convene a debate on the advantages and disadvantages of various energy resources. Have the debate judged by a panel including representatives from science, business, energy suppliers, citizens at large, and others.

19. Explore forecasts of future lifestyles. Then discuss what it might be like to be a child or adolescent in the future. Consider education, family structure, recreation, and so on. Focus on identifying possible and preferable futures in this area.

20. Design and make models of futuristic clothing. Put these on display with explanations of design features and the reasons why particular fashions might evolve.

21. Consulting school and community resources, identify future trends in music, art, sculpture, dance, drama, and other cultural areas. Consider how social and technological trends that have been forecast might influence these aspects of living.

22. Interview physicians about current medical research that has implications for future living. Develop a model of possible health care delivery systems.

23. Discuss and illustrate various aspects of the physical and intellectual development of human beings. Considering possibilities in biomechanical engineering, try to predict some future evolution. Which possibilities seem most likely? Which are most preferable? What are some moral/ethical issues involved in biomedical engineering?

24. Invite a panel of representatives from various religions to the class. Ask them to discuss the place and power of church, religions, and spiritual values in future life. Also, focus on present trends that might suggest future possibilities in this area.

25. Using a map of the United States and/or the world, reorganize states/countries into a new geopolitical structure. Consider such variables as energy resources, political beliefs, and cultural values and customs.

26. Examine future weather forecasts regarding inadvertent climate modification (hot and cold). Make a geographic weather map based upon these possibilities. What are the implications for food resources, lifestyles, population migration, and other aspects of living?

27. Design a space station capable of supporting the living needs of one thousand or more people. In terms of occupations, age, political and philosophical beliefs, interests, etc., discuss what mix of people you would want living in the space station.

28. Write a five-day journal segment for a person living on a space station in the year 2000.

29. Assume the class has been appointed to develop recommendations for building a preferable future for the world. Form small groups around such areas as communications, medicine, transportation, lifestyles, economics, politics, energy, food, etc. Also develop a process for integrating recommendations of the small groups into a general design for a preferable world future.

30. Develop a dictionary addendum including words that could or should be added to our language. Begin by noting words or terms that have emerged recently, such as "hi-tech" and "punk rock." New words should be considered to denote futuristic products, foods, sports, vehicles, communications devices, etc.

31. Design the inside of a futuristic automobile. Consider such factors as computer technology, safety, energy, lifestyles, etc.

Prepare a written or taped explanation of various aspects of the model, as well as a description of its place in the future of transportation.

32. Form small groups, and ask each to design a new sport or game. Alternatives might be based on present types or may be completely new. They may be competitive or noncompetitive. If possible, the whole group should try out various sports or games designed by the separate small groups.

33. Develop a new form of economic currency for the future. Consideration might be given to goods, information, money, resources, etc. Explain implications of the new currency for social, political, and economic structures. Can the currency be accumulated? If so, how? How would it be used? Would it change the present socioeconomic class structure?

34. Interview officials from local schools, businesses, and industries to determine present and future (planned) use of technology in the workplace. Determine the use of communications devices such as teleconferencing hardware and computers. Also investigate the possible impact of robots and other technologies.

35. Have students select a currently vacant or undeveloped parcel of land in their community and recommend the most appropriate use of that land in the future (e.g., residential, commercial, recreational, agricultural). Recommendations should take into account such factors as: (a) topography, (b) soil composition, (c) weather patterns, (d) past use of the land, (e) uses of surrounding parcels of land, (f) community needs, and (g) zoning regulations. (Note: Soil survey maps and soil testing are available through Cooperative Extension Bureaus.)

36. Prepare and administer a questionnaire that asks senior and junior class members to indicate future plans (e.g., educational, occupational, lifestyle). Tabulate the results and summarize the findings. Are these findings consistent with projected national and global trends? If not, discuss alternative occupational choices for those students selecting areas for which there may ultimately be a greater supply of trained personnel than these fields can accommodate.

37. Plan a week of nutritious meals representing what you believe the majority of human beings should be eating in the year 2000. Prepare at least one main dish from these menus and serve it to the rest of the class. Menu planning and food preparation can be done as a small-group activity. Food preparation can be coordinated among the various groups so that a buffet meal could be served. (Note: *Diet for a Small Planet*

by Frances Moore Lappé and *Recipes for a Small Planet* by Ellen Buchman Ewald might prove useful resources for this activity.)

38. Design a future elementary, middle level, or high school. Consider what would be learned, how learning would take place, how the school would be organized, and what roles teachers, students, administrators, and others would play.

39. Prepare a table of contents and brief narrative for a world history book written in the year 2000. Consider possible or probable major events in areas such as geopolitics, cultural values, environmental issues, war and peace, and world hunger.

40. Discuss the possibility of learning/education without attending school. Consider educational resources in the community, home computers, holography, biochemical learning, etc.

41. Devise a school program, elementary and secondary, involving subject areas and extracurricular activities that could be common in the future. Role-play one day in a future school. Students should take parts of all personnel—administrators, teachers, etc. Have lunch in the classroom in order to maintain the activity throughout an entire day.

42. Plan a trip around the "new" world. Discuss what you will travel in, what clothing and supplies you will need, etc. Make a travel guide of what you will now see in each country. Draw pictures for an overhead to go with your travel guide, and devise a narration to go with it.

43. Have the group identify about ten major problems/issues they believe will face our world in the next fifty years. Have individuals determine the priorities of these issues by using a cross-impact matrix. Tabulate the individual and group results for discussion. What major events or incidents could happen to solve or complicate the problems?

44. Find copies of journals, magazines, and books written before 1950. Search for articles or ideas about what the future might be like. Develop a list of various forecasts and determine their accuracy (particularly those concerning the present time).

45. Contact local government and education offices to secure data on past and present facts regarding the local community. Overall census data would be most helpful, but local statistics on population, births, school enrollments, etc., may be used. Extrapolate these data for ten to thirty years. Then analyze local facilities, cultural and recreational resources, business opportunities, employment opportunities, etc., to determine what changes, if any, would need to be made in the local community to adapt to the local future.

RESOURCES

■ ■   There is a growing list of resources owing to increased interest in the futures field. Journals, magazines, newspapers, films, and books have all been developed around the futures theme. Following are some examples.

■   **Magazines**

1. Probably the best ongoing source of information is *The Futurist,* journal of the World Futures Society, 4916 St. Elmo Avenue, Washington, D.C. 20014. Examples include:

   "How the Future May Surprise Us," April 1983
   "What May Happen in the Next 100 Years," October 1982
   "Crime in the Year 2000," April 1981
   "World Future Society Book Catalog," October 1983
   "Prospects for the Automobile," February 1980
   "Christianity in the Coming Decades," June 1979
   "The Computer Home," February 1982
   "Robots and the Economy," December 1984
   "Living on the Moon: Will Humans Develop an Unearthly Culture?" April 1985

2. Other magazines and newspapers include occasional articles, such as the following:

   "Prediction: Sunny Side Up," *Time,* September 19, 1983
   "21st Century Retirement May Be Easier," *USA Today,* August 1983
   "From a Textbook Written in 2001," *School Update,* April 1, 1983
   "What the Next 50 Years Will Bring," *US News and World Report,* May 9, 1983
   "Thinking about Education in the Year 2000," *Phi Delta Kappan,* May 1983
   "Making It to the 21st Century," *Popular Science,* May 1982
   "A Solar Home for a Sunless Climate," *Popular Science,* December 1983

■   **Films/Videotapes**

Films and videotapes typically available through county or regional clearinghouses include:

   Future Shock: a documentary based on Toffler's book
   Conserving Our Forests Today: how forest lands are protected and renewed for the future

Air Pollution: a discussion of long-range remedies
The Story of Our Money System: how our system evolved
Man Uses and Changes the Land: planning for the use of limited
   resources
Our Changing Cities: technology and cities
Planning Ahead—The Racer: planning to realize aspirations
People Need People: interdependency of workers
Make a Present for the Future: making of a time capsule
Life beyond Earth: possibilities for extraterrestrial life

■ Books

Brenneman, Richard J. *Fuller's Earth: A Day with Bucky and the
   Kids.* New York: St. Martin's Press, 1984.
Clarke, Arthur C. *Profiles of the Future.* New York: Harper &
   Row, 1973.
Corn, Joseph J., and Horrigan, Brian. *Yesterday's Tomorrows:
   Past Visions of the American Future.* New York: Summit Books,
   1984.
Dickson, Paul. *The Future File.* New York: Rawson Associates,
   1977.
Kahn, Herman. *The Next 200 Years,* Washington, D.C.: World
   Futures Society.
Naisbitt, John. *Megatrends.* New York: Warner Books, 1982.
Glines, Don H. *Educational Futures.* Vols. 1–5. Millville, Minn.
   Anvil Press, 1978–1980.
Toffler, Alvin. *Future Shock.* New York: Random House, 1970.
———. *The Third Wave.* New York: Random House, 1981.

MEASURING DEVICES

■ ■ Following are some ideas for developing means to analyze learners'
progress toward the objectives.

1. *Evaluation Projects*
   As students develop forecasts, models, etc., look for accuracy
   of present trend descriptions, reasonable use of time/change
   concepts, imaginative ideas, use of resources, and defensible
   arguments for forecasts.
2. *Oral and Written Reports*
   In addition to those items mentioned in (1) above, oral and
   written reports may be assessed in terms of manner of
   presentation.

3. *Pre- and Post-Unit Inventories*
   The teacher might construct a checklist of brief future facts or forecasts that learners might respond to at the beginning of the unit by assessing whether they see each item as possible or preferable. Given again at the end of the unit, the checklist may be analyzed for change of attitudes toward the future.

4. *Student Journals*
   See the "Self-Evaluation Activity" described immediately after this section.

5. *Paper-and-Pencil Tests*
   A variety of paper-and-pencil tests could be developed to assess knowledge of future facts and forecasts, futurists, and other subject matter.

SELF-EVALUATION

■ ■ In order for students to develop clear and accurate self-concepts, they need to learn the skills of self-evaluation. Following is a procedure that may be used in any subject, unit, or other learning experience.

1. At the beginning of a new unit or marking period, share with students the objectives that the class will undertake. Discuss these so that everyone understands what they mean. Also discuss planned activities and criteria for measuring objectives.

2. At the end of each class (or at least every other day), give the students a few minutes to record on paper their reactions to the class. What were they supposed to learn? What did they learn? Did they encounter problems? Was homework completed? Did anything interfere with learning, inside or outside of the class? Provide a storage space for students' folders, and have each day's log stored there.

3. At the end of each week, have students review their daily logs and write a summary for that week.

4. At the end of the unit or marking period, have students review their daily and weekly logs. Also review the objectives and criteria from (1) above. Then have students write a self-evaluation considering the questions in (2) above in relation to the objectives.

5. Review the written statements with each student. (This takes only a few minutes per student.) If you agree with what is written, cosign the statement. If not—and these cases should be few—write a brief statement of your views. Arrange to have the statements mailed to students' homes (perhaps with report

cards). Be prepared for parent conference requests if there is a difference between what you and the student have written.

6. As a variation, you may ask students for permission to review their logs from time to time. You may want to write your own comments in them or to meet with individuals.

This self-evaluation procedure not only helps students develop self-analysis skills, but provides an anecdotal record for parents without requiring the teacher to write about each student. It also helps students to keep track of their progress and focus on their own learning. At the same time, if they review logs periodically, teachers may be alerted to emerging problems. Finally, the process encourages student involvement in planning and evaluation of learning.

COOPERATIVE LEARNING—THE JIGSAW METHOD

■ ■ Research indicates that learning is enhanced when students work co-operatively and when they teach each other. However, many teachers have had less than satisfactory experiences with small-group techniques. Following is a structured small-group method that provides for cooperative learning and peer teaching.

1. Having identified a unit topic, identify five or six subtopics within it. For example:

   Studying the Future
   1. Communication Technology
   2. Transportation
   3. Lifestyle
   4. Occupations
   5. Medical Technology

2. Form small groups of four to six students around each subtopic. For a specified period (about one to two weeks), have each small group study its topic extensively so that each member becomes an "expert." The teacher should provide resources, information, suggestions, etc.

3. After the "expert" groups have completed their study, meet with each group to design a teaching strategy (e.g., a lesson plan) for its topic.

4. Form new interdisciplinary small groups composed of one representative from each of the former "expert" groups. Over another period of one to two weeks, each member teaches the rest of the interdisciplinary group about his or her topic.

5. The interdisciplinary group may culminate its work with a project involving all subtopics, a test, or some other activity.

Research has shown that this method promotes (1) academic achievement, since it is based on peer teaching, (2) self-esteem, since each member has an important role in the group, and (3) human relations, since the key idea is cooperation. Process problems (such as the degree of individual work) may arise, but these should be dealt with as learning opportunities in the affective domain. Numbers of subtopics and group membership may vary according to the size of the whole class.

By the end of the experience, all the students have been exposed to all of the various subtopics, each class member has served as an "expert" while doing peer teaching, and all the students have engaged in cooperative learning.

APPENDIX B
Goal Statement of 1938 Educational Policies Commission

THE OBJECTIVES OF SELF-REALIZATION

■ ■ *The Inquiring Mind*   The educated person has an appetite for learning.

Speech   The educated person can speak the mother tongue clearly.

Reading   The educated person reads the mother tongue effectively.

Writing   The educated person writes the mother tongue efficiently.

Number   The educated person solves his problems of counting and calculating.

Sight and Hearing   The educated person is skilled in listening and observing.

Health Knowledge   The educated person understands the basic facts concerning health and disease.

Health Habits   The educated person protects his own health and that of his dependents.

Public Health   The educated person works to improve the health of the community.

Recreation   The educated person is participant and spectator to many sports and other pastimes.

Intellectual Interests   The educated person has mental resources for the use of leisure.

Esthetic Interests   The educated person appreciates beauty.

Character   The educated person gives responsible direction to his own life.

THE OBJECTIVES OF HUMAN RELATIONSHIP

■ ■ *Respect for Humanity*   The educated person puts human relationships first.

Friendships   The educated person enjoys a rich, sincere, and varied social life.

Cooperation   The educated person can work and play with others.

Courtesy   The educated person observes the amenities of social behavior.

Appreciation of the Home   The educated person appreciates the family as a social institution.

Conservation of the Home   The educated person conserves family ideals.

Homemaking   The educated person is skilled in homemaking.

Democracy in the Home   The educated person maintains democratic family relationships.

THE OBJECTIVES OF ECONOMIC EFFICIENCY

■ ■ *Work*

The educated producer knows the satisfaction of good workmanship.

Occupational Information

The educated producer understands the requirements and opportunities for various jobs.

Occupational Choice

The educated producer has selected his occupation.

Occupational Efficiency

The educated producer succeeds in his chosen vocation.

Occupational Adjustment

The educated producer maintains and improves his efficiency.

Occupational Appreciation

The educated producer appreciates the social value of his work.

Personal Economics

The educated consumer plans the economics of his own life.

Consumer Judgment

The educated consumer develops standards for guiding his expenditures.

Efficiency in Buying

The educated consumer is an informed and skilled buyer.

Consumer Protection

The educated consumer takes appropriate measures to safeguard his interests.

THE OBJECTIVES OF CIVIC RESPONSIBILITY

■ ■ *Social Justice*

The educated citizen is sensitive to the disparities of human circumstance.

Social Activity

The educated citizen acts to correct unsatisfactory conditions.

Social Understanding

The educated citizen seeks to understand social structures and social processes.

Critical Judgment

The educated citizen has defenses against propaganda.

Tolerance

The educated citizen respects honest differences of opinion.

Conservation

The educated citizen has a regard for the nation's resources.

Social Applications of Science

The educated citizen measures scientific advance by its contribution to the general welfare.

World Citizenship

The educated citizen is a cooperating member of the world community.

Law Observance

The educated citizen respects the law.

Economic Literacy

The educated citizen is economically literate.

Political Citizenship

The educated citizen accepts his civic duties.

Devotion to Democracy

The educated citizen acts upon an unswerving loyalty to democratic ideals.

APPENDIX C
Goals for Elementary, Secondary, and Continuing Education (New York State Board of Regents, 1982)

GOAL 1

■ ■ Mastery of the following basic skills of communication and reasoning essential to live a full and productive life:

1.1 Reading
1.2 Listening
1.3 Viewing
1.4 Speaking
1.5 Writing
1.6 Computing
1.7 Thinking logically
1.8 Thinking creatively
1.9 Acquiring and using information stored in print and electronic form

GOAL 2

■ ■ Knowledge of the following disciplines at a level required to participate in an ever more complex world:

2.1 The Arts
2.2 English
2.3 History
2.4 Foreign Language
2.5 Social Sciences
2.6 Mathematics
2.7 Natural Sciences
2.8 Knowledge of the basic methods of inquiry in each field
2.9 Interdisciplinary efforts to focus knowledge on problems

GOAL 3

■ ■ Knowledge and appreciation of our culture and capacity for creativity, recreation, and self-renewal, including:

3.1 Knowledge of major forms of visual art
3.2 Knowledge of major forms of music
3.3 Knowledge of major forms of literature
3.4 Knowledge of major forms of drama
3.5 Appreciation of the diversity of mankind's historic and cultural heritage
3.6 Appreciation of beauty
3.7 Development of individual creative talents
3.8 Wise use of leisure time
3.9 Promotion of increased use of and appreciation for community resources that reflect our cultural heritage and achievements (museums, historic sites, performing arts groups, etc.)

GOAL 4

■ ■ Understanding the processes of effective citizenship in order to participate in and contribute to the government of our society, including:

4.1 Knowledge about political, economic, and legal systems with an emphasis on democratic institutions and on the global interdependence of these systems
4.2 Knowledge of the American political process at the national, state, and local levels
4.3 Knowledge about taxation and fiscal and economic policy
4.4 Acquisition of the values of civil responsibility

GOAL 5

■ ■ Knowledge of the natural environment and the relationship between one's own acts and the quality of that environment, including:

5.1 Awareness of one's relationship to the natural environment
5.2 Preservation and wise use of resources
5.3 Understanding of the effects on the environment of man's activities and values—technology, population growth, energy use

GOAL 6

■ ■ Occupational competence necessary to secure employment in the world students will face as adults, commensurate with ability and aspiration, and to the individual and to those served, including:

6.1 Development of work skills and habits
6.2 Development of awareness of work opportunities
6.3 Opportunity for occupational training and retraining

GOAL 7

■ ■ Ability to sustain lifetime learning in order to adapt to the new demands, opportunities, and values of a changing world, including:

7.1 Knowledge of contemporary society
7.2 Knowledge of alternative futures
7.3 Learning skills
7.4 Personal planning skills
7.5 Problem defining and solving skills

GOAL 8

■ ■ Understanding human relations—respect for and ability to relate to other people in our own and other nations—including those of different sexes, races, colors, national origins, religions, and other cultural heritages, including:

8.1 Respect for and knowledge of other social, cultural, and ethnic groups
8.2 Understanding one's relationship to one's natural, economic, and social environment
8.3 Respect for the community of man
8.4 Understanding of home and family relationships and involvement in the home community and society in general

GOAL 9

■ ■ Ability to develop and maintain one's mental, physical, and emotional health including:

9.1 Basic understanding of human development
9.2 Knowledge of good health habits and the conditions necessary for physical well-being
9.3 Knowledge of the conditions necessary for emotional well-being
9.4 Knowledge of the physical and health problems caused by

alcohol and substance abuse and other personally harmful activities

9.5 Knowledge of sound community health practices

9.6 Knowledge of safety principles and practices

9.7 Development of physical fitness

9.8 Development of a sense of self-esteem

GOAL 10

■ ■ Competence in the process of developing values which are essential to individual dignity and humane civilization, including:

10.1 Knowledge of the diversity of values

10.2 Skill in making value-based choices

10.3 Commitment to one's own values and acceptance of diversity of values in society

10.4 Respect for law, others, self, and property

APPENDIX D
Attica School District—Learner Goals

CONCERNS

- ■ ■ **Area I: (Philosophy) Living a Happy and Productive Life**

   One mission of the Attica School District is to develop the skills, knowledge, and attitudes which will lead to a happy and productive life. Such a life is characterized by:

   1. Satisfaction with whatever career is chosen and the ability to advance in or change careers
   2. The enjoyment of personal interests, travel, hobbies, and cultural activities
   3. The attainment of economic advantages which allow for a feeling of financial security
   4. A sense of self-respect and esteem in social groups
   5. Continuous pursuit of self-inspired learning
   6. Continuous physical and mental health
   7. A sense of moral decency in conducting personal, social, and business affairs
   8. Access to and participation in community and government affairs

- ■ **Area II: (Sociology) Characteristics of Contemporary and Future Society**

   Every person must learn to deal with the society in which they live. Thus one mission of the Attica School District is to help people develop the skills, knowledges, and attitudes which will aid in this process of living. Among the important characteristics of the present and future society are the following observations:

   1. Through better health care, people can expect to live increasingly longer lives. Along with this, the proportion of older persons living in our society is expected to continue to increase.
   2. Our society is experiencing a change in family structure. Increasing numbers of people are living in homes which differ from the traditional family structure.
   3. We live in a fragile environment. There is an increasing need for humans to understand the interrelationship between themselves and their natural environment.

4. The past fifty years have seen the development of more complex and sophisticated technology in medicine, communications, travel, and virtually all other aspects of human life.
5. Difficulties in military, political, economic, and energy resource areas have made it increasingly clear that peoples around the world are interdependent and should learn to work cooperatively.
6. Sophisticated technology in the area of transportation has allowed for greater career and leisure mobility.
7. Economics of our society have become increasingly complex and thus more difficult to comprehend and deal with.
8. In the past decade, our world has experienced a significant rise in acts of violence through terrorism, political anarchy, and crime.
9. With increases in technology, people will have growing amounts of leisure time.

■ Area III: (Psychology) Basic Human Needs

All human beings have basic needs which should be fulfilled to contribute to their social, physical, and psychological well-being. The Attica Central Schools should help individuals meet these needs and be organized to provide an environment in which they are enhanced.

1. All human beings need:
   a. Assurance of necessary food, clothing, and shelter and to be physically safe (free of bodily harm)
   b. A calming, uplifting, encouraging, loving environment to give them a feeling of well-being
2. Freedom from unnecessary guilt—All human beings need the assurance that they are not a total failure because of failing in a specific endeavor.
3. Interaction with human beings—All human beings need to socialize yet also be free to have privacy.
4. Self-worth—All human beings need a persistent sense of dignity.
5. Acceptance by others—All human beings need to feel the acceptance and respect of family, peers, and other persons.
6. Control of one's life—All human beings need the freedom to make their own choices with a sense of order and structure.
7. Value—All human beings need a values structure to help in decision-making about behavior.
8. Flexibility—All human beings need to be able to adapt to their environment.
9. Leisure—All human beings need time to be free from the pressures of life (to relax and pursue their personal interests).

GOALS

■ ■   The Attica Central School District believes that it has the responsibility to help its citizens, young and old, to develop the skills, knowledge, attitudes, and behaviors which are needed in the areas listed below. It should be realized that the schools are not solely responsible for this development. Parents, religious institutions, and the community as a whole also have responsibilities in each area. Wherever appropriate and possible, therefore, the Attica School District will help its citizens:

1. *To Function Effectively in Everyday Living*
   This involves skill in:
   a. communications
   b. computation
   c. responsible work habits
   d. making decisions
   e. planning and management of time
   f. money management
   g. acquiring and using information
2. *To Understand and Respect Others*
   This involves dealing with persons:
   a. of other ages
   b. of different ethnic and racial groups
   c. of different socio-economic levels
   d. who are handicapped physically and/or emotionally
   e. who have different lifestyles
   f. who are employers, employees, or clients
   g. who have different careers or occupations
3. *To Maintain Physical Health*
   This involves awareness and use of concepts such as:
   a. physical fitness
   b. personal hygiene
   c. dealing with common illnesses
   d. nutrition
   e. physical safety
   f. the negative effects of alcohol and drugs
   g. physical growth and development
4. *To Maintain Mental Health*
   This involves:
   a. a positive sense of self-worth
   b. being accepted by others
   c. dealing appropriately with one's emotions
   d. psychological security
5. *To Use Leisure Time in Personally Satisfying Ways*
   This might involve activities such as:

     a. athletics
     b. cultural pursuits
     c. hobbies
     d. travel

6. *To Participate in and Make Contributions to Community, State, National, and World Affairs*
   This involves ideas such as:
   a. understanding and respecting the democratic form of government and way of life
   b. voting in elections
   c. participating in community organizations
   d. working cooperatively with others
   e. being aware of community agencies

7. *To Engage in Lifelong Learning*
   This would involve:
   a. self-motivated learning
   b. supporting and participating in continuing education programs
   c. keeping abreast of current events
   d. using community resources such as the library, schools, extension agencies, and the like

8. *To Be Flexible in Dealing with Life Problems*
   Such problems may include:
   a. career or job changes
   b. death or illness
   c. geographic relocation
   d. natural disasters
   e. family living problems
   f. technological change
   g. diminishing resources

9. *To Understand and Deal with the Aging Process*
   This involves:
   a. awareness of physical changes
   b. planning for personal, economic, living, and social needs
   c. awareness of community agencies for age group services

10. *To Maintain and Improve the Quality of Our Environment*
    This involves concepts such as:
    a. awareness of how one's values and activities may affect the environment
    b. wise use of technology
    c. wise use of natural resources

11. *To Select and Prepare for a Satisfying Career*
    This would involve:
    a. awareness of career choices
    b. knowledge about what various occupations involve
    c. legal decisions governing access to occupations

12. *To Engage in Critical Thinking*
    This leads to skill in:
    a. analyzing choices
    b. making responsible moral and value decisions
    c. solving problems
    d. evaluating information
13. *To Be Effective Parents*
    This involves:
    a. understanding children's actions and behaviors
    b. understanding children with special needs
    c. providing children with a healthy and enriched home environment

APPENDIX E
Examples of "General Objectives for the High Schools" (French and Associates, 1957)

1. Goal: Growing Toward Self-Realization
   1.1 *General Objective:* Developing Behaviors Indicative of Intellectual Self-Realization
      1.12 Improving in His Ability to Communicate Ideas and to Recognize and Use Good Standards
         1.121 Commands and uses the basic skills of reading for information, ideas, opinions, stimulation, and leisure.

   Illustrative Behaviors
   a) Adjusts his reading rate and his method of reading (skimming, taking notes for detail or for enjoyment only) to the material at hand.
   b) Seeks consciously to attain his best reading rate and comprehension.
   c) Reads with increasing speed, comprehension, and appreciation.
   d) Makes use of newpapers, magazines, and other mass media to keep abreast of current events and to keep himself informed on important issues and developments and other matters of interest to him, but guards against the influence of propaganda, emotional appeals, bias, and prejudices.
   e) Reads current books, magazines and journals, and the "classics" dealing with one or more special interests; e.g., science, art, drama, government, literature, music, homemaking, or biography.
   f) Reads with discrimination for information or recreation books and periodicals of various types and dealing with various themes, including some of the "classics" which have influenced our intellectual climate.
   g) Reads to find out what is happening and why; to get at the truth; to obtain directions for carrying out a project or for using new tools or equipment; and to acquire more knowledge of a field of his special interest, etc.

h) Reads fairly difficult and complicated writing if it deals with a particular need or interest.

i) Makes a deliberate effort to relate new (to him) knowledge and ideas gained from reading to what he already knows or has experienced first hand.

1.122   Expresses his ideas in speech, writing, or in some artistic form with increasing clarity and correctness.

Illustrative Behaviors

a) Writes and speaks with sufficient clarity and in good enough form to communicate with others.

b) Organizes material which is to be presented in written or oral form into a meaningful sequence of ideas and puts them into reasonably good sentences and paragraphs.

c) Spells correctly the words he uses in ordinary written discourse and uses the dictionary if uncertain of spelling.

d) Seeks to find words which express his meaning accurately and which add variety and interest to the subjects about which he is writing.

e) Shows some individuality in expression whether it be in speaking, writing, artistic creation, or mechanical design.

f) Can speak before at least a small group in a pleasing manner and voice without being overcome by embarrassment or experiencing undue strain.

g) Accepts responsibility for correctness and honesty in his own speaking and writing: does not knowingly plagiarize.

h) Writes usable outlines or summaries of important writings which he must understand and remember.

i) Writes social and business letters which are correct in form and clear in expression.

2. *Goal:* Growing in Ability to Maintain Desirable Small Group Relationships

2.13   *General Objective:* Developing Behaviors Indicative of the Kinds of Competence Needed as a Member of Small Organized Groups.

2.131   Joins organized groups when their purposes relate to his tastes and interests, and develops the personal characteristics which contribute to successful small group membership.

Illustrative Behaviors

a) Is actively identifying himself with organizations or groups with intellectual, cultural, or social service interests as well as those with purely social interests.

b) Uses good judgment in the number of groups he joins, so that his interest will not be too widely dissipated and his contributions, therefore, limited.

c) Participates with others in organizing school activities outside the classroom, and contributes to or supports worthwhile proposals. Registers his disapproval of proposals which seem unacceptable to him.

d) Shows the understanding and skill necessary to participate effectively in the affairs of an organized group; becomes a participant in school government; attends school functions and can discharge the duties of office or committee membership if called upon.

e) Sees in club activities opportunities for the growth of the members.

f) Cooperates with others from a sense of feeling the unity of group endeavor, but knows when to work alone.

g) Is able to raise important questions and to present information and his own experiences which provide new insights and information into the problems under consideration.

h) Is developing appropriate standards by which to appreciate and evaluate his performance and that of others in a group.

i) Cooperates with others in setting up acceptable purposes and plans for judging the success of school activities and for building a standard of behavior for school affairs.

j) Is able to devise ways to relate the activities of the school to the activities of other agencies in the community for recreation, leisure interests, and character building.

3. *Goal:* Growing in the Ability to Maintain the Relationships Imposed by Membership in Large Organizations

3.11   *General Objective:* Becoming Intellectually Able to Follow Developments on the World and National Levels and to Formulate Opinions About Proposed Solutions to Some of the Prinicipal Problems and Issues.

3.111   Is developing an interest in, and understanding of, world events, conditions, and organizations.

Illustrative Behaviors

a)   Recognizes that survival demands that the peoples of the world learn to live together without war; is aware of the more likely preventives of war, and supports by word and deed as occasion permits efforts to make these operative.

b)   Recognizes conditions and problems in his own and other countries which threaten world peace; supports measures to improve such conditions and approves of measures for helping the peoples of underdeveloped areas to improve their standards of living.

c)   Understands why no national state, such as the United States, can alone fortify itself militarily and economically with the free or would-be-free nations that have the courage to resist imperialism.

d)   Supports efforts of international agencies, such as the United Nations, to reduce poverty, ignorance, and disease in underdeveloped countries by acceptable means.

e)   Recognizes that some type of world integration is desirable and studies the various possibilities of achieving more effective integration.

f)   Knows and contrasts some of the basic concepts and practices of democratic and totalitarian states concerning: family life, morality and religion, schools and formal education, government and political parties, economic organization and regulation, civil liberties and rights, public opinion, and class differences.

g)   Examines critically proposed measures for international control of atomic weapons and disarmament.

h) Accepts obligation to serve in the armed forces and to support the nation's defense program in order to check aggressors and prevent war unless this is contrary to conscience.

i) Gradually begins to recognize fundamental differences in people and learns to understand and live with them amicably: (a) develops respect for them; (b) recognizes his own prejudices and tries to control them; (c) seeks to develop some common interests with those who are different.

j) Identifies himself sufficiently with people of different nations and cultures to have a desire to understand their viewpoints and policies on international questions, and is interested in movements which help to interpret to Americans the goals, cultures, and problems of other nations.

3.112 Endeavors to become well informed on the backgrounds of the larger problems of our nation and the world and to make an intelligent analysis of the issues involved.

Illustrative Behaviors

a) Enters into study and discussion of controversial issues (political, economic, and social; local, national, and international) with a willingness to look at all sides of the controversy and weigh consequences in terms of conscious values.

b) Recognizes that change is inevitable; that cultures and institutions which fail to adjust to changing conditions decline and are replaced by more adaptable cultures and institutions.

c) Is learning to apply the advances of science to community organization and planning (transportation, communication, employment) and such other community problems as can be similarly studied.

d) On the basis of his knowledge of world's geography and its people, examines the evidence concerned with the so-called "superiority" or so-called "inferiority" of any group.

e) Understands and can explain adequately enough of the world's different social customs to document the view that "there is no one way of adapting to one's environment."

f) Knows that most of the world's peoples have for centuries fatalistically suffered personal indignity, poverty, hunger, and disease, but that they are now rapidly acquiring the belief that they are not necessarily bound to their present lot.

g) Reflects upon the chief characteristics of American ideology and uses this frame of reference in analyzing the national and international issues on which he must take a stand.

h) Believes that everyone has the responsibility of keeping informed about public problems and of the actions taken on them by those in public office.

i) Follows legislative programs in city, state, and national legislatures and in the United Nations in order to be able to express considered opinions to his representatives and to others when he feels it important to do so.

j) Reads magazines and books which discuss national and world issues and keeps informed on current problems.

Index

Grades, skipping, 211
Grading curve, 191
Gran, Eldon, 287
Gregorc, Anthony, 161
Gronlund, Norman, 230, 232
Grouping of learners, 197–201
Growth and development in learning, 151–57
Growth, professional, 371
    and staff development/inservice education, 316–17
"Guiding Principles for Future Curriculum Planning,"
    340
Gwynn, J. Minor, 150, 152–53, 361, 365, 372

H

Harmin, Willis, 99
Harnack, Robert, 31, 68, 254, 336–37
Hass, Glen, 31, 57
Hastings, J. Thomas, 274–75
Hatch Act, 309, 311, 313
Havighurst, Robert, 102–3, 156, 380
Hegel, Georg, 76
Hemispheric dominance, 160
Herrick, Virgil, 66, 271, 276–78, 280–81
Heterogeneous grouping of learners, 197–98
Hidden curriculum, 48–49, 58, 189–93
High school
    curriculum settings at, 23–26
    general objectives, 134–36
High technology, 368
Homogeneous grouping of learners, 197–201
Horney, Karen, 104
Howe, Harold, 368
Hoy, Wayne, 190
Hull, C. L., 145
Humanistic school climate, 190–91
Hutchins, Robert, 79

I

Idealism, 75–77, 118, 169
Identical elements theory, 149–50
Identity crisis, 155
"Imperative Educational Needs for Youth," 122, 124
Inservice education, 316–27, 371
    components of, 324
    guidelines for, 318–19
    personalizing, 323–27
    in practice, 319–23
    and professional growth, 316–17
Individual Educational Plan (IEP), 210
Individualization of instruction, 242
Information services, 213–15
Information society, 362–65, 366
    working in, 93–95

Institutional goals, 116–17, 125
Instruction
    definition of, 57
    phases, 241–42
Instructional objectives, 229–34
Intellectual development, 151–54
Intended learnings, curriculum as, 32
Interdisciplinary curriculum planning, 50
Interdisciplinary team teaching, 170–71, 195–96, 203
Interest
    grouping by, 199
    variable in teaching–learning situations, 156
Introductory activities, 241, 243
IQ, grouping by, 200–201

J

Jackson, Philip, 34, 190
Jacobson, Willard, 374
Jennings, Irene, 375
Johnson, Mauritz, 30
Joseph, Earl, 364
Judd, Charles H., 150

K

Kagan, Jerome, 158
Kelley, Earl, 27–28, 102–4, 142–43, 375–77, 382
Kilpatrick, William, 81, 240
Kliebard, Herbert, 66
Kohlberg, Lawrence, 241
Krug, Edward, 66, 299–301, 317, 341–43
    advising on goals, 306
    concerns in improving curriculum, 298, 303–4
    curriculum, defining, 30
    curriculum planning, 57
    evaluation as a punitive measure, 271
    learning experience, 107–8
    nature and purpose of subject matter, 27
    student–teacher planning, 339–40
    transfer of training, 149

L

Langone, John, 379
Language arts skill levels, variable in teacher–learning situation, 156
LaPointe, Archie, 374
Lay and professional interaction, 381
    cyclic model for, 307–16
Lay concerns in improving curriculum, 298–303
LD (learning disabled), 209
Learner. See also Pupil; Student
    -centered curriculum, subject-centered versus, 59–
        60

Credits (continued)

Page 274: Bloom, B., Hastings, J. T., and Madaus, G. *Handbook on Formative and Summative Evaluation of Student Learning.* Copyright © 1971 McGraw-Hill Book Company. Reproduced by permission of the publisher.

Page 87: Counts, G. S. *Dare the Schools Build a New Social Order?* by George S. Counts, John Day Co., Inc. (pp. 191–192). Copyright 1932 by George S. Counts. Reprinted by permission of Harper & Row, Publishers, Inc.

Pages 123 and 124: Educational Policies Commission. *The Purposes of Education in American Democracy* (1938) and *Education for All American Youth* (1944) by permission of the National Education Association, Washington, D.C.

Page 284: Eisner, E. "Using Professional Judgment," *Applied Strategies for Curriculum Evaluation.* Washington, D.C.: ASCD, 1981. Reprinted with permission of the Association for Supervision and Curriculum Development and Elliot Eisner. Copyright © 1981 by the Association for Supervision and Curriculum Development. All rights reserved.

Page 135: French, W. and Associates. From *Behavioral Goals for General Education in the High School* by Will French. © 1957 by the Russell Sage Foundation. Reprinted by permission of Basic Books, Inc., Publishers.

Page 246: Gall, M. *Handbook for Evaluating and Selecting Curriculum Materials.* Copyright © 1981 Allyn and Bacon. Reprinted by permission of the publisher.

Page 232: Gronlund, N. E. *Stating Objectives for Classroom Instruction,* 2nd. ed. Reprinted with permission of Macmillan Publishing Co., Inc. Copyright © 1985 by Norman E. Gronlund.

Page 152: Gwynn, J. M. and Chase, J. B. *Curriculum Principles and Social Trends.* 4th ed. Reprinted with permission of Macmillan Publishing Company. Copyright © 1964 by Macmillan Publishing Company.

Page 103: Havighurst, R. J. *Developmental Tasks and Education,* Third edition by Robert J. Havighurst. Copyright © 1972 by Longman Inc. Reprinted by permission of Longman Inc., New York.

Page 280: Herrick, V. E. "The Evaluation of Change in Programs of In-Service Education," in *In-Service Education for Teachers, Supervisors, and Administrators,* 56th Yearbook, Part 1 of the National Society for the Study of Education, ed. Nelson B. Henry. Chicago: University of Chicago Press, 1957, pp. 327–329, with permission of the publisher.

Page 79: Hutchins, R. M. "The Basis of Education," *The Conflict in Education* (pp. 71–72). Copyright 1953 by Harper & Row, Publishers, Inc. Reprinted by permission of Harper & Row, Publishers, Inc.

Page 34: Jackson, P. W. "Curriculum and Its Discontents," *Curriculum Inquiry* 10:2 (1980): 159, 171, with permission of John Wiley & Sons, Inc.

Page 132: Kearney, N. C. From *Elementary School Objectives* by Nolan C. Kearney. © 1953 by the Russell Sage Foundation. Reprinted by permission of Basic Books, Inc., Publishers.

Page 376: Kelley, E. C. *In Defense of Youth* (pp. 144–145). © 1962 by Prentice-Hall, Inc. Reprinted by permission of Prentice-Hall, Inc., Englewood Cliffs, New Jersey 07632.

Page 233: Krathwohl, D. R. et al. *Taxonomy of Educational Objectives: Handbook II: Affective Domain.* Copyright © 1964 by Longman Inc. Reprinted by permission of Longman Inc., New York.